Working Class Man

Praise for *WORKING CLASS BOY*

Working Class Boy is a stunning piece of work – relentless, earnest, shockingly vivid. Barnes ... doesn't just have a scarifying story to tell. He has a grippingly effective way of telling it: one that does full justice to the grim facts without overcooking them ... there are no requests for pity here, no wallowing in victimhood. Above all there is a bracing intolerance of bullshit. You can't fake such a tone. You have to earn it.
– *The Australian*

Nothing will prepare you for the power of Jimmy's memoir. A fierce, graphic, bawdy account of his working class childhood – truly harrowing, and yet often tender and funny. I couldn't put it down because, above all, it is also a story of resilience and bravery.
– Sam Neill

Barnes' way of addressing the reader directly, while largely ignoring his rock-star status, edges towards a unique voice.
– *The Listener*

This is volume one of the book [Jimmy Barnes] needed to write to expel his demons ... It finishes as Cold Chisel starts, and I'm hanging out for the next instalment. What a life.
– Jennifer Byrne, *Australian Women's Weekly*

Reading about [Barnes's] harrowing early life gives a greater understanding of both the belting lyrics and the softer, sometimes haunting, music he has produced ... This moving account ... shows in grim detail the enormous effort Jimmy had to put in to become the man he is.

— *Booksellers New Zealand*

Visceral, brave, honest. A deep, guttural howl of a book, it speaks of the pain and hurt that haunt so many men. And it may just save lives.

— Magda Szubanski

Barnes writes with verve and style to present a fascinating story of flawed and compelling personalities, not least his own. The result is unexpectedly compelling.

— *Rolling Stone*

Jimmy Barnes

Working Class Man

HarperCollins*Publishers*

We gratefully acknowledge the permission granted by copyright holders to reproduce the copyright material in this book. All reasonable attempts have been made to contact the copyright holders; the publisher would be interested to hear from anyone not acknowledged here, or acknowledged incorrectly.

HarperCollins*Publishers*

First published in Australia in 2017
by HarperCollins*Publishers* Australia Pty Limited
ABN 36 009 913 517
harpercollins.com.au

HarperCollins*Publishers*
Level 13, 201 Elizabeth Street, Sydney NSW 2000, Australia
Unit D1, 63 Apollo Drive, Rosedale, Auckland 0632, New Zealand
A 53, Sector 57, Noida, UP, India
1 London Bridge Street, London, SE1 9GF, United Kingdom
2 Bloor Street East, 20th floor, Toronto, Ontario M4W 1A8, Canada
195 Broadway, New York NY 10007, USA

National Library of Australia Cataloguing-in-Publication data:

Barnes, Jimmy, author.
Working class man / Jimmy Barnes.
978 1 4607 5214 2 (hardback)
978 1 4607 0701 2 (ebook)
Subjects: Barnes, Jimmy.
Cold Chisel (Musical group)
Rock musicians – Australia – Biography.
Rock groups – Australia – Biography.

Cover design by Darren Holt, HarperCollins Design Studio
Front cover image © Patrick Jones
Back cover image by shutterstock.com
Author photo © Scott Hull
Picture section design by HarperCollins Design Studio
Internal photographs: page xxii, courtesy of Cold Chisel; page 248, Patrick Jones Studio; page 364, Dan Boud, courtesy of Cold Chisel
Typeset in Bembo Std by Kirby Jones
Printed and bound in Australia by Griffin Press
The papers used by HarperCollins in the manufacture of this book are a natural, recyclable product made from wood grown in sustainable plantation forests.
The fibre source and manufacturing processes meet recognised international environmental standards, and carry certification.

For my Jane,
I love you.
I have loved you.
I will always love you.

And for my children.
Your father has made a lot of mistakes.
But when I look at you I know
that I have done something right.

For my grandchildren.
This is a story from the dark past.
Now you are here everything is all right.

For Oliver and Snoop.
You have lived through this
with me. But even in the
thick of it, you never judged me,
and you wagged your tails
whenever you saw me.

I love you all.

CONTENTS

PART 2   THE BEGINNING OF THE END

PART 3   A NEW BEGINNING

It's hard to believe that this is book two of my memoirs. Who would have thought that I would remember any of my life, especially considering I spent so much time and money trying to forget it all? But I do. I remember most of it. Some of it is not pretty and some of it is just plain painful to relive. But I have done my best to write it down, for you to read and for me to make sense of.

When I started writing my first book, *Working Class Boy*, I had no idea how it would finish. I knew I had things that I had to write down. I knew I had things that I had to get out of my system. But as the writing process progressed, I found more and more to write about. The simple act of sitting at the computer unlocked a lot of memories that had been hidden somewhere in the darkest places in my mind. Fuzzy and hard to see at first, they came into focus the more I wrote. I can see now that these events were waiting until I was ready and able to deal with them before they presented themselves to me. So the whole process was enlightening and disturbing at the same time. I found that once these hidden gems of family history were out and on paper, things seemed to feel better. Then of course I went on the road, talking about the book, sharing my darkest secrets with the world.

I was surprised, at first, how many people the book touched. But the more I toured the more I realised that there were a lot of people who went through similar childhoods to myself. I was not alone. I have been stopped in the street and after shows and total strangers have broken down and cried with me as they thanked me for starting a conversation about family violence. And I know that I have started healing because this is no longer locked inside me. It's out there, I can start to let it go now.

I have met people who are still living in violent, abusive relationships. I have had to suggest that they get help. I am not qualified to help people with this. My only qualification is that I have lived through it. There are people out there who are qualified to talk about this. Rosie Batty, through her foundation, the Luke Batty Foundation, is working tirelessly to help women and families find help. To find peace. To feel safe. But we can all do something to help. I have found that being able to talk about this has broken down barriers that had previously stopped me from getting on with my life. If you know someone who is living with family violence, reach out to them. Let them know that they're not alone.

The other problem I can see, that caused grief and violence and abuse in my life, was poverty. We live in 'the lucky country', but look around. There are families all over Australia struggling to put food on the table or to keep a roof over their children's heads. Yet we allow our governments to cut spending on schools and on health care for families that need it most. I don't want to stand on a soap box and preach, or take sides with any political party here, but we need to reach out to those families less fortunate than we might be. If we ignore these social issues they will get worse. Most people who grow up like I did, grow up with problems, just like I did. I was lucky to get to a point in my life where I had the chance to deal with some of those problems. There were many times when I thought I wasn't going to make it. There are a lot of us who don't make it. Our jails are overcrowded and the suicide rate, particularly among our young people, is way too high. These are cries for help that no one is hearing. We have to listen. People all over this country are suffering.

YOU DON'T HAVE TO have read my first book to read this one. But if you do, it will explain a lot of things. From the time I was born until I was seventeen, the building blocks of my life were never that strong. I had no role models to speak of except my stepfather Reg Barnes, and by the time Reg came along I was already damaged goods. My adult years, and I do use that term loosely, were spent crashing through life, waiting to fall. Some of you will recognise me at this point because, unfortunately, I did all of this in the public eye. It's all there for everyone to see.

I couldn't leave my childhood behind. It was too painful to forget. So I built a life around the mess that I was left with. I stumbled around in the dark trying to make sense of what I was dealing with, falling flat on my face most of the time. When I found my feet I ran again until I hit another wall. My life has been an adventure to say the least. Along the way I found the love of my life and we had a beautiful family. But I almost let them slip through my fingers so many times. I flirted with death regularly. Almost every night. I stared into its eyes and never learned a thing.

In my first book I faced the damage that a broken home and a broken heart can bring. In this book I face the impact that a childhood like mine can have on a man. Don't get me wrong. I'm not blaming anyone for any of this. We all do the best with what we have. But here the blame rests squarely on my shoulders.

The book picks up where the last left off, in the back of that truck with my newfound family, Cold Chisel, as I ran from my past. I have retraced my rampage through the '70s and '80s into the '90s and the new millennium. I have had incredible highs in my life but there were despicable lows too. My childhood has affected everyone I have ever come in touch with: my wife, my children, my friends and the people who listened to our music. In the end I asked for help. I used to think that if someone asked for help they were weak. But the toughest thing I ever did was reach out and ask for help. And that was when I started to heal. It took courage. I will no doubt make more mistakes in my life, but not like before. We all make mistakes. We all have problems. It's how we tackle those mistakes and problems that defines us. Good luck, you are not alone. If you or someone you know is in need of crisis or suicide prevention support, please call Lifeline on 13 11 14 or visit www.lifeline.org.au/gethelp

This second book covers a lot of time, from seventeen up until now. I have written about what I felt was important to me. There are a lot of people whose paths have crossed mine along the way. I couldn't write about you all, but you have all helped me in one way or another. So, thank you. I hope that knowing me hasn't held you back. There are a few of you out there I wish I had never met, but I try to be philosophical.

I drank and smoked and snorted my way through a lot of this life and I ask you to cut me some slack. I have tried to remember what happened but of course some of it is a bit hazy and blurred. I have also tried to bare it all. The truth. Warts and all. There are a few things I have kept close to my chest because they are no one's business but mine. I hope you understand.

Lastly, I don't think I'm finished yet. I love life and will try to love and laugh for many years to come. In which case, maybe you'll see book three in a few more years. I'm not slowing down.

Jimmy Barnes

PROLOGUE

———

AUCKLAND, 2012

I AM ALONE IN the darkness. With my eyes squeezed shut I scream.

'Ahhhhhhhhhhhhhhhhhh!'

It comes straight from the darkest depths of my soul. My heart is pounding. I can feel the blood rushing through my veins. I move around the room, slowly at first but gathering speed. Every night it's the same thing. Alone, I wait to see if I am going to make it. Wait until I am told that I am all right.

'Ahhhhhhhhhhhhhhhhhhhhhhhhhhhhh!'

The sound is stronger. Louder and higher. *Bang!* I slam my fist into the wall, leaving indentations of my knuckles. *Bang!* I hit it again. This time I nearly go through to the other side.

'Pleeeeeeeeeeeease Pleeeeeeeassssse he-elp meeeeeeeeeee!'

It spews from deep inside of me, tearing at my throat on its way out of my body and into the room. A room that is dirty with graffiti scrawled across the walls. I lash out again at the filthy, stained walls. *Bang! Bang!* I hit again and again. There is movement in the room. It's nearly time.

'Ahhhhhhhhhhhhhhhhhhhhhhh!'

It's a call that only those who really know me understand. Even they don't know why I go through this every night. I feel like I am expelling the poison from deep inside of me, out of my system. I have to purge myself of all the toxic energy that is in my way, blocking me. I look into the mirror that is covered in condensation. The room feels like an oven. There is smoke coming under the door. I can see the shadow of the man I once was looking back at me, asking the same questions. Every night it is the same questions.

'Can I get through this? Will I survive tonight? Am I good enough?'

I take one last look at the face in the mirror. I am not going down tonight. Not without a fight anyway. I'm as ready as I'll ever be to do this.

The door flies open and a blinding light fills the room. The muffled noise I have been hearing in the background has turned to a roar. It's the same thing every night. The same ritual, every single night before I go on stage.

'GOOD EVENING, NEW ZEALAND!'

Bang! The band kicks in like a freight train, unstoppable and relentless. Just like my life. It rolls down the track way too fast and the only thing holding it down is the speed at which I'm travelling. With every song, we take it up a notch in tempo, in volume and in intensity. My world is spinning out of control but up here I can still find myself. Whatever happens to me for the rest of the day is gone. All that matters is them and me. The connection that is formed every night on stage between me and the audience. By the end of the set it sounds like a hurricane tearing through each town that we visit. And then it grinds to a screaming halt. Jackie, my son, crashes down on as many drums as he can hit at once and it is over.

'Thank you.'

I hold up a towel and a bottle of water and shake the sweat from my hair. The crowd is screaming for more but we have given enough. Two encores and a two-hour set. I walk off stage, the same way I walk off every night. The booze that I poured down my throat while on stage has taken me beyond reach. As we leave the venue people thump the car, begging us to stop and talk. Girls in short skirts and high heels, too much eye makeup and lipstick freshly applied, smiling at me through the windows of the slow-moving car, looking for a good time. Guys with wild eyes and bulging pockets, full of God knows what, wanting to party until the next show, sway in front of the car. I've seen them all before and probably have taken them up on their offers. I can't remember.

Unable to talk to me anymore, my wife Jane sits in the car saying nothing. We drive in silence to the hotel. The casino in Auckland is the best hotel in town and we have booked a big suite. The biggest they have. Maybe it will be big enough so that we won't have to talk anymore. We are both sick of talking. Talking and nothing ever changing. Jane has tried everything to reach me. Everything to help me. But I am beyond help. I stare at the road, wishing the car would travel faster so we could get there and I could consume every drug that I have hidden in my bag. We pull into the driveway and move to the elevator with our heads down, trying not to be stopped by the Saturday night crowd of party animals and chronic gamblers, all down on their luck and looking for somewhere to get fucked up. We get to the room and lock the door. The quiet is good for a minute and then I turn on the television to break the deafening silence. We take all that we have as quickly as we can. Trying hard not to say anything that would start a fight, I pace the room from end to end. Trying to wear myself out and stop myself from walking away. Jane falls into bed and I follow a little later, trying not to wake her up.

THERE IS NO LIGHT coming into this room. The air conditioning is screaming as it blows the cold stale drug-filled smoke from one room to the next in our hotel suite. Only hours before, we flew into Auckland on a tour that felt the same as the last, that felt the same as the one before. It's as if we desperately try to keep moving, knowing that if we stop too long, one of us might die. The motion is all that is keeping our hearts beating. I have dragged Jane all the way from her old life, full of hope, into my world, my own personal hell, and there is no way out. Not for me anyway.

I can hear Jane sleeping; she breathes in and then breathes out, her lungs gasping for air. The only time we seem to breathe just air is when we are passed out. Otherwise we are trying to force something toxic into our bodies. Anything, as long as it stops the pain.

Next to me on the bedside table I have placed everything I could find in the minibar. Scotch, vodka, bourbon, gin. I am in the process of pouring it all down my throat as fast and as quietly as I can, so as not to wake her. I am gagging as I wash down as many sleeping tablets as I can. This is how I get to sleep these days. In the haze I think about it all ending. Not waking up. Never having to face myself again. The red light on the television even seems bright to me as I pull an eye mask over my eyes and pray for peace.

I wake to the sound of Jane in the next room, sending empty bottles out the door with the room service girl. My eyes are nearly stuck together but I prise them apart and look at the time.

Ten o'clock. I walk into the lounge. Jane is trying to be upbeat and happy. I can see by the red rings around her eyes she's been crying again but she smiles at me anyway.

'Let's eat something and then go for a walk and get some fresh air.' Jane starts every day trying to be positive but I can tell it's getting harder. 'I don't want to do this anymore. Can we just start again, please?'

I nod my head and try to smile. 'Sure baby, let's do that.'

The lounge room is the size of a basketball court and everywhere I look I see something that reminds me of something else I did wrong the night before. How can we be living in such luxury and feel like we have so little? We are just being ungrateful. We have everything in the world but we don't appreciate it.

I head to the dressing room to get some clothes. I pick up my jeans from the floor and pull them on and then I see it.

The end of last night suddenly runs through my head like an old newsreel. Scratchy and unclear. I remember drinking the minibar but I don't remember getting back up. But I know I did. I can see the evidence right there in front of my eyes. Tied around the clothes rail is the dressing gown cord, just where I must have left it. It all comes flooding back. The rail, the cord and me with the cord around my neck waiting to die. But I didn't. It's not that easy to die, apparently.

I quickly take the cord down and place it back with the dressing gown. No one must ever know about this. I don't want to remember this. This will never happen again.

PART 1

THE
BEGINNING

I was a serial runner

ON THE WAY TO ARMIDALE, 1974

*W*HOOSH. THE TRUCK LURCHED to the left as a semitrailer roared by. We all held our breath as the wind gripped us in its twisted hands, picking us up for a second before throwing us back onto the winding road. *Bang.* We all breathed out.

It was the beginning of 1974 and I was finally leaving Adelaide, the place that had been my home since my family fled Scotland in 1961. We always seemed to be running from somewhere. My ancestors had run from famine in Ireland to find a new life in Scotland. But all they found was pain and more hunger. Eventually my folks had to start running again. This time they ended up in Australia. This was the last chance. The end of the line. We would have nowhere left to run. So this had to be it, the place where we would find peace. Where the family could stop being afraid and get on with living. But it didn't work out.

Now I was running away from my family. I had tried this many times as a young kid but all I ever managed to do was escape for a few hours. I was a serial runner. Running as far as the sea then stopping. Standing, wide-eyed and alone, looking out to the ocean, trying to breathe in the cool clean air before I made my way back to Elizabeth and the life that was slowly suffocating me. I came from a long line of runners. The whole family took turns escaping. My brother John left home at thirteen years of age because of what was happening to him in the place where he should have felt safe, our house. My mum left because she could no longer stand the sight of Dad or us or even herself in the mirror. Dad ran away because he knew he had let us all down and couldn't face anything anymore. My big sisters ran from all of us and I ran from all of them. The only ones who couldn't run away were my little brother and sister. If they ran at all it was to the place in their heads where kids go when they don't want to see what is happening around them.

This time I was running to New South Wales with the band. Cold Chisel. We were following our leader, Don Walker. Don was a bearded university student. He dressed like a country boy: straight-leg jeans and shirt always tucked in perfectly. He never looked ruffled in any way; not a hippy by any stretch of the imagination. He looked more like a mountain man, with thick hair and intelligent eyes that always seemed to be watching, taking in everything. He always thought long and hard before he spoke.

Don was the piano player but he was much more than just that. He was the guy the rest of us looked to for advice and guidance. He was a little older than us and we all saw him as a sort of big brother.

'Now Jim. Why don't you give this record a listen? I know he's not wearing silver platform boots like the other bands you listen to, which might put you off a bit, but he's a pretty good songwriter. I've got a feeling you'll like it,' Don said to me one day. He was being a little sarcastic but that's what his sense of humour was like. I didn't mind it. I could give as much as I got. He then proceeded to play *Greetings from Asbury Park, N.J.*, Bruce Springsteen's first album. He was right, I loved it. The words Bruce sang painted pictures, they told stories. Some I could relate to and some sounded like the scripts to old movies I'd seen on TV.

'It's great, Don. But I've seen photos of him and he always seems a little underdressed to me. What do you think?'

Don smiled. 'If you like that one, take this one too, and give it a listen later.' He was holding *Highway 61 Revisited* by Bob Dylan.

'No, you keep it. One badly dressed hippy a day is my limit.'

Later on, I would discover it. *Highway 61 Revisted* was a great album. Over the years I would listen to it many times. I remember the first time I heard 'It Takes a Lot to Laugh, It Takes a Train to Cry', I could almost feel the wind blowing through my hair. It was as if I was sitting on the back of an open carriage of a freight train leaving town. The words transported me away from the life I knew, and I loved it. I hoped that one day I would write songs like this. I'm still hoping, I haven't given up yet.

Don was leaving for a year to finish his Honours degree in quantum mechanics, which would be as useful to him as a bicycle to a fish. Rock'n'roll is not rocket science, you know. The only degree I ever got was the third degree from the police. But Don was smart and we all knew it. I was smart too, despite how I behaved. Don knew this and encouraged me to broaden my horizons a little.

'There's a lot of good music out there, Jim, that you probably haven't heard, you know. I'll see if I can find more for you if you like,' Don said one day as he packed up his room at the university in Adelaide.

'Yeah. That'll be good.'

Besides the music I'd grown up with at home, if I didn't hear it on the radio in one of my mate's cars as we drove around

Elizabeth looking for fights, or on the jukebox while I was batting my eyes and flirting with the girls wearing tight skirts in the coffee shop, then there was a good chance I missed it. We came from different planets, Don and I. But as different as we were, I think that we were very similar in a lot of ways too. Both wanting something that was there for the taking. Something that was calling out to us. Both scrambling, looking for ways to grab onto it. A dream, a life, a future. Whatever you call it, we wanted it.

He wanted his parents to be happy. So did I. He wanted to live up to the expectations they had for him. So did I. But we went about it in very different ways. He got his uni degree, hoping that would make them happy. I got a job in a factory and tried my best to be the loser they always thought I would be. I guess we were same, same but different.

THE TRUCK WE WERE leaving town in was an old Tip Top baker's truck. It wasn't very big but it was perfect for us. We didn't have a lot of money or gear at the time. So we piled everything we needed to make music into the truck and filled the rest of the space with a mattress so that we would have something to sit on. Threw what little luggage we had on top of the gear and we hit the road.

Cold Chisel, even then, felt special to me and I was sure it did to the others too. There was something that happened from day one that excited all of us. A certain spark when we played music that we hadn't felt before.

These four guys would eventually become my family. The family I always needed. We would laugh and cry together and have huge fights too. When I fought at home with my real family, someone always got hurt, a deep hurt that took too long to heal. But the band would fight and then go on stage and it would all be forgotten. The music pulled us through everything. This became a bond that not even sharing the same blood could match. We had each other's backs.

Don came from a different place musically to the rest of us. He liked Charlie Mingus and Bob Dylan and a lot of American bands like The Doors, music I'd never really listened to that much. The rest of us liked British rock, blues and soul music.

Steve Prestwich had come from a band that played progressive rock. Their repertoire was filled with Yes songs. He knew every song and rhythm that Bill Bruford, the Yes drummer, ever played. I was more of a no man myself – 'No I can't count that, no I can't sing to that and no I don't like your face or your fucking band.'

Steve was an immigrant, just like me. His family moved from Liverpool in England and ended up in Elizabeth. But our families were very different. His dad was a musician and his mum was a beautiful woman who loved her family dearly. Steve, instead of joining gangs and fighting like I did, was a gentle, easy-going, almost hippy-ish sort of guy and a very serious musician. But he had a razor-sharp tongue and I wasn't always sure if he was kidding, so I was a little wary of him. I would watch him for a while in case I had to belt him.

Ian Moss, our guitar player, listened to a lot of different types of music but was obsessed with Ritchie Blackmore and Deep Purple. Ian was born and bred in the dead centre, an Alice Springs boy who moved to Adelaide to finish high school. He seemed to look down at his feet a lot. I could tell that he was gentle and sensitive, not like most of the guys I grew up with. But when he did look at you, his eyes seemed to look deep inside you, searching, looking for something; something he hoped would make it easier to reach out and connect with.

Les Kaczmarek, our original bass player, liked Golden Earring and other weird European bands. It didn't matter, as long as they were hard rock. Les was a middle-class Polish boy. He had lived with his mum and dad until we left town in the back of our truck. He didn't live with them because he needed to, not financially anyway. I got the feeling that he stayed at home because he loved his mum. He was the driving force behind getting this strange group of guys together. He had the best, shiniest and newest equipment that I had ever seen. I had never been in a band with a guy whose amplifiers were so big. Even at this time he looked like he was ready to be playing stadiums. But like the rest of us his playing was still barely out of the garage.

I listened to anything my big brother John liked. Jimi Hendrix and Jeff Beck. In the end, all these different styles seemed to gel together somehow when we crashed our way naively through the songs we played in the rehearsal room. It sounded exciting.

Although we all had our own taste in music, we all listened to Don. We thought he had a plan. A plan that included getting somewhere in the music business. A plan that included a future for all of us. I for one had never had a real future before. This was the reason that I was ready to travel across the country in a truck with a bunch of guys I didn't really know.

The back of the truck was as black as night and it wasn't easy to see one another, or anything else for that matter. I'm sure that like me the other guys were chewing their lips, wondering if they were doing the right thing. Every now and then a wash of light splashed across our faces as we huddled in the darkness.

Whoosh, another truck barrelled by. The little Tip Top truck swayed and shook and for a moment crossed the white line that split the highway in two. This line was our only protection from the horrors the impact of an oncoming semi could bring. We'd all be tossed sideways as our van grabbed the road again and straightened up one more time.

Michael, who was driving, was our first roadie and came from Elizabeth too. He wasn't in any sort of gang but I got the feeling he had been chased by a few, maybe even by me and my mates. He was a bit of a gentle soul. His hair was longish and stringy and his eyes always seemed to be slightly red. I thought he must suffer from allergies until I worked out he was a big pot smoker. He wasn't in this game for fame. He just wanted to hear nice music and smoke dope, so he was happy to carry our gear and mix the sound. Michael's passion was music from the southern states of America. The Allman Brothers was his favourite band and he was singing their songs to himself as he was driving.

'Fuck, take it easy would you, Michael? You'll get us killed,' I screamed at him and then sat quietly hoping that we weren't going to die before we even left the Adelaide Hills.

'You guys just sit quietly and drink. You're in good hands, boys,' he yelled over the seat and put his foot flat to the floor. The engine screamed but the truck hardly gained any speed at all. It would be a long drive.

We sat, saying very little. We didn't really feel comfortable enough with each other to make idle chitchat. Not while we were waiting for death to occur at any moment, anyway. The boys had a slab of beer and were slowly starting to loosen up. I didn't like beer. I was already quarter of the way through a bottle of whisky.

'You want one of these, Jim?' Ian asked, offering me a beer.

'Don't like beer. It's for girls.'

Ian just laughed to himself.

After a few beers, the others were cracking bad jokes and singing songs in three-part harmony. I thought that these guys were geeks. Nice boys, not like the guys I hung around with, but I liked them anyway.

So Michael was driving and we took turns sitting in the front with him. Whoever was in the back spent most of the time singing and being thrown around the truck. Who said rock'n'roll is not glamorous? But we were free and with every mile we put between ourselves and Adelaide, I could feel a weight lifting from my shoulders. I had come to hate the place and as long as it was fading into the distance in the rear-view mirror I was happy. In fact, at that time, if I never saw Adelaide again it would be too soon.

This was really the start of our brotherhood. Before that, we were just individuals thrown together by chance, hoping to make some music for fun. Now we were held together by something different; now it was us against the world. These guys needed me and I needed them and it would stay that way until we broke up in 1983. Except for the odd time we fought and stormed off. When I say *we* stormed off, I mean *I* stormed off, because I seemed to be the only one who did it. The others just laughed and let me go, as if they knew I'd be back. Maybe they didn't care if I didn't come back. But I always did. And right in time for the next gig.

The whisky and beer soon began to override the darkness and we all loosened up. We laughed and sang and told lies for the first six hours or so then it got quiet. You can only sing 'Happy Together' so many times before you start to get a bit snappy with each other.

'That's not the part you were singing before,' I said.

'Don't fuckin' tell me what part I was singing. I'm the fuckin' guy who showed you the song, remember,' Steve snapped in his Liverpudlian accent. He was leading the choir.

'I've known this song for years. I love The Tortoises,' I sniggered.

'They're fucking Turtles, you fucking twat,' Steve shouted and we all laughed.

'I know, I know. Tortoises, Turtles, all the same aren't they?'

We stopped at a roadhouse for coffee and something to eat. I fell out of the truck and staggered into the truckstop. The boys seemed to be a bit intimidated by the big truck drivers, some of them covered in tattoos and all of them wearing blue singlets.

'Don't worry, boys. I've dated tougher looking girls than these blokes,' I joked. I did feel quite at home. This wasn't scary at all.

'Can I get a coffee and what have you got to eat?' I said to the waitress as she walked past, trying to ignore us.

She had to think for a second and then replied, 'We have toasted sandwiches and, oh yeah, we've got toasted sandwiches and that's about it, I'm afraid. It's the middle of the bloody night, you know.'

I ordered coffee and a toasted ham, cheese and tomato sandwich. Steve ordered chips and bread and butter. This was what we lived on for the next few years. Roadhouse food and bad coffee.

Before long we were back in the truck, singing and drinking again. Loving life and ready for anything the road wanted to throw at us.

By the time we were getting close to our destination, none of us could feel our teeth, our legs, or our arses for that matter from sitting in the truck. We had driven about eight hundred miles, dodging kamikaze truck drivers and kangaroos with death wishes. We had run out of songs to sing and booze to drink and we were happy to just get anywhere in one piece. The back of the truck smelled like a brewery and was full of empty bottles and half-eaten toasted sandwiches. We were dishevelled but excited about our new lives.

Around four in the morning the truck started to make a few strange noises.

'Shit. What's that noise?' a voice from the darkness in the back whispered.

'Don't know, boys. But I got to tell you, it's not good,' Michael announced as the truck came to a grinding halt and refused to move another inch. Luckily we had made it to the outskirts of a small town and could walk to a phone box.

'I reckon the baker's ripped you off, Mick.'

'Fuck off.'

We knew we were in the mountains somewhere to the west of Sydney but had no idea where exactly. None of us knew anything at all about cars or trucks, so we had to call the NRMA. A guy came and towed us to a petrol station and left us there for a mechanic to help us the next morning. We all needed sleep and started fighting to get a place where we could lie down. It was first in, best dressed. That meant some of us had to sleep on the concrete outside. It was like camping, only on concrete, which I didn't mind because at least you weren't likely to have spiders crawling all over you.

We were that tired and drunk that we managed to sleep until after sun up. I remember waking up and scratching my head, wondering who the bloke standing over me was. He was kicking my shoes.

'Hey. Get up. You can't sleep there, mate. This is a bloody petrol station, not a bloody campsite.' He obviously wasn't good in the morning.

'It looked like a bloody campsite to me, all right. And don't kick my shoes. Mate.' I wasn't good in the morning either. I didn't like being woken up at the best of times, never mind by this guy.

It appeared we had slept in the driveway of a garage in the outer suburbs of Sydney. We slowly worked out what was going on and where we were. Penrith was what the sign said, wherever that was. We managed to scrape together enough money to get the truck moving again and headed into Sydney.

I'm not sure where, but we stayed in the city for the day. I think at one of Michael's friend's houses. We walked around Sydney looking like country mice, staring at the buildings and the people. Some of us were even dressed like country folk. No shoes, and jeans that were just a wee bit too short, with crochet around the bottom. Now that I think about it, that's what Adelaide was, a big country town. A big country town full of serial killers.

As the sun was sinking over the harbour, covering the city in rays of brilliant red light, I crossed the Sydney Harbour Bridge for the first time in my life. And we started our long slow trip up the coast. This would be the first of many times I would travel this highway. We lived on that road and we lost friends on that road. We sang about it in 'Houndog' and complained about it every time we had to drive it to a gig. By the time the band broke up I knew every turn and hill and every bump and pothole on the highway. I'd slept on that road, I'd walked it, driven it, hitchhiked it. Eventually I knew where to stop for the best coffee, what roadhouse made the best food and where you might find something a bit stronger to drink if you winked at the right waitress. I even knew where you might find a bed if you were a smooth talker. This road became part of my life.

WE GOT TO ARMIDALE, New South Wales, and suddenly it felt like we were in Woodstock circa 1969. There were hippies everywhere. But not just hippies. The hippy population was mixed with a lot of country folk. Farmers with big hats and moleskin trousers walking around the streets, looking at the weirdos in cheesecloth who smiled at them as they passed by. I wasn't sure about either of them. I didn't know any farmers. And I didn't think you could trust people who smiled as much as the hippies did.

I'd never spent any time with people like this before. If you dressed like a farmer or a hippy in Elizabeth, you were screaming out to be beaten. Most of the Adelaide hippies lived in the hills or somewhere out of sight. I don't mean 'outtasight, man' either.

But everyone seemed to get along and all the people I met were very warm and friendly. It wasn't that long until I began to drop my guard. It seemed I didn't need to be ready to fight anyone. Within a month I was wearing cheesecloth and smoking pot and listening to Crosby, Stills & Nash and eating only vegetables. The girls in the area appeared to eat only vegetables and rock singers, which suited me down to the ground.

WE BEGAN LOOKING FOR gigs and had no trouble getting work at the local university, colleges and schools. We were the only band that remotely resembled a rock band within a hundred miles, so we managed to get gigs from Tamworth all the way up to Glen Innes and everywhere in between.

We found ourselves a place to stay, a little farm twenty-five miles out of Armidale, on the way to Tamworth, at a place called Kentucky. The house was next to an apple orchard. It wasn't too flash, but it was clean and it was cheap and there was no one near us for miles and miles. We loved it, we could play music whenever we wanted to and no one cared. We could walk out to the trees outside the house and pick apples to eat, which we did a lot because we didn't have much money. There were always a few slices of bread and butter lying around, so we didn't starve. And, let me tell you, getting an apple straight off the tree is the only way to eat one.

There were a few drawbacks. To go to the toilet we had to take a shovel and go out into the paddock, and we had to build a fire in the stove or else we had no hot water. If we wanted to go into town we all had to go, because if you decided to stay home, you were basically trapped, with no vehicle, ten miles from the main road and twenty-five miles from town. It could get a bit lonely and a little scary out there alone. I was always first in the truck, ready to go to town and drink or do whatever we were going to do. Just as long as I wasn't left behind, I was happy.

We found some contacts through friends of Don who sorted us out with pot and there was no shortage of booze, so everything was all right. Even I was happy smoking pot. It seemed that the environment around New England suited stoners and I didn't feel worried about letting my guard down.

I was becoming relaxed in my new surroundings. There was no trouble at the house. A few little arguments but nothing serious. We all got on like a house on fire. There were a few nights where we nearly did set the house on fire, come to think of it. We became good mates. Mick seemed to be getting a little withdrawn but we all just presumed he missed his mum's cooking or was smoking too much pot – this was more likely – and shrugged it off.

I was missing nothing from home at all. I had nothing to miss. These guys were my family now. I was happy. Waking up in the country without having to see Elizabeth or the inside of the foundry suited me down to the ground.

CHAPTER TWO

Thunderbolt's Rock

ON THE FARM, 1974

T HE GIGS WERE DIFFERENT every night. We'd get one gig at the teacher's college and that would be wild and boozy and then we'd play at the university and the place would be full of hippies. I remember playing one night at the university and the crowd seemed really small but we started the set anyway. Right next to the stage there was a small window which was next to a drainpipe that ran one storey down to the ground floor. The band had just started when I noticed a leg coming through this very small window. The leg was attached to a foot that was not wearing shoes and I noticed that there were beads tied around the ankle. The foot was followed by a pair of ripped and torn flared pants with crochet around the bottom. Next came the very thin vegan-looking waist of a young hippy girl followed by a head of unbrushed, blonde hair. As her leg touched the floor in front of the band it started dancing, even before the rest of her body was through the window. By the time she was completely inside she was in full motion, interpretive dancing around the dance floor in front of me, with a huge smile. She had shining, if not slightly bloodshot, eyes, and was staring at me. Close behind her, about twenty more hippies danced their way through the window and onto the dance floor. They all seemed to love the band.

This particular group of people became the core of our support in Armidale for the next six months. We were, by this point, wearing no shoes and flares ourselves, so we fitted right in with the audience. After the show we left the hall and followed our newfound friends to a farm where the young vegan girl lived and that's where I stayed for the next few nights, listening to Van Morrison and smoking weed and eating vegetables. I never realised I liked Van or vegetables that much, but suddenly he was my favourite singer. This lasted until I left her farm. Then I went back to listening to Deep Purple and eating steak whenever I could.

MICHAEL OUR ROADIE WAS becoming more and more depressed. He decided he needed a friend to talk to because none of us wanted to talk to him anymore, so he bought a dog, a cute-looking little beagle.

As the dog got older he started eating anything that wasn't put up high, including guitar leads, shoes and records, and we all stopped liking this poor little dog when he pissed on the PA. His popularity was dwindling to the point of non-existence when one day we arrived home from a shopping trip, just before dark. There, on the floor, were the tell-tale signs of the party the dog had been having – a trail of aluminium foil, covered in teeth marks and ripped to pieces all through the lounge. The rubbish bin had been raided and rubbish was scattered all over the kitchen floor. 'Michael, I think your dog has eaten the hash. We're going to have to kill it,' I shouted back towards the truck.

I followed the trail of silver paper, like a tracker, looking for the culprit. I was going to have to give this dog a good talking to.

Then I spotted him, just his tail at first, wagging ever so slightly. He was lying behind the door to the front bedroom. So I snuck up, and jumped around from behind the door.

'Hey you little bastard, what the fuck have you done?' I yelled, expecting the dog to hit the ceiling. But to my surprise he didn't move. The poor dog lay on his side with his tongue hanging out of his mouth. He still didn't move, except for his eyes, which followed me around the room like the Mona Lisa, and then rolled around his head like a dog insane.

I couldn't be mad at him as I had felt the very same way many times after a big night. I'd eaten a lot of rubbish in my day too, so I immediately knew what I had to do.

'Are you all right, man? Hey, one of you guys get him some water. He's really fucking stoned.' I picked him up and carried him into the lounge room where it was warmer and whispered, 'Ian, get him a drink of water.'

The dog drank as if he'd just crossed the Simpson Desert on foot. Steve covered him with a blanket and turned down the lights. 'It's a bit too bright for the wee bastard.'

Ian lit some incense and I put on *Dark Side of the Moon* by Pink Floyd. And then we stood back looking at him. 'He looks happy there doesn't he?' I said.

After about twenty-four hours he got up and started walking around but something had changed. He no longer looked for things to piss on, or to tear apart. No, he had become a pacifist and a hippy dog. So we did the only right thing. We packed him into the car and took him out to the farm where the cute young hippy girl with the dishevelled blonde hair and the small waist and the crochet around the bottom of her jeans lived and gave him to her. He never chased another cat or ate another bone. I believe he lived out his days happily eating lentils and barking along to George Harrison albums.

LIVING IN ARMIDALE, I had almost forgotten what it was like to have to worry about watching your back. Then we got our first gig in Glen Innes. Now Glen Innes looks like a lot of other Australian country towns, so we just set up the gear and went about playing our set as per usual. But this was not a normal pub and they weren't a normal crowd. These were hardcore country boys who wanted a good time. A good time being a skinful of booze, a slap on the face from a young girl and a good fight.

I stood on the stage singing for a couple of sets, watching the crowd, and something felt very familiar about the place. No one was dancing while the band was playing, but that was normal in a lot of places. They were drinking lots and lots. That was pretty normal too. But it wasn't until the third set when we started playing our harder stuff that the place exploded. It was as if the first chord of one of our harder rock songs was the bell ringing to start the fight. As Mossy played the opening chords, I watched as every bloke in the place turned to the bloke next to him and proceeded to tear into them. The whole place broke into a bar-room brawl. It looked like a scene in a western movie. One person punched someone, who fell onto someone else, who turned and punched them and so on, and so on, until the whole pub was swinging and punching each other. Suddenly I felt comfortable and started winding the band up to play louder so that we weren't drowned out by the sound of breaking glass and screaming girls. This was just like home.

After the show we were worried that the publican would blame us for the riot. 'I hope he fucking pays us. Look at the fucking state of this place,' Steve said as he looked around the room, which was being hosed out by this point.

But we did get paid. In fact, the publican turned to us and said, 'Thanks boys, that was great. One of the best shows we've ever had. You guys are going to have to come back more often.' He smiled as he tucked his ripped shirt back into his pants. 'I'll book you right now if you'd like me to. The crowd loved you. You could lose a few of those slower songs you played at the start, but it was great once it got going.'

We all smiled nervously.

'Well, I suppose you want your money, eh?'

We stood and looked at him and nodded.

'Hey guys. Why don't you stick around and have a drink with me and a few of the local lads? Maybe I can win my money back in pool?' He laughed but I got the feeling he was serious.

The locals were all black-eyed and standing around in ripped T-shirts smiling at us, with teeth missing and blood trickling from their noses.

'Shit. You know we'd love to but we have a long drive ahead of us and it's getting late. We should hit it. Thanks for asking though,' Ian said politely and we all headed out the door. We jumped into the back of our little truck and left town as fast as it would take us, laughing and counting the money we had made, all the way back home.

A LOT OF THE people we met were like Don, studying to be scientists or mathematicians and whatnot. But they all seemed to be a lot looser than Don. They were taking drugs and drank like fish, whereas Don hardly drank at all and I'd never seen him look at drugs at this stage. But they all got up every morning to study or teach or whatever they did. I would sleep until lunchtime and then get up wondering where I was, how I got there and what I had done. Then I would shake off the cobwebs and start to think about the next gig.

One guy, Phil, had worked out a way to send opium from South-East Asia to himself, or to a post box at the university actually. Phil was a funny, intelligent man. He had travelled the world and had a story about everything. He became a bit of a mentor to us younger guys, guiding us through the ins and outs of living and working around a university campus. He had a thick head of curly hair and drove a VW that always seemed to have smoke billowing from the windows and Pink Floyd blaring out as he drove around Armidale.

He had smoked quite a lot of opium on his travels overseas and told us wondrous tales. 'Boys, you would have loved this. I was lying on a bed in Bangkok, in a room lit only by candles, the smell of cheap perfume, Nag Champa and opium filling the air. I was being massaged by a couple of naked, well-oiled, beautiful golden-skinned Thai girls at the time. Every now and then one of the girls would grab hold of the pipe. That's the opium pipe by the way, not a euphemism, you dirty little bastards. And then she'd bring it to my mouth, while the other little angel would lean over me, sliding her slippery body over mine, and light it for me. And then, then, well, you can just imagine what happened then. Some things you have to experience for yourselves.'

He laughed out loud, looking at us as if we were his students and he was the master. We were hanging on his every word. Well, he had me sold on smoking opium. The massages and the naked girls just sealed the deal. In my head I was already buying the massage oil and booking an airline ticket.

Luckily for us, one of Phil's parcels arrived just in time for a party we were having at the orchard on the coming Saturday afternoon. We were all really excited by the prospect of trying this wondrous drug for ourselves. Where we were going to find the golden-skinned Asian beauties was something we would have to work out once we had the opium.

The big day came. We had the whole day planned. Phil would arrive with the opium late in the afternoon. In the meantime, we would have a few drinks, play some music and generally get a bit loose. Another friend turned up with bottles of magic mushroom juice for us to drink. Mushrooms were a bit of a staple up there in

New England and we'd all had them before, so they wouldn't be a worry. We cranked up the music, rolled a few spliffs and started drinking mushy juice and Coke.

The day was going really well. I had invited a young lady called Nicki who I'd met at one of our gigs at the local high school. She turned up looking absolutely gorgeous. Nicki and I were good mates the whole time we were in the area. She was a great girl. I was trying to control myself a bit and not be so wild that I scared her off. But this girl, I soon found out, could hold her own with the best of them. I wasn't a problem.

Everything was perfect, the sun was shining, the music was pumping, beautiful Nicki was with me and we could not leave each other alone. I felt like I'd died and gone to heaven even before Phil arrived with his stash. We went into the kitchen, where he pulled out a block of golden, almost black, treacle-like stuff. It looked a bit like hash to me.

I stared at it for a minute and said, 'Is that it?'

'Wait a minute, would you?' he said and proceeded to pull out the pipe he'd told us that he smuggled in from South-East Asia.

'Where did you hide that? It's pretty big.'

'Never you mind, young fellow.'

I quickly tried to stop thinking about that. I was more interested in what was in front of me. 'I'm already flying, Phil, so I'm ready to give this a good go.'

'All in good time, young man.'

Phil told us a few stories as he prepared his party trick. I, of course, didn't really want to listen. I wanted to eat the whole fucking block immediately. But he talked me down.

'Listen, mate. Grown men have disappeared off the face of the earth after just one pipe of this magnificently evil concoction I have in my hand. And you – you, young fella, are about to try it.' He laughed. 'Wealthy sailors travelling the world have stumbled upon this stuff and given away everything, their boats, their money, even their families, in exchange for a life being massaged on a bed in Thailand smoking this golden treasure.'

If he was trying to scare me off he was going about it all the wrong way.

Finally, he got down to business. He got the tiniest piece of opium on a pin and started burning it over a flickering candle flame. Was it my imagination, or did Led Zeppelin's *Kashmir* start spinning on the turntable? No, it couldn't be, that album wouldn't even be released for another year. Man, this stuff was good. The treacle then expanded into a tiny ball. It was getting bigger as you used it. I liked that.

Phil placed the ball on the pipe.

'Here we go, lads.'

As he put a light to it he breathed in. A thick cloud of blue smoke swirled up into his mouth and nose. His eyes rolled back in his head and he let out a low moan as if he was in the throes of some incredible orgasm. He held it in, it seemed for an eternity. We all stood around saying nothing, barely breathing. Then he let the smoke billow from his lips until it filled the room and turned it from a country kitchen in New South Wales into a Siamese den of pleasure.

Opening up his already bloodshot eyes, he stared at me with a crazed expression and said, 'Fuck, that's good. Who's next?'

'I'm ready,' I said, jumping to the front of the queue.

Everyone else waited in line. They were all excited about what they were about to do, but they were all slightly afraid as well. Not me. I was in. I had my first pipe. I stood, waiting to be swept away from reality, which was going to be difficult, because I hadn't seen reality for a long, long time. Everyone else quickly had their turn. I stood there, quietly waiting. I was willing it to take me and transport me to a new level of consciousness. A place of peace and beautiful colours and, of course, naked girls.

But nothing happened. Everyone else was obviously floating around the room so I reached up and pulled Phil back to the ground and said, 'Hey, fill her up again, chief. I think my one must have been too small.'

He restocked the pipe.

'Thanks.'

I grabbed the pipe and I breathed in the smoke like a free diver before going down into the deep blue sea. I held it in until my lungs nearly exploded and then breathed out, imagining myself breaking through the surface of the Mediterranean. Nothing happened.

'Give me that shit and we can all have a few more rounds,' I said.

'You have to wait. Don't rush, man. This stuff will creep up on you.'

'I'm here for a good time not a long time,' I said, restocking the pipe. Before long, I'd had nine or ten pipes. It seemed to have no effect on me. I decided to cut to the chase and started eating it raw.

'Are you sure this is opium?' I asked. 'I think you've been ripped off.'

But no. It definitely was. It appeared that opium didn't work on me. What a cruel twist of fate this was. What had I done to deserve this? Why am I asking you? Everyone else was as high as Afghani kites and I was straighter than the road out of town. Nicki was having a great time, as were the rest of the gang so I shook it off and we went on with the party. But I was not going to give up so easily. Every now and again I took a little more and swallowed it.

I forget how much I had but at some point I was talking to one of the guests. 'I love this album. The guitar playing is …' When suddenly, mid-sentence … I couldn't speak. I couldn't move and I could barely stand. My tongue didn't seem to fit my mouth anymore. Was it even my tongue, I wondered. It might have been Nicki's. I couldn't tell. Someone must have helped me, probably the beautiful Nicki, because I remember floating just above the ground into the lounge room and then lying down on what looked like a cloud. I later found out it was the couch. The one light globe hanging in the centre of the room shone down on me like the northern lights, throwing colours in all directions and shadows that swayed on the walls like beautiful Indian dancers. The music coming from Michael's cheap little stereo sounded like choirs of angels were in the room, standing right next to me in fact, singing at the top of their heavenly voices. Nicki, who was looking even more beautiful by this point, had by some miracle turned into a golden-skinned Asian masseuse. I had reached Nirvana.

AROUND THIS TIME, MY big brother John somehow talked his way into the band. 'Come on son, this will be great, two singers. Eh? Much better than just one. We can have a great time.' His tone sounded familiar. I knew I was getting conned. Just like when we were kids.

All through my childhood, I remember him saying things like, 'Hey Jim, come here quick!' He'd be whispering as if something great was about to happen.

'What is it, John?' I'd say.

'Keep it down,' he'd whisper, looking around the room to make sure no one else was listening. 'I've got a job that only you can do. Now don't tell the other kids.'

By then I'd be sitting at the bottom of his bed, like a puppy waiting for scraps. 'Great, what is it, John?'

'I need you to go out to the kitchen and make me a cup of tea and some toast.' His tone would get secretive here. 'But keep it quiet or they'll all be wanting to do it.'

I'm not dumb and never was, but his delivery was great, and I fell for it every time. Almost before he finished talking I'd find myself out in the kitchen in stealth mode, acting like a secret agent, doing whatever he asked me to do.

Now he promised, 'I'll be there to back you up if these guys give you a hard time.'

'John, these guys don't give anybody a hard time,' I tried to tell him.

'Well, I'd be there if they do. Come on, Jim, it'll be great. The brothers back, united as one. Come on.'

John talked me into it and then he talked the band into it too. We didn't take a lot of convincing. He was the singer that the band originally wanted so they loved his voice. John could sing, play piano, guitar and was an amazing drummer. He could also fight better than most people and seemed to be afraid of nothing. He was a dangerous individual when cornered. If his back was to the wall he would lash out with a fury I had never seen in anyone else. It wouldn't be until many years later that I would work out that he was afraid of everything, just like me.

He moved into the house in Kentucky and started doing gigs. John and I always sang together at home so we could harmonise well and we both liked to rock. So really he was a bit of an ally for me, helping me push the band closer and closer to becoming a hard rock band.

Before long John wanted us to wear makeup and stand on top of the PA system in robes, screaming and pointing at the crowd. 'Come on guys, try it. This will freak these fucking hippies right out, I promise you,' he said one afternoon at rehearsals.

'But we don't want to wear makeup.'

'I do,' Steve said.

'Come on, guys. All the big bands are doing it.'

'Who?' Ian said.

'I don't fucking know. You know who I'm talking about. All

they big fucking bands. Let's not get bogged down with details.'
John could have been a politician. He was very convincing.

'Yeah all right. I'll wear it too, but I'm not wearing a robe.
Fuck it,' I agreed. John had me again.

This period of glam rock didn't last long and it wasn't really
glamorous. We looked a bit stupid. Unfortunately, there are
photos of me in makeup and a robe. Not many, thank God. He
was right though, it did freak out the hippies. I think the glam
phase ended when John left the band. When I say left, I mean was
sacked.

John had joined the band at a bit of a bad time. Michael
was becoming even more depressed and had been driving us all
mad for months. He would sit and play the first Jackson Browne
album over and over and over until we all wanted to slash our
wrists. Well, I actually wanted to slash his wrists but I didn't
tell the boys this. They were pacifists. Don't get me wrong, the
album was beautiful but by the four-hundredth listen it started
to wear a little thin. We would plead with him, 'Come on man,
play something else. Anything fucking else.'

But he'd snap back, 'This is my stereo. If you want to play
something else you should buy your own.'

'Are you fucking serious? You sound like a spoilt little kid,' I
shouted at him, almost stamping my feet.

'Yeah, well, this kid owns the stereo, so fuck you.'

I wanted to hit him so hard but I kept my cool. None of us
was about to buy a stereo so we would leave the room and try to
make noise in the studio space to drown out Jackson.

But John was not known for keeping his cool and after a
short time his patience snapped. He walked into the lounge room
and smashed Michael's Jackson Browne record over his head.

'And as for your fucking stupid little stereo, this is what I
think of it.' He turned and kicked it across the room. It smashed
into pieces.

By the time the rest of us could get into the room, Michael was laying back over one of the lounge chairs, turning blue, with John's hands around his neck.

'I fucking asked you to take it off, but no, you wanted to play it over and over. Well now I'm going to rock you on the fucking water until you drown, you fucking idiot.' John had snapped and there was no turning back. If any of the boys said a word they would be next.

'I think that's enough, John. I don't think he'll ever play Jackson Browne again,' I said, placing my hand on John's shoulder.

'Good. Good. Right then.' John straightened up his clothes and walked out of the room as if nothing had happened.

We had all dreamed of taking Michael out and nailing him to an apple tree and leaving him for the birds to eat, or hogtying him and burying him in the paddock for the farmer to run over in his tractor, but we had all held our urges under control. Every single one of us had thought about doing the same thing, but John had actually done it. The rest of the boys could all be annoying in their own way and they must have been worried about suffering a similar fate.

One of them was elected spokesperson; I can't remember who. 'We think John should leave the band now. That was out of line. What if he did that to one of us?'

They were right to be worried. I knew John would never hit me but I wasn't sure if he felt the same about them. If they pissed him off one night after a few drinks he might belt one of them. Besides, they already had me to deal with. That was bad enough. So John was asked to leave, very politely, and shipped back to Adelaide. He was disappointed, but I think a little bit happy he was getting away from us, and all the hippies who hung around us.

BY NOW IT WAS winter. It was so cold that most nights or early mornings we would be fighting for space next to the stove, the main source of heat for the whole house.

'Hey, you've been sitting there for hours. Let someone else get close for a minute.' This would be the standard morning chitchat as we began stumbling out of bed, bleary-eyed and freezing cold. 'At least if you're going to hog the fire, put the kettle on. Do fucking something useful.'

One day we decided to go into Armidale. It was cold and wet and we all thought it would be good to eat something and go to the movies. Mossy decided to stay back.

'I'll just stay here and do a bit of guitar practice, I think,' he said, wearing nothing but a towel. It was five o'clock in the afternoon and he hadn't got dressed yet.

'Are you sure? It could be a long cold night out here,' I tried to warn him.

'Na mate, I'm good. I'll get a fire going and stuff. It'll be great. See you guys later.'

'You might want to put some clothes on soon. It's getting cold.'

He practised guitar all day and all night by the way, and it seemed like every time I saw him he was naked or near to it, with his guitar, playing scales and Ritchie Blackmore and Jeff Beck licks.

'Yeah, yeah, I will in a minute.'

So we all jumped into the truck just before dark and headed off. 'See you mate. We'll be back about midnight with some beer and stuff. Watch out for ghosts.'

One of us always had to volunteer to drive the truck home, which meant no drinking. I hardly ever drove, now that I think about it. We went to the pub and had a few drinks and something to eat. We had a great night and headed home around twelve. As we left town the temperature dropped rapidly and by the time we were halfway home it was snowing quite heavily. We drove slowly down the highway, trying desperately not to slip off the road and die. We made it to the Kentucky turn-off. It was dirt road from there on and the snow was lying heavy on the ground.

About a mile from the highway and ten miles from our house, the truck came to a screaming halt. Mick thought he saw something out on the road ahead of us.

'What the fuck is that?' he shouted. 'Hey guys, there's something big and weird-looking out on the road.'

Everyone in the back was tossed around but we found our feet and jumped out to see what was confronting us. There, in the middle of the road about two hundred yards away, was a large hairy figure. Whatever it was stumbled as it lurched across the snow-covered road. It was obviously afraid of the light, preferring to hide in the shadows, as it was pulling away from us. But it was too late. It was caught in the high beam of our truck lights. It seemed to freeze, and stood there staring back at us, as if it was trying to work out who or what it was that had interrupted its nocturnal stroll. None of us could work out what it was.

'Is it a fucking yeti?'

No one had heard of any sightings of yetis around Kentucky. So we quickly ruled that out.

'A gorilla?' someone asked.

'Not in Australia, you fucking idiot.'

Not far from where we had stopped was a large rock known as Thunderbolt's Rock. Apparently the bushranger known as Captain Thunderbolt and his gang used to jump out from behind the rock and shout, 'Stand and deliver!' and rob stage coaches at gunpoint, a hundred or so years before. We had heard local legends of his ghost being seen in the area.

'Maybe it's Thunderbolt's ghost?' I said.

That got a bit of an uncomfortable laugh. 'Could be.'

The figure turned and walked towards us. Slowly at first, with a menacing, awkward gait, picking up speed as it crossed the snow-covered ground. Our eyes adjusted to the light and we worked out what it was. It was not a yeti or a gorilla. It wasn't even Thunderbolt holding his pistol at the ready. It was Ian, and he was stark naked, and that wasn't a pistol.

'What the fuck are you doing out here?'

'I looked out the window and saw the snow falling and it looked so beautiful. So I thought I'd go for a walk.'

'Where's your clothes, mate?' I asked. I was freezing just looking at him.

'I was only just stepping outside the door. I didn't think I needed any.'

It seemed that even though he was naked at the time, or maybe especially because he was naked at the time, Ian had decided to brave the cold. He lost track of distance and time and ended up ten miles from the house, alone in the darkness, naked in the snow. We found him standing in the middle of a dirt road staring at the sky. Luckily it was us who found him, as he could have scared some poor farmer's wife to death. We got him into the truck and drove home. No one said a word. What could you say about something like this? It was an uncomfortable short ride. No one knew where to look, so we just looked down, in silence.

Next day Mossy got up and acted like nothing had happened. Luckily for him and us, his fingers and other extremities had not been damaged by frostbite and he lived to play guitar again. Mossy was always on another planet, but we loved him.

THE YEAR WENT BY quickly. Pretty soon it was September and we were getting itchy feet. We began to think that we'd learned as much as we could from playing in country towns. It was time to get back to the big smoke. Adelaide. Don was heading into the final few months of his degree and needed to work hard so we wouldn't be seeing him much anyway.

'You blokes just head back down there and start doing some work. I'll join you after Christmas and we can get stuck into things together,' he said.

I had been happy staying in the country. Mainly because I didn't want to see Adelaide again. But after being away for this short period, I had forgotten what I was running from and the thought of going back to Adelaide sounded pretty good.

'Yeah, it'll be great to see my mates again. I can catch up with the family I guess too.' As I spoke I could feel my enthusiasm dwindling. Did we really have to go back to Adelaide? Life was easy up here. Our lease on the farm was up but we could find somewhere else to live. Maybe closer to town. We'd made some good friends up here. Nicki was here. I wasn't fighting in gangs or taking too many drugs or even drinking as much as I used to.

Les spoke up. 'We'll die as a band unless we challenge ourselves a bit. We can do anything up here and get away with it.'

He was right. It was time to leave. We said our goodbyes to our good friends. Some we would forget and others we remember forever. Michael couldn't bring himself to leave. He fitted right in, these were his people. He took what was left of his record collection, scratched copies of The Allman Brothers records he had brought with him and the brand new copy of Jackson Browne he'd been forced to buy, and off he went to live with a bunch of hippies somewhere out of Armidale. None of us have seen him since, but I'm sure if we ever head up that way we could find him. He probably has dreadlocks by now, if he still has hair. He'd be sitting red-eyed in the corner of a remote farmhouse singing 'Jamaica Say You Will' in his slightly flat and somewhat unattractive to the human ear singing voice. Still traumatised by his run-in with my brother John. I can just hear him. 'Man, you should have seen him. He came at me like an animal, man. Wow. It was scary. Like, who doesn't like Jackson Browne, man? I mean, really.'

CHAPTER THREE

*take the shirt off their backs ... or
rip your head off your shoulders*

LARGS PIER HOTEL, ADELAIDE 1974–75

Back to Adelaide we went. The band looked for work and managed to play shows all over town. It seemed that the trip to the country had done us a lot of good. We played hard and fast. Glen Innes must have sharpened us up a little. We got a few reviews and even got some interest from promoters.

The first place to really get us was the Largs Pier Hotel. It was a great pub that led the way in Adelaide rock'n'roll for years. These people knew how to party and the fact that we'd been going crazy in northern New South Wales for a few months served us well. If you wanted to jump on the tables at this pub you had to book a spot. Everyone was either on the table or under it. If you put your drink down no one tried to spike it, they just drank it. There were a few complaints about people getting felt up and having their arses pinched at the Pier, but we guys got used to it after a while and just let the girls get away with it. You wouldn't want to have to fight these chicks.

'Get us a drink Jim, would ya?' Suzi said as she slid across the dance floor. I waited until her partner Dennis spun her once around the floor and then back to me. She was screaming with excitement. She loved to dance and especially with Dennis.

'Sure, what do you want?' I didn't mind, as I got free drinks whenever we played there.

'A jug of ouzo and Coke thanks luv. No ice.'

'Coming up. What's Tooley having?'

We all called him Tooley, but his real name was Dennis O'Toole. Dennis drove a crane on the wharfs at Port Adelaide. He was born in the area, spent his whole life living in the area and would probably die in the area too. Tooley was one of those guys who, if he won a trip to Paris, would say, 'Paris. Why would I want to go there? Can you get freshly caught flathead and blue swimmer crabs off the fishing boats as they pull up to the wharf in the Port River? Can you watch Port Adelaide play football on the telly on a Saturday night? I don't think so. Why would I want to go to Paris? I got everything I need right here. You can shove Paris up your arse.'

He wore straight-leg jeans and T-shirts most days, maybe a dress shirt on a Saturday night so he could look smart when he danced with his favourite girl. He drove a Holden and lived with his mum and dad. He swore he was never going to leave home. 'Somebody's got to watch out for Mum. She's not getting any younger, you know.'

Tooley was the most Australian guy I ever met.

THEY LOVED TO DRINK at this pub. Most of the clientele were big, tattooed, musclebound, ugly motherfuckers in blue singlets and shorts. And that was just the chicks. No, not really. Not all of them anyway. Saturday nights most of the girls dressed to the nines, their hair tied back and their dresses hiked up high, smelling like the makeup section of a department store. There were some beautiful girls. The blokes were all smooth-talking, hard-drinking, fast-car-driving, salt-of-the-earth, working-class Australian blokes who knew how to have a good time. They would punch and kick each other for fun but if anyone else had tried to do the same they would have been killed. These were the sort of mates you read about in books, the kind of guys who joined the army to fight in Gallipoli because their friends were going. The kind of blokes who would take the shirt off their backs to give you if you needed it, or rip your head off your shoulders if you deserved it. They drank hard, lived fast, laughed and cried together, all in this beautiful pub. We were lucky enough to get the chance to play for them and they took us to their hearts.

I spent every cent I made drinking in that pub and when I had no money, I was still there, because one of our mates always had enough to go around. And if for any reason none of us had money, the publican would let us drink for free. This place was home to me and the band and a bunch of wild misfits just like us. In the Pier we found a place where we belonged, and for a lot of us, this was the first time we had felt that.

I remember singing there one night and I heard the distinct bang of a shotgun over the roar of the band. The roof above the stage collapsed on me. The band went quiet.

'What are you stopping for? Fuck, come on mate. Play your fucking guitar. We're just having a good time!' One of the guys liked the band so much he had gone to his car and got his shotgun and blown a hole in the roof above us. This was his way of showing us his appreciation. This place was like the Wild West.

Football teams from Broken Hill and marauding bikie gangs from Melbourne all turned up on the steps of the Pier, hoping to beat the locals, whose fighting ability was legendary, only to be beaten to a pulp and sent packing with their tails between their legs and their teeth missing. The Pier was a tough pub. It was where we learned to hold our own in the rock'n'roll business. By the time we were dealing with the big guns and thugs in the music business, we had seen it all. Nothing scared us.

LES HAD MOVED BACK in with his parents. He really didn't want to leave in the first place. I moved back in with Mum and my stepfather Reg in Elizabeth for a little while.

My mum had lived a harsh life. And even though she'd made it through that life and didn't have to fight anymore, she still felt more comfortable when trouble was happening. The worse the trouble, the more comfortable she was, so much so that if it wasn't happening she would start it herself. Reg was the opposite. He just wanted to stay home and have peace. They were a match made in hell. He would have been content to live a simple life without anybody judging him, look after his newfound family and stay low under the radar, but that was never going to happen. Not with my mum anyway. By the time I went to stay with them again, Mum was sick of him. She needed to escape from him and his quiet fucking life, and he knew it. I didn't want to be there and I got out as soon as I could.

BEING BACK IN ADELAIDE was a bit of a roller coaster. We were playing the same circuit, the same gigs, over and over, so the same people worked out they could see us whenever they wanted. If they didn't come out Thursday, they could see us Friday somewhere else, or even the next week if they really wanted to. We would go from full houses to empty houses and then back to full houses, all within a month. We were like goldfish swimming around in a very small fishbowl, only unlike goldfish, we remembered everything and everybody we had seen. We were going crazy.

We did runs to Port Lincoln and back, stopping anywhere in between we could. Our crew at the time included Ian's big brother, Peter Moss, who had joined us when we got back from Armidale. He was our sound guy and truck driver, and he was a man of few words.

'Are you all right, Peter?' I would ask.

'Ahhh, yeah,' was all he would say.

'Can I get you a drink, mate?'

He never wasted a good sentence. 'Ahhh, yeah.'

Even if I asked for more I never got it. 'How did the band sound tonight? Were we loud enough?'

'Ahhhh, yeah. I guess so.'

But he was a great guy. Loyal and hardworking. He smoked too many cigarettes and he liked a beer but didn't really need much more than that to make him happy.

Tooley and Mick McDermott, another good mate of mine from the Pier, were helping out too. They set up our gear and then drank with me all night. These guys knew how to drink.

I started hanging around with a guy from the Pier called Alan Dallow. Big Al, as he was known around the Pier, was six-foot-two with not an ounce of fat on him. He was quick on his feet and had a sharp wit that could easily provoke a reaction and often did. Alan and I would drink jugs of scotch and Coke all night, every night of the week. We were the first ones at the bar and the last to leave. We knew all the bouncers and the barmen and were on a first name basis with every waitress that ever worked a shift at the Pier.

Alan and myself used to terrorise everybody who came near us, even our mates. We became inseparable, travelling to shows all over the state on Alan's motorbike. He rode a Honda 750 k1. Alan was a bit of a mechanic, so his bike flew and saved us from many a dangerous situation. He was a good-looking guy and all the girls had a bit of a soft spot for him. We went out with two girls who we'd met at the Pier. Brioni was a quiet little girl who looked like a doll. She had long blonde hair and used to dress in a cheongsam. I was smitten by her when I saw her knocking back drinks at the bar of the Pier. Cathy was her sister and she could drink like one of the guys. She was a great girl too and both of them would hang around the gang at the Pier. So after every show we'd jump on Alan's bike and make a beeline back to Largs to drink and hang out with the girls. It was an on again, off again sort of thing but we had a good time with them while it was on.

Alan was afraid of no one. He loved to fight, but not to hurt people, he did it just for fun. So he would get into fights with people who deserved to be punched. Gangs of marauding hooligans from all over the state were knocked to the ground by Big Al. I was his sidekick, never really having that much to do but always there just in case he needed backup.

One night we were riding down the road near Elizabeth somewhere and Alan spotted this big guy hitting a girl. I don't know how he saw it, we were travelling at about a hundred miles an hour on his bike, but he spotted this domestic out of the corner of his eye. He turned the bike around and pulled up next to this monster who was back-handing his girlfriend, knocking her to the ground in the middle of the day, out on the street. People were walking past and doing nothing. This guy was so big and ugly that he scared everyone off.

Alan walked up and said, 'That's enough, mate.'

And the guy turned around and walked towards him. He roared something in caveman at Alan, in a voice that would have made most men tremble with fear.

'Are you for fuckin' real?' Alan laughed. He had that look on his face like he was thinking, good, finally someone who might be able to fight and he walked up and hit this guy so hard that his jaw swung in the breeze, broken. He collapsed on the street in a pile, and Alan just stood and laughed at the state of this wife-beating moron.

What Alan didn't see was the guy's wife, who had had her eyes blacked and her teeth knocked out by the thug, get up and run at Alan screaming like a banshee.

'Don't you hit my man!' she yelled, and punched, kicked and spat at Alan, who quickly stepped back and held her at arm's length from himself. She was still swinging like a windmill as Alan waved at me.

'Quick, get back to the bike. She's crazy,' he shouted. Then he pulled his arm away and ran for the bike, managing to get on and moving before she could get her bearings and attack for a second time. We sped down the road in silence and after a few miles, Alan turned to me and said, 'If I ever stop to help anyone again, no matter who it is, I want you to slap me. All right?'

WE WERE GETTING WORK through a new Adelaide booking agency called Jovan. Jovan was basically Vince Lovegrove and his wife, Helen, a good rock'n'roll team. They both looked like rock stars and were wilder than most of the bands they booked. Vince loved the spotlight and basked in it as often as possible, while Helen was happy in the shadows doing all the hard work. She loved Vince and was used to him. He had spent a lot of his adult life in that spotlight. As a young man he had sung in a wild band called The Valentines, sharing the singing duties with Bon Scott, and although those days were gone, he still acted like more of a pop star than anybody else I ever met. He was dramatic and funny and loved life. He had a story for every situation and was always happy to tell it to you. Helen, on the other hand, was dry and equally as funny, if not funnier.

One day we went around to Vince and Helen's house with a proposition. We didn't really expect them to agree.

'We need to step things up. Take it to the next level. We're getting a lot of work and we need a manager,' I said.

Vince sat listening. 'I know how much work you're getting. I'm giving it all to you.'

'But if you managed us you could get us work at places you don't run, too.'

Vince laughed to himself. 'Yeah, you're right there.' He looked at Helen. 'What do you think? Can we do it?'

I think it was Vince who officially managed us, but we all knew that Helen was doing the hard yards. We had watched her running the office for months.

'It'll mean a lot of work but why not?' she smiled. 'Let's all have a drink to celebrate.'

They put us in pubs and clubs all over Adelaide. They had their hands in the running of the Pier Hotel, the Pooraka Hotel, the Mansfield Park Hotel and a number of others, including the Mediterranean Hotel in the middle of the city. The Mediterranean was the home of a gig called Countdown, the same as the TV show. It was in the middle of Hindley Street, at the sleazy end of town. It was the Kings Cross of Adelaide. You could get laid or laid to rest on Hindley Street, it all depended on how lucky you felt. If you wanted something illegal or wild you could find it on that street. I felt more threatened there than I did in the Cross. People were out of control, so we fitted in just perfectly.

BY EARLY 1975, DON was ready to rejoin the band and he felt it was time to get serious. 'I think it's time to start learning some original songs.' While he was studying, he had written a whole repertoire for us. 'We've got to stop playing cover songs. Now that I'm back we could take a break and learn new material.'

The rest of the band looked at each other. We were worried. 'But the audiences are loving the songs we're playing.' I didn't want to throw away anything that was working.

But Don had decided that if we were ever going to make it, we needed to be playing our own material. And we needed to do it now. We were still playing Led Zeppelin songs – faster and harder than Led Zeppelin ever did, but the fact was they were still not our songs. We all knew we needed to make the change. I must say Cold Chisel have never been afraid to shake things up a bit. Especially Don. And this is a trait that has helped us sustain people's interest for over forty years.

Vince wasn't so sure it was time to change though. 'Why fix it if it isn't broke? People are loving the way the band plays. You guys are crazy.'

I had a feeling Vince didn't want Don back at all. He had no control over him. We were already filling rooms, and Don just meant more gear, less room on the stage and more people to share what little money we were making. I also think that Vince knew that the rest of us would do almost anything he said, and he wasn't sure if he would wield the same power over Don.

'If you guys drop all those songs, the crowds will leave you and go to someone else. I'm telling you.' He kept trying but it was decided. Don was one of the band and we wanted him back in. So Don rejoined us and we took a bit of a break to learn our new original repertoire.

COLD CHISEL HAD FIRST got together and spent quite a few months practising at the Women's Liberation Hall in the centre of Adelaide. As a struggling young band, we didn't have a lot of money but these fine women were kind enough to let us use the premises for next to nothing. We never got in their way and they never bothered us, and we began rehearsing there again when we returned from Armidale. That is, until one day when Vince Lovegrove came in to watch us work.

Now Vince had the attention span of a small soap dish and before long grew bored with us struggling through our songs. To amuse himself, unbeknown to us, he sat and wrote a few messages in the women's comments book. Vince was not politically correct; he was an opinionated bloke who didn't mind sharing his opinion with whoever would listen. And as the women who frequented the hall were not there to tell him to shut the fuck up, he ranted on and on about where he thought a woman's place was. We finished the rehearsal and left thinking we would be back the following week. I'm not sure exactly what Vince wrote but it was clearly offensive and we were told in no uncertain terms to hit the fucking road and never come back. We couldn't blame them. Vince could offend anyone. When Helen heard about this she was disgusted, but she had to laugh a little. She always told us Vince could be an idiot sometimes.

We found a new practice hall behind a church in Hindmarsh, on the same street where I had lived with my mum and Reg. I'd probably sung in the choir there.

IT WAS AROUND THIS time that we changed bass players too. Les had started the band, and we all loved him for that. But what he wanted to do and what the rest of us wanted had changed. Les was happy playing covers all night, and he didn't want Don to run the band. In Don's absence he had taken over running things, and he liked it. With Don back, that would all change and he knew it. Our musical tastes had changed too. We were heading in a different direction now.

It was hard though. We'd been together from the start, travelling in the back of the truck together. But at some point, up in Armidale, the gap had grown and it was only a matter of time until he had to go. Phil Small joined the band.

Phil had been in a band with Ian for a short time while Ian was still at school. Phil tells me that Ian used to turn up to play dressed in his school uniform. Phil was now in a blues band with his brother and a few mates and Ian felt that he would be the perfect guy for the job.

Phil was not only the perfect man for the job musically but was also one of the nicest guys in the world. He was the exact opposite of Les. He was quiet and even a little shy. He was a blues guy. He never dressed too flash or said too much. His bass playing reflected his personality. He was straight to the point, solid and soulful. He listened to what everybody had to say and then carefully made up his mind before joining the conversation. Phil was the sort of guy you would want for a best mate. He was honest and supportive, funny and compassionate. He never started trouble, in fact, he hated violence of any kind. He was a gentleman in every sense of the word.

WITH THE ADDITION OF Phil and the return of Don the band began to feel complete. We were moving into a new phase. The whole thing kicked up a gear. This was it. New songs, a new attitude and we would be soaring off into the stratosphere.

We spent about a month learning and relearning the songs that Don had written. Arranging them as we went along. Working all day and night until we got them right. They sounded really good to us. Maybe a little more mid-paced than we were used to but good all the same. We knew that some of them might be a little slower than our audience was ready for, but we pushed ahead. The month flew by and eventually we had two sets of material consisting mostly of Don's new songs and a few covers that had survived the cull. We moved the gear to the Mediterranean Hotel, ready for the reveal. Our regular crowd must have been chomping at the bit to see us because there they were, lined up ready to hear the band they knew and loved.

Unfortunately, we were no longer the band they knew and loved; we were a band who had just learned a bunch of new songs, written by a guy who'd spent the last year or so studying physics and living in college with a bunch of dorks. He was totally out of touch with where the band had moved on to, and the songs didn't work for us at all that night.

The place emptied quickly, and by the end of the second set we could hear crickets rubbing their legs together. We were alone in Countdown with nothing but the memories of our old crowd looking very angry and bemused and mumbling under their breath as they left the hall as fast as their feet would carry them. It was a disaster. We were shattered. Even Don knew that the songs weren't right. Next day we went to see Vince and decided never to play the songs again. There were a couple that worked, but not many. We went back to playing the old songs even harder and faster than we did before, with more anger and just a touch of embarrassment.

Things settled down and we went on working our way around South Australia. The songs came. Don worked up new songs for us every day and slowly but surely we started to get our own sound, a combination of the raw power the band had learned from playing live to hostile strangers in pubs and the songs that Don was writing. We slowly found a way to marry the two together. We were on our way.

IAN, STEVE AND DON shared a house with Peter Moss. I spent a lot of time at that house but never lived there. I think this was a good thing for the other three. The last thing they needed was me and a bunch of my drunken mates hanging around the house looking for trouble. But regardless of what they wanted, I still did hang around a bit.

I lived with John, my brother, in a tiny house near a pub called the Arkaba Hotel, just off Glen Osmond Road. We had two small bedrooms. One for me and one for John and his Great Dane. The dog was the size of a bear. As you can imagine, a dog this size needed a lot of exercise. Unfortunately, John didn't walk the dog as much as he should have. Consequently, the dog went crazy from being locked up so much.

One morning John let the dog out into our very small backyard to have a pee, then went back to sleep. By the time he woke and went out to check on the dog, it had jumped the fence into the neighbour's yard, and ripped all his washing off the clothesline. What was left of his clothes lay in pools of mud around the backyard. John quickly jumped the fence and managed to get the dog back over, then proceeded to pick up all the guy's shredded clothes and hang what was left of them back up on the clothesline, as if no one had touched them. The guy next door never said anything to us. I think he was scared of John and the dog.

The house was not comfortable or particularly clean, like most houses that I shared with John over the years. It was a place to crash if we needed to. Otherwise we were out on the town.

MOST YOUNG BANDS DON'T have a lot of money to spend on promotional material. Cold Chisel was no different. We couldn't wait for our name to be on everyone's lips, but that takes time.

We wanted to be big now, so we figured we needed our posters plastered around town. But we couldn't afford to buy posters to put up. What was worse, we really didn't have that many shows to promote. It was decided that we would write our name directly onto walls around town. I think this was Don Walker's idea. All he needed to do was find someone who wasn't afraid of getting into trouble. Someone who liked to get on people's nerves. Someone he could talk into doing it. Someone stupid enough to not care about getting caught. He came to me.

'Sure, I'll do it. It'll be good fun,' I said.

'That's good, Jim. It'll be for the greater good of the band but you'd better not get caught. It wouldn't look good, one of the band doing this. We want people to think it was done by diehard fans. Not the singer. You know what I mean?' Don said in his slow Queensland drawl. I'd heard him use the same tone of voice as he tried to talk agents into booking the band into a pub that didn't want us.

'Yeah, no worries, Don. Nobody's going to catch me,' I said, rubbing my hands together. 'Big Alan will help me. We'll go on his bike so we can get away quickly.'

Alan was sitting on the couch, not really listening to us. 'What? What did you say?' He looked at me with a blank face.

'I was just saying you and me would go around town painting the name of the band on people's walls, won't we?'

'Fuckin' oath!' he said, getting up. 'Are we going now?'

'No, I think we should think about it a bit. At least we should wait until it gets dark,' I said, looking like I had a plan. I didn't.

'Yeah, yeah, good idea. I like that about you Jim. You're an ideas man. Will we have to fight anybody?' Alan was getting excited now, I could tell.

'Maybe. We'll do what we have to do, Al. Let's just wait and see.'

'Cool. But it'll be more fun if there's some fighting involved.'

'I know, mate.'

My plan was to wait until after midnight then head out on Alan's motorbike and hit as many places as we could in as short a time as possible. Then get back to the house before the cops caught us. It was a Monday night, so there wouldn't be too many people out and about. It would be a piece of cake.

Before midnight, Alan and I had a few drinks and a line of speed just to sharpen our very dull wits and then headed off.

'Let's just hit the usual walls where they put up posters and that should do us,' I said, sounding like I knew exactly what I was doing.

'I know a couple of places that would be good to splash a bit of paint onto,' Alan laughed. I could tell immediately that things might get out of hand. We headed out into the dark night. Unfortunately, it wasn't dark enough.

While we were busy writing 'COLD CHISEL' in two-foot-high letters on a brick wall in Alberton, some do-gooder stopped his car and shouted, 'You blokes shouldn't be doing that. That's public property!'

Alan turned, hoping for an argument, and walked towards the car. 'What's your problem, you fuckin' bozo?'

The guy took one look at him and sped off, the car fishtailing as he fled the area as fast as he could.

'What a pussy,' Alan sniggered.

'Okay Alan, let's go before he gets the cops.'

We put on our helmets and jumped on the bike.

We spent the next two hours painting walls all over the suburbs of Adelaide. We wrote on the wall of the local Prospect Police Station. That was Alan's idea. We even found a beautiful big white wall that surrounded the house of the then biggest promoter in Adelaide. He ran quite a few gigs around town and on Sunday nights he ran a gay evening. It was the only thing open late and most musicians ended up there at some point in the night. People from all walks of life rubbed shoulders at the club: judges and criminals, musicians and gangsters, all sharing tables, listening to music and watching drag shows. The highlight of the night occurred about 1 a.m. That's when the weekly 'slave market' was held. Punters who had had way too much to drink would offer themselves up for auction to be some lucky bidder's 'slave' for the next few hours. I never volunteered to be sold, or bought anybody myself. But people would pay up the money and take whoever they bought out the door and leave. What they did was their business, I guess.

Anyway, that promoter probably wouldn't like us much after this night.

'What do you think, mate? This'll look really good. And fuck him, he doesn't give us many gigs anyway,' I said.

'He definitely won't give us any gigs now,' Alan laughed.

We wrote it so large that 'VOTE 1 COLD CHISEL' was easy to read for the next few months as you drove past his house, even at high speed. He tried to scrub it off but it refused to be gone. He painted over it but it still bled through. He would not forget us in a hurry.

We were satisfied that we had done our job as well as we could. 'The band is going to be so happy with us,' I shouted against the wind as we roared towards home at high speed.

We were nearly home when I yelled out to Alan, 'Stop. Stop the fuckin' bike!'

Alan locked up the brakes and the bike screamed to a stop. 'We can't miss this chance, can we?'

There, right in front of us, was a big new wooden fence. The sun was coming up, but I figured we had just enough time to do it then get to fuck out of there. The band lived just around the corner, so we could escape quickly before anyone noticed us. This fence looked down the main street that led from the city to the airport. By seven in the morning it would be gridlocked and would stay that way for hours. No one would be able to sit in their car without seeing the name 'COLD CHISEL' in big black letters.

'I'll do the painting, you keep an eye out for any cars,' I said to Alan as I leapt from the back of his bike.

This was the big finish, the pièce de résistance. We were exhausted. We took off and turned the corner and headed down the street back to the house.

I was woken by the sound of Peter, who was responsible for our truck. He was screaming out at the top of his voice. 'What the fuck is that?'

I looked out the window and there, written on the side of our truck in big black letters, was the word 'FRANK'.

'I don't know. We never did it. It definitely wasn't there when we got home. I don't think,' I said, rubbing my eyes.

We found out later that the guy who owned the last fence that we vandalised knew of the band and knew where we lived. Apparently his name was Frank. He left us a note under the windscreen wipers telling us never to touch his property again or he'd carve his name into our foreheads.

'That's pretty funny,' I said and went back to bed. Peter spent the next four hours getting Frank's name off the truck.

CHAPTER FOUR

Deep Purple overdosed on methedrine

FRATERNITY, 1975 OR THEREABOUTS

S OMEWHERE DURING THIS PERIOD, a harmonica player named John Ayres started turning up at our gigs. John, or Uncle as he was known, was a crazy guy with his hair shaved all the way from the crown of his head down to where his beard started under his chin. This included his eyebrows, so he looked like a cross between an alien and a garden gnome. Uncle played harp for Fraternity, one of the bands I used to look up to at the Pier Hotel. They started out as a sort of hippy band, with recorder solos and gnome beards. But they were great. They ended up changing their name to Fang, moving to the UK and becoming a hard rock band. By the time they got back to Australia they were jaded and on the verge of breaking up. But some new blood was injected into them via a few new members, and they were in the process of reinventing themselves when their singer, Bon Scott, left and joined another band.

Bon was tired from slogging it out with Fraternity in the UK. By the time they returned to Adelaide he was over it. In May 1974 he was riding a motorbike around town and drinking way too much. A bad combination. He had a serious accident and recovery took a long time. It was during this time Bon and I became friends. I had looked up to Bon for years. Even though Fraternity had limited success in the rest of Australia, in Adelaide they were huge. I had always watched local Adelaide bands and admired them even when they didn't talk to me. These were guys from the same town I was living in. Hometown heroes, I guess. But a lot of the local bands were pop stars. They seemed to have more attitude than they should have had. Bon was different. He was a good guy. He drank down at the Pier with the locals and that's where I started hanging out with him. At this time, I remember Bon's drink of choice was a Harvey Wallbanger, a weird mix of vodka, Galliano and orange juice. Bon didn't have a lot of orange juice with his. I drank these with him one night. I could never look at Galliano again. Ever.

Bon was a hard-rocking guy from his head to his toes. He had the swagger of a rock singer and the look of a rock singer, but unlike most of the other people around Adelaide who tried to be rock stars he had the goods to back it up. He could sing higher and drink more than most, and more than one time drank me into the ground. Even I was shocked by how much he could consume. But he was a funny, warm, down-to-earth bloke, and he stayed that way for as long as I knew him. No matter how famous he got, he never changed.

The band that Bon was to join were from Sydney. They already had a reputation as a band that was going places. They knew how to rock. Before Bon joined them, I had seen them at Chequers Nightclub in Sydney on our way back from Armidale, and was blown away by the power of the two guitar players. They were a great band who needed a great singer, and

Bon was a great singer. The band he joined was called AC/DC. Bon and AC/DC were a match made in heaven. They went on to make a few of the best rock'n'roll records ever.

SO FRATERNITY FOUND THEMSELVES in the market for a new singer and my brother John was in the market for a new band, and he decided to join Fraternity. It was all going great when suddenly the drummer, a guy called JF, left the band. JF had had a big fight with Bruce Howe, the bass player and leader of the band. My brother, who always had a plan B, said, 'No worries. I'll play drums and we can find another singer.' At that time, he was more comfortable behind the kit.

This was around the time Uncle started turning up at our shows. We got him up to play with us at the Pooraka Hotel and it was pretty wild. After the show he cornered us and said, 'Maybe I could get up and do some more shows with you guys.' He was a charmer.

'Yeah, that sounds good.' We all agreed.

'Well, maybe you could pay me a little wage. You know, just for petrol and pot. My band is building a PA system so we need all the cash we can get.'

Whatever his band was building had fuck-all to do with us, but our crowd loved him being up there and so did we.

'Yeah, all right, we could pay a little bit. We don't make that much.'

We all had the feeling we were being conned, but in a nice way, so we hired him anyway. I was loving the energy that he had, and the volume he played at. He was deafening. I always liked people who grabbed my attention. It wasn't long until my brother John was hanging around too. And Uncle and John came up with a scheme to get me to leave Cold Chisel and join Fraternity.

I talked before about how John had a way of getting me to do whatever he wanted. Uncle and John's Fraternity proposition was a bit like that. Before I knew what was happening, they had me leaving Cold Chisel, a band that I loved, and joining a band that no one had heard. This was the plan.

'It'll be so good, Jim. You and me in the same band.' I had heard this before when John joined Cold Chisel. It didn't work out that time. 'I'll play drums and you'll be out front singing. We'll kick arse, I'm telling you.' John could see it all in his head. 'We will kill it. How could we go wrong, eh?'

Uncle watched on as John spun his story. Even he was impressed.

'Listen Jim, these guys have been around for a long time. They've played overseas. They have a shitload of experience. With a bit of energy from us two we'll blow the business wide open.'

I looked at John and could see in his eyes that he believed what he was saying. This meant a lot to him.

'What do you think, Uncle?' John asked, looking for support.

Uncle was almost as sucked in as I was. 'Ah, yeah mate. This could be the start of something really good for all of us.'

Even though he had no eyebrows – maybe because he had no eyebrows – he always looked a little startled. Naive looking, like a deer in the headlights. But I felt I could trust him. Uncle was a bit crazy, but he had a good heart. I looked at the two of them and decided then and there to join Fraternity.

Fraternity mark two was a really good band, made up of these great players who had years of experience in the music business. Bruce Howe and Uncle had toured the world with Fraternity mark one. Mauri Berg, the guitar player, was from a band called Headband. They had been huge in Adelaide when I was a young fellow. We had John on drums and a young virtuoso named Peter Bersee on electric violin and second guitar. This guy was amazing but had never been in a rock band before, so he was a wild card. He kept getting tangled up in his guitar cord and falling over. It was great to watch, funny as hell.

We would rehearse in the cellar of the Fraternity house in Prospect. In that cellar Bruce would read the riot act to us all. 'Listen, if you play drums like that on the night, the crowd will walk out the fucking door. And I don't want to be fucking there if they do, okay?'

John didn't take criticism well. It was a family trait. 'What's wrong with the way I'm playing?'

I could see John wanted to hit him. Bruce would be red in the face. He had told John a million times what he wanted. 'Just keep it simple and in time. Try to play the kick drum with the fucking bass. That's all. You don't have to get all fancy with it. You're not in a fucking cabaret band now, you know.'

Bruce yelled at everyone. Most of the time no one listened. But I did. I listened to everything he told me. 'You don't need fucking vibrato, Jim. Hit the fucking note and hit it clean. Don't wobble it around. You're in a rock band. Don't slide up the notes, just hit them pure and clean. It's fucking that simple.'

I filed everything away, never forgetting it.

The band built its own equipment, guitar amps and PA system. This was all new to me, as we didn't really even know how to turn ours on. I was very impressed by it all. We rehearsed and went about announcing our first show at the Largs Pier Hotel.

The band were really something special; they sounded like a cross between Little Feat and J. Geils Band. Uncle and Bruce had written most of the songs and they sounded different to any songs I'd sung before. They were heavily influenced by Captain Beefheart. They were loud and aggressive, and the combination of their experience, and the out of control factor that John and I brought to them, was very exciting.

A couple of the guys' wives decided to make me a stage outfit. There is a photo of me somewhere wearing a pair of patchwork satin pants. How they talked me into them I'll never know. I looked ridiculous.

Well, the big day came and we put the final touches on the PA. It had never been fired up before the gig, so anything could have gone wrong, but surprisingly it all worked. The PA consisted of these massive bass bins that were made up of two open boxes, each containing four front-mounted fifteen-inch speakers that were bolted together, forming a monstrous wall of subsonic sound that could make a human being lose control of their bowels. On top of that, on each side, were two midrange speaker boxes, called 45/60s, this alone was as big as most PAs I'd seen in pubs in Australia. Then on top of that were these two large fifteen-cell multi-cellular horns. Uncle had stolen the horns from a drive-in movie theatre. The cops caught him but somehow he managed to keep the speakers. Then a ninety-degree JBL horn and tweeters. This setup was as big as what bands used when they were playing outdoors.

The stage gear was no smaller. Each guitar amp contained four fifteen-inch speakers, as did the harmonica box, and the bass player had eight fifteen-inch speakers, all with huge, hand-wired amplifiers. The reason I'm telling you all this is to paint a picture of what was about to happen when we turned on this wall of speakers for the first time, which was only minutes before we went on stage at the Pier.

The scene was set, the band members were nervous and pacing around backstage. We were ready. Or were we?

'Where the fuck's Swanee? I haven't seen him for a while,' shouted Bruce. Bruce was a bit of a worrier. 'I fuckin' knew something would fuck up. Now we won't be able to go on and we'll never get booked again. This is all fucked.'

'Settle down, Bruce, he was here ten minutes ago. He must be having a drink with some of the boys in the front bar. He'll turn up,' I said, trying to cover for John. I hadn't seen him for a while either.

'Oh Jesus, I fuckin' hope so. We have to talk through the endings of the songs, and he's the one who fucks them up, not me. I know the fucking things. If he'd stayed sober for one day he'd know 'em too. I fucking tell you, it's fucked. This is not a professional outfit.' Bruce was pacing back and forth in the dressing room, whipping himself into a frenzy.

'He'll be so pissed that he won't be able to play, mark my words. Fuck it, I'm getting a beer too. Might as well be pissed, none of you guys take this shit seriously. This band could be huge if you guys pulled your weight. Fuck.'

'I'll send someone to find him. You just have a beer and calm down,' I said.

Well, they found John and sure enough, Bruce was right. He was so drunk he could hardly stand up. He was naked in a shower in one of the upstairs rooms with the publican's daughter. One of the roadies quickly got her out of there before anyone spotted her and told her dad. He turned the cold water on full and held John under the shower until John could understand his voice, then he dragged him downstairs and into the backstage area just as we were due to go on.

'This is just fuckin' great. You better play well or this will be the end of this fuckin' band, I tell you,' yelled Bruce.

'Yeah, yeah, yeah,' John slurred at Bruce. He didn't even have time to dress. He went on stage for the first gig the band ever did dressed only in his underwear. He swayed and staggered as he walked on. One of the roadies pushed him towards his kit and put a bucket next to him in case he threw up.

'Good evening.' We were off and running.

The set started with a roar. The audience was jammed up against the front of the stage with their arms in the air, eagerly waiting for our first song. *Bang!* We hit the first chord of the first song and all the windows of the pub cracked, from the front of the room to the back. Within seconds there was at least thirty yards between us and the front row, who by now had their hands over their ears, trying in vain to save what was left of their rapidly diminishing hearing. Bruce scowled at John for the first ten minutes, hitting him on the head with his bass every time he slowed down, but besides that we were rocking. We assaulted the poor audience that night, from the start of the set until the finish, and they seemed to love it.

The next day, in the daily paper, was the only review we ever had. It said that we sounded like 'Deep Purple overdosed on methedrine'. We loved that and stuck it up on the fridge at the Fraternity house until we broke up not long after. We did a tour of Port Pirie, Port Augusta, Whyalla and Port Lincoln and that was about it really.

In the short time I was in Fraternity I learned more about singing than I had in years. Bruce was a brutal taskmaster and demanded that the singer give everything he had and then some. I can see why Bon was such a good singer; he had been in that band for many years. I believe that Bruce was instrumental in making me the singer that I am today, so if you don't like it, go and see him.

ONE DAY, LATE IN 1975, John and I were at the Largs Pier when one of the barmen walked up to me. 'There's an old bloke in the front bar and he's looking for you.'

'Is he a cop?' I immediately asked, half-serious. It was always better to be safe than sorry.

'No mate, this guy's not dressed like a cop. He's a bit pissed too and he's with some bird who's swearing like a sailor at anyone who looks at her. You'd better come and see them before they find any trouble.'

The front bar at the Pier was a good place to find trouble. The locals didn't take well to strangers. I'd seen many of them thrown out on their arses.

'Why would I go see them? Am I supposed to know them?' I was too busy recovering from a bad hangover to worry about some old bloke and a strange woman in the bar.

'Well, he reckons he's related to you.' John looked at me. Suddenly he looked worried.

'Could be one of the Barnes family,' I thought. There were a few of them in the area.

'Well if he's related to me, he knows where to find me,' I said.

'He reckons he's your dad and he's telling everyone in the bar he's come back to see you.' The barman didn't have time to argue with me and left. John and I didn't say a word.

Now, I knew that Reg Barnes didn't drink much, if at all. And he certainly wouldn't be drunk at the front bar of the Pier. So it wasn't him. I stood scratching my head. Maybe it was my real dad? Jim Swan. Couldn't be. I hadn't seen him since he left years earlier. What was he doing back, and at the Pier as well? I followed John to find out.

In the bar we spotted him. He still looked like my dad. He always had a kind face unless he was fighting someone. He looked calm and gentle. We could hear his voice across the room; it was soft and a bit raspy, like smooth sandpaper. But I knew the tone and so did John. It was reassuring and warm and he was as charming as I remembered him. I knew it was definitely Dad. He looked a lot worse than when I had seen him last. I remember thinking he looked pretty bad then, so that was saying something.

Was he all right? I was worried about him, just like I had been all those years before, when he should have been worrying about me. But he still had that look in his eyes. The one that made people trust him immediately. I could tell people were already warming to him in the bar.

I'd heard stories that Dad had left with another woman from Elizabeth but I never knew it for a fact until then. I remembered her face. Her voice was like a knife. It could be heard across the whole bar. 'Whose buy is it? Come on, someone get they fuckin' drinks in. I'm dyin' of thirst.'

I tried to ignore her and walked over to Dad. John was already in his arms. I stood still and said, 'Hi Dad. How are you?' I think my lip was quivering.

Dad looked me in the eye, and in that same voice that used to tell me everything was going to be all right, said, 'Hello ma son. Oh, I've missed ye so much. I really have. Gie us a kiss.'

He put his arms around me. I could smell cigarettes and booze on him, but it didn't matter. It smelled like him. He had me ready to forgive everything from the first word he spoke. I just wanted to never let him go again.

Dad went on to tell us how he and Margaret had been living somewhere between Streaky Bay and Whyalla.

'Sometimes we lived right oot o' the boot o' the car. It was terrific, boys. Whit freedom we had. Naebody in the world tae tell us what tae dae. As far away from yer ma as I could get.' Dad could even make living in your car sound like an adventure. He had a way with words. He was probably homeless, but that didn't matter.

'But I'm back now and here wi' you two. Maybe I'll take yous away wi' me next time. You'll love it. No a care in the world.'

I had a lot I wanted to say. I wanted to tell him he should have been around to keep an eye on us, but then I remembered; even when he was around he couldn't keep his eye on us. I needed a drink suddenly.

Dad told us stories of his adventures. 'You should see the fish you catch in Streaky Bay, boys. Big and juicy and they practically throw themsels at ye. You don't need a boat. You hardly need a line. I tell ye, you'd have to be an eejit not to catch them.'

It was like I was six years old again, hitchhiking to work with my dad. John and I sat waiting on every word.

'Ye just cook them right there on the beach. And sleep under the stars. It's a great life, I tell ye.'

I sat on the edge of the chair on one side of him and John sat on the other side. We were both trying to ignore Margaret.

'Why don't ye get in a few drinks and I'll tell ye more.'

I jumped up without thinking. But I had a bad feeling in my stomach as I walked to the bar.

'There you go, Dad.'

'Right, son.' Dad lowered his voice. He didn't want anyone but me to hear this, I could tell. 'D'ye think you boys can spot me a few dollars? Just until I get settled.'

I felt sick. Dad hadn't come back to see us. He was passing through and needed money.

'I was reading the paper and I saw ye were doin' okay and I just thought ye might be able to lend me a wee bit, just until I get on ma feet.'

Luckily for us, John and I didn't have any money or we would have given him the lot. He told us lots of sob stories about how he always meant to be in contact but couldn't find us. Even though we knew why he was there, we were still happy to see him.

Dad stuck around for a short time then headed through to Melbourne. I wouldn't see much of him until we started touring there a lot more. John stayed in contact. Dad and I had a lot to work out. But it would have to wait.

CHAPTER FIVE

this is what you have to be prepared to do

BACK WITH COLD CHISEL, 1976

I ENDED UP GOING to see Cold Chisel playing a few gigs when they got back from an Eastern States tour without me. The band had stepped things up a notch or two and were playing better than ever. They had spent a bit of time in Trafalgar Studios in Sydney doing some demos, maybe with Charles Fisher, the producer who would later expose the world to Savage Garden. Anyway, Don seemed to have really got his songs together. They sounded like a new band. I jumped up with them at one or two shows before rejoining permanently in May 1976. During that time people were starting to notice us. In fact Charles Fisher had come to Adelaide a few times to see us, I guess hoping to produce us when and if we got signed. But that didn't happen. He must have given up on us.

FIGHTS WERE COMMON AT our shows but very rarely did they spill onto the stage. Occasionally things got out of control while we were playing but most of the fighting went on outside the gigs.

The audience we were pulling was very mixed. Some were girls, which we all loved, and then there were mad music boffins, who liked our songs or Ian's guitar playing. But there were also a lot of guys, some of them in gangs, some of them just having a night out. Sometimes these gangs clashed outside the shows and it could get very frightening, especially for the younger fans, worried that they might get caught in the middle.

I was always trying to defuse the fights inside the halls, but sometimes I failed. One night in Glenelg I saw a scuffle break out in the crowd. Two gangs of skinheads had set upon each other and things were getting pretty rough. The bouncers managed to drag the offenders outside and when I left the gig about half an hour later it was all coming to a head. There in front of me were two guys lying on the ground, getting the living shit kicked out of them by about twenty skinheads.

Now, I've seen a lot of fighting, and I've been in gangs, but this sort of behaviour always felt completely wrong to me. So what could I do? I jumped into the middle of it to try to save the guys on the ground. Most of the people involved were part of our audience and had been cheering for us just minutes before, but when I jumped in, they didn't give a shit who I was. They all turned on me like animals. As hard as I tried, it wasn't long until I was on the ground and they were kicking into me, too.

It was raining leather and steel-capped boots on me and I was getting beaten to a pulp when, in a sort of haze, I saw guys flying across the carpark. One by one the guys beating me were being dragged off and were becoming victims. Two very hard-looking blokes, skinheads themselves, were dragging them off and pummelling them one by one. Eventually they got me out and stood me up. Everyone else in the gang stood back, either out of respect for these guys or out of pure fear. Eventually the two of them took me to one side and tried to explain what had happened.

Apparently, the two skinheads had broken their code by doing something wrong to one of their own gang. I was bleeding from the mouth and nose so I wasn't really listening but I got the message that they were giving these guys a beating because they deserved it, and I had jumped in to help the wrong guys.

All right, I had been an idiot for getting involved and they made that very clear, but they liked the way I had jumped in because I thought it was the right thing to do. They became my friends from that day on and none of the Adelaide skinheads ever bothered us or our gigs again. They would turn up en masse to watch us but they were on their best behaviour because of my two friends, Billy and Oscar. Oscar, I found out later, was one of the Pier boys. I hadn't met him because he had started hanging with the skinhead gang but he was a great guy. He still pops up backstage at gigs in Adelaide, normally working security, and we always have time for each other, to say hello, or have a laugh and talk about the good old days.

Billy Rowe became a dear friend of mine. I found out later that Billy and I came from the same area out near Elizabeth and that we both had tough childhoods. He started working for Cold Chisel and travelling around Australia with me and the boys from that day on. He was very creative and it seemed he was just waiting for life to give him a break, and it happened that day, when he jumped in to save my arse.

Life has a way of working out for the better sometimes, but not always. I don't know if Billy would have survived gang life in Adelaide or if he would have ended up in jail, but that day Cold Chisel found a great friend and he found a friend in us. We also found a great lighting guy. Billy and Big Al became our regular crew, and not a tougher or nicer crew ever worked for a band.

They were my best mates. We all came together on the road and all found some sort of escape, even peace, on tour with Cold Chisel.

AFTER A WHILE THINGS got too hard for Vince and Helen to manage. What with a band, a family and an agency, something had to go and I think we were the first. Our disastrous set of original songs at the Mediterranean might have had something to do with it too. We found new management in the form of a one-time roadie from one of Swanee's old bands. A guy called Ray Hearn. Ray had come a long way since his roadie days and knew a lot about music. He was passionate about it. I liked Ray because I once saw him single-handedly move a Hammond organ, which is a very hard thing to do.

Ray was a bit of an alternative guy but he liked us anyway, maybe because we were wilder than most of the other so-called rock bands in Adelaide. He took us to a new agency, CBA, and things were going really well. He got us a couple of gigs with Split Enz, who were touring Adelaide at the same time as a band called Skyhooks.

Split Enz were a very arty but they played well and wrote very good songs. Tim, the singer, had a beautiful voice. A few years later, Tim's young brother Neil would join the band and they would rocket even further up the charts, but even before Neil came along they were a cracking band.

Skyhooks weren't as good musically and had a lot more attitude. They were arty too – but more like a glam band that didn't play their instruments that well, although if you look at how well they targeted their audience, you have to admire them. They were one of those bands you either loved or hated. I hated them at first. They were bigger than Ben Hur, partly because they had come along as the TV show *Countdown* took off. They were the perfect band for these times. They wrote songs about places that people could relate to. Their hometown, Melbourne, seemed to dominate their songs, but kids all over Australia related to their sense of humour. Apart from them and Split Enz, who dressed in outrageous clothing, every other band looked like a blues band – jeans, long hair and T-shirts. They didn't work to their audiences, they played with their backs to the crowd and jammed self-indulgently for hours on end. Skyhooks had short sharp pop songs, presented by a band dressed up as clowns in satin and silk and wearing far too much makeup. They were perfect for TV and they tore the Australian rock scene apart.

Cold Chisel didn't wear any makeup and we didn't have clothes made of satin. We weren't on TV. We didn't have a plan or a direction and most importantly, we didn't stick our tongues out. We had nothing going for us. I should have been feeling pretty down about life and the music business in general. And then Ray decided to give us a reality check. He took us to see Skyhooks at the Mediterranean.

He shook his head and looked at us and shouted over the noise of Skyhooks, 'Well, boys ...' Whenever anyone starts a sentence like that, you know it won't end well. 'Lads, if you want to make it in the music business today, this is what you have to be prepared to do,' he said, looking towards the stage. 'Dress up a bit. Get an image. Something way out. Something catchy.'

He looked us up and down. We were just off stage and were dressed like most of the audience. I quickly tucked my shirt in.

'The other thing you need to do is write some good pop songs.' We all looked at Don. This was his job. We didn't know how to do it. 'Write some songs about Adelaide, for instance.'

This was getting plain uncomfortable now. I looked Ray up and down. He was wearing ill-fitting jeans, thongs and a T-shirt with the name of a bad band on it.

'It probably wouldn't hurt if you stuck your tongue out occasionally too.'

No, he never really mentioned tongues but he might as well have. I swallowed all that was left of my drink and tried my best not to hit him with the glass.

'Anything else?' I was already moving towards the bar.

'Na. That's about it.'

'Good.'

We went about finding a new manager to champion our cause. It took a while but the people at the new agency, CBA, were making quite a bit of money from us so sometime in 1976 they put in a good word with a manager who was working with them, a bloke called Geoff Skewes. Now Geoff was as far from our type of person as you could find. He was a bit of a yuppie manager, who drove a BMW and made more money than any of his acts did, which wasn't really that hard, as his acts didn't make any money. But we needed someone to do the job, so we took him up on his offer and joined his stable of acts.

Stable is a pretty good word for it actually. His stable included Stars, another band we had been doing gigs with around the traps. They looked like they should have been playing music on horseback. They were a reasonably good band but, more importantly, they had come up with a gimmick. They wore cowboy hats and boots and badges with their name on them and sang songs about horses and guns and shooting up the town and stuff like that. They might very well have been saving up for horses for all I know. To top things off they looked cute and had more girls following them than we did. With all this going for them, obviously they got preferential treatment from Geoff. This pissed us off, as we had so much belief in ourselves that we couldn't see why he didn't think we were the best band he had.

The demos that Cold Chisel had done in Trafalgar Studios without me sounded pretty good. As Geoff and his posse were heading interstate to find themselves a deal, we gave him our demos in the hope he would corral us a deal too. He went to

Mushroom Records in Melbourne and played Stars and Cold Chisel to Michael Gudinski, the best independent music man in Australia. Michael had a reputation for knowing what was going to work and what wasn't. He was sharp and used his own money to back whatever he saw a glimmer of hope in. He had signed both Split Enz and Skyhooks before anyone else even noticed them. (How could anyone have missed them is what I want to know.) Michael took one look at Stars' hats, boots, sheriffs' badges and pretty faces and then one look at our bad press photos, without hats or badges or boots, and shouted, 'Boys, you've got a fucking deal!'

And he signed Stars to a lucrative recording contract. We were left in the paddock. Any contract, by the way, was a lucrative contract when you didn't have one.

WE DID A FEW more demos at Peppers Studios in Adelaide. A couple of these songs actually made it onto the first album. I think 'Northbound Train' and 'Just How Many Times' were in this bunch of songs. The studio wasn't great, which was fine because we weren't that great either, we just thought we were. You need to be confident to get ahead in music. The studio didn't have the best gear or the best isolation happening. I remember doing 'Just How Many Times', and as the song was finishing and the sound was fading out, leaving the audience holding their collective breaths – at least that's what we thought they'd be doing – someone from the studio office went to the toilet, and you could hear it flush on the recording because the vocal booth was right next to it. We didn't have time or money to do it again so that was it, there was a toilet flushing on the song. That sort of summed up the demos actually.

Things got a bit lean for us for a while there as Geoff got more and more caught up with Stars, recording and touring.

Eventually Geoff had to go and we were looking for a manager again. As we weren't doing anything, I decided I had to get out of Adelaide for a week or two. We had no work booked and I was going stir crazy. I took the job as stage roadie for Stars, who were heading off to Sydney to do some gigs. The boys from Stars were good guys. I only make fun of the cowboy thing because they were my mates. I was basically their singing roadie. I never carried a lot of gear but I sang whenever they needed me. I would go to the gigs early and help set up and the band would turn up and do their thing and towards the end of the night they would get me up to sing and that would work for all of us. The gig got more exciting because suddenly they had two singers, one with boots, badge with name and hat, and one without, working the crowd, and I would get noticed by people, other musicians and industry types and, more importantly to me, girls. By the way, in case you didn't work it out, I never got the boots, badge or hat. I didn't stay long enough to earn my cowboy gear. We were staying in some dodgy hotel in Coogee Bay, but thanks to the boys getting me up to sing I don't think I ever slept there. I was always out drinking or getting up to no good. So the whole trip was a bit of a holiday for me.

___

CHAPTER SIX

play every show like it is your last

ON THE ROAD, 1976

WE DROVE FROM TOWN to town, playing every gig that would have us and a few that didn't want us. Every night we got better and every night we pulled more people, well, most nights anyway.

There were a few nights when we played to empty houses. One that sticks in my mind was in Geraldton, Western Australia. We were booked to play a pub on Thursday and Friday night and it was looking pretty good. Thursday was packed to the rafters and we killed them, left them yelling for more. At the end of the night we were having a few drinks with the bouncers and I made a comment about how good it would be on Friday, going on how busy Thursday was. One of them turned to me and said, 'Oh no, tomorrow they all go to the drive-in.' We just laughed, thinking he was kidding. Next night we went on stage at eight-thirty and there was not one person in the audience. Apparently, they all went to the drive-in. The bouncer caught my eye and smiled.

He was right, but what could we do? So we took requests from the barman and all the staff and played covers all night. No one turned up and after a few sets they let us stop so they could save money on staff. We treated it like a rehearsal and just had fun playing. The bouncers and barmaids were cheering and laughing with us, and we all had a good night.

I learned a lesson that night. It doesn't matter if the house is empty or packed, you play every show like it is your last. Give it everything. The manager of the gig liked us, and because we played regardless of the fact that no one was there, he hired us again. That's how we built our following, one gig at a time.

THE BAND STARTED DOING shows in Sydney and Melbourne. Melbourne took to us right away, so we spent a lot of time there. There were dozens of pubs waiting to pay a young band next to nothing to play for them. In fact, a lot of Saturdays we could play two or three pubs in the same day. These shows bleed into one another, but a typical Saturday would consist of a lunchtime show at one hotel, an early support at another pub and then a late-night session at a club in St Kilda, at a place called Bananas.

Lunchtime shows were normally quite sedate. People nursing hangovers from the night before, me included. I would vaguely remember finishing the lunchtime gig. We drank a lot but we rocked and got wilder than the audience were expecting at lunch. It was good for everyone involved. I would only have foggy memories of the second gig. One of them I kind of remember. We were loud and aggressive and not really happy to be at the Croxton Park Hotel, supporting a band that weren't better than us but were better known than we were. They were called Supernaut. They had one big hit, a song called 'I Like It Both Ways'. I'm not sure how many ways I heard that song, but I didn't like any way it came. So I wasn't happy to be on first.

I thought we were a million times better than they were, but the mobs of young screaming girls who came to their shows thought differently. Anyway, we went on and got a pretty good reception and left the stage to a smattering of applause. Supernaut came on to a deafening roar from the crowd.

'Good evening!' the singer shouted. Then with the first crash of the first chord, of the first song, the band let off a huge display of pyrotechnics. *Bang!* The power for the whole pub blew. *Poof!* The whole place filled with thick grey smoke. It looked like it was burning down and everyone had to be evacuated. The band ran shrieking, side by side with the punters, from the smoke-filled room. Fire engines and police cars turned up with sirens screaming and lights flashing. The firemen and police who went through the pub wearing breathing apparatus weren't happy with the situation at all. There was no fire, just smoke. The publican, who had spent a fortune promoting the night, expecting to sell a truckload of beer, was furious with the band's lighting guy for being so stupid. The support band – us – was trying not to laugh too much, but it was very difficult. And the hordes of young girls, with eyes weeping from the thought of being that close to their idols, went home, coughing but still thinking that it was one of the best gigs they'd ever been to. Even though the band they paid to see only got to play a single note.

'I touched him. He bumped into me in the dark. Did you see him?' One girl wept as she sat in the gutter while the singer was led away, coughing into a towel, by the stage crew to a waiting car.

'He coughed on me. Oh, he's so cute!'

So I guess the second show wasn't a complete waste of time. By the time we got to the third show, we were a mess. I'd have no memories of it at all. I think the crew had to carry me in. I heard that it was a great gig. And we all partied through until sun up.

WE LOVED MELBOURNE BUT we didn't want to live there. The time came to move on to Sydney in the spring of 1976, and we left with mixed emotions. Everyone we had met in Melbourne would tell us how much better Melbourne was than Sydney. They told us we sounded more like a Melbourne band than a Sydney band, but for the life of me I couldn't work out what a Melbourne band or Sydney band sounded like. I thought, if anything, we sounded like an Adelaide band, although I never admitted that to anyone before now. They also told us how much better life was in Melbourne than in Sydney, the gigs were better, the weather was better, the hotels were better. Oh my God, how could we possibly find a hotel as bad as Melbourne's Majestic Hotel in Sydney? There couldn't possibly be another like it. But there was. I soon came to realise that there were hotels just like it all over Australia. In fact, we managed to find them all over the world.

We rolled into Sydney to work and to see what we thought of the place. We found a place to stay, a motel near Tamarama Beach, in the eastern suburbs of Sydney. Sounds posh, but it wasn't. The motel was on a hill at the back of Bondi Road and might have been nice in about 1960, but not anymore. It was too far from the beach to see the water and too close to the main road to hear the surf over the roaring of the local hoons' cars as they sped down to the beach, hoping to impress the local chicks. It was a classic motel, where you can park your car outside your room. There have been a few of these motels where I've been tempted to drive the car inside the room, but not this one.

We holed up in it for about six weeks, over the spring of '76. The owner was an English chap, who obviously had dreams of moving to Australia and buying a motel on Bondi Beach and he and his family becoming surf bums. But this was not the motel for that. It was run-down and dirty and no one wanted to stay, which is why we ended up there. It was really cheap. In fact, the guy let us stay and only pay him as our money came through.

THE BAND HAD FOUND a few allies in Sydney on the trip they did without me. One of those allies was a great music guy named Sebastian Chase. Sab, as he is known, was managing Dragon, a very wild band from New Zealand, and also a band called Rose Tattoo, who were equally wild. I knew a few of the Tatts from a band called Buster Brown, who we'd worked with in Adelaide. Both of these bands had bad – or good – reputations; it depended how you looked at it. For me they had great reputations. They liked to party and play music and get crazy. What could be wrong with that? So it seemed to me that we were right up Sab's alley. He talked us into staying in Sydney. He was going to manage us. It sounded good, as Don had been reluctantly looking after everything and it was driving him nuts. He had no time to write music or even enjoy playing in the band, he was too busy trying to keep our heads above water.

In retrospect, I think Sab had the toughest job in music at that time, between the three bands he was trying to look after. The Tatts were always drawing attention, normally from the police. They looked like they were out for trouble, and maybe they were, but they were a great rock band. I think the obvious tattoos and henna-red cropped hair made them a scary proposition to the police. The most dangerous to my mind was one of the founding members, Ian Rilen. Ian was a rebel. He was rock'n'roll and everything it stood for, freedom, rebellion and equality. Ian first came to my attention in The Band of Light, a Sydney blues-based rock group that I was a big fan of. He had been in a lot of bands that helped change the face of Australian rock before he joined the Tatts in 1976.

So Sab was trying to get this band across to people – and then there was Dragon. Dragon, besides being a bunch of real troublemakers, were a brilliant pop band. When we joined up with Sab, they had just released their first big single in Australia, called 'This Time', and it shot up the charts. I use the term 'shot up' very carefully because that happens to be the biggest problem Dragon had in those days. Some of the members were junkies. Their original drummer had died of an overdose in 1975 and they were very out of it by the time the record hit the shops. But they were about to become huge and Sab was trying to steady the ship – a ship that was already heading for the rocks.

THE AUSTRALIAN MUSIC SCENE had a dark history that people didn't talk about – heroin. For a long time, I'd been watching and working with bands and I'd noticed pockets of roadies and musicians who didn't seem as, how can I say it, grounded. I don't know if that's the right word but there were people who were vaguer or darker than others; not all the time, it depended when you caught them. But I soon worked out what was going on behind closed doors. Hard drugs. Heroin was something akin to the bogeyman. Our parents had warned us about it and the little media we were exposed to told stories about drug-crazed killers and degenerate jazz musicians, sneaking away and injecting heroin. There was definitely a stigma attached to it. Well, I started meeting heroin users and most of them I wouldn't have suspected, so they couldn't have been that bad. But they did hide it.

I remember seeing the Tatts play at the Bondi Lifesaver, a famous venue in the Sydney scene. I was standing at the mixing desk, enjoying the band. One of my friends, a guy called Panther, was the sound guy. I don't know if 'sound' is the right word to describe Panther, but he was my good mate and we had a lot of fun together. I knew that he dabbled in some serious drugs but he always kept it together when he worked. I don't know how he got the name Panther. He wasn't particularly sleek or fast on his feet, but his eyes did glow yellow in the dark.

Well, this night Panther seemed to be having too much fun. I noticed that Rose Tattoo was getting louder and louder. Not unusual for them. They were a fucking loud band. But this night the sound was changing every few bars. I looked over and there was Panther with his hands on the master faders, nodding off. As he fell asleep he leaned onto the desk, pushing the faders and the volume up. I gave him a nudge just before he blew up the system. His head snapped back and his eyes rolled open as he looked at me and smiled, with the butt of a cigarette almost burning his lip. He yelled, 'They sound fucking great, don't they?'

I laughed and I had to agree. 'Yes mate, they do sound fuckin' great,' I said. The Tatts played on and Panther went back to sleep.

Most of the heroin users I knew only dabbled. When I saw someone lost in it, I was really saddened. Not because it was worse than anything else to be addicted to, because I'd seen alcoholics who were nastier, I'd seen potheads who were more desperate and I myself had certainly been more smashed. But this was different, it was as if shame was a part of the high. I don't really know what the high was, it wasn't my drug of choice. I did try it by accident one night and I'll tell you about that in a minute. But like all drugs it changed the user and this one seemed to erode all self-worth from anyone who came close to it.

Dragon was a great band that survived for decades in spite of heroin tearing them apart. It's hard enough to get by in the music business, never mind bringing heroin into the equation. The fact that Dragon were so good and had so many hits is a testament to their great talent.

But Sab had to deal with those guys and he didn't have time for us, so after a short while something had to give and again, we were the first to go. I don't think the Tatts lasted much longer.

We were back to square one, with Don grudgingly doing the work of a manager instead of enjoying the music and writing songs.

HEROIN. I TRIED IT by accident one night. I was flying when I left our show in the suburbs of Sydney somewhere. We drove into the Cross to find some real trouble. I found it at a party I'd heard about, in one of the hotels on Macleay Street. An American band, which I can't remember the name of, was playing in town and they were having a big party at one of the suites in this hotel. I managed to talk my way in. I usually did.

I stood next to a wardrobe, looking for something to do. I managed to find a few drinks while I waited for the party to really take off. People were in all sorts of states, staggering from room to room. At one point a young woman walked past and smiled at me. She was a beautiful girl and she was staring at me. I offered her my hand and we disappeared into the wardrobe. The room was packed but no one seemed to notice or care. We banged and bumped away inside the cupboard for about twenty minutes and then fell back out into the room. She smiled again and kept walking. I straightened up my clothing and looked around the room. Now what could I do?

I noticed two suspicious-looking blokes ducking into the toilet. I knew what they were up to. They were taking drugs and I wanted some. I burst in as if I didn't know that they were there.

'Oh, sorry guys. Hey, what are you up to?' I asked, but it was obvious what they were doing. One of them had a big bag of white powder that he was in the process of emptying onto the counter.

'Do you mind if I join you? I knew you wouldn't,' I said before they could answer. I loved uppers and coke – but who could afford it? Anyway, it looked like these guys had plenty to go around.

They didn't seem to mind. 'Ah, no, ah, help yourself.'
Sssnnniiiiifffffff.

I already was. I took most of the mound they had poured out in one huge snort. 'Thanks, guys!' I was out of the door before they could say a word.

This coke really burned my nose. My legs buckled and the room took a definite shift to the left. I wasn't sure if my feet were working properly. 'Fuck. That wasn't coke. What was it?'

I started to panic. It must have been smack. Heroin. I had no idea how it would affect me. But I knew I had been a real hog and consumed a lot of it. I had to get out of the place fast. I staggered towards the door. With each step the room spun a little more. By the time I was in the lift I was bouncing off the walls. I could no longer tell which way was up and which way was down. I fell out of the lift and through the front doors of the hotel and the last thing I saw was the sidewalk crashing towards me. I was rolling around in the gutter of one of the main streets of the Cross.

'Fuck, what have I done? I'm going to die,' I thought to myself. I was falling in and out of consciousness. I looked up and there in front of me was a young Aboriginal girl.

'Are you all right?' she was asking me. Her eyes were bright and warm.

'Help me, I think I've overdosed on something.'

I passed out.

I woke a few times during the next twenty-four hours. I had no idea where I was. I vaguely remembered being loaded into a cab and driven somewhere. And I was lying on a mattress on a floor. Every now and then I would see an angel floating above me, wiping my brow.

'Are you all right? Just stay there. You've been very sick, but I'm here to look after you.'

I drifted off again. I woke up after a few more hours. I was better than I had been but I was thirsty and I smelled of vomit.

'Here. Drink this. It'll help you.' The same angel I had seen in the Cross was sitting on the floor next to me. She was nursing me. I didn't know who she was. But she was beautiful. I passed out again.

When I awoke next, I was alone. I sat up and the days before slowly came back to me. Where was I, and how did I get here? I stood up and called out, 'Hello?', quietly at first. 'Hello. Is anybody there?'

I didn't get an answer. I found my shoes, put them on and left. I was somewhere in Redfern. I had a picture in my head of a pretty young girl who had helped me. But I couldn't find her to thank her. To this day I don't know who she was. But she saved my life. I know it. If she hadn't helped me I would have been found dead in a gutter in the Cross. If you read this and remember me, thank you, whoever you are.

FROM THE TIME THE band hit the road, my drinking started elevating. Every night I had a little more and every night I got a little bit wilder. There was good wild, and destructive wild, and for a while the good wild was winning. The show got better, more intense, and the audiences loved us more and more, but my stage antics became unpredictable. Some nights I didn't remember finishing shows. In fact, I notice that writing this is harder than writing about my younger years. Those years were lost in the darkness because of fear and trauma, whereas these years, since leaving home, were lost in a sea of booze and cheap drugs – and eventually not-so-cheap drugs.

At the start, I would only drink a little bit on stage. Then there were the odd times that we took drugs on stage, whether by accident, like if a show came in at the last moment and we'd already taken them, or just because I wanted to try it out, to see if it was fun. But things started to snowball quickly. My drinking was fine at first, because if I drank too much then I couldn't do the show – it was that simple – but later, somewhere along the road, I worked out that if I swallowed a handful of cheap speed pills I could drink all I wanted to and not stumble.

My behaviour was like that of someone who was blind drunk, but I didn't fall over.

I knew I came from a long line of alcoholics but I never allowed myself to think about it. My take was that if you could keep up a front and no one noticed how bad you were, you didn't have a problem. I was also convinced that there was no problem if you could afford to drink – if you didn't feel desperate or seem desperate to other people, then there was no issue. As long as there were drinks and drugs available, I was all right. In the music business, as in my life in general, there always seemed to be drinks and drugs around if you looked for them. I knew how to look, and how to get hold of most things I needed. This way of thinking – or not really thinking, when I look back on it now – was going to cause me big problems as time went by and my habits got more and more out of hand.

Another thing that went along with this whole merry-go-round was, once you got out of control on stage, what did you do after you left the stage – be out of control then too? That meant more drinking and more fighting and lots and lots of sex. There seemed to be no end to the availability of drugs and booze, and there certainly wasn't any shortage of sex either.

Even before I joined the band I was never short of someone to sleep with, but after joining things just got crazier and crazier. Just like the drugs and booze, the more I had, the more I wanted. I'm not going to sit here and brag about this. I'm not proud of all I've done. This behaviour has been nothing but destructive in my life. It started out as something that filled a gap, something that made me feel good about myself, but after a short time all these encounters added to my feelings of not being worthy and I began to dislike myself even more. This of course started long before I recognised what was going on. These feelings, as much as I pushed them to the back of my head, were slowly driving me to a point where I could see no way back. I was fucked, and nothing, I thought, could be done about it. I couldn't stop getting smashed, I liked it too much, because when I wasn't smashed I had to live with myself, this bloke I had been running from since I was a small child. If I didn't like myself as a kid, who had done nothing wrong, how I was going to live with myself as an adult, whose every step was one giant leap into self-loathing? I was on the road to ruin. The highway to ... no, someone else wrote that, but we were all on the same road. I think some of us had more baggage than others to carry, but it was hard for everyone on that journey.

Fame and adulation are not healthy, they really screw with a person's focus in life and sense of reality, and if you add mind-altering substances into that mix the road becomes even more treacherous. I was travelling through my life at breakneck speed wearing a blindfold.

I think in the early days I was easier for the band to put up with, but as things progressed, I became more and more volatile. We used to finish shows and if the band didn't go as crazy as I did, I would scream and yell. Most nights they went along with me and everything seemed fine. Whether they were unhappy or not, I've never had the heart to ask them. You'll have to wait for their books to come out. But like I said, most nights were cool. It was like cooking in a lot of ways, add a little of this, and a little of that, and, oops too much, add a little more of this to counteract that, and so on and so on. If all goes well, the final result is good or at least bearable, but one slight miscalculation and all hell breaks loose. I would be flying at a hundred miles an hour, jumping out of the plane without a parachute, attacking anybody that disagreed with me. So quite often I would end up fighting with someone, or storming off alone or with someone who wanted to do the same things as me. There was always someone who wanted to do the same as me. They just didn't want to do it every night of the week.

STEVE WAS FOND OF a drink too, and sometimes he would get enough under his belt to become unbearable. Even if he didn't, he might get up enough courage to tell me to fuck off, and then it would be on. He would say something and head-butt me – he always seemed to be coming up when I wasn't looking and head-butting me – then I would tear into him with everything I had. To an outsider it looked like we hated each other, but it was the opposite really. We were the best of mates. We'd both seen the tough side of life and survived with our sense of humour intact.

I have to say, for a pacifist, Steve liked to fight, and knew how to start trouble. He wasn't good at it, but he had a go. I would jump all over him and punch the shit out of him but Steve had a secret weapon, his head. Steve's head was as hard as a rock, and he had these big Liverpudlian front teeth that were, as far as we could tell, unbreakable. He told stories of diving into a swimming pool and smashing his teeth onto the bottom and cracking the tiles. Whether this was true or not I'm not sure, but I know that I punched him hard in the teeth so many times, and the next day when we woke up there would be Steve, not a mark on him, while my hands would be cut to ribbons by those teeth. Steve also had a habit of getting drunk and the next day not remembering anything that happened. I would wake up still steaming and angry and walk out and bump into Steve and he would be smiling, showing those big teeth, and offering to buy breakfast. He was a hard guy to stay mad at because he was so funny.

The other guys didn't fight with either of us. They were reserved and quiet and hardly raised their voices. I know it wasn't because they were scared of me or Steve; it just wasn't in their nature to be aggressive.

I still have difficulties with problem-solving. If something is too hard to fix I tend to throw it across the room, but I don't fight anymore. My aggressive side softened a lot when I met Jane, which I will tell you about when I get to that point in my life.

IN THE MEANTIME, WE kept driving from one end of the country to the other, doing what we loved – playing music. The fights weren't happening all that often. I think the band let me be wild because they liked me and they liked what it did for the shows. Some nights were crazier than others but most went down so well that the promoters wanted us back, which is exactly what we wanted too.

Some gigs took us in and really treated us well. The Mawson Hotel in Caves Beach, the Pier in Adelaide, the Bombay Rock in Melbourne, Hernando's Hideaway in Perth, and many other gigs across the country. Whenever we hit one of these pubs the band cut loose. I think we did some of our best shows in these places that allowed us the freedom to go crazy.

We lived in and played at the Rising Sun Hotel in Broken Hill, a wild town filled with miners and girls. We tore this place down. They fed us, they gave us free booze and treated us like we were part of the family. There was always a smiling face behind the bar, ready to make the rest of the night go as well as the gig. So we would drive from state to state playing in pubs and getting run out of town and then hit an old favourite and recharge our batteries.

DON'S SONGS WERE REALLY starting to strike a chord with the crowd, and with us. We were playing them better and better and the band just kept getting tougher and tougher. The right people were taking notice, but we still fell back on Led Zeppelin covers more than we should have.

'Come on, guys. Surely we could drop the Zeppelin covers now? Our own songs are as good as any of them,' Don would say to us over and over, only to be met with a wall of self-doubt from the rest of us, especially me.

'I like playing them. We smash them anyway. We play them better than Zeppelin do.' I'm sure I was trying to convince myself as much as Don. 'The crowd always go crazy when we start them. So what's the problem?'

'We should have already driven them crazy with our songs for a couple of hours. We don't need to play somebody else's songs to finish them off. Plus, I'm sick of playing them. I don't want to be in a covers band all my life.'

Don was right again, but I still had that nagging fear. Were we good enough? 'We're not a fucking covers band. But I think we should play "Rock'n'roll" in the encore just to finish them off. It fucking works,' I said.

For a long time, we ended up doing whatever I said. I'm not sure I didn't subconsciously sabotage the set so that the only way it could be saved was to do what I wanted. It sounds like childish behaviour by a singer with arrested development, doesn't it? I had no idea what arrested development was at this time. I only knew that if we ever did something that was challenging, I was afraid.

It was only once the rest of the band got on side with Don that our covers-to-originals ratio changed. I would try to convince them I was right, but in the end I wasn't and they knew it and so did I. Eventually the only covers we played were songs that we wanted to play. Well, a lot of the time, *they* wanted to play them.

'Why don't we play that Dylan song "Mozambique"?' one of them suggested.

'Yeah that'll be great, I love that song.' Ian would be enthused.

'There must be a Dylan song that rocks,' I would say under my breath.

But Steve was running with it by this point. 'Yeah, that's got a good groove.'

'But we're a fucking rock'n'roll band.'

'I know but it'd be great to play some different types of songs, wouldn't it? Like an African groove would be good. We don't play anything like that. I'm fuckin' bored playing the same shit all the time. Come on. Fuck it. Let's do it.' Steve was always happy to throw in his two cents worth.

'We don't need to play songs with an African groove. We're not fucking African, are we?'

'Neither is Bob Dylan but he does it.'

'But he fucking wrote it. Besides, we're not playing in Africa, so we don't need to play African fucking music. Do we? Play something that rocks.' My head would be spinning.

'You just always want to play the same old shit, don't you? Come on man, fucking try something new,' Steve would tell me.

Eventually I stopped fighting them. 'Yeah, all right then. But I think Ian should sing it.' If it was something I didn't think would work, Ian was singing it as far as I was concerned. 'You could sell this one really well, Ian. Give it a go,' I'd try to convince him.

'Aw, I'm not sure. I think that you should be singing it,' Ian said looking at me.

'Come on you lazy fuckin' bastard. Sing it. You're the fucking singer,' Steve would say. He'd be laughing and taunting me by this point. 'If I can play drums, you can sing the fuckin' thing.'

'Fine. I'll fucking sing it. But don't blame me if it fucks up the set.'

And guess what? It worked. 'Mozambique' was in the set for a while with me singing it, albeit a little more rock than the original and a lot harder than the band pictured it. The crowd loved it. What do I know?

Don would suggest we cover a song at soundcheck and we would learn it and make it work and do it that night. It wasn't always to please or excite the crowd. In fact, I would see the confusion on their faces when we would pull out an obscure Conway Twitty or Bob Dylan cover or the like. The set would take a momentary dip while we satisfied what I thought was our self-centred musical indulgence and then, when it was over, we'd whip it back into warp speed. Most of the time these would not have been the songs that I would have chosen, but I went along with it anyway, and tried to make the band play them hard and fast.

In the end, I realised that they were right. Playing these covers gave us an insight into how to play and write different types of songs. Songs that would free us up from the idea that we had to play straight four-on-the-floor music. And this would eventually take the band to bigger and better places musically, especially once we started recording seriously.

CHAPTER SEVEN

Pig, Bear, Beaver, Spider ...

A NOTE ON ROADIES

Some of my best friends throughout my time in the music business have been the guys who carried the gear. There was a quiet strength and dignity to most of them that appealed to me. They took next to none of the money, very little of the glory and did most of the work. They fought for the band and cheered for the band when there was no one else to cheer. Every night when we came off stage it was the crew who would tell us how it was. Good, bad or indifferent. When we felt like chucking it in they took us out for a drink and told us how important it was to keep going. Not for ourselves but for those punters who got out every night, rain, hail or shine, to see and support live music. They laughed at us and with us. And they always had our backs. I know so many good men and women who have worked tirelessly behind the scenes in this business, making sure it moves.

For a while in the 1970s every roadie in Australia seemed to be named after an animal. There was Pig, Bear, Beaver, Spider,

Panther, another Bear, another Pig. It was like a zoo out there on the road. Most were hardworking blokes who were the reason that shows made it to the stage. They hardly slept, hardly ate and drank anything that was offered to them. When they did sleep it was in the truck, in the hire car, in road cases, in toilets, in the dressing room and with whoever would have them.

But there were a few wild ones too. One night we were booked to play at Chequers in Sydney. Pig was a roadie who worked with Rose Tattoo and he was an animal. He announced to us all that he was marrying a nice young girl from the south of Sydney somewhere and asked a bunch of us to come along. We thought he was kidding. What self-respecting nice girl would marry him and invite us along? The ceremony was to be at 6.30 in the evening so we could go to the wedding, have a few drinks and still get to the show in time to play. Myself and the boys from Rose Tattoo went along as his side of the family. In the backyard of this house in the suburbs the lines were drawn. The bride's family, a bunch of straight, hardworking, no-bullshit Australians, on one side, staring in disbelief at the groom's family. Us. We must have looked like the Addams Family. Angry and the boys covered from head to toe in tatts. Me in black leather pants and jacket with studs all over it, still drunk from the night before. And a selection of wild animals who loitered, rather than stood around, drinking copious amounts of beer and whisky straight from the bottle. Pig, Bear, Panther and a couple of others were well and truly pissed by the time we got there. Spider was crying in his drink. Pig had already insulted the bride's father and there was a lot of tension in the air. The big brother of the bride disappeared and came back with a half a dozen of his mates.

As the ceremony started, Pig turned and said something under his breath to the father of the bride and then he proceeded to smash him in the face. Both parties dropped their drinks and started belting into each other. It was a bloodbath. We fought our way out of the backyard. One of the boys had a van and a bunch of us jumped in it. Pig came running after us, falling over and busting his already bloody face on the road. We stopped and picked him up. He was absolutely blind drunk so we threw him in the back and drove off at speed. We screamed around a few corners. Unbeknown to us in the front, the back door wasn't shut properly and was sliding open. I looked back and realised that Pig was gone. We just kept going. I had to get to Chequers for the gig.

About three hours later, when I was singing on stage, I saw the silhouette of a man staggering across the dance floor. He walked like an animal, funnily enough, limping and dragging one foot behind him. It was Pig. He told us he woke up as we went around a corner. He was sliding across the floor and out the door. He hit the road at about thirty miles an hour. Needless to say the marriage ended before it started. I'm sure the young girl's family were happy about that.

Pig had gravel marks across his face. I thought it was an improvement. He didn't seem to mind that he had gotten married and divorced in the same night. The same hour in fact. He just laughed about it. This would be a good story to tell the boys in the truck after a show and a big line of speed.

'Thanks guys, for coming. That was a great fucking party, wasn't it?'

What could we say?

'Yeah, Pig. Let us know when you get married next time. We'll be there for sure.'

Pig smiled through broken teeth and busted lips. 'Fuckin' oath. You guys are the fuckin' best mates a roadie could have. Let's find another drink somewhere, eh?'

CHAPTER EIGHT

very positive fucking forward movement

THE CLUBS, 1977–1978

IN SYDNEY, WE WOULD play five sets a night at Chequers Nightclub. Half hour on, half hour off was the way they liked it. This was a famous old nightclub that had been witness to the birth of some of Australia's best bands. It had seen its fair share of the worst bands too. And it had seen many a band die in the arse.

I first saw AC/DC in that room. They were fresh faced and young. So was I, come to think of it. Malcolm, with silver platform boots, looked like he was in a glam band. And Angus's school uniform was freshly made by his sister. But even then they were ferocious. I knew they were going places.

When we started playing there it was right in the middle of the disco days. Disco ruled. So we would go on stage and play to an empty dance floor and then the DJ would put on 'Play That Funky Music', flick a switch and the mirror ball would start to spin. The dance floor would be packed, full of blokes with huge collars on their shirts and way too much chest hair showing, and girls with faces covered in too much makeup and dresses cut way too low. We didn't know where all these people were coming from. Our audience didn't wear white suits or low-cut dresses, but there they were on the dance floor as soon as we finished. They must have been hiding under the tables while we were on because I never seemed to see them. It was very strange, but it just made us work harder.

We did some great shows at Chequers. We did a few shockers too. Cold Chisel didn't fuck up too often but I guess disco music wore us down for a while. We lifted our game and before long we were at our best again. We played at the club night after night, and eventually we started seeing people taking off their jackets, rolling up their sleeves and staying on the floor when we came on.

The girls began standing down the front, looking at us differently. Nodding to their friends and talking to each other as if they were ordering at a takeaway restaurant, only it seemed that we were what was on the menu.

'Oh, I like that bass player. He's so cute. He looks like JPY.' They would talk to each other and shout out to Phil while we played. 'Over here. Come and stand over here. Oh, and that guitar player's nice too. Why is he not wearing shoes?'

Then I would walk past dripping sweat on them and put them off.

We still weren't a dance band by any stretch of the imagination, but people started to like what we were playing. Slowly but surely, we were building a following at Chequers and around the traps in Sydney.

Chequers had one of those dressing rooms with no privacy. Behind the stage there was a space big enough for maybe one person. It was first in, best dressed. The rest of us sat on a bench seat in the corridor. We would be changing while waiters with plates of Chinese food walked past and laughed at us, shouting, 'Don't stand around here, we got food to serve.'

It was one of those gigs where you didn't stay in the dressing room long anyway, unless you liked getting bitten by fleas. So we'd get changed and get on stage as soon as we could, and when we weren't playing we would be up at the bar, looking for free drinks and girls.

The people who ran Chequers treated us well, gave us free drinks when we needed them most and always encouraged us to keep going. The staff were the first to start cheering for us. I think we got booked again because they liked us, long before the crowd started responding. But something was happening all around the country – people were starting to take notice.

Still, not one of the record companies seemed to warm to us. Every night of the week we would be out there playing killer shows. Unfortunately, every night they could also find Steve and I after those shows, having drunk all the free booze we could, throwing punches and yelling at each other out in the street. They all thought we were going to implode, so they never signed us. But at least they knew that people liked what we were doing, so we felt that we were getting somewhere.

AT CHEQUERS I USED to see a woman who was always extremely well dressed. She wasn't a teenager like most of the crowds we played to. She was elegant and beautiful. She would stand in the corner alone and sip cocktails with umbrellas sticking out of them. As the lights from the club danced around her, she looked like a beauty from a '40s movie. And I imagined that she was alone because she was so amazing that no one could work up the courage to talk to her. It didn't take long until we were waving to each other across the crowded room and I could see her watching me on the stage.

After one gig, I had drunk enough to walk up to her. 'I couldn't help notice you were staring at me,' I said in my coolest voice.

'I thought you'd never notice. Boys are so slow.' She put her hand on mine and smiled at me. Within minutes we were out of the club, into a cab and on the way to her apartment in Elizabeth Bay. The apartment was big, the kind of place a singer like me could never afford. It overlooked the harbour.

'Nice view from here,' I said looking back at her, the harbour behind me. I told you I was smooth. She excused herself for a moment and I was left standing alone on the balcony, admiring the harbour, wondering what it would be like to live in such a beautiful place with such a beautiful girl. But it wasn't long until the harbour view paled into insignificance. She walked back into the room. The lights were dimmed but I could see her skin shining in the moonlight. She had removed her clothes and was standing in the middle of the room waiting for me. Within seconds we were writhing around on the floor. My hands were all over her when she whispered something in my ear.

I stopped what I was doing. 'Would you repeat what you just said?'

I could have been wrong but it sounded to me like she said, 'We had best be quick as my boyfriend will be home very soon.'

She whispered his name. I froze. It was a name I recognised – an extremely well known, and extremely violent, Sydney gangster.

'Would you say that again please?' I asked uncomfortably. She repeated herself and much to my horror, I had heard right. I have never gotten dressed and out of a place quicker in my life. If the doorbell had rung I would have jumped a hundred feet off the balcony into the pitch-black, shark-infested waters of the beautiful Sydney Harbour without a second thought.

I saw her again the next night we played at Chequers. We both waved politely to each other from a distance. But for a second, just a second, everything seemed to be moving in slow motion. Her eyes met mine, and sparkled. Or was that the mirror ball? Before she turned away, she smiled at me, and for a fleeting second, I considered taking him on. But I was way too young to die. And anyway, I had another set to do.

WE MADE NO MONEY playing at those half-empty inner-city gigs but every week or two we would jump in the truck and drive out of town to Wollongong, or up to Newcastle, and *bang!*, the places would be packed to the rafters, full of punters who wanted to drink and listen to real music. Rock'n'roll music. And believe me they knew how to drink. They were out for a good time and as fast as the barmen poured the drinks, they threw them back and shouted for more. Every time we ventured to either of these places the crowds got bigger and bigger. We would fill up one hall or pub and then move on to a bigger one next trip. Publicans told us time and again that hands down our crowds drank more per head than any other band playing in their venues, and they loved us for it. This started in Newcastle and Wollongong and a few other working-class towns around the country and spread like a virus until the same thing was happening everywhere.

Most nights after playing in Newcastle, I would find someone to drink with, be it some surfie from Redhead Beach or a girl that I'd met at the gig. I would insist that we stay back for a few quick drinks. The guys by this point just wanted to get home. I always seemed to have more energy than them, so they would leave me behind to find my own way back to Sydney. Next day or even later that night you could find me walking along the side of the highway with my thumb stuck out, looking bleary-eyed and tired, but always happy, hoping for a lift back to Sydney in time for the next show. Laughing quietly to myself about the trouble I had started during, and after, the show.

Wollongong was the same. We'd play to great audiences for over two hours, until we had just about played everything we knew, or were too tired to play anymore. And we'd be collapsed in the corner of the dressing room when someone would turn up at the window – which was two floors up, they had to shimmy up a pole to get there – to tell us how good the gig was and to get back fucking on because they weren't done yet and didn't want to go home. So out we'd go again to this room full of drunken punters who'd refused to leave and were threatening to wreck the joint if we didn't play more. It was crazy.

BACK IN SYDNEY, EARLY in 1977, we were told we would be playing a few nights in an Oxford Street wine bar called French's Tavern, for little or no money. In the words of the guy who booked us at the agency, 'This will be the start of some very positive fucking forward movement for you boys.'

'Couldn't we make some positive fucking forward movement and make enough money to eat as well?' I asked naively.

'Don't be so fucking stupid. This will be a good run for you. You'll get free fucking booze and the place will be full of those fucking trendy inner-city chicks. You know, the ones with more dollars than sense.' So we basically played shows for as much wine as we could drink. I hated wine.

We had been playing to crowds all over Sydney but mainly out in the suburbs. Oxford Street was not our strong suit. Radio Birdman were the band everybody liked around this area. Cold Chisel were never an inner-city band. We were never that cool. And we didn't want to be. Punks didn't like us because we were too wild for them. I remember when the whole punk thing exploded and people started spitting on bands and shit like that. I just hated it.

'Anybody who fucking spits on me will be spitting fucking teeth, get it?' I snarled at audiences all over the country.

The odd punk who got carried away and did it would have me jumping off the stage and onto their heads. I had fights with support bands and their audiences night after night. A couple of years later, a punk band played some shows with us and the singer and I nearly came to blows. I can't remember what he said but I do remember running the back of his head into the wall with my hands wrapped around his throat. At a guess, I'd say that we both might have had a little too much to drink. In those days, rock'n'roll was fuelled by lots of booze and speed and fights were quite common at gigs. Well, they were at our gigs anyway.

But we did make some good friends at French's, friendships that have stood the test of time. Midnight Oil were the next band after we finished our little run at French's Tavern. They came down a couple of nights for a glass of wine or two and to see how we were doing. We became friends immediately. I remember the first day I saw The Oils. I thought they were a frightening rock'n'roll band. Powerhouse drummer, killer guitar players and then there was that singer. Peter Garrett is one of the greatest front men to come out of Sydney, or anywhere else in the world come to think about it. On stage, he is a scary man, menacing and intense, but off stage you couldn't meet a gentler soul. We have stayed good mates and over the years we have done some fantastic shows together.

AFTER ONE OF THESE nights at French's, Ian was talking to some girls and got invited to a party. 'Hey guys, there's a couple of cute blondes out there and they want me to go with them to some place up the Cross,' he announced in the band room. The band room, as it was at most shows, was a toilet somewhere in the back of the gig.

'Are they nice guys?' I asked, almost ignoring him while finishing a bottle of Stone's Green Ginger Wine.

'Do you need some help?' Don said, looking for anywhere to go as long as it was out of French's and away from me.

So Don and Ian headed off to the party. The venue was a squat in Darlinghurst Road. I didn't want to go. The place would be full of hippies and heroin addicts. Not really my scene. The squat was an old hotel that was falling down, but for a few years before it crumbled, it would be home to all sorts of wild and wonderful people and parties. Ian even lived there for a while.

The girls soon disappeared and so did Ian. Don found himself alone at the party. Looking around for someone to talk to, he found a few guys from the Tatts, with eyes as wide as saucers. They were grinding their teeth and looked like they were chewing their own tongues out. They were talking with a loud, cocky-sounding guy in one corner of the room. 'I've been living in England for years now and to come back here and see the way this industry is run makes me laugh.'

'What do you fucking mean?' one of the Tatts protested.

'I'm just saying it's amateur hour around here, that's all.'

'Fuck off back to England then if you don't like it.' The boys from Rose Tattoo were proudly Australian.

Don sidled over and listened in.

'There are no fucking good managers in this country. There's plenty of talent but you need someone to show them what to do with it.'

'And you're the fucking man for the job, eh? I don't fucking think so.' The Tatts were bored with all this business talk and walked away, looking for a beer or anything else they could consume, leaving Don and the music industry critic looking at each other.

'Hi, I'm Don Walker. I play in a band called Cold Chisel. I couldn't help but hear what you were saying.'

'Oh yeah. My name's Rod Willis.'

'We're one of those bands that needs to find a good manager. There aren't any, as far as I can see. If you want to have a coffee, we could have a talk about your ideas.'

'Yeah okay then, if you want to talk about it give me a call next week.' Rod gave Don his number and walked away. He had Don's attention. Don would meet him two days later and Rod Willis would become an integral part of Cold Chisel's success. But first Rod would go to Chequers to see us play five sets in a battle with the DJ and disco music. We won that night. He saw us on a great night, he loved the band and it was just a matter of time until he and Don met up again. He went on to manage us for the next thirty-two years.

At the time he met Don, Rod had a job booking bands at the Harbour Premier Agency with a bloke called Chris Murphy, a fast-talking music agent with more movements than a tin of worms. Chris went on to manage INXS. With his cut-throat style of management and the band's raw talent, they took Australian music to the world. I've heard that Chris has said he was considering managing us at one point. But if he was, we never knew about it. We never wanted to have much to do with him at all. Rod was our man.

Rod had some big ideas from day one. The first thing he said to Don was, 'When do you guys rehearse?'

Don looked at him blankly and said, 'Er, we don't. Not much anyway.'

Rod was stunned. 'What? Why not? Are you fucking kidding me?'

'No, I'm not. We don't have time to rehearse. We have to get to and from gigs. We don't have any spare time. We're a working band. We rehearse at soundchecks.'

Rod now looked at him blankly. 'I'm not saying I know it all, but here's an idea. Maybe if you did, you could inject a few new songs into your set and who fucking knows, you just might get a reaction from the punters who've seen you before. You know what I mean?'

Don agreed straightaway. Finally, he had an ally. He had been trying to tell us the same thing forever, but we didn't listen. I was always way too hungover to rehearse.

So, grudgingly, we went into a rehearsal hall and learned a few new songs. One of them was 'Khe Sanh'.

CHAPTER NINE

a reputation for being very volatile

SIGNING AT LAST, 1977

COLD CHISEL MUST HAVE played to everyone in Australia individually before we got signed to a record deal. The band had a reputation for being very volatile, which we were, and everyone thought that we would fall apart at any minute, which we knew we wouldn't. We were like brothers; sometimes we would be happy and get on fantastic, other times we were at each other's throats.

Eventually, in September 1977, we were signed to WEA Records but it wasn't easy. At first the only company interested in us was the music publisher, Rondor. By the way, there are two copyrights in every song. The first belongs to the person or band who made the recording – like Cold Chisel – and the record company controls this. The second belongs to whoever wrote the song – mostly Don Walker – and that's usually controlled by the music publisher. Anyway, Rondor's boss, John Bromell, would become our publisher, and he also cooked up a scheme to get us a deal with a record company. He was a bit of a rogue who had seen the best and worst the music industry had to offer. And luckily for us, he loved the band.

John conspired with Rod and Peter Rix, a guy who was managing some big acts at the time. Peter would pretend he managed us, as a favour to John. Peter had a lot of clout in the industry and the record companies might take him seriously, whereas Rod had no track record at this time. Their idea was to fool WEA, one of the biggest record companies in the world, into believing that every other record company in the country, in particular their mortal enemy CBS, wanted to sign us. And in fact, CBS were waiting with contracts already drawn up, just needing us to sign on the dotted line. WEA, who didn't like to be beaten to a band by anybody, especially CBS, rushed over and offered us a deal. A deal, by the way, that by new band standards was pretty good.

As soon as the deal was signed, Peter retired from our management and Rod took over. The same day we signed the recording contract, Don and I signed a publishing deal with Rondor. Signing with John was the least we could do. He was a rogue but he was a very smart rogue and he knew that signing Don Walker was one of the best deals he had done in a long time. Compared to the rest of us, Don made more money because he wrote the songs. But we all know first deals aren't good, so maybe he didn't make as much as we thought.

Within a week we went from being dead in the water, covered in marks where record companies had been prodding us with ten foot poles, to being a good signing. We were baffled by the whole deal. How did they pull this off? But it wasn't long until WEA's signing looked like a smart move.

THE BAND WANTED TO make a record more than anything, but, at the same time, we were terrified about not getting it right. WEA, the record company, were very supportive but they wanted us to deliver. I'm sure they were putting pressure on us but we didn't really care what they thought; we wanted them to like us, but too bad if they didn't. The only pressure we felt, we put on ourselves. By the time we recorded we were a cracking live band. In fact I would go as far as to say that on a good night we were great, as good as anybody in the world. We were hard, fast, ferocious and tight as hell. We left nothing in reserve. Every ounce of energy and sweat we had, we poured out onto the stage. We left gigs shattered and exhausted and so did our audience.

Capturing that energy in the studio would prove to be more difficult than we thought. We got into the studio in January 1978 with Peter Walker as producer. He was a guy that we all admired. Peter used to play guitar in Bakery, a band from Perth. He was not your average rock guitar player. He didn't wear black jeans and cowboy boots. He was quite conservative really. He was thin and very short-sighted. He wore thick glasses or else he would have been as blind as a bat. Peter could play the guitar though. As a band we had watched in amazement as he tore it up on stage at Bakery shows.

But Bakery was not Cold Chisel; they were a blues band. Peter was a laidback guy and we should have known he wouldn't understand what we were trying to capture. Bakery, even in their wildest dreams, never played a show as hard and as fast and as loud as Cold Chisel played every night of the week. He didn't know what we were chasing. So we chased our tails trying to make things perfect, spending more time getting the right compression or the great snare sound instead of catching what we did best, playing with intensity and passion. I don't believe that we caught that in the studio until many years later, when we recorded *The Last Wave of Summer* album. But I'll tell you about that when we get there, okay?

It took three months to make the first album. Let me rephrase that. It took our whole career up until then, and it probably took all of Don's life as a writer, to get to that point, and then it took us three months in the studio with Peter Walker. Peter liked to share his experiences with us so we would spend ten minutes on a song and then four hours hearing a story about Bakery on the road. We were such fans, we just sat around him, listening like kids enjoying a bedtime story. He also liked to explain the ins and outs of recording to us.

'Now guys, I'm going to tell you about analogue delay, then we'll test some out on Ian's guitar, okay?'

I could only hear so much about compression ratios before I wanted to blow a gasket and get really drunk. After these long talks the band would quite often have to regroup so I could sober up a bit and we could start again. Then we would spend ten minutes recording and sit down for another long talk on when and where to use reverb and how to set delay times. I would listen for a short time and then go and look for pins to stick into my eyes.

Recording seemed to be a lot about sitting around waiting for shit to happen. I never had the patience to sit and wait for anything. If I wanted something, I took it. But I couldn't reach across the mixing desk and just do something, one, because I had no clue what to do and two, because that was Peter's job. I much preferred playing live, where you could see the whites of people's eyes and you knew instantly what was good and what was bad. If it was good they clapped and if it was bad they threw bottles, simple. And if you didn't like the audience you could jump out and swing at them.

Sitting around doing things over and over, until they had no feel or dynamics, was not what I thought being in a rock band was all about. I wanted it to be explosive and earth shattering and it just wasn't. Recording was making something in a dark room with no one to bounce things off, and then waiting three months until it was finished, and then another three months until it came out – only to listen six months later and say to yourself, 'Oh, I wish I'd done this or that.'

Even today I use the studio to get what I want and then get out. It's not where the best music is made. I think that music becomes something special when it's played in front of people and sparks start to fly between the audience and the band. I have never understood those bands that don't like to play live. I'm the opposite; in fact, I live for it.

It wasn't all Peter's fault. The band wanted to sit around and talk and hang in the studio. Nowadays we go to work with a positive idea of what we want and how we want to do it. If we want to sit and talk, we go out to dinner, not into a two-thousand-dollar-a-day studio. We were young and stupid.

We finished the record and realised how much we had to learn to take the band to the next level. It seemed that being in a band was a continuously changing, growing process. Even when you thought you'd learned something, suddenly you'd find a better way of doing it and then it would take a while until you mastered that and by the time you got it, it had changed. You started out making music for fun and then you spent a long time finding ways of getting the job done. Once you learned enough you went right back to doing what you started out doing in the first place – making music for fun. What a strange business.

THINGS WERE MOVING FASTER and faster – one night in Adelaide, the next night in Melbourne and the next night in Sydney. We were playing all over the country, we never seemed to take a night off. We'd do our own shows one night and a support the next.

We played at the Bondi Lifesaver one night in March 1978 with Skyhooks, and Greg Macainsh, their main songwriter, loved Don's songs so he went back and talked us up around the

Melbourne radio scene. 'This band I saw in Sydney, they're called Cold Chisel and they have some great songs. There was one about Vietnam that was a killer.' So even before our record was released there was a buzz about 'Khe Sanh'.

I can sit and say that the album doesn't sound like we did. I can say it all day long here but that would miss the point. The album did sound like us, but the band's sense of urgency was missing. The intensity that had been built up from the day we met, the edge we honed at every gig, was dulled. We had spent every night sharpening our tools so that when we hit the stage we were deadly. All that was thrown aside. All the things that we'd learned about live performance were of no use to us. The studio was a different animal. That's what we were told.

'Oh yeah. That might work when you're on stage but that's not how it works in here. You guys need to listen to me and I'll show you how it's done.' This was the language used by every producer or studio engineer we met for a long time. It seemed to me that they were protecting their jobs by keeping the two worlds as far apart as they could. In fact, what we wanted to do in the studio was what we were doing every night on stage. All they had to do was throw a mic in front of us and capture it. We needed someone who let us use the tools we had. This would take us years to master.

Our first album, *Cold Chisel*, was full of good songs written by Don, but we didn't really know how to get them on tape. Peter Walker was our mate and in hindsight he did a fairly good job. 'Khe Sanh' was an exceptional song. It was recorded a lot lighter than the band actually played it live, but the lyrics were angry, the message was important and the song cut through on its own merits. It is one of the most played and easily recognisable songs ever recorded in this country, so Peter obviously did something right. But if you'd been around to see the band live in 1977 and 1978, you'd know we sounded nothing like that album. We were a ferocious, loud, out of control rock'n'roll band and our record sounded soft. How did that happen?

EVEN BEFORE MAKING THE first album we had noticed that there was a lot more pressure on the band to come up with the goods. We were filling houses all over the country and with those full houses came a huge responsibility to the punters who were lining up for tickets. These guys were making it possible for us to have a say on how we wanted to perform. Before the houses were full we were at the mercy of the promoters or the venues, but now they needed us and the only people we had to please were the audience. We had just come to terms with that pressure when suddenly, in April 1978, we had an album out and a whole new lot of problems arose. Now we had people in magazines talking us up and the record company putting their own spin on things, which we didn't always agree with.

People would come and see us for the first time, expecting to hear a band that sounded like the *Cold Chisel* album, and we were nothing like that. We played those songs the way we had been playing them to packed houses before we recorded it. Delicate songs like 'Just How Many Times' for instance, instead of being wispy and haunting, were being delivered by a battering ram of a band. 'One Long Day', a song that in the studio was bluesy and piano driven, became a grinding rock song. In fact most of the songs were nothing like the album; everything became hard and fast and edgy and just rock.

I KNOW THAT IN the period from when we met to when we started recording, I had not only worked out what the audiences wanted from us but also what I thought we did best. We had played night after night in sweaty dirty pubs where most people didn't give a fuck about you and we had figured out what it took to make them sit up and take notice. And sometimes that was different to what the band itself wanted to play. Ian would always want to play blues and jazz rock, Steve would be continually trying to make the band funky, and all I knew was that whenever we started doing either of those things people sat down or walked out.

It was as if the rest of the guys had a bit of a chip on their shoulders and wanted to be cool. The last fucking thing I wanted was to be cool. I wanted us to be red hot. I wanted people to walk out of a venue either loving us or fucking hating us. I didn't want them to sit on the fence. If they didn't like us they could fuck off and stay away and if they liked us they could bring their mates along and know that we would always give everything we had to them. I didn't want to be in a funk band or a reggae band and I certainly didn't want to be in the same room as a jazz rock band. So I would do everything I could to make the band get off their arses and hit the audience square between the eyes.

I used to stand and look at Steve until he pushed a song harder or faster, I would climb on Ian's back and yell in his ear, I would sit on Don's piano and pour whisky down his throat even though I knew he didn't like it. Phil just stood his ground and played. He wasn't too tall so he had a low centre of gravity, which meant I could jump on him without knocking him over, but I rarely did. Phil stayed back towards his bass amp. Maybe he felt safer back there. Out of the way of my storming around. He didn't need me messing up his almost perfect hair. His shirt was always neatly tucked in and he always looked in control. So I left him alone most of the time. He was too cute to attack. Anyway, I picked on Ian because he was out front with me and I felt that this was what we were supposed to be doing. Entertaining at all costs. Even if it meant that we spilled our own blood. I was happy to spill mine for the sake of the show and if I had to I would spill

Ian's. But Phil was off limits. Steve normally finished the show with some sort of blood loss from smashing his hands on the snare or the cymbals. The audience liked it and so did I. I would turn Ian's amps up to full, put everything on ten when he wasn't looking. I drove the band crazy trying to make more of a rock band out of them.

I look back now and see that it wasn't just about what the audience wanted. It was about what I wanted. My life had always been out of my control, from the time I was a child until the time I joined the band. And I joined a band because I could not control myself. I wanted to drink myself into oblivion because I had nothing to live for. I joined the band at sixteen and a half and I didn't expect to live to twenty-one. I wanted everything around me to be out of control because that was when I felt comfortable. I could hide in among the chaos and no one would see what a fuck-up I was. So whenever the boys tried to settle the whole thing down, I did my best to sabotage it. I needed the chaos.

By the time we were signed I was living on whisky and cheap speed. I hardly slept unless I passed out and I never sang straight. With all the chemicals that were running through my veins, no band could play hard enough for me, so I was constantly pushing them harder and harder. Wanting more of everything: more volume, more lights, more booze, more speed, more sex, more fame, just more, that was all I knew. I had started my life with nothing and now I wanted everything and I wanted it all at once.

Anyone who tried to travel with me or keep up with me was left burnt out and damaged. Even back then I would have moments when I would surprise myself with how much punishment my own body could take. I wasn't consciously trying to kill myself but I knew that everyone had a limit and I just couldn't seem to find mine. Hardened drinkers, junkies and professional hellraisers would fall around me, and I just seemed to keep going. I didn't show signs of slowing down. I think that when I began to realise that I wasn't going to die young, I started pushing it harder just because I could.

My job didn't require that I was an animal, it demanded it. I was painting myself into a corner and eventually my world would come crashing down around me, but not for a long, long time. I will tell you all about that later. I don't think you're ready for it yet. Back to Cold Chisel.

OUR SECOND RELEASE WAS an EP we recorded at the Regent Theatre in Sydney in October 1978. It was a ball-tearing gig that was put on by Double J, when it was a new and progressive rock'n'roll station that played all sorts of young Australian music. Those were the days.

On the bill were some good mates of ours, Midnight Oil. The show was hosted by a flying, surfing pig that was in *Tracks*, a famous surf magazine at the time. His name was Captain Goodvibes, the Pig of Steel, and he was very funny. He started life as a pork chop and turned into a super pig after being exposed to radiation. He loved to drink and take drugs and surf. He was awesome. He would swing across the stage on a rope and every time he did the crowd would roar. So we were in for a great night.

The Oils played and were brilliant, as usual, but there was just one problem. The venue was a beautiful old theatre and the security were worried about our rock audience ripping the place apart and jumping on their seats. They really clamped down on anyone getting up during the Oils set.

Because this show was being recorded, we wanted it to be as wild as we could make it. This wasn't going to happen with the crowd sitting down. We sat around backstage and worked out a plan to fix the situation. We walked on stage and instead of starting with one of our usual songs, we tore into an upstanding version of the national anthem, which was 'God Save the Queen' at that time. We knew that during The Oils, every time small groups of people would try to stand up, the bouncers would quickly sit them down so they didn't get out of control. But if we got them all to stand up at once they were fucked. What decent Australian security guy could make an audience sit down during the anthem? Once they were all up, it was all over and we had them jumping for the whole show. The theatre wasn't wrecked, but it certainly shook at its foundations that night.

We came up with the name for the record after a drinking session where we were all throwing around ideas.

I think WEA had given me a Jerry Lee Lewis record around that time and I loved it, as I do most Jerry Lee stuff. One of the songs on that record was called 'You're Sixteen, You're Beautiful and You're Mine'. Now, in light of The Killer marrying his first cousin, who, by the way was only thirteen, I happened to say, 'His record would have been better if it was called "You're Thirteen, You're Beautiful and You're Mine".'

We all laughed out loud. That was the name we needed. It was perfect for our EP and it stuck.

The cover of the EP was made while we were on tour down in Melbourne. Some dear friends of ours lived in this great place on Punt Road, by the Yarra River. Every time we hit Melbourne that's where I went first. The girls who lived there were Georgina and Jan. Georgina was cute, with raven dark hair, and a free spirit. Jan was a beautiful blonde girl who could party as hard as anyone I've ever met. Jan and I hit it off from the moment we met and were great friends for years. She was wild.

The girls threw huge parties at their house. The place took on legendary status after a while. It was sort of a rave before raves started, only we knew everyone who turned up. If we didn't, they either fitted in, or were chucked out on their arses before they could start any trouble. The house was a second home to me. Everyone who was there looked out for everyone else, so it got wild but no one got hurt.

On many a night I had to save a dear friend of mine, James Freud, who would later go on to join The Models, from getting beaten up at the house. The problem was that James was just too damn good looking and all the girls loved him, which of course meant most of the boys hated him.

'You look like a fucking poof with that fucking eye makeup on. Why don't you take that shit off?' Roadies and other blokes who thought they were really butch would start on James as soon as they saw him.

But James didn't just sit and take it. He was a funny guy. 'Give us a kiss and I'll tell you who else is gay in the room.'

They just couldn't cope with him. 'You fucking fag. I'm gonna bash your fucking head in.'

That's when I'd step in. If anyone wanted to hit James, they had to hit me first. By the way, James wasn't gay. He just liked wearing makeup. But it didn't matter to me, I just hated people who were arseholes.

'Give him a fucking break, would you? He's my mate. Just fuck off out of here or I'll do you in.' I was normally too crazed to take on. Full of whisky and speed, so they would walk away. I don't know what happened to James when I wasn't there. Maybe he could fight too, I never asked him.

The bathroom had been decorated by the girls and was wall-to-wall covered with great nude shots of beautiful girls, topped with a coat of varnish. It looked amazing and was a very popular spot in the house for lots of different reasons.

We needed a place to do a photo shoot for the cover of the EP and someone, I'm not sure who, suggested this bathroom. As it was very small, only Ian and myself were in the photos, instead of the whole band. We got into doing the shot and I said, 'I feel a bit weird doing a photo shoot in a toilet with Ian, with all the naked girls all over the walls.'

Ian agreed. 'I think it would be better with a real girl in here too.'

Georgina was the only girl around at the time. Jan was in the lounge room putting on some music.

'Georgina, will you come in this photo with Ian and me?' I said.

Now Georgina was a great girl, and not overly shy. She jumped at the chance. She laughed and said, 'Sure. Let me in there with you, boys.'

But the photographer had a vision. 'Sorry, but you do know that you have to be naked or at least nearly naked, don't you?'

She laughed. 'Of course. I knew that. Not a problem. I'll just get my gear off. Watch out boys, here I come.'

But still the camera demanded more. 'Hey Georgie, can we hang your underwear on the guitar too?'

'Whatever you need to do,' she laughed.

Then the photographer said, 'You know, Georgie, it would look really good if you were on your knees biting the underwear.'

Georgie, not wanting to be a spoilsport, said, 'Lucky I was here, eh? This would have been a boring photo.'

We scrawled the title of the EP on the mirror with Jan's lipstick and *boom!*, we had a cover. The record went on to become a real collector's item, and at that time was by far the closest thing you could buy if you wanted to hear what Cold Chisel really sounded like. Live and loud.

CHAPTER TEN

you clowns had your chance

A NOTE ON SUPPORTS

OVER THE YEARS WE played a lot of supports. Supports open up for the main band, by the way. We never really liked doing them but we picked up a lot of fans.

Sometimes we would be treated well and other times we wouldn't. A few bands were a bit cold towards us, others were out and out rude. I learned from this that no matter who is opening for you, you have to give them a good chance to get their message out. Nowadays I make sure that if a band opens for us, we show some respect for them and do what we can to make their job easier. If we're not good enough to follow them, that's our problem – but it hasn't happened yet.

There is a long list of bands that were all right to us. But there's a shorter list of bands who didn't give a shit. Little Feat sang in one of their songs, 'The same dudes you misuse on your way up you might meet up on your way down'. I think about this when I see a young band starting out. If you give them a little leg up, it might just be the break they need to go further. Who knows, you might be supporting them one day.

Little Feat were one of the bands who didn't give a shit about who was opening for them. We all really loved Little Feat's music, and I still do, so when we got the chance to open up for them we were very excited. Come the night of the show, we arrived at the Adelaide Festival Theatre ready to meet and work with them.

They came nowhere near us. Never said a word. In fact, they made it harder for us to play than they needed to. They wouldn't give us any room to set up. We weren't allowed to move a thing.

There used to be a roadie called Bear ... one of three Bears I knew, by the way. Anyway, Bear, as his name suggests, was a big unit. He was our mate after this day, but before this incident, he hardly spoke to us. But he was always a pro, he did his job. He was working in the Australian crew on the Little Feat tour. The overseas road crew did not want us on their stage at all. And so they refused to give us any space suitable to set up and play.

We were about to give up when Bear came to the rescue. He walked on stage and shouted, 'Let the fucking young band set up, you fucking arseholes.' His voice was not soft and he wasn't asking anything, he was telling them. The American crew stood there looking at him, not knowing what they should do. 'Well if you won't move your fucking gear I will.' He walked on stage and began unplugging things and pushing them out of the way.

'You, hey, you can't touch that,' one of the Americans said.

'Just fucking watch me, mate. You clowns had your chance.'

The other crew said nothing. Bear moved their gear to the side of the stage. Suddenly we had plenty of room to set up.

He turned to us. 'Well, are you going to stand there all fucking day or are you going to set up? We have a fucking show to do.'

This was only the start of what would be an eventful night. I heard that a couple of the Little Feat guys had problems with drugs. Couldn't really understand what they were talking about. I never had any problems with drugs. Well, there were a couple of times that I couldn't find any. Does that count?

These guys apparently had a problem with heroin. Maybe that's why the crew were so uptight. Maybe they were trying to cope with the problems that really hard drugs can create and that's why they were arseholes.

I heard that someone from the band told the local WEA representative to find them some heroin before they'd go on, or they wouldn't play. Now this rep didn't look like the type of guy who knew where to find anything, never mind heroin at short notice in Adelaide in 1976. But he must have had some dodgy mates. I know he had to run all over town to find it, but at quarter to nine, just after we finished our set, he came running into the backstage area. He was dressed in a slightly sweaty blue satin tour jacket with the logo of some West Coast American band on it. This was the traditional dress of the late '70s record company rep. He was sweating profusely and looked extremely worried. He didn't see us or have time to worry about us. He was ushered immediately into Little Feat's dressing room to deliver the goods.

Well, he must have managed to find it. I guess I underestimated him. Fifteen minutes later most of the band walked out of the room towards the stage. I say most of them walked. A couple of them looked a little the worse for wear and sort of staggered. The drummer was carried to the stage by two of their roadies. He had his arm over each guy's shoulders and his feet were dragging behind him.

'There is no fucking way this guy is going to be able to play tonight,' I heard Bear whisper to one of the stage guys.

'He will, he was like this last night as well.' The stage guy smiled. They propped him up at the kit and left him swaying on his stool. Then he counted in the first song and proceeded to play better than any drummer I had ever seen. Whatever the record company guy scored seemed to agree with him.

I NEARLY GOT INTO a fight with Johnny O'Keefe at the Largs Pier Hotel one night. It was on a cold Sunday night, a good night to stay home and watch the television. Which was what a lot of people decided to do, judging by the crowd anyway. We were his support band at the last minute and the gig was half full. Our mates didn't know we were playing and anyway, although they loved Johnny, it had been a long time since he was at his best.

He wasn't happy at all. He was staggering around backstage, I think a bit out of it. It seemed to me like he was a man looking for trouble – I knew that look well – and he nearly found it. Maybe he was just pissed off that he was playing in a half-filled pub after all those years. But that was no excuse. He should have been happy to still be playing at all as far as I was concerned.

I walked up and said, 'Hey Johnny, I'm Jimmy Barnes. I sing for your support band tonight. I'm a big fan of your work.'

He muttered something that I didn't hear properly but I knew it wasn't nice, and suddenly I wanted to punch his lights out.

'But this is The Wild One,' I thought to myself. 'This was the guy who made me, and the rest of the country, want to shout. Johnny O'Fucking Keefe.'

No excuse for rudeness. He was a nasty piece of work and could have done with a good slapping.

'Have a good show, you fucking arsehole,' I mumbled under my breath as I walked away. I didn't belt him. He didn't look so tough to me. He did have a couple of huge security guys with him, although I can't quite remember all the details. It was the Pier so I was mindless at the time, but not like him. I was having a good time, he wasn't. I didn't stick around to watch him sing. I'd seen enough.

WE DID A SHOW at Victoria Park in Sydney with Sherbet, the biggest band in the land at the time. They had hit after hit and everybody loved them. I had watched them play in Adelaide in a pub, but they had become huge, filling stadiums and halls all over the country. By the time we played together at Victoria Park, I remember they had to be taken out of the gig in an armoured truck, the kind you use to pick up money from the bank. I couldn't believe the reaction they were getting. Girls were passing out from screaming, it was like The Beatles or something. I watched them pile into the armoured van, wondering to myself how it would feel to be that big. Suddenly, in the middle of all the mayhem and madness, Daryl Braithwaite looked across at me and shouted, 'Hey quick, you better jump in here mate, you're coming with us.'

'What?' I said as I snapped back to reality.

'Come on. Come with us. Quickly.'

I jumped in, grinning from ear to ear. The van was being rocked from side to side by gangs of young girls. They would have torn Sherbet apart if they'd got their hands on them. The band were just laughing as if this was normal.

No one was after me but it felt good to be in the thick of it. As we drove out of the gig I got a taste of what being a big star felt like. The girls were now throwing themselves down on the road, trying to get to the band.

'This is fucking crazy, isn't it?' I shouted across the back of the van.

'This shit happens all the time,' one of the band said casually. It was great fun to see it all from their perspective. The Sherbet guys looked after me that night. That's what musicians should do. Stick up for one another. When I talk to young bands coming up I tell them to remember, 'The same people you abuse on your way up you might meet up on your way down.'

CHAPTER ELEVEN

I'll be in the pub if you need me

IN THE STUDIO, 1978

Our second studio album, *Breakfast at Sweethearts*, was not all we wanted it to be, not because the songs weren't good, but because we didn't enjoy making it and didn't really achieve what we were after.

The whole studio process was still foreign to us. We'd spent five years on the road, playing in front of audiences, changing songs as we went along, desperately trying to get some sort of reaction from the crowds. I'd be bouncing off the walls most nights. Normally by the end of a good night, the songs sounded nothing like the songs we had written or learned, somewhere way up in tempo and way beyond where the band was happy to play.

But in the studio things didn't work that way. We had already found this out with the first record. We were asked to play the songs over and over, slower and slower until all the life had been wrung out of them. We would all be left looking at each other, worried, while the producer promised it would sound better when we let him mix it. The big lesson we eventually learned was that if something doesn't sound good when you put it down, no amount of mixing is going to make it any better. Of course, we all know that now, but back then we were at the mercy of the people we let take control of our records. You live and learn.

We wanted to play new songs in our set and to do that we needed to get a bunch of them out there on a record. We needed the right studio and the right producer for our much-anticipated second record – when I say much anticipated, I mean much anticipated by us, the band – but we didn't find them.

We wanted to rock more and get more of a live sound, so we decided to record at Alberts studios, which was turning out some great-sounding rock records – AC/DC, The Angels and Stevie Wright were a few – so off to Alberts we went. Now, everyone knows that it takes more than just the right studio to make a record, but I'm not sure we did.

No one told us that Alberts had more than one studio. Alberts Studio One was the room where all the great records were made. I had sat in Studio One with George Young and Harry Vanda, watching them record AC/DC. Young and Vanda had been the driving force behind The Easybeats, and were now entrenched at Alberts, writing and producing rock, pop and soul music. Everything they touched turned to gold. I knew how great that room felt.

Cold Chisel headed into Alberts only to find we were in Studio Two, which was a bit of a turkey. I'm not sure if the management booked it, the record company or the producer, but whoever did made a big mistake. Studio Two felt like you were in the dentist. Pulling good sounds in that room was a lot like pulling teeth, slow and painful.

WEA wanted us to have a producer, instead of a musician, make the record, and that would have been a good idea, had it been a good producer. They also wanted someone with a track record, someone who had produced hits, and Richard Batchens had been involved in a lot of Australian records. The one that caught our eye was *Goodbye Tiger*, an album by Richard Clapton, a fantastic songwriter we all respected. This record, we know now, resonated with us not because of the production but because of Richard Clapton's great songs. It was a great record but not really a rock record. For some reason we thought using his producer might work for us. So when WEA suggested Richard Batchens we foolishly agreed.

I don't know how he got his good reputation, because he didn't seem to know what he was doing. You generally have to have some respect for the producer to place your career in his or her hands. I wanted to place his head in his hands. I would have felt sorry for him, but we had so much riding on the record and I didn't think he did the songs justice.

I got to the point, when I was singing the final vocals for the record, that I would sing and then take off as quickly as I could, not even sticking around to see if he had got what was needed.

When it came to mixing the record, I remember we would all be in the studio, trying to make it work.

'Hey Richard. Excuse me.' I would start the day off with a nice tone.

'What?' He was so polite.

'Do you think we could turn up the vocals a bit please?'

'I wish you'd just shut up. I'm busy here.'

There was silence. Smoke was coming out of my ears as one of the band tried to calm me down.

'Hey Don, can I talk to you? Outside,' I snarled through my teeth. 'Mate, I reckon this fucking guy hasn't got a clue what he's doing. He's fucking up our songs.'

'I know. They're my songs.'

'What'll we do?'

'Let's just give him a go and see if he pulls it together. He might be in the middle of something and we don't know it.'

'Yeah. All right.'

A few minutes later Don said, 'Hey Richard, sorry to interrupt, but can you turn that organ up a little for me? Just to see if it works.'

'Not without turning the floor tom up.'

'Er, what do you mean?'

'I've bounced some of the tracks together to make the mixing a bit easier. We do it all the time in the producing business.'

Don went pale. We all knew our baby, the new record, was fucked.

'Hey Don, I'll be in the pub if you need me. I can't stay here any longer,' I yelled across the room.

Don sat, not answering me for a while, the voice of Richard the producer still ringing in his head. 'Yeah, ah, no. I think I'd better stay here.'

Richard leaned over the mixing console, talking to himself, and seemed to be out of his depth. To make things worse he seemed angry at us for asking him to be there. In my opinion, the guy couldn't mix a cake never mind a record. The album was unlistenable to me.

Miraculously the record, released February 1979, was a hit and took the band one more step up the Australian music industry ladder. I think the album's success was ultimately all down to a bunch of great songs that Don had written, and the hordes of punters who got drunk with us and listened to those songs every night.

CHAPTER TWELVE

do yourself a favour

COUNTDOWN, 1978–79

*D*IGA *DIGA DIGA DIGA Diga Diga Diga Diga Countdown!*
The intro for the TV show sounded like a bad drum fill. But *Countdown* would become the most powerful show in Australian music history. Every week on Sunday night the whole country stopped and sat in front of their TV sets and tuned them to the ABC at six o'clock, waiting for the drum fill that would announce the start of the entertainment. What new band would we see this week? Would Molly be able to speak? Why did we care so much? Often we would see the same old songs repeated from last week. Just like listening to Top 40 radio, the playlist was fairly small, which meant as a young band you didn't have much chance of getting on the show. But if you did, it could break you wide open. Bands that had no profile or following would leap to the top of the charts and become overnight pop stars, with screaming fans who wanted a piece of them. All their dreams would come true.

Cold Chisel didn't want that sort of success. We had worked for years, touring the country relentlessly, trying to build a solid foundation for a career that was real and based on our ability to write and play good music. But even then I would sit and watch *Countdown*, amazed at some of the rubbish that made it onto the show and subsequently onto the charts. 'S–S–S–Single Bed' by Fox or 'I Like It Both Ways' by Supernaut – Molly seemed to be bending over forwards to promote this song. But the audience swallowed them up and couldn't wait for their next taste. Eventually Cold Chisel was asked onto the show, but under *Countdown*'s rules. This was their show and while we were under their roof we would do it their way. It was like they were talking to kids.

We got to rehearsal only to be told, 'Guys, you're going to have to change the lyrics to "Khe Sanh" if you want to get on the show.' A representative told us this while I was watching Rod Stewart writhe and scream about 'Hot Legs' and what he wanted to do with them. 'You can't say "Their legs were often open but their minds were always closed" on national TV. No way. It's obscene.'

Meanwhile, Hush leered and thrust their hips at girls so young they should have been with their mothers, and Mark Hunter from Dragon sang 'Are You Old Enough?', drowned out by prepubescent girls screaming and wanting to throw their underwear at him.

It didn't make any sense to us. 'We're never going to change our words for you,' we announced, and were quickly told we would not be appearing. 'So do yourself a favour and get out of our sight!'

We knew what a couple of appearances could do for us but we didn't want to compromise ourselves. WEA, our record company, was begging us to make some effort for them. Why did we have to be so stubborn?

'Fuck guys, come on. Skyhooks play on there all the time.'

We weren't impressed.

'Even AC/DC go on the show.'

This was true, even if it was with Bon dressed as a schoolgirl. That was very funny and I wondered if *Countdown* saw the irony, Bon driving the young girls wild while dressed as a young girl, covered in tattoos and with lipstick smeared across his face. That was good TV. Even Iggy Pop appeared, spitting on and scaring the shit out of the kids standing in the front row waiting to see John Paul Young.

Eventually, and reluctantly, we agreed to play. It was around the time of our second album's release. 'Breakfast at Sweethearts' was the song we played. I use the term 'played' very loosely here. *Countdown* would not let bands play live. That would have given them too much control. Don and Steve sat pretending to be playing chess while Ian and Phil pretended to play their guitars, looking smooth, waiting for their close ups. This was not the way our band behaved. We never sat still.

We wanted to smash up the show. But that would have to wait. Instead, we were miming a song about a café in Sydney that was frequented by junkies and hookers. And I was walking around a set that was made to look like the Marble Bar at the Sydney Hilton, where we had shot the cover of the album late one night. We would never have been allowed into the real Marble Bar while it was open by the way. We weren't the kind of guys that went there. But here I was, miming the song while chewing my lips, with my eyes darting from side to side, residue of the speed I'd had the night before.

We hated it. We felt we had sold out. But we also felt the impact almost immediately. Record sales jumped. The live shows were even more packed. The band had made a leap from a medium-sized bar band to across-the-board acceptance. We were suddenly like an overnight success. But we had done the hard yards. We were completely prepared for what was to come. We knew how to build a show. We knew how to take hold of an audience. A lot of the bands that went on *Countdown* didn't, and were gone as quickly as they had arrived. But we were only just getting started and if the people from *Countdown* wanted to help us, we'd let them. It didn't mean we liked them or their fucking show and they knew it.

AROUND THIS TIME, ROD Willis teamed up with John Woodruff and Ray Hearn, one of our old Adelaide managers, to form Dirty Pool. Dirty Pool both managed and booked The Angels, Cold Chisel and Flowers (later called Icehouse), but this is a very simple description of what they did. Before Dirty Pool came along, bands in Australia had been subject to the same poor conditions for years. If you wanted to perform you had to go through one of the agencies that had a stranglehold on virtually all live work in this country. These monopolies in each city took high commissions and charged flat fees for shows, regardless of a band's following. It wasn't unusual for a band to sell $5000 worth of tickets and fill a pub with drinkers but still only get paid $750. That fee had to cover PA/lighting costs, crew wages, travel and commissions before the musicians received their first dollar. Someone was making lots more money than they should have been and it definitely wasn't the bands.

Dirty Pool demolished that system by introducing 'door deals', where bands kept nearly all of the ticket receipts and therefore got paid according to the number of people who turned up to see them. This meant popular bands could keep ticket prices down and still end up making a lot more money than they used to make on flat fees, and that made punters happy and bands even happier. Lots more people started going to gigs and lots more pubs started booking bands because 'door deals' meant the publicans didn't have to risk paying a fee and having nobody turn up. Live music exploded around Australia. Dirty Pool helped save an industry that was coughing up blood and turned it into a very big business.

FOR A WHILE, THE band had moved into the Plaza Hotel in Kings Cross. Don ended up staying there for several years. It was so dirty the rats were looking for better digs. I stayed one night there and then decided to take my chances in the big world outside the Cross.

The Plaza was a stone's throw from the infamous Manzil Room, the place where most rock bands drank after they had played in Sydney. It was the scene of many a nasty fight between drunken country boys and drug-rattled Croatian gangsters. Punters were found dead in the alleys and even in the skip bins outside.

The hotel was almost across the street from where the Les Girls shows had been a huge part of Sydney nightlife in days gone by. Now the alley where the hotel stood was a little darker and the building was a lot dingier. The street outside the hotel had become a place of work for some of the young ladies who lived in the hotel. They could take their clients upstairs, get their business done and then belt something into their arms that helped them not to think about who they were fucking next. Then it was back down the stairs and out onto the street.

'Hi girls. Not working too hard I hope,' I would say as I made my way out of the Manzil Room and past the hotel.

'Never, Jimmy. It's a quiet night tonight. Want to come up for a freebie?'

'No. I've had it. Gotta go home.'

The sun would be coming up and the girls wouldn't look quite as pretty as they had twelve hours earlier. Below the reception of the Plaza was a Lebanese takeaway. It looked dirty and small but the food was great. I staggered into this place at all hours of the day and night, drunk and stoned. If I was heading home, they would make a special coffee to help finish me off, a double shot of espresso with a large squirt of liquid hash oil from a sauce bottle.

'Here you go, Jimmy. You drink this down and you will sleep like a prince, my friend.'

I never argued. 'Shall I give you some money for that?' I asked.

They laughed at me. 'Don't be foolish. You don't think we make our money from this takeaway, do you? There is plenty of this oil to go around. We like you, Jimmy. Now go home.'

Anyway, like I said, I'd decided not to live in the Plaza. I had everything I needed in a small kit bag. Leather pants that had been sweated in so many times they almost stood up and walked to gigs by themselves. A couple of black T-shirts and an oversize off-pink shirt that I wore on stage. I remember buying it in a shop in Double Bay one afternoon.

'Could I have a look at the biggest, ugliest shirt in the shop?'

'Any particular colour, sir?'

'Na, any colour. Wait, what do you have in pink?'

'We have this pink shirt but I don't think your father will like it, sir. It's very ugly, sir.'

'Perfect, I'll take it. Don't bother wrapping it. Just shove it in a bag.'

'As you wish, sir. Will there be anything else? I have a huge, vile pair of pants that will go with that.'

'Na, that's it. Cheers.'

In my kit bag there were also one or two pairs of socks and underwear that I would wash in the sink wherever I ended up, a cassette of Johnny Burnette and the Rock'n'Roll Trio that I took to every party I went to and forced them to play as loud as their

1. **With Les Kaczmarek in Adelaide, 1973.** I think there was a special on checked cheesecloth shirts. Les and I swooped in and bought a couple. (BARNES FAMILY COLLECTION) 2. **This mid-1970s shot** captures us playing an early gig at a high school dance. The program described us as 'one of Adelaide's top bands'. (BARNES FAMILY COLLECTION) 3. **Steve outside the farm** in Kentucky, northern NSW, in 1974, next to our truck. Yes, it was small, but it was still a truck. (GARY SKINNER, COURTESY OF MICHAEL LAWRENCE)

1. Armidale Town Hall, 23 February 1974. The gigs got wilder later on, but this one looks pretty tame. No sign of Don. Maybe he had a uni lecture that night. (Barnes Family Collection) **2. Cold Chisel and friends in Armidale, 1974.** I was going to comment on how Don is dressed here, then I looked at what I was wearing. Next to me is our roadie, Michael Porter. (Gary Skinner, courtesy of Michael Lawrence)

1. My brother John joined the band and decided that we should all wear makeup. He went first. (Gary Skinner, courtesy of Michael Lawrence) **2. It wasn't long** till I followed. Damn, I knew this would turn up one day. (Barnes Family Collection) **3. Cold Chisel in Armidale, 1974.** I'm not sure if I'm wearing a lot of makeup or just had no sleep the night before. (Gary Skinner, courtesy of Michael Lawrence)

1. **An early publicity shot** of Cold Chisel, taken at Adelaide Railway Station in 1975. (Barnes Family Collection) **2. Vince Lovegrove,** our first manager, was well known on the Adelaide scene, singing solo and in bands and writing for music magazine *Go-Set*. (Barnes Family Collection) **3. In the 1960s,** Vince (bottom right) was a member of pop band The Valentines, along with Bon Scott (centre right). Obviously from here 'It's a Long Way to the Top (If You Wanna Rock 'n' Roll)'.

1. **Fraternity, with me singing,** at the Largs Pier Hotel in 1975. A couple of the band members' wives had decided to make me trousers. They were so excited that I felt I had to wear them. (BARNES FAMILY COLLECTION) 2. **My mate Ben Quilty's** painting of the Largs Pier Hotel. This is what it looked like on many a night when I left. (COURTESY OF BEN QUILTY) 3. **Poster for a Largs Pier show.** 'Four solid hours' – the punters got their money's worth. (COURTESY OF COLD CHISEL) 4. **Soon we spread our wings,** heading to the eastern states. Here we're performing at the first Sydney Festival, at the Haymarket in January 1977. (BOB KING)

1. Signing our first record deal, with WEA, in September 1977. Our manager Rod Willis is at top right and Dave Sinclair from the record label is at top left. (**Philip Mortlock**) **2. Opening for Sherbet**, at Victoria Park, Sydney, on 15 January 1978. After the show, I left the venue with them – in an armoured van. (**Bob King**)

1. Supporting Peter Frampton, November 1978. I'm wearing a red leather outfit made by Madame Lash, a well known Sydney dominatrix. (Marc Christowski) **2. At the Dirty Pool office,** in Bondi, doing interviews for *Breakfast at Sweethearts* – note the album beside me. (Philip Mortlock) **3. Lining up** in a dark alley for a band publicity shot, 1979. (Philip Mortlock) **4. Cold Chisel** at our Paddington house in 1980 – the Brown Street days. (Philip Mortlock)

1. This photo of Jane and me was taken by Rick Brewster at an open-air gig in Townsville in July 1980. (**RICK BREWSTER**) **2. Jane, at far right,** with her mum, siblings and cousins, when they were leaving Thailand for Australia in 1963. (**BARNES FAMILY COLLECTION**) **3. Jane and I got married** on 22 May 1981, in a Sydney city registry office. (**PHILIP MORTLOCK**) **4. After the ceremony,** attended by close friends and family, we partied back at our place – before I headed off to play a gig. (**PHILIP MORTLOCK**)

1. Making billy tea on the epic road trip up the east coast with a pregnant Jane, which ended abruptly when our Mahalia arrived early. **2. Mahalia, Jane and me**, just after we moved into our Bowral farm. **3. Giving 'Two Up'**, Jane's horse, a pep talk: 'Please don't throw the kid off.' **4. Jane on my horse 'Big Jim'**. She was always a better rider than me. **5. Mahalia and me,** living the country life, in the early Bowral days. (ALL IMAGES: BARNES FAMILY COLLECTION)

1. **The cover shoot for East, 1980.** I think I have the headband on upside down. (GREG NOAKES)
2. **Playing my** black and white Fender Telecaster on *Countdown*, 1980. My first guitar, it got stolen a few years later in Germany. I still miss it. (GREG NOAKES) 3. **This show** at the Capitol Theatre, Sydney, in 1980, was recorded for the *Swingshift* live album. 'Hey mate, get your hand off my arse. I'm trying to climb the PA.' (PHILIP MORTLOCK) 4. **'Big Alan' Dallow with his son,** my nephew James. I sang about my good mate in 'Letter to Alan'. (BARNES FAMILY COLLECTION) 5. **Billy Rowe worked** for Cold Chisel alongside Big Alan, before we lost them both in a tragic truck crash. (BARNES FAMILY COLLECTION)

1. I used to dive off the stage long before stage diving was a thing. At the Bombay Rock in Melbourne, the audience got wise to me and parted like the Red Sea. This was the result. (**Barnes Family Collection**)

2. The calm before the storm at the 1981 *Countdown/TV Week* Music and Video Awards. Moments later we started smashing up the set. (**Bob King**) **3. 'Family' photo,** beside our tour bus in the USA, in 1981. The first big cracks appeared between us during this tour. (**Courtesy of Cold Chisel**)

4. Me and Phil looking for trouble somewhere in America. I think we found it. (**Barnes Family Collection**)

5. Mark Opitz producing *Circus Animals* at Paradise Studios, Sydney, in 1982. (**Mark Opitz**)

6. For the album cover photo shoot, we towed a caravan out into the desert near Lake Eyre. You can just see me peeking out of it, behind Don. (**Courtesy of Phil Small**)

1. The tent we used for the Circus Animals tour. We had a circus and we were animals. (BARNES FAMILY COLLECTION) **2. I was also the trapeze artist,** flying high above the crowd. (PATRICK JONES STUDIO) **3. Climbing on Don's piano.** 'Hey, does this hair come off?' (BOB KING) **4. Artist Martin Sharp** designed this poster for the tour. (COURTESY OF THE ESTATE OF MARTIN SHARP/VISCOPY/COLD CHISEL) **5. On the road,** if anyone got drunk and passed out, we'd always do something stupid to them – like put a bucket on their head. Our sound guy, Gerry Georgettis, is driving here. (COURTESY OF COLD CHISEL) **6. We did a series of gigs** in jails for inmates. We certainly got all their attention and they were intense shows. This is Steve and me laughing nervously at Pentridge in Melbourne, on 2 June 1982. (GREG NOAKES)

1. Waiting backstage before one of the final Last Stand shows in 1983, at the Entertainment Centre in Sydney. (BARNES FAMILY COLLECTION) **2. This classic photo** of the Last Stand audience captures the passion of our fans. (GREG NOAKES) **3. These days,** it seems like a million people claim to have had one of the 50,000 tickets to our final Last Stand gigs. (COURTESY OF COLD CHISEL) **4. I wanted to give it everything** and get right in among the crowd. Lucky I had the security guys to haul me out. (GREG NOAKES) **5. Singing from the inside,** looking out. (BOB KING) **6. A moment lost in thought,** before I drank the rest of the vodka and went off again. (BOB KING)

1. **'Pretty little thing**, there's a smokin' moon.' Me and the dancers on the Last Wave of Summer tour. (TONY MOTT) 2. **A Last Wave** backstage pass. (COURTESY OF COLD CHISEL) 3. **Jane backstage** during the Ringside tour, in 2003. (ROBERT HAMBLING) 4. **Rehearsing with Ian and Steve** on the Ringside tour. We were probably trying to work out how to deal with that revolving stage. (ROBERT HAMBLING)
5. **A backstage pass** for the Ringside tour. (COURTESY OF COLD CHISEL)

1. This was the last official photo of Cold Chisel with Steve Prestwich, taken backstage at the V8 Supercars show at the Olympic Stadium, Sydney, on 5 December 2009. (GREG WEIGHT, COURTESY OF COLD CHISEL) **2. Rehearsing for the NRL Grand Final,** with Charley Drayton on drums. (BARNES FAMILY COLLECTION) **3. To give you an idea** of how many people it takes to put together a big show, this is most of the team behind 2011's Light the Nitro tour, onstage at the Sydney Entertainment Centre. (TONY MOTT, COURTESY OF COLD CHISEL). **4. Me and Charley,** outside the Townsville Casino. (BARNES FAMILY COLLECTION). **5. The band backstage** at the Sydney Entertainment Centre in December 2015, along with our co-managers John O'Donnell (far left) and John Watson (far right), and publicist Rina Ferris (centre). (BOB KING)

1. A publicity shot for the One Night Stand tour, with Charley Drayton. This is our current line-up. God, we look serious. (DAN BOUD, COURTESY OF COLD CHISEL) **2. Taking our final bows** at the Sydney Entertainment Centre's Last Stand on 18 December 2015. The band just kept playing and playing that night. We didn't want it to end. (TONY MOTT)

stereo could handle, and that was it. I had no home for two years or so. Every night I just ended up somewhere. Someone's couch. Someone's bed if I got lucky, or someone's floor if I didn't. I was quite happy to drink until everything closed and then try to sort it out. I always found somewhere to crash. This lifestyle got me into a lot of tight situations, if you get my drift.

---

CHAPTER THIRTEEN

not really groupies

A NOTE ON FANS

I REMEMBER WHEN WE first started out, if I thought I saw a person at two shows I was over the moon.

'Hey, guys. There's a girl out there who was at the last show. I think she likes the band!'

After having a look out front, Don would tell me, 'No, Jim. She works for the agency. She's counting how many people are at the show.'

But I never listened to him. As far as I was concerned she was a fan and she was following us around. We were on our way to the top.

By the time people really did start to turn up night after night it was different. By this point we were too caught up in putting on the show to worry about it too much. Well at least until the show was over. Then we would bump into them at the bar.

In the early days a lot of girls would turn up to stand in front of Phil. He was the first one of us to have a following of young girls. Phil was always well groomed, not a hair out of place, with clean, well-pressed clothes. Whereas I was normally drug crazed and covered in sweat and pacing from side to side looking for trouble. And if I couldn't find any I would start it.

Ian had a bit of a following too. He was a good-looking young fella with no shoes and even though he didn't dress as well as Phil, he was always being watched by girls with big doe eyes, who were waiting for him to notice them. He didn't notice them as much or as soon as they wanted. Ian was always head down, face covered by his thick curly hair as he concentrated on what was coming out of his amps, twisting and flicking dials on his guitar, wringing the wildest sound he could out of it.

'Hey Ian, did you see that girl out there blowing kisses at you all night? She was very cute,' I would announce in the dressing room after the show.

'Er, no. I, er, was having trouble hearing any top end from my amp. It was weird, it was changing all night. I was sure I had the volume set on seven and then I would look at it and it was flat out. I never touched it.'

I would walk away, never looking back, not wanting Ian to know that I had been changing his volume all night. Not to fuck him up but to make the band sound heavier and louder. If I'd asked him, he might not have done it. If I could have found a control for Steve, he would have been hitting harder too. But I did find that if I made Ian play louder, the rest of the band followed, maybe because they couldn't hear themselves.

Don was a bit of a dark horse. The girls who liked him didn't stand in front of the stage. They were way too cool to be seen up the front. But sure enough, after the show we'd see Don leaving for drinks with a beautiful young girl.

There were usually a few girls trying to catch a broken drumstick from Steve, but he was always too busy keeping time and worrying about the rest of us to worry about girls.

FANS CAME IN ALL shapes and sizes. For most of our career, Cold Chisel was followed around by gangs of blokes. Blokes who I'd drunk with or fought with. Guys who came out every night to see if they could work out how Ian pulled the sound that he did or how he played so fast. Young musicians standing just away from the front, watching to see who was driving the band. Just when they thought they had it worked out, it would change. Depending on which song we were playing it would take another path. A lot of the time I would be the one dictating the pace of the songs, but Don stood his ground when he had to, keeping the band playing at a solid speed despite my efforts to drive it towards certain death. When Don or Steve did that, it was usually the right thing for the song. The band always let me do my thing, pushing and shoving each song about because they knew that I was working off the crowd. If the crowd needed it to go faster, I made the band play faster. If they were getting bored, I made the band play something else. But when it came down to the real nitty-gritty of a song, every member knew that they had to hold the song at the right speed regardless of what I was doing. So really the music was a result of a push and pull between myself and the rest of the band. And this was our secret ingredient. This was what created the tension between the band members. This was what made us exciting to watch. Our fans, I think, knew this and they watched the game we played very night, waiting to see who would win the tug-o-war. Every night something different happened. We could play the same set but it was never the same in reality. Phil and Steve were mostly oblivious to the battle between Ian and myself. They played in a world of their own, unless I was jumping on their backs. Then they either ignored me or had to go with me, depending on how much they could take.

AFTER A FEW *COUNTDOWN* appearances, I noticed that the cool musician types were standing further back. It was like they were pissed off with us for going on *Countdown*, like we had sold out or something. Their place at the front was filled by lots of young, good-looking girls. This suited me down to the ground. I always hated the cool muso types who came to our shows. They were no fun afterwards.

'Yes, so Ian, I noticed that you used your front pickup on that new song tonight. Do you think the tone makes the difference to the mood? Oh and by the way, have you changed the valves in your amp since last night? It's much brighter.'

This was the last thing I wanted to do after a show. Talk about equipment.

'Can you get to fuck out of here? You are driving me crazy. Who cares what fucking pickup he used? And leave our drinks alone. Buy your own. Get out of here before I change your fucking valves.'

Then I would fill the room with girls and be ready to kick on all night.

Over the years our relationship with the fans changed. We were never a band that had groupies. There were girls who followed us around but not really groupies. After a while, the after-shows changed for us. It became more important to have time to recover and figure out what had worked and what hadn't. We would talk about what we needed to do to take the show to the next level. When I got bored with that I would leave and look for girls. One of us had to do it. I took one for the team.

CHAPTER FOURTEEN

your taxi is here

MOTEL 7, 1979

L IFE WAS A BLUR. Nothing made sense to me. I would wake up and get in the car and drive to the next town on the tour itinerary. Then try to get myself together in time to do the show. Every town felt the same, every show ended the same. I would get drunk and try to whip the band into a frenzy and then find somewhere to go or someone to sleep with. If that didn't happen, I had to spend the night alone and out of it, which was like a fate worse than death. I didn't like most other people's company, but I hated my own.

That's the way it was on 29 November 1979, when the Pooled Resources Tour rolled into Canberra. We pulled up to another motel for another show. The tour was Cold Chisel with The Angels and Flowers, soon to become Icehouse. Both were good bands but both were boring as batshit to hang around with after shows. Their idea of a good night was smoking pot, drinking tea and singing Mamas & Papas songs. Mine was slightly different.

I didn't want to talk or sing, or sit still for that matter. It was mayhem or nothing for me and it was starting to show on my face.

We had come off the back of a huge tour called Set Fire to the Town, where we played all over the country and destroyed everywhere we went. What we didn't set fire to, we demolished by hand. That was the plan for this tour too – play music and create havoc everywhere. It was an easy brief for us. We had been doing that for years, well, I had.

But by now, I felt tired, and like I was completely alone in the world. Even my best friends, the other guys in the band, were beginning to turn on me. Well, let's just say they didn't like hanging around with me after shows.

So we settled into our rooms at the Motel 7 in Canberra and I tried to work out how to shake the cobwebs off from the night before.

'Hey guys, you want to throw some Frisbee?' I heard a dorky voice say from outside in the carpark. I recognised it. One of The Angels.

'I hope to fuck these guys don't start laughing and yelling outside my door,' I thought to myself. Then I heard a car or two pull into the carpark and stop, followed by the sound of a voice I didn't recognise. It was a girl.

'Great to see you,' she said.

'Yeah, hi there,' said the dorky voice again.

I got up and walked out just as the group disappeared into one of the rooms. I stood alone in the carpark for a minute, taking in the sun. Canberra was normally a cold, cold place. The kind of town that looked better in the rear-view mirror. But today it was sunny and warm. I don't think I'd seen it in the daytime before. I usually left as soon as I could after a show. It all looked quite nice, but I had a feeling that would change later.

Before long there was the sound of laughter and the distinct smell of pot coming from The Angels' room. I was a bit bored by this time. So bored in fact that I decided to walk into the room and see what was going on.

The door was wide open, so naturally I invited myself in. They were all nice guys, they wouldn't mind me saying hello. As I walked in I could see them sitting around the room, on chairs and beds and the floor.

'Hi,' one of them said in that voice that I'd recognised outside my door. It was Rick Brewster.

'Hi. How's it going? Have you guys soundchecked yet?'

I was looking around the room and that was when it happened. It was four o'clock in the afternoon, 29 November 1979. I remember it like it was yesterday. Sitting in the corner of the room, not saying a word, was the most beautiful girl I had ever seen. She looked like a princess, not someone you would see in the Motel 7 in the outer suburbs of Canberra. But it wouldn't have mattered where I'd seen her. The impact would have been the same. She was something else. Like no one I'd ever seen. I couldn't take my eyes off her. I tried not to stare but I think I might have. Her hair was long and dark and her fringe was almost covering her beautiful eyes. I sat waiting for a sound to leave her mouth. A mouth that was slightly pouted, her beautiful, slightly buck teeth biting her top lip as if she didn't really want to be there. But here she was. She never said a word. She never even looked at me, I don't think she even knew I was in the room. My heart was racing, I had to leave the room for a minute so I could breathe.

I stepped outside and thought about what had happened. Who was she? How was I going to get to talk to her? Would she want to talk to someone as horrible as me? Not a chance. Girls like her weren't meant to be with guys like me.

I went back into the room, just as Buzz Bidstrup, The Angels' drummer, said, 'Hey Jimmy, we're going to head down to the gig soon. Oh, by the way, this is Victoria and Jane, some friends of ours. Jane's come down from Sydney to see the show. And this is Jimmy. Jimmy sings with Cold Chisel.'

One of the girls was laughing and chatting and looking confidently around the room as if she owned the place. She might have, for all I knew at the time. She stopped and looked at me and smiled. 'Hi, I'm Victoria Pollock.' She seemed to be a nice girl. I liked her then and we are still friends to this day.

'Hi. How are you?'

The other girl, the one that I couldn't take my eyes off, sat in the corner and said nothing. Her name must be Jane, I quickly worked out. She didn't look like a Jane. She was exotic-looking, from Asia or somewhere I hadn't been.

'We're just going to throw the Frisbee around a bit then head to the gig,' Buzz announced and they all got up. I was hungover and the last thing I wanted to do was run around throwing a Frisbee. Cold Chisel didn't throw Frisbees. The Angels did.

'Do you mind if I join you?' I was suddenly interested in exercise.

'Sure man, come on.' Buzz was always friendly with everyone. I liked him. So out we went and threw a small plastic disk around the hotel carpark for a short while.

Jane never spoke to me at all. I don't think she even noticed me. I thought to myself, 'Maybe she doesn't speak English.'

I was smitten. I wanted to be nice and happy and maybe catch her attention but it never happened. It wasn't long until I'd had enough of Frisbee and went back to my room. But I couldn't stop myself from thinking about her.

Then I heard a car start up and I jumped up and looked out of the window, just in time to see her get into the car and drive off. My heart sank. Would I see her again? Would she be at the show? I could only hope.

I'D MET A LOT of girls in my life but no one had ever stopped me in my tracks like that girl, that day. Her name was Jane Mahoney, not a very exotic name for a girl so mysterious. I later found out that she was born in Thailand. Her real name, her Thai name, was Ratana Dejakaisaya and she moved to Canberra when she was five years old. The first book she read in English was *Fun with Dick and Jane* so she picked the name Jane for her English name. She was brought up by her mother, Kusumphorn, a strikingly beautiful woman in her own right and her stepfather John, who was a diplomat and a gentleman. Not only did she speak five languages but she spoke better English than I did. She was way out of my class but I loved her from the minute I saw her. Jane would change my life.

THAT NIGHT WE PLAYED at the Canberra Showground Pavilion. On the tour, The Angels and Cold Chisel shared the top billing, so we played last one night, they played last the next and so on. This particular night we went on before them as fate would have it.

So, after our show, I was standing side of stage watching The Angels when suddenly there she was. The girl from the room, the one who didn't speak to me or look at me. Now she was standing right next to me. I tried to be cool. This wasn't something I was good at. I'd never been cool.

I looked over and she was looking straight at me.

'Hi.'

She smiled at me. That was cool. I wondered what to say next.

'Did you like the show?'

The music was screaming so loud off the stage she could hardly speak. She nodded her head.

Had I really said that? I had to get it together, quickly. 'Do you go out with one of these guys?' I was shouting just as the song abruptly finished. 'Sorry.' I lowered my voice and motioned towards The Angels. Why had I asked that? I was digging a hole.

'No,' she said in a matter of fact way.

'Great, ah sorry, I mean, oh.' I was fumbling for words. I took a deep breath and quickly removed both my feet from my mouth. 'What are you doing after the show?' Oh my God, that was dumb.

Luckily for me she seemed a lot more confident than I was. She looked at me and said, 'We're having a few drinks later at my friend's house, would you like to come?' It appeared she spoke perfect English. I felt stupid for thinking she didn't. How dumb was I?

'Ah. Yeah, um sure. Yeah, that would be nice. Ah, just me or should I bring the others?' I asked awkwardly. By this point, I was the one who was having trouble speaking English. In fact, I was having trouble speaking at all.

'Yes. You can bring your friends. You can all come. Follow us if you like. We're all going straight after the show. It will be fun.' She smiled at me. I almost melted.

I stopped drinking so that I wouldn't get too out of control. I didn't want to scare her away. I had to make her like me. She was so beautiful. Inside I was saying to myself, 'Now stay cool, don't look too excited or too keen. Play a bit hard to get. Stay calm.' But outside I quickly said, 'Sure, that'd be great.'

What a smooth talker I was.

So we all went back to her friend Victoria's mum and dad's house. I thought this was a little strange. We didn't get invited anywhere that someone's parents lived. Parents didn't seem to like us. We weren't parent material, I don't think.

From that first minute I saw Jane, I put myself under pressure. I wanted to be the best I could be. I wanted to be someone that she liked. I wanted to be better than I thought I really was. So I tried and I tried, but the other me, the wild one, kept shining through.

BEFORE WE ARRIVED IN Canberra, Steve had broken his wrist in a stupid and avoidable accident.

His replacement was a bloke called Trevor Young. Trevor was a wild boy. He was a good man but he didn't care or need to care what other people thought of him. My life revolved around people liking me. This night I was out of my depth.

Jane was from a different world, a place where everything was as it seemed. People didn't play games or dive in out of their depth. She had to see that I was a fraud.

The whole night I was pretending to be normal. To be nice. To be likable even if I wasn't. She was so special. She was smart. She was confident, she was full of life. I tried. I thought I had her believing that I was someone she could like.

I sat listening to Jane talk. I thought it was all going well. I was being as charming as I could. Not breaking things or threatening any of the other blokes who were talking to Jane.

Out of the blue Jane smiled at me and asked, 'Shall I play a song for you?'

'I would love that. I didn't know you sang or played music.'

I was intrigued. Jane picked up an acoustic guitar and sat in front of me and began to play and sing 'Puff the Magic Dragon'.

I sat staring at her. I could see Trevor, out of the corner of my eye, getting wound up. But he stayed out of the way and caused trouble in the other room so I thought I was all right. Jane finished the song and I clapped. 'That was great.'

No one had ever played a song like that to me before. She was so cute. Everything seemed perfect as I sat as close to her as I could, watching her every move. The way her lips curled as she laughed.

Suddenly Trevor shattered the moment. I looked up just in time to see him fall through a window, spilling beer all over the nice white carpet.

'Fuck, that was lucky,' he yelled in the kind of booming working-class Melbourne accent that would make Paul Hogan sound like Prince Charles. The whole room turned and looked at him. 'Fuck, I only spilled my fucking beer. Luckily I didn't waste any scotch, that would have been a real fucking mess.'

He was looking around the room, hoping someone would tell him to slow down a bit so he could smash them in the face. But everyone just looked away. Everyone but me. I looked up to the heavens, wondering, 'Why me?'

Then Trevor roared again. 'Oh fuck. Oops. Sorry about that. Ha ha ha.' His voice carried through the whole house. This time he'd broken a glass.

Victoria scowled at him.

'What are you fucking looking at? What's your problem?' He laughed, spitting beer from his mouth.

'You are my problem.' Vicki's tongue was like acid when she spoke to him.

'It was only a fucking glass. I told you to give me a plastic one. I'm useless when I'm this fucking pissed.'

He was out of control and I could see Jane wanted him out of her friend's house before he wrecked it. She was right, he would have wrecked it. The Angels and the rest of Chisel were too scared to say a word. Trevor was a loose cannon. On any other night so might I have been, but tonight she was there.

I jumped up and tried to cover for him. He knew me and knew I wasn't scared of him. He wasn't really violent, just loud. But he was way too far out of it for everybody else to cope with. He had to go. And to get rid of him, so did I.

'Give me a chance. I'm not that bad. Look at me, I'm all right. I know you like me.' This is what was going through my head but I couldn't say any of it to her. Meanwhile Jane had figured out what she had to do to stop the damage. And I was part of that damage. I had to go. She disappeared.

Five minutes later she was back. 'Your taxi is here.' Her voice was sympathetic but stern. She wanted me to leave.

'I never called a cab,' I pleaded with her. I was shattered. I had nothing left. There was nothing else I could try or say that would change her mind.

'Well, there is a taxi here with your name on the booking.'

I walked to the already open door. It was too late for any more excuses. But as I walked out, she gave me a piece of paper. I stopped, right in front of her.

'Here's my phone number,' she whispered. 'I'll come and see you off at the airport tomorrow.'

I looked at her in disbelief. 'Yeah, all right. It was nice to meet you.'

I glared at Trevor. I wanted to kill him. It was over. Probably just as well. This girl couldn't have liked me once she got to know me.

'See you tomorrow then.' She half smiled at me.

'Yeah, sure. Thanks for having us over.'

The door was shut.

'Why me, God?' I thought. 'Why did Steve break his wrist right now? Why did I meet such a great girl when Trevor Young was playing drums with me?'

Why was I asking God? There was nothing he could do. By the way, speaking of God, the first time I ever saw Trevor Young play drums, he was playing with Lobby Loyde and the Coloured Balls. They had a hit song called 'God' and were playing to a sea of swastika-tattooed, bald-headed skinheads, recently released from or soon to visit prison, somewhere in the suburbs of Melbourne.

But this was different. Trevor didn't fit in here and neither did I.

I turned around and there was Trevor, looking like a slightly rabid Rottweiler on methamphetamines, pulling on a leash, looking right at me.

'Let's find a fuckin' bar with some real filthy chicks and have some real fun, eh? Ha ha ha.'

'No. I think I'll go home.'

I went to the motel. I don't think I had ever felt so low. It was probably for the best. I wasn't any better than Trevor. I didn't belong with someone so beautiful. Canberra was a cold, cold, lonely place. Did I tell you that already? Colder that night than I had ever felt it before.

I fell asleep in the Motel 7. When I woke up it all seemed like a bad dream.

WE GOT TO THE airport to move on to the next town. There was something heavy in my heart and I couldn't get rid of it. I wasn't used to feeling like this. In fact, I wasn't used to feeling at all.

As I walked into the airport I saw her. I couldn't believe it. There she was, just like she'd said she would be. I had never been so happy to see anybody in my life. She looked like an angel. A beautiful smiling angel. I almost couldn't breathe. I knew she liked me. I could tell. I was filled with a sense of hope and a sense of hopelessness at the same time. My life changed that day.

I CALLED HER AS soon as I got back to Sydney, a few days later. By this time I'd moved into a house in Kensington. I wasn't confident of the outcome but I called her. I had to. 'Hi, it's me, Jimmy. Remember, you gave me your number in Canberra.'

'Oh yes. How are you?' She sounded warm and friendly.

'I was wondering if you wanted to catch up some time. You said you might.'

'Yes. All right. That would be nice.'

'I'm having a bit of a party at my place at Kensington. I was hoping you might want to come. You know, you said you wanted to catch up. Say hello.'

I was nervous. What if she really didn't want to? What if she'd changed her mind and didn't like me after all? I could understand that. I mean, I didn't like me much.

'Yes, that would be nice. When is it?'

Jane didn't sound like other girls I knew. She was well mannered. She sounded like she came from overseas somewhere. Not English, definitely not English but not Australian either – but whatever it was, it sounded good to me.

'When is the party? I need to know when it is happening.'

I was so rattled that I hadn't even given her the time or date. 'Er, sorry. Yeah, it's this Saturday. We have a day off and I thought I might be able to see you.'

'That's all right. I'd love to come. I'll see you about eight or so.'

That was the time normal people had parties. But I wanted to see her before anyone else turned up.

'Why not come a little earlier and we can sit and talk. If you like. But you don't have to. I was just saying it would be nice.'

'I'll see you then.'

She was gone. Shit, I couldn't believe it. She was going to come. This was fantastic. Suddenly I was excited. I was going to see her. I'd better clean up my room.

I was sharing the house with Bernadette. I had gone out with Bernadette for a short time but it hadn't really worked out. The problem was, I hadn't really told her that it hadn't worked out and I wasn't sure she understood that we weren't still going out. I mean, we lived in the same house, but that didn't necessarily mean we were still going out, did it?

I started to worry. Maybe she didn't know we weren't still going out. The more I thought about it, the more it worried me. That night in bed I tried to bring it up and that's when it dawned on me. We were still sharing a room. A bed. Shit, she doesn't know. How could she? She was a girl. She wasn't the same as me. I was going to have to talk it over with her before Saturday.

Bernadette took the news well. I think she was relieved in fact. I was too wild for her. She moved into the spare room as soon as we spoke. Things seemed to get a little better between us from then on. She looked happy again. It was nice. So that made me relax. I didn't mean to hurt anybody and I was so glad that things went well. That's when the phone rang.

'Hi.' It was Jan, the girl who shared the Punt Road house where we shot our EP cover. I had been seeing her on and off for a long time.

'Er, hi.' I didn't think that Jan thought we were going steady either. So that wasn't a problem.

'I'm in town for a few days and I thought I'd stay with you.'

'Ah, yeah, sure. That's cool.'

'Only if you want me to. If it's a hassle just tell me.'

'No-no-no, that would be great. When are you getting here?' I was slowly starting to panic.

'I arrive Saturday afternoon. I heard you guys were having a party and I thought I'd surprise you.' Jan often surprised me.

'Terrific. That's great. Yeah, I can't wait to see you.'

'Okay then, I'll see you Saturday. I'll wear something special.'

'Great, see you then.'

I was in trouble. How had I got this all so wrong? I really wanted to see Jane but I hadn't counted on all this confusion. I had only had a drink with Jane one night. It wasn't like we were going steady. In fact, I wasn't going steady with anyone as far as I knew. It would work itself out, or so I hoped.

I was getting more nervous the more I thought about it. What would Jane think of me? Would she even care? But I cared, so I had to try to sort it out.

'Hi, it's Jimmy,' I mumbled.

'Oh hi, Jimmy.' Jan sounded happy to hear from me. I didn't call that often.

'Listen, I was thinking about Saturday,' I said.

'Yes. What about it?' She sounded worried.

'Maybe you should just stay in Melbourne and I'll see you when I'm down there next week?' I tried to sound as casual as I could. After all, this was just a casual relationship. Shit, there was that word. Relationship. It always made me nervous.

'No, it's cool. I want to come up and see some friends anyway. As long as you don't mind me staying with you.'

'No-no-no, of course not. I'll see you then.' I was stuttering.

'Great. Can't wait. Bye.'

'Yeah bye.'

Oh shit. What was I going to do? I thought I could explain all this to Jane before anyone arrived. That's what I'd do. I'd deal with it when I had to.

SATURDAY AFTERNOON I WAS sitting on the front porch with my two dogs. Spike was a Staffordshire bull terrier and Duke was a German shepherd. I was also looking after a Great Dane for a friend of mine. All three dogs looked like they shouldn't be messed with, but they were all very friendly. I looked down the street and saw a car pull up. Jane was driving. She drove a Mini Cooper S. She looked very stylish and I smiled and waved as she parked her car. I walked to the gate to greet her.

As she got out of the car I made a quiet noise. 'Sssssss.'

The dogs' ears all pricked up and they looked around to see who I could want them to attack.

'Sssssss,' I said again and they ran out the gate, barking like the Hound of the Baskervilles at Jane.

Jane screamed and jumped back into her car.

'Boys. Boys. Come. Come here,' I barked back at the dogs and they ran towards me wagging their tails.

Jane got out of the car again and looked around.

'Sssssss,' I whispered but this time Jane could hear me. The dogs went into attack mode and ran at her.

She jumped back in the car, yelling from the slightly opened window, 'Why did you do that?'

I was laughing out loud.

'That's not funny. I don't like it or you.' She was clearly upset.

'Sorry, it was a joke. They won't hurt you. Come on in, I won't do it again.'

Jane looked worried but the dogs were back in the yard, standing behind me by this time, so she slowly, nervously, got out of the car and headed to the gate.

'Sssss,' I started one last time but grabbed the dogs before they could run. I didn't think I could get away with it again.

Jane wasn't happy with the way our second date had started but she soon settled down. 'My dog is bigger than any of these little runts,' she laughed and proceeded to tell me about the hound she owned, a huge Great Dane with an appetite for small dogs. I knew I liked her when I first met her but now I was sure.

The party went well. Things were a bit uncomfortable at first but Jane was so cool and poised and never let anything upset her. I thought she was amazing. Bernadette was fine too, but Jan wasn't sure about either of them. Or me for that matter. She left early. Jane and I laughed our way through the evening. I liked everything about her and she forgave me for sicking the dogs on her. I wanted to see her again and soon.

SHE LIVED IN BEN Boyd Street in Neutral Bay and I arranged to see her the following week. I went over and sat while Jane and her friends played bad music and smoked bongs. These were not the sort of parties I was used to, but I was on my best behaviour. Until one night. 'Can I borrow your Mini? I've got a show to do and I'm really late.'

Jane was happy to lend it to me. But after the show I got drunk and couldn't drive it back to her. The next day I went away on tour, leaving the car at my house. Jane tracked it down and rang the house to get her car back. Jan from Punt Road, the other girlfriend I never had, was back again and answered the phone. 'Yeah, he's gone. The keys are here but you know he doesn't care about you. He's my boyfriend, not yours.'

Jane was furious, not about me but about the car. 'I wouldn't have him as a boyfriend. I only want my car, that's all.' And she hung up.

When Jane tracked me down, somewhere in Melbourne, it wasn't to let me know she had the car back but to tell me in no uncertain terms, 'You have no manners and a gentleman would never take someone's car and not bring it back. And I never want to see you again.'

She was right, I was no gentleman. I felt bad and tried to call her. Eventually she answered one of my calls, and luckily for me, she gave me another chance.

CHAPTER FIFTEEN

what a girl she was

SYDNEY, 1980

Early in 1980, I moved in with Jane in Neutral Bay. It appeared she liked me too. We were from different worlds but when those worlds collided, sparks flew. We laughed a lot and we had big fights but, most important of all, we liked being together. But I was in a rock'n'roll band, touring relentlessly, and Jane was at university, studying. She liked pretty, girly things, like Laura Ashley print clothes and flowers and soft music, whereas I wore leather jackets and ripped denim and lived in cheap motels and screamed for a living. And I didn't know who or what Laura Ashley was.

Her world looked, sounded and smelled different to mine. I liked being in her world a lot, but I was a stranger in a strange land. I had never felt the way I did with her, but I was scared at the same time. I had an underlying feeling that I didn't belong in her world. Jane tried her best to make me feel a part of it, but nothing she could do would fix the problems I had. I met her sisters, they were great girls: confident, poised and beautiful. They were also normal, happy, and they all got on together. This was new to me. My family couldn't be in the same room for very long before one of us started a fight. I never wanted our two families to meet.

Although Jane smoked pot, she was very straight. Well, compared to the people I knew. Until Jane met me the idea of snorting drugs was crazy to her. When she saw me snorting a line of speed one day, she was shocked.

'What are you doing, Jimmy?'

I thought everybody knew about drugs. 'I'm just having a line. Do you want one?' I didn't know that she had never seen speed before, let alone done it.

She nervously watched me chop and lay out a line and then she said, 'Are you going to breathe those solids into your lungs? You're not, are you?'

I laughed. I thought she was kidding. 'You bet I am.'

Ssnniiiiiffff! I snorted up a long white line of speed. It burned like hell and Jane panicked.

'Are you all right, Jimmy?'

My eyes were watering and my face was grimacing and I let out a groan. 'Ahhhhh. Fuck. What? Yeah, baby, I'm good. I'm great in fact. Do you want one too?'

Jane looked at me like I was crazy. I was slightly crazed but only a little bit crazy at this point. A few days later, Jane decided to try a line too. I wish I had never given it to her. She didn't need this shit. I didn't need this shit. But she did it and almost from day one we fought even more. Speed makes a person aggressive. Jane and I were both full-on people, so this just made us worse.

Jane became intolerant of idiots. I was used to them. I met them every day in my world. We would try to go out for a quiet drink. We would smoke pot and then sneak into a club and sit up the back. Order a few drinks and sit and play Space Invaders.

Space Invaders was a new thing and was huge at the time, with tables in coffee shops and bars all over the country. So this night we were in a bar in the Cross drinking and playing games. There was a band playing up the front but we weren't watching them.

A guy walked up out of the blue and shouted over the music, 'Hey Jimmy. Jimmy. Hey, remember me?'

I could tell he was drunk just by the tone of his voice. I looked at him quickly between shots and said, 'Nope.'

But he persisted. 'Come on, Barnesy. You fucking remember me, don't you?'

I looked up again. 'No, I don't.'

He was getting annoying by this point. 'Hey Barnesy, come on, man. The last two times you've seen me, you've fucking belted me. Come on, man.'

This made sense to me so I looked up again and said, 'Keep it up and it'll be fucking three times.'

But this guy wouldn't give up. He kept hassling me. 'Your memory's fucked, Barnsey. You know me, don't you?'

I was shuffling my feet into position so I could jump up and smash him. Suddenly I spotted Jane getting up at the other side of the table and *bang!* She hit him in the face. Dropped him where he stood.

As he lay on the floor I looked at her. What a girl she was. She turned to me and said, 'I thought I'd do it to save you doing it. Besides, you would have hurt him.'

The guy was carried out of the club by a couple of bouncers, bleeding from Jane's blow, but he still kept shouting, 'Jesus, Barnesy! Your memory's fucked. You know me!'

I looked at Jane and smiled. I hated her having to put up with my life and the people it attracted. 'Do you want to go home?'

She smiled and picked up her bag. 'Sure. Let's go.'

But not every night went so well. Other times we would end up arguing with each other. Jane would scream at me and walk off down the street alone. I always followed her just in case she needed me. We started fighting more and more. It wasn't only the people around me that rubbed Jane the wrong way. My behaviour was bad too. I drank too much and I took too many drugs. I would go out for a drink and not come home for days. Something had to give.

AFTER A COUPLE OF months, Jane announced that she was leaving. 'Since I met you I have quit uni and I started taking hard drugs. I am not this sort of person. I don't want to live like this anymore.'

I had known the day would come. In fact, I knew I had driven her to it. She chose to try to live rather than stay and die with me. I would have done the same if I was her.

I pleaded with her to stay. 'I can change. I love you. Don't leave.' But we both knew I wasn't going to change.

'I'm going to live with my parents in Japan. It would be better if you didn't follow me.'

JANE LEFT FOR JAPAN in April 1980, and I was heartbroken. I had fucked up the best thing in my life. It would not be the last time I did this.

But she made one mistake. She told me where she was going. It would have been better if she had just left. I would have been in pain, but not this pain. I knew where she was and I thought she didn't want me. This was a pain I'd thought I'd never feel again. I'd spent most of my life not ever letting anyone get close enough to hurt me. But I was hurting now. I hadn't seen it coming. I knew I liked her a lot but I'd liked other girls before her. This was different. Jane going away left a hole inside me. It wasn't even the emptiness that I had become used to as a child. This was something else.

I tried all the things that had masked pain for me in the past. I drank more, I took more drugs, I filled the gap every way I could. But it was still there. Gnawing away at my insides. Nothing worked.

Jane would call me from Japan and for a while everything brightened up. Then as soon as she was off the phone I was left with a vast sense of loss. I wanted to run to Japan and see her. But we were in the middle of making the album *East*, an album that was starting to feel right. There were a lot of reasons for this. The band was tight, the sort of tight you can only get from doing thousands of shows, and that helped the recording process immensely. The other big difference between *East* and the previous two records was Mark Opitz, a young producer fresh from working at Alberts. He had been an engineer for Vanda and Young and it appeared he had watched what they were doing quite closely, whether they knew this or not. Mark came to us with a refreshing style that brought the best out of us.

We had started off trying him out just for a single. WEA were desperate for us to have a hit. I heard recently that they were sick of waiting and were on the verge of dropping us unless we had a breakthrough. We certainly weren't aware of that at the time. We were oblivious to record companies and anything they wanted. We only did what we wanted. Anyway, we had spent a few days with Mark in late 1979 recording at Paradise, a new studio, to get a feel for each other. The result was 'Choirgirl', the first single off *East*. Jane told me later that before her mum Phorn moved to Japan, she heard the song on the radio while they were in a car together. The song came out around the time of the first boat people crisis. So refugees were talked about on the radio all the time.

'Looking like a choirgirl. Crying like a refugee ...'

'Listen to these stupid people,' Phorn laughed.

'Looking like a choirgirl. Crying like a refugee ...'

'Why are they singing about refugees? Silly people. They would probably think that we were refugees too.' Jane and her mum both laughed as 'Choirgirl' sang out from the radio.

That song was never really understood by the public. It sold well and was all over the radio but no one ever picked up on what it was about. They all thought it was a sweet pop song about doctors and nurses. It was in fact a very dark song about abortion. But we never told anyone.

Mark helped us start to find our sound – the sound that we had when we played live – in the studio. Not only that but he helped us find a whole new set of dynamics that would enhance the band's live sound. Softer, cleaner, but still aggressive enough to fit into our live show. It was the start of a good friendship. The song was a hit and everyone, including the band, wanted us to make the new album with Mark.

AFTER THE FIASCO THAT was *Breakfast at Sweethearts* I owed it to the band and myself to see the new record through. But as important as the record was, my thoughts were constantly with Jane. When I should have been immersed in a song, I was waiting on a call.

I even wrote a song about Jane leaving. 'Rising Sun' was written because that was all I was thinking about. What was Jane doing? Had I lost her? How was I going to win her back? I thought that writing a song about her would impress her, let her know how much she meant to me. So I grabbed my only guitar, a black and white Fender Telecaster. I remember I bought this guitar because it looked like the one Bruce Springsteen was playing on the cover of *Born to Run*. Maybe I thought if I had the same guitar, some of that songwriting magic would rub off on me. But Bruce was safe. It would take a lot more than a Fender to help me write songs.

Twelve months earlier, a fan had handed me a cassette of Johnny Burnette and the Rock'n'Roll Trio as I was leaving a show – the cassette I used to carry around in my kit bag, remember? He looked like an old-school rocker: no front teeth, with slicked back hair and a leather jacket. I remember him saying, 'Hey Jimmy. Why don't you have a listen to this? This is the best rock'n'roll album ever written.'

He had a bit of a glint in his eye, and as I was about to drive overnight, interstate with the band, I was looking for something new to listen to for the next few hours. 'Thanks mate. I'll give it a go. But if it's shit, you know it's going out the window, don't you?'

'Yeah mate, I know. But trust me, you'll love this.'

I was sceptical but he was confident so I jumped in the car and banged it into the cassette player. It stayed there until the band couldn't listen to it anymore. I loved it. I never knew the guy who gave it to me but if he's reading this, thanks. You saved my drive and inspired me to write some rock'n'roll.

So I drew on what I had. I'd spent months listening to that cassette. I wanted to write a rockabilly song and 'Rising Sun' was what I got. It was just a little story but it rocked. It was a bit shallow but I can look back at it now and see that I was thinking about much deeper things. I just couldn't write about them yet.

COLD CHISEL ALWAYS TEETERED on the edge of getting too nice for my liking. I spent most of my time in the band trying to stop that happening. I only wanted to write rock songs. Steve was writing pop. Very good pop, but lighter than Don and I were writing. Ian was experimenting with funk and so was Phil, so it was up to Don and myself to write up-tempo songs.

Don spent a lot of time writing for *East*. He came up with a lot of songs about outsiders. We were outsiders, and we were surrounded by outsiders and misfits. There was something about the outcasts from society that fascinated him. Maybe that's why he liked me. I felt like I'd been locked up all my life. These were my people. Don was trying to understand these people and I was trying to outrun them. Don's songs got too close for comfort for me sometimes. When he presented 'Standing on the Outside' to the band, I felt like I was singing a song that came from somewhere deep inside my soul. I had been standing on the outside all my life, never being allowed to taste or touch the world that was always just out of my reach. 'Star Hotel' let me sing about not being good enough, not being wanted or worth anything, and wanting to tear the world down because of it.

So this record was special to me on many levels but I still couldn't wait until we finished it and our shows, so I could go to see Jane. But I was preparing for the worst. If she didn't want me I would not allow myself to get hurt. I planned to go on to the UK, catch up with an old girlfriend and visit Scotland for the first time. I was setting myself up for failure. Jane and I continued to speak every day, and every night I would get hammered and give myself another reason to feel that she didn't need me in her life. Still, the calls got longer and longer until the day I left.

LIFE ON THE ROAD is as far from reality as you can get. You spend eight to ten hours a day driving to somewhere that you know nothing about, and when you get there, you're too tired to feel anything or see anything the place has to offer. Instead, you go to an area where real light doesn't shine, a place where real people aren't allowed, and that's where you stay until you walk out onto a stage and into a world that is made up of people's hopes and expectations being pushed at you. Expectations that you have no hope of meeting or even understanding, so you twist and turn and go berserk until you drag the audience kicking and screaming into the mess that you have created, using volume, booze and drugs and whatever else comes to hand. Sometimes it explodes into something spectacular and other times it just fizzles out, lost in smoke and mirrors. Whatever happens, it rarely feels real, and unless you can detach from it somehow, it will drag you down.

We had the music to keep us grounded, but our roadies Billy and Alan didn't, and as much as we tried to make them feel a part of it, it was our world and not theirs. Although these two guys were real hard men compared to the rest of Chisel, we had been doing this for a long time and it was our lives. These guys were just visitors in our lives, and they started to crumble under the pressure that a couple of years on the road can have on a person. It ground Billy and Alan down and eventually killed them.

After a few years on the road with us, they drifted off and worked with other people, but it was never the same. They thought they'd found a home working with my brother's band, but on the night of 12 April 1980, somewhere just out of Canberra, Billy, Alan and another roadie called John Affleck were driving on a straight road, with next to no trees for miles. They blew a front tyre and the truck crashed into the one tree by the side of that road in five miles. John told me later that he thought Billy, who was in the front passenger seat, was killed outright. Alan, who was driving, was trapped behind the wheel, and flames were starting to flare up under the truck. John, who had been sleeping in the bunk behind the seats, was knocked out cold by the impact, but Alan managed to wake him up and drag him to the front so he could get out of the wreck, knowing that he himself was trapped and had no escape. The truck burst into flames seconds after John fell out, and Billy and Alan were gone.

Both guys left a part of themselves with us. I sing about that night every night with Cold Chisel in one of Don's songs, 'Letter to Alan', and after all these years my heart still hurts every time. Billy left behind a family who miss him dearly and Alan, who had fathered a beautiful boy he called James with my sister Linda, left a boy who still needs and misses his dad.

The road had taken Billy and Alan, but our memories keep them alive, and they are in my heart especially as Don and I start the opening verse of that song.

When it's time for your reflection
As you wait till help arrives
See our good friend's face on the dashboard
And to know you cannot leave that cab alive
Do you know I reach for you, from later times

CHAPTER SIXTEEN

Rising Sun

TOKYO, 1980

THE NIGHT BEFORE I left for Tokyo in May 1980, I was so smashed I don't even remember packing my bags. I was sharing a house in Sydney and we were living like pigs. The place was a mess, clothes and filth everywhere. I couldn't wait to escape. Somehow, I managed to get to the airport and onto the plane where I drank myself to sleep again. I caught a taxi from Narita Airport in Tokyo to Jane's parents' house in the Australian embassy compound. They had agreed to let me stay. It took hours and cost a fortune.

When I arrived at the door, I must have smelled like a brewery. This was the first time I met Jane's parents, John and Phorn. I had tried to tuck in my shirt and put on deodorant and chewed some gum but it wasn't enough. I was a mess and if it was me answering the door, I would have slammed it in my face.

'Hello. Can I help you?' The voice on the intercom sounded friendly enough.

'Yeah, it's Jimmy here to see Jane.'

There was silence for a second.

'Who is it again?'

'It's Jimmy. Jimmy Barnes. I'm here to see Jane.'

I heard a click.

'Come on in.'

JOHN MAHONEY WAS A career diplomat who had been with Foreign Affairs for most of his working life. He was a hardworking and honest bloke who was climbing his way up the Foreign Affairs ladder. Eventually he would represent Australia abroad as one of the country's High Commissioners. He met his beautiful wife, Kusumphorn, on his first posting abroad, in Bangkok, Thailand. Phorn, as she was known, came from a well-to-do family. Her father was a wealthy Chinese merchant who had seven wives and twenty-six children. She had divorced Jane's real father Khun Suvit a few years earlier. John met Phorn while she was working at the Australian Embassy in Bangkok. He fell in love with her immediately. Phorn had three beautiful little girls: Ratana, or Jane as I knew her, Pimpa, or Kaye as she had become, and Jep. John fell in love with the children too. John and Phorn were married and the family moved back to Canberra for a short while before his job took them to some of the best cities in the world, Rome, Moscow and Kuala Lumpur to name a few. John and Phorn had two boys of their own, Robert and Richard.

When I met them, they were the opposite of my family. They were happy and loving. The children were well travelled and well balanced and educated. They were nothing like the families I grew up with in Adelaide. I found it very hard to be comfortable with them at first.

JANE'S PARENTS WELCOMED ME in and we went into the lounge to get to know each other. My mouth was dry and my hands were sweating as I shook her father's hand for the first time. He held my hand longer than I expected and looked at me. I looked down, I couldn't look at him. I had seen the disappointment in their eyes. This was not the kind of man they wanted their beautiful daughter to hang around with. But they were nice. Over their shoulders I could see Jane smiling at me, and for a moment I completely forgot about her parents. I'd hoped that arriving on her doorstep with a song I had written for her would impress her but, when I later got the chance to play 'Rising Sun' for her, she wasn't that impressed, and I had to wonder whether she was really that impressed by me.

John laid out the rules of the house to Jane and me. 'Now, you two, don't think that this is some sort of hotel you can fall in and out of. This is our home and as long as you are staying with us, under my roof, it will be by our rules.'

I recognised the voice from the intercom. He didn't sound quite as friendly as he had when I was outside. I was even more worried now. Reg Barnes had used these same words to my sisters when they brought boys home. They never stuck to his rules. Not even for a minute. But I had the feeling this would be different. I wanted them to like me too, so I promised myself I would be on my best behaviour. As soon as I sobered up.

'You can stay with us, young man, but don't for a minute think that you two will in the same room. In fact, we don't even want you two to be alone together in this house. Do you understand?'

This seemed a little strange to me as Jane and I had been living together in Sydney, but it was their house and I would have to stick to their rules. I guess.

Jane smiled at me and then looked sternly at her father. 'Oh, Dad. He has only just got here. Be nice.'

'Now, your room will be just up here near our room and we would like you to make yourself at home. This is our home and we keep it nice and tidy and we expect the same from you.'

I was still looking at the ground. 'Yes of course, sir.' I wanted to get away for a minute and gather my thoughts. 'I'll just go and unpack my clothes and have a shower.' I could smell myself more every minute I stood there.

'Yes, a shower would be good but the maid has already unpacked your clothes for you.' John continued talking to me but I couldn't hear him. I was too busy panicking. What? What maid? I'd never had a maid do anything. Shit, what was in my bags? I couldn't remember packing them. Oh my God. Had it gotten warm in here suddenly? I was sweating now. I could feel the sweat forming on my neck and then chilling before running down my back.

'Don't worry, Jimmy. They're not as fierce as they act.'

I looked at Jane and then at them. They looked fierce.

'Of course you will have dinner with us this evening. Nothing fancy, just a shabu–shabu.'

I guessed that shabu–shabu was some sort of food group. I only hoped it kept still while I ate it. 'Yes, of course. Ah, ah, thank you for allowing me to stay.' I reached out my hand again. Again Jane's father held onto it for what felt like a lifetime. He was looking straight into my eyes. I tried not to blink but I know I did.

'Thank you both so much.' I reached out to shake Jane's mum's hand but she had already turned away.

Jane blew me a little kiss.

In my room, on the shelf, I could see the contents of my bag. All folded neatly and placed in little piles. I could smell them too. My clothes stood out from everything else I could smell. Jane's family home smelled perfect. Not like any home I'd ever smelled before. These were different smells. Sweet smells I didn't recognise. Something from another world. Flowers and spices. And then there were my clothes.

In my bag had been my clean clothes. Well, clothes that had been washed but hadn't been dried properly. Slightly musty smelling. Then there were my leather pants. I had come off stage the night before I left and thrown them into the bag. Maybe I'd need them? I don't know why I packed them. But they were wet and smelled of the sweat from the hundred shows that they'd seen since they were last cleaned. And then I looked at the bottom shelf and there were my shoes. A pair of work boots with steel cap toes. That would be handy if I got a job in a factory or if I wanted to join a skinhead gang. A pair of Adidas Rome running shoes that I had worn on stage for the last tour. And then, sitting alone at the end of the line of second-hand shoes, was one women's stiletto-heeled shoe. Fuck. Was that in my bag? How did that get there? It must belong to one of my flatmates. Oh my God. The maid would surely report back to Jane's parents.

I showered, scrubbing myself until my skin was nearly peeled off. But I could still smell vodka. I stood sniffing each piece of clothing, trying to find the least offensive things to wear. Looked at myself in the mirror and tried to straighten my hair. I hadn't really combed it in about five years so I could only do so much. Then I went back out to face the music.

JOHN WAS WAITING WHEN I came out of my room. 'You ever play squash, young fellow?'

Jane interrupted. 'Dad, he just got here!'

I smiled at her. I had this under control. I wondered if this was some sort of test. I had played squash once or twice but would I say I knew how to play the game? 'Yes sir. I love playing squash,' I lied. 'Maybe we could have a game sometime.'

Now I thought that this was just conversation. Anyway, they didn't play squash in Japan, did they? The nearest court must be in Malaysia somewhere.

'Great, why don't we go and have a quick game before dinner. Shake off the cobwebs from your flight. What do you think?'

Now I was nursing the mother of all hangovers but I tried not to let on. I thought I could use diplomacy to get out of the confrontation. 'I know you're a busy man. I don't want to bother you or waste your time going out to find a squash court at such short notice and all. So maybe another time. In Australia perhaps?' I thought he was just trying to make me feel at home so I had given him an out.

'It's not a problem. We have our own private court right here in the building. Come on, get your gear on, young fellow, and we'll see what you can do. Ha ha ha.'

Suddenly I got the feeling that I was in trouble. But how much trouble could he give me? I was much younger than him and he wasn't a small man. Not fat, mind you, but I could surely tire him out after a little while.

'Love to. I'll get my sneakers and shorts on and be right with you.' I'd already made up my mind that I would make it look like I was trying very hard but I would let him win in the end. It would make him feel good about himself and get us off to a good start.

We walked downstairs to the court and I couldn't help notice that John had a spring in his step and an air of confidence about him. He couldn't be that good though. Could he?

'I hope you are ready for a flogging, young fellow, because you don't really look like a squash player to me.'

Even if he couldn't play, I had to admit his psychological gamesmanship was good. What did squash players look like? Did they look like him? I wasn't sure. 'Well, we'll soon see about that, eh? You can serve.'

John served and moved to the centre of the court and that was where he stayed for the rest of the game. Myself, on the other hand, saw a lot more of the court than he did. John hardly moved anything except his wrists. And that was enough to have me running flat out from side to side, only stopping occasionally because I had smashed into the wall or fallen onto the floor with exhaustion. By the end of five games I thought I was going to have a heart attack. My face was so red it was about to explode and my lungs were screaming out for me to stop and lay down and die.

This was John's plan. I could see it now. He didn't like Jane's choice of friends and he was going to kill me right here on the squash court.

'Another game? Ha ha ha.' He was beginning to sound evil by this point.

'I'd love to but I think the jetlag is getting the better of me. Shall we stop and just call it a draw?'

There was no way I was going to get away with this. I could tell John was very competitive.

'Well, considering you haven't won a point, a draw is the last thing I'd have thought of. I think that I have flogged you, young fellow. If you've had enough we can call it quits, but I could keep going for a few more games.'

I knew and he knew that I was beaten and no amount of small talk or excuses was going to change that.

'If you don't mind. I think I have to stop. If I don't I think I might die. You're very good at this, aren't you?'

John was a gracious winner and patted me on the back and said, 'Let's call it quits before you do yourself an injury. I have played this game all my life. I get the impression you haven't.'

'Was I that bad?'

'Sorry but yes you were. Let's go.'

I limped back into the house. I was tired, hungover and now felt like I'd run a marathon as well. I had another shower and then we sat down for dinner. I was pale and could hardly speak. The shabu-shabu sat motionless on the plate waiting to be dipped into the boiling soup. For some reason, I felt that I was a lot like dinner, sitting motionless, waiting to be boiled.

'I've been reading a lot about you and your band in the Australian papers. We get them all here, you know. Sounds like an interesting life you lead.' As John spoke I suddenly remembered the headlines in the papers in Australia for the last week. 'The Thousand Girls of Jimmy Barnes.' A month or so earlier I had been woken in the middle of the night by a phone call. It was a reporter from a very smutty newspaper called *Truth*. Now the only truth *Truth* published was in the form guide for the races and even that could have been contested. The rest of the paper was filled with nude photos and stories about aliens and sex. Sometimes there were aliens and sex in the same story.

Anyway, the first thing the reporter said was, 'Hey Jimmy, how many girls do you think you've slept with?'

I, having been woken from a deep sleep, wasn't thinking clearly or I would have told him to fuck off. I mumbled and groaned and said, 'Oh fuck. Are you serious? I don't know, thousands.'

Then I hung up and went back to sleep and forgot about it until I saw the newspaper posters. 'This week, Jimmy Barnes tells us about the thousand girls he has slept with. In a five-part series we examine the life of Cold Chisel's wild young singer.'

'How the fuck did they make a story out of that?' I thought. I was glad Jane wasn't there to deal with it. Of course I never imagined her or her parents reading it in Japan. So I just ignored it until that moment at dinner.

Drip. Drip. Drip. I was starting to sweat.

'Dad, let him eat. He's tired.' Jane could obviously see I was dying. But I kept digging a hole so I could crawl into it.

'Ah, ah, em. You can't believe all you read in the papers. They, ah, they, em, make up a lot of stuff, you know.' I had nearly choked on a piece of slightly cooked squid. I think that's what it was. My face was red. Jane's parents sat examining my every move. Waiting for me to break.

Drip. Drip. Drip. I could feel the sweat again running cold down my back. 'I don't read the papers myself. They're full of rubbish, I think.' I was sinking into my chair.

Drip. Drip. Drip. It must have been collecting on my chair by now. Fear was oozing out of my pores. I was sure they could smell it.

'I suppose you make a lot of money in your business then?' John said, taking the pressure off me for a minute. 'What do you take home a week, if you don't mind me asking?'

Drip. Drip. Drip. I was drowning by this point. The sweat was gathering on my forehead and falling onto the prawns that lay looking at me from my plate. Even they wanted to know how I would get out of this.

'Ahem, yes well. It's not that simple. Ahem, you see we, ah, sink a lot of what we make back into the band. So we don't make a lot in our hands.'

John was starting to look closer at me, as if he was trying to see what I was hiding. 'So do you take a decent wage or does the band pay all your expenses? And what about tax? Who deals with all that?'

Drip. Drip. Drip. 'Not a big wage, but enough to get by on.' Now I was lying. I couldn't tell them my real wage. Even I knew that twenty-five dollars a week was not a lot of money. 'Less tax and expenses. Yes, that's right. Oh, you know, I get by.'

John let me off the hook. 'Oh that's good. Of course, it's none of my business. Glad things are going so well.'

I excused myself. 'I'm so worn out I think I have to go to bed. Thanks for having me here.'

'Goodnight. I think we all need an early night. It's been a big day,' John said.

We all got up and I headed to my room.

Jane stood up and gave me a kiss on the cheek.

'See you tomorrow.'

I kept walking to the safety of my room and shut the door. I wasn't convinced that they didn't hate me, but they seemed nice enough.

AFTER A GOOD NIGHT's sleep things seemed a little better. I opened my bedroom door and was confronted by a very strange smell. Now I had definitely never smelled this before. My eyes were burning and I could hear John and Phorn talking in the kitchen.

'Jesus, Phorn, if the maids have to make *kapi* can you get them to make it outside? The whole house is going to smell like this for days now.' *Kapi*, I found out much later, is a Thai delicacy made from aged and fermented shrimp paste and tastes much better than it smells.

Jane was working at the embassy all day so I was on my own. I left the house and I spent the day walking around Tokyo. I didn't go far from the embassy. In Tokyo I felt like a complete alien. The simple act of walking around trying to find a cup of coffee was a huge challenge. I'd never been in Asia before and I loved it. The doors of the taxis opened by themselves and the interiors were so clean you could have eaten off them. This was a lot different to Sydney cabs. In Sydney people bled and spewed and God knows what else on the seats of the cabs and I always felt I was going to catch something when I used them. I loved Japan and I still do.

I returned to the house to meet Jane. John was right, I could still smell the shrimp paste, but I sort of liked it. I waited in my room until Jane came home from work, then we went out and had dinner and a lot to drink. Jane introduced me to a few of her friends. They were all from a different world to mine but they were nice. They worked in shipping and banking and other jobs I'd only read about. But I just wanted to be alone with Jane.

We got home reasonably early but a bit under the weather and I went to bed. After a little while my door opened and Jane came in to see if I was all right. She just wanted to cuddle and say hi. Then I heard Phorn yell out, 'Jane. Jane. Are you in there? We don't want you two in there alone. We already told you that.'

Jane kissed me and went to talk with them. Now the walls weren't that thick and Jane had left the door slightly ajar, so I could hear everything that was said. They were understandably upset.

'I told you that I didn't want you going into his room at night, young lady,' John said firmly.

Then I heard Phorn raise her voice. 'You stay out of there. What are you doing in there anyway? We don't even know him. Or his family. Can he even read and write?'

Now, Jane's mum and dad had been very nice but I'd had enough to drink to make me a little intolerant. I wasn't going to stay in my room while they spoke like this about me. If they didn't like me, which I could understand, then I wouldn't stay in their house. So I got up and packed my bag before the maid could. Jane came past the room and I told her I was leaving. Jane decided she was coming with me.

'Where are we going to go?' she asked.

'I'll find somewhere. Anywhere.'

We checked into one of the big hotels near the Tokyo Tower and went out to drink some more. Jane had introduced me to a restaurant called Inakaya. I loved it and I think we ate there about four times over the next few days. I have compulsive tendencies, in case you didn't know. If I like something, I do it to death and then do it some more. This is something that has caused me a lot of problems over the years. Anyway, we drank and ate and ate and drank and then drank some more, every night staggering back to the hotel and falling asleep in each other's arms. It was great, although I noticed that drinking so much sake seemed to make me a bit aggressive. I know what you're thinking – I'm aggressive anyway, and you're right. But I think that the lead in the petrol from so many cars and the sake were a lethal combination. I was nearly getting into fights with strangers just walking down the street. Eventually Jane and I started to fight a little too.

AFTER A PARTICULARLY BIG night we walked into my hotel. I noticed that there were what appeared to be hotel security following us through the lobby right to the lifts. I pressed the button to call the lift when one of the men said, 'Excuse me sir. You cannot take any prostitutes up to your room.'

I stopped and looked around. There was only Jane and myself standing there.

'What did you say?' I snapped.

'No prostitutes are allowed in guest rooms, sir.'

He was looking at Jane. I was dressed in faded blue jeans with holes in them and a leather jacket. Jane was in a short, short miniskirt with thick eye makeup and a leather jacket and we had both been staggering through the lobby of the hotel. They had mistaken Jane for a hooker and I was ready to kill them.

When you check into hotels overseas they ask for your passport and Jane had some sort of diplomatic stamp in hers. If they had checked before they acted they might have been a little more careful what they said. But now it was too late.

'Hey mate. This is my girlfriend, you fucking idiot. Now get out of my way.' And I pushed my way past them. But they followed us upstairs and stopped us again. I went nuts. 'Go downstairs and get my bill ready. I am checking out and your hotel is going to be in big trouble. I am a famous rock star in Australia and this will be all over the papers.' (I don't pull the rock star card unless I'm really desperate and drunk, by the way.) 'And this young lady is the daughter of an Australian diplomat. You guys have really fucked up.'

Jane and I went to our room to pack our bags. We were furious. I punched holes in the walls and smashed the television set and generally threw everything in the room around. Then we went downstairs.

'I'm not staying in this fucking country another minute,' I announced to Jane, expecting her to join me. 'I hate this place,' I went on as I stormed around the hotel.

We got to reception and the staff had obviously realised their error and were waiting to apologise. 'Very sorry, sir. Please accept our apology and let us make it up to you by offering you your room for free.'

They bowed graciously and waited for my reply. It was too late to back down. I hadn't fitted in anywhere since I'd left Australia. I was out of my class at Jane's family home and out of my depth in Tokyo. I was embarrassed and angry and the only way I knew how to deal with the situation was the way my mum had dealt with things: smash up the place and burn every bridge that I had crossed.

'I accept nothing, mate. It's fucking hara-kiri for you, pal. Now fuck off and give me my passport.'

As we left the hotel I wasn't sure what I was doing. I was in a blind rage. Had I thought Jane would come with me or had I not thought at all? I think it was the latter.

'Where are we going to go now, baby?' I looked at Jane. She paid no attention to me. She had already organised for someone to pick her up and I was alone.

'Take me to Narita Airport and don't spare the fucking horsepower.' The cab driver didn't know what I was talking about so I told him slowly, 'Please take me to the airport.'

I jumped on the first plane that would take me to Britain. As it took off I could see the sun rising in the east. Over the next few hours I drank the plane out of sake. I had fucked it all up again.

CHAPTER SEVENTEEN

this hotel's a cesspool

PLAZA HOTEL, KINGS CROSS, 1980

M Y FIRST TRIP TO Scotland was an eye opener. I immediately knew that this was where I was from. Everywhere I looked I saw glimpses of myself in the people I met. On the street, in the bars, in fact everywhere. Some of the people reminded me of good things in my life but a lot reminded me of the bad. So I was happy to have gone there but I was also happy to leave. I wasn't quite ready to confront all my demons yet. I had to get back to Australia. The album had been released and we were ready to start work again.

The band had run off in all directions looking for inspiration and a chance to put some distance between us. We had lived in each other's pockets for a long time. I think that if we hadn't gotten away from each other we might have broken up earlier than we did.

Just like my pilgrimage to Scotland, Don had made a pilgrimage to New York, in search of ideas. I'm sure he found some in the coffee shops and bars of downtown New York. I figured Don had spoken to every character that inhabited the Cross and he needed some new people to write about. New York was full of wild and wonderful people. I don't know if that's what inspired him, but his new songs were darker and more worldly.

So, after a short break, we all assembled back in Sydney with a new lease on life. Rested and ready to work. Well, ready to work anyway. I hadn't really rested that much. I'd hardly slept while I was away unless I passed out cold. In the UK I drank a lot, smoked a lot and snorted a lot of drugs. Speed, coke, whatever I could lay my hands on. So it was good to get back to work and some sort of routine before I died.

EAST WAS A SMASH. A huge success. Much bigger than any of us had imagined. Of course *Countdown* was right behind us. They were in our corner now. The people who ran *Countdown*, including Molly, were smart, and they knew that we were good for their show. They didn't need to be fighting with all the best rock bands in the country. They already had a feud going on with Midnight Oil, who refused to have anything to do with them. But we knew that as much as we disliked aspects of the show, it was better to use it for our own good than fight against it. Next time we played, we were allowed to have live vocals. 'Cheap Wine' became almost a regular on the show. They even played the film clip we made for the song. I was blasted across TV screens all over the country, half naked and wearing eyeliner. We were wearing them down, bit by bit. Record sales kept climbing and so did the numbers of people who came through the doors at our shows. We would use *Countdown* as much as they used us.

We shot the cover for *East* the day I arrived back from overseas. We were set up in an apartment in Elizabeth Bay somewhere, in the same block of apartments where we would eventually shoot the film clip for 'Cheap Wine'. The idea was to base the cover on a famous artwork, *The Death of Marat* by Jacques-Louis David. Revolutionary Jean-Paul Marat was murdered in the bath and this painting was one of the most famous images of the French Revolution, one of the first times politics and art collided. *East* was an album where Don, in particular, had lyrically painted a picture of an underlying feeling of discontent with social justice in our country. This idea, this image, seemed to fit with that feeling. I turned up for the shoot with a headband that I had picked up in Tokyo. The headband had a bit of a story to go along with it. There had been protests in the streets of Tokyo while I was there. The protesters called it the Spring Offensive and a lot of the marchers wore headbands with slogans like 'Death Before Dishonour' and 'Fight for Freedom' written on them. I liked the idea of this so I grabbed one of their headbands, not knowing what I would do with it. For some reason I brought it along to the photoshoot. It seemed perfect for the shot, so I wrapped it around my head and lay in the bath. Everyone loved the image. I wore the headband for years.

It wasn't until about ten years later that a Japanese fan stopped me after a show and told me, 'Hey Jimmy. On the cover of your album *East*, you have the headband on upside down.'

What could I do? I laughed and pretended I knew all along.

THE GUYS IN THE band will all have different memories of things like this but I remember us meeting at the Plaza Hotel. Don wrote a song about this place:

I've been living
In the Plaza Hotel
It ain't the Hilton
But I live well.

Ian had to sing this song because I refused to.

Anyway, at this meeting I said to the band and management, 'I want a pay rise.'

'Er, not really a good time to be asking for more money at the moment.'

'Why the fuck not? We've just done a sold-out tour. Don't you guys want more money to live on? Look where you're living.' I looked around the sleazy hotel room, trying to make eye contact with one of the band.' Any one of them would do.

'Na. I don't need any more,' Steve said. 'What would I fucking spend it on anyway? I got everything I need, I can drink at the gigs and I've got money for chip butties and I got a place to stay. What fucking else do I want?'

'Look at this fucking place. It's a shithole,' I pleaded.

'Looks good to me,' Steve quickly shot back, in his thick Liverpudlian accent that made everything sound like a joke. Maybe he was kidding. I wasn't sure anymore.

'Well, I need more,' I stated. 'Twenty-five fucking dollars a week is not enough for me to live on. We're one of the biggest bands in the country and I think I should be able to earn enough to rent a house.'

Don was next to speak up. 'You could stay in the hotel like me.' Now Don was in a different position to the rest of us. He was making a lot of money from his publishing by this time. None of us begrudged him making the money because he worked really hard, writing some of the best songs we had ever heard for the band. I felt privileged to be singing them. But Don could afford to stay anywhere he wanted. He liked living in the Cross. I think the filth and the desperation of the place were inspiring to him somehow. But not to me. I'd seen enough filth and I'd lived through enough desperation.

'This hotel's a cesspool. It's full of cockroaches. They ran over me in bed when I was sleeping when I stayed here!'

'You could just pull your bed away from the wall a bit,' Steve quipped.

'I did. They fucking pulled it back.' We all laughed; it was an old joke but a goody. But I was sort of serious. 'The place is full of hookers and drug dealers.'

'And you have a problem with that suddenly, do you?'

I wanted to punch Steve in the face. 'No, I don't actually, but the doors don't lock properly and you have to share a bathroom with the hookers' fucking filthy old drunken clients. It's fucked.' I was sick of talking about it. Couldn't they see that? 'And that's why I won't stay here.'

'I think it's okay.' Ian had finally joined the argument.

I glared at him. 'Glad you like it. You stay here. I don't fucking want to. Anyway, I want more money.'

'You'll just waste it if we give it to you,' Rod said, baiting me.

'I'm allowed to waste my own fucking money. Where the fuck is it anyway? Give me some.'

'Well. Now is not a good time.'

'Why not?'

'It's a business thing, Jim. You wouldn't understand. It's about cash flow or the lack of it, if you really must know.'

'Yes, as a matter of fact I do need to fucking know.'

'The accountant tells me that this is not a good time to outlay money. We've invested all the money in a few projects that should pay you guys big dividends if you can just be a little bit patient.' Rod's voice always became calm and monotone when he tried to sell us on something. He was a hard boy and there was always an underlying touch of aggression to what he said, but he never tried to intimidate us. He had been on the road too long, like us, and he could just sound aggressive at times. I'm glad I never had to fight him. I reckon he could go, but I trusted Rod with my life. He was one of us. He was honest as the day is long and hardworking, but I still wasn't sure we were investing wisely.

'Like what?' I asked.

'Listen, you ungrateful bastards don't know the work that your accountant is doing behind the scenes.' Rod's voice was raised slightly. He knew our accountant was honest and doing his best too. So did we.

'Is he even a real accountant yet?' I was asking for trouble now. This subject always got Rod's back up. Our accountant was doing an accounting course through the mail at one time. 'He might be out of his depth.' I kept digging.

'I think he's doing the right things with your money,' Rod defended him.

'Like what?'

'Well, he's invested in a really great gold scheme we heard about. Nobody has caught onto it yet. You guys are going to clean up.'

This particular scheme ended up being known as the 'bottom of the harbour scheme'. It was illegal and that's why no one was talking about it. We lost a fortune. It's an expensive exercise to run a band at the best of times, but when what little money you have is involved in schemes like this, it doesn't help.

'Well, I hope it pays off soon.'

It never did, but at least none of us went to jail. Another thing we did on his advice was buy a block of apartments in Glebe. 'You guys are going to make a killing with this. We got them for two hundred and seventy-five thousand dollars. We can strata title them and sell them off and you will make at least a cool million. Can't go wrong.'

Famous last words there. We sold them four years later for less than we paid for them. It appears we were the only people to lose money from the property boom in Sydney.

'Well, meeting over then,' Rod said.

'Wait a minute. I can't live on twenty-five dollars a week.'

'Leave it with me and I'll look at the books and see what we can do. Good talking. Very productive, I thought.' Rod smiled and walked to the door.

'Fuck, Rod.'

He stopped. 'I'll do my best,' he said and winked at me.

'Thanks.'

'We really should have meetings like this, every week. We get so much more done. Bye.' Then he disappeared into the corridor and was gone, quicker than one of the hookers' clients.

'What the fuck happened? I never got an answer?'

'Oh, don't worry, he'll get back to you,' Don drawled. 'Anybody want to get a coffee?'

'Yeah, I'm in,' Steve and Ian said at once.

'Yeah, me too, I'm starving.' Phil was up and heading for the door.

The band walked off, leaving me alone with my friends the cockroaches in their lovely hotel. This had been a typical Cold Chisel meeting.

I was propositioned by a young lady as I walked down the hall towards the stairs.

'Sorry love. You're asking the wrong bloke. I'm a musician. I'm broke. Maybe another time.'

AFTER SIX MONTHS JANE moved back to Sydney and we moved in with some friends while we found a place to live. My old friend Vince Lovegrove and his girlfriend of the time let Jane and I live at their house for a while, but it was too wild a time for all concerned. Vince was crazier than I was, so we needed to find our own house. Jane's best friend Victoria was spending more and more time in Sydney and I introduced her to Mark Opitz. They immediately took to each other, so we all thought it would be a good idea to move in together. Jane found us a house in Brown Street in Paddington.

It was a huge terrace house, much nicer than anywhere I'd ever stayed before. I was used to living in hovels but Jane needed somewhere nice. I liked it. Jane made a home for us. The house was on three levels and Jane and I decided we were moving into the ground floor. So we took the ballroom on the ground floor as our bedroom. We didn't have lot of furniture but it was a great room. And we had room to dance if we liked. No, I never really danced. Mark and Victoria moved in together onto the second floor. I was working with Mark and living with him. We all became the best of friends. Mark and I talked about music all day and night, driving the girls crazy. He had a great sense of melody and had a million ideas on how I could make music, with or without Cold Chisel. Mark and I talked about making solo records long before I actually made one.

COUNTDOWN AND *TV WEEK* ran the Australian Music and Video Awards. *TV Week* was a television guide that included one photo of whichever band they chose to fill the centre spot of their cheap magazine each week. Record companies fought hand to hand to get their bands into that magazine. It meant you got free advertising at newsstands and even on television. And of course, this gave the featured band an opportunity to sell more records. So both *Countdown* and *TV Week* knew that bands would do whatever they wanted to sell more records. But Cold Chisel knew that they could only push us so far. Then we would turn on them.

By the time *East* tore up to the top end of the charts and stayed there for six months, we were in the driver's seat and they knew it. They wanted us to be on the *Countdown/TV Week* Music and Video Awards show in March 1981 because they knew we would win quite a few of their awards. But we insisted that we'd only play if we could do it completely live, the way real bands do. They were appalled. No one played live on television. Not on their show anyway. But we stood our ground. If they wanted us on, it would be on our terms. The shoe was on the other foot.

They weren't happy, but what could they do? They had to agree. It was decided that we would go on towards the end of the show and play a song. Not the song they wanted either, but a song that we would choose. We informed them that we would play an album track, not a single, because we were a serious band. We all decided on 'My Turn to Cry', a song I had written. It wasn't the strongest song on the album but we had plans to make it a real show stopper.

We set about buying cheap guitars that we could dress up to look like our real gear. We changed the stickers at the top of the neck, carefully replacing the ones that were there with Fender stickers so they would suspect nothing. Then we went into a secret studio session and rearranged the song to add a little spice to the night.

They never caught on. We had trouble keeping the smiles off our faces on the day when we went in to rehearse the album version of the song for the evening's broadcast. It all went smoothly. They were happy. Well, as happy as they could be. We weren't their puppets anymore.

The show started. We had informed them that we would not be picking up any awards we might win, as we wanted to have a big impact when we played live. It would be better television, we assured them. Then, after winning seven of the awards up for grabs, including Most Popular Group and Best Album, we hit the stage. The performance was explosive from the start. If you didn't know us, like most people, you would have thought we were up to something. I walked on with an open bottle of vodka that I had already half drunk. Phil was dressed in a Nazi uniform.

I could see the worried looks of the TV crew as we burst into our song. Then, at a prearranged spot, the band changed the song into something else. It went like clockwork. We went from a song about love lost to me screaming at the cameras like a maniac, telling them,

> I never saw you at the Astra Hotel
> I never saw you at the Largs Pier Hotel
> I never saw you down on Fitzroy Street
> And now you want to use my face to sell *TV Week*.

I then raised my mic stand above my head and smashed it onto the floor. Pieces shattered and flew everywhere. The band all did the same, smashing their respective instruments to pieces. The final words to the song were, 'Eat this.'

Mossy's guitar was the last thing to be seen, flying through the air, as the curtain was quickly brought down in an attempt to make us stop. The guitar banged to the floor, barely missing Molly as he walked out with his mouth open. He was speechless. This was a rare occasion. When it was all over there was an awkward silence, except for the noise of our guitars feeding back as the roadies turned off our equipment. It was only quiet for a second and then the crowd went crazy. We walked off stage and straight out the back door, giggling like schoolboys, and left. We didn't go to the afterparty. I doubt we would have been welcomed. We had organised our own celebration, much bigger and a lot more fun than anything they had in mind. The television world was shocked and angry with us. The punters, the only ones who really mattered, loved us. The night was a great success.

News filtered back to our party. Angry messages were passed on to us. 'You guys are finished. This is the end of your careers.'

We didn't give a shit. We had made our statement. We were happy. Our careers weren't over. In fact, over the last year, the band had become even bigger and thousands more diehard fans turned up every night to see us play music and fight for our rights. Every night I would arrive at our shows and there would be queues of punters lined up around the block and down the street. We were out of control. We played sixty-four shows in eighty-eight days on the Youth in Asia tour, finishing at the Capitol Theatre in Sydney, where we recorded *Swingshift*, a double live album. Then we went straight out again, on the Summer Offensive Tour. We were like stormtroopers, marching across Australia. We were on top of the world and there was only one way we could go. Down. But that wouldn't happen for a long time. I drank more, partied harder and pushed the band to play faster and faster. My drug intake was increasing everyday as I woke up wondering what I had done the night before. I smashed up pubs and clubs all over the country, the walls and roofs crumbling down around us. The pace we were keeping was blistering. More towns, more girls, more booze, more drugs, and all in less time. Longer sets, faster songs and even longer drives after shows. Eventually, this pace would bring us to our knees.

CHAPTER EIGHTEEN

what are we doing with our lives?

BROWN STREET, PADDINGTON, 1981

ONE DAY OUT OF the blue, when Jane and I were lying in bed, she said to me, 'So what are we doing?'

I wasn't doing anything. I was just lying there. I didn't understand what she meant. 'What do you want to do? I'll do whatever you want,' I said, trying to sound enthusiastic.

'No, I mean what are we doing with our lives? Are we just going to live like this and get stoned all day and night or are we going to get serious about things?'

Jane had obviously been thinking a lot more about our future than I had. I was happy to spend at least the near future, if not longer, just getting stoned, but now that she mentioned it, what were we doing?

'What do you mean, baby? What do you want to do?' I was too stoned to respond any better, but I was straightening up rapidly. I sat up and looked at her.

'Well, if we are not going to get married I might move on and do something with my life,' she said.

I was wide awake and completely straight now. 'What do you mean? Why would you go anywhere?' I was worried.

'If we're not getting married I am going to go to America and continue studying.'

I sat thinking for a second. I knew that I couldn't think about this too long or I would lose Jane. 'Yeah. I think we should get married too. Let's do it.' It wasn't very romantic of me but I loved Jane. I just hadn't thought about marriage until that moment.

I WAS WORRIED. NOT about marrying Jane but the idea of the wedding. Surely that meant that my family and Jane's family would all have to be there? I didn't want them to be in the same room. My mum was not from the same world as Jane's mum.

Luckily Jane wanted to get married straightaway. She didn't want a big wedding. I think she didn't want our parents getting together either. We looked into a civil ceremony. We would have to apply and wait four weeks. But we didn't have that long. Cold Chisel was starting a big tour in three and a half weeks and the only way we could speed up the proceedings was to ask permission and show the details of the tour, airline tickets etc. We set a date, 22 May 1981. All we had to do was take in the proof. But we never got around to it. They married us anyway, in the Registry Office that afternoon, and I did a show at the Comb and Cutter Hotel in Blacktown that evening. How romantic of me.

I look back on a lot of these times and wonder how I ended up with such a great girl. Besides feeling unworthy, I was a complete idiot. If I could do it all again I would, but with more style. The style that my Jane always deserved.

ONE THING THAT HAPPENED when I was young that changed my life for the better was the birth of my son David Campbell. David was conceived and born before I joined Cold Chisel. I was very young, as was David's mum, Kim. We found each other one night while leaving a community hall show I was doing with my first band.

Although I never meant to have a child, I see that night as one of the most important moments in my life. We were so young and we ended up in each other's arms only because we needed to feel loved, even if it was just for one night. But I found a love that night that has been growing stronger ever since, the love I have for my son David. He was adopted and raised by his biological grandmother, Joan. It has been complicated at times – life is complicated – but things worked out for the best. I know this and I see it every time I see him smile.

I told Jane about David before we were married. I was worried about telling her. But I shouldn't have been. David was important to me, but the fact that I already had a son in Adelaide might, I felt, put Jane off having a relationship with me. I wanted her to know that this was my responsibility and not hers. I would understand if she wanted nothing to do with David. In fact, I would understand if she wanted nothing to do with me. But I underestimated Jane, not for the first or last time. If I had a son, Jane wanted to meet him, be a part of his life. If he was a part of me then she would love him too. If he was a part of me then he was a part of her. It was that simple.

I tried to explain why I hadn't seen a lot of David, the circumstances that dictated our relationship. She said, 'Nothing or no one could keep me away from my child. You need to be in his life. He needs you and you need him.'

I felt stupid for not reacting the same way. Of course she was right, but where I came from, and my relationship with David's mother and his grandmother, Joan, was something Jane knew nothing about. I told her about the circumstances around David's birth and the relationship or lack of relationship that I had with Joan, who, by the way, David believed was his mother.

I never got on with Joan. I'm sure it was a lot to do with my age and my background but basically I didn't like her that much. And more importantly, she didn't like me at all. But she brought David up, and whether I liked her or not, she obviously did something right. You just have to look at him to see that. She never wanted money from me to help look after David. In fact, David was never to know that I had anything to do with him. So how could I bring anything to his life? I couldn't see him. I had no money to give him and I lived in a different state to him. I lived in a different world to him. But David lived in the world that I had run away from. The world I hated. And I left him in the middle of it. What could I do? I couldn't look after myself, never mind him. This caused me incredible pain. So I did what I did with everything that caused me pain. I ran from it. This made me feel a new guilt. I was starting to behave the same as my parents. No care and no responsibility. This could have been my family motto. I wonder how you say that in Latin. We could have written it on our coat of arms if we could have afforded a coat to write it on.

Jane pushed me into re-establishing contact with Joan and more importantly, with David. I thought seeing him would hurt but it didn't. The more I saw him, the better I felt. David was always a good boy. He was soft, gentle and loving. As far as he knew, I was a friend of the family. It must have been confusing for him. I visited whenever I was in Adelaide. I'm not sure he knew what I did for a living but I couldn't have looked like the rest of the family friends.

I would turn up at the door and be taken to the lounge room and left with him. 'David, this 'ere is your Uncle Jim. He's come to spend a bit of time wiff you, son,' Joan would say in a stern English working-class voice and then leave the room.

I would sit down, not knowing what to say or do. 'So. How are you?'

David would look at me and say, 'Hello.' And then nothing.

'Are these your toys over here?' I would say, stating the obvious, trying to get him to talk to me.

Then David would get up and play. 'Do you want to play with me?' It was as if David knew how uncomfortable I was and tried to make it easier for me.

'Yeah. That'd be nice.'

We would spend half an hour talking and playing then I would have to leave. 'I have to go now but would you mind if I came back to see you again?'

He would look at me with eyes that said he knew who I was, even though he couldn't have, and say, 'Yeah, that would be nice.'

He would kiss my cheek. I would make an uncomfortable attempt at a hug and then we'd walk to the kitchen where Joan was waiting, drinking tea.

'David must never, ever know about you, Jim. You know it would break his little 'eart. And nun of us want that, do we?' she would say as she saw me out the door.

It was painful but I loved seeing him. He looked like me. Well, he did to me anyway. I could see myself in him. But he was softer, much softer than I was. Maybe it was a good thing he didn't know me. Or my family. We'd only hurt him too.

By the end of Cold Chisel, I saw him more and more. Jane came with me a few times to meet him. He was immediately more comfortable with her than he was with me. She was great with children. But Joan made it harder each time I went. I would ring and she would be horrible on the phone. Eventually though, we got to spend time with David alone. He came with us for a picnic in the Hills. But as soon as we were away from Joan, David would start to get sick. He would have migraines. Joan would tell me later that they were emotional. 'It's too hard on the poor little fing. I don't fink it's good for him to be wiff you alone. He's better off 'ere wiff me.'

I knew that this was going to get worse before it got better.

THE BAND HIT THE road, and married life and Cold Chisel were thrown together. Cold Chisel had always been five guys fighting as one. Every now and then one more body would join the gang: Peter Moss; Alan Dallow; Billy Rowe; Gerry Georgettis, our new sound guy; Harry Parsons, our foldback operator; even Rod Willis. Rod of course was one of us. Once Rod joined he was there for decades. But there were never any girls who could come between us. Girlfriends came and went but when push came to shove, the band always came first. That all changed when I met Jane. From the minute I met her, the band took a backseat. They knew it too and they didn't like it. This was the beginning of the end.

Jane and I were in it together. Us against the world, and that included everyone, even Cold Chisel, and in particular the management. Jane was the first person to say to me, 'Hey, considering how many people come to see you and how many records you are selling every day, you don't make a lot of money. Don't you think that's a little strange?'

I'd never really cared that much. I had brought it up once, at that band meeting at the Plaza I told you about, but it was never mentioned again.

'Yeah. I think you're right, now that I think about it.'

Jane wanted to make sure I was all right, and not getting taken advantage of. 'Why don't you ask for more money? You're married now and you know we want to have a family sooner or later. You should know exactly where all your money goes. It's just good business.'

I felt a little stupid. Of course I should know where it all went. But it never mattered really until then.

'Yeah, I'll ask about it next time we meet.' I didn't. But I would soon, and it would cause problems.

CHAPTER NINETEEN

a small fish in a big sewer

ON THE WAY TO THE USA, 1981

I GREW UP THINKING that American music was the best in the world. I heard my mum and dad sing along with black American singers when I was young, even before we moved halfway around the world to Australia. It seemed nearly everyone in post-war Britain listened to the radio, hoping to hear songs fresh off the American charts. Songs about leaving your chewing gum on the bedpost didn't cut it anymore. Vera Lynn had been replaced by Ray Charles and Nat King Cole. 'We'll Meet Again' was gone and 'Your Cheatin' Heart' and 'Hit the Road Jack' became anthems for women like my mum, who were sick of cheating husbands telling them what they could and couldn't do. My mum would sing these songs at parties when she'd had a few, her eyes drilling a hole straight through my father while she sang them. He never noticed that these songs were sung especially for him. He was oblivious to anything that my mum felt or cared about. And of course, night after night, he kept singing love songs to anyone else who'd listen. But never to my mum.

So American music was part of the soundtrack of my life even before I took any notice of it. Of course these songs were mixed with Scottish songs too, songs by people like Andy Stewart, singing about bonnie Scotland. These were the songs that my parents would sing together when they'd both drunk enough to put aside their differences and get along with each other. This never happened until the end of the night. Right before they started to really fight.

IT WASN'T UNTIL I was older that I found songs that touched me too. They were songs that I heard on the radio, songs that spoke to me about rebellion and freedom and sex.

My favourite lyrics of all time would have to be 'Wop bop a loo bop a lop bam boom'. Even the sound of Little Richard's microphone distorting appealed to me. I didn't know why it was doing it, that was too technical for me at the time, but I knew he was screaming at the top of his voice and I liked that. I wanted to scream too. And adults couldn't deal with the rawness of what he was doing. So that was enough for me. I was sold. From then on, anything that irritated my parents appealed to me. Whether it was Wilson Pickett or Chuck Berry, it didn't matter, as long as it annoyed them.

As I got older I escaped life by listening to rock'n'roll music. First the sound I loved came from America and then, once it had been trodden down by the scared white folk that lived there, it was reinvented by the British.

I would hear about new artists coming out of England with their fresh new sound, but somehow it was familiar to me. It took a few years before I made the connection and traced it back to the music my brother had listened to. The music of The Beatles and The Rolling Stones sounded like pale, insipid versions of the songs I'd heard years before, coming from the likes of Howlin' Wolf and Muddy Waters and of course Chuck Berry. But they were British, just like me, and that, somehow, made it easier for me to relate to them and sing along with them.

Eventually, I would be singing along with Australian singers, most of whom were immigrants, just like me. These singers would be the real reason that I got into bands. These blokes beat down the doors in this country and allowed singers like me to walk straight through them. Singers like Johnny O'Keefe and of course my favourite, Billy Thorpe. But that would be just the start.

I REMEMBER HEARING 'ALL Right Now' by Free and 'Black Night' by Deep Purple on the radio. I think I heard them back to back, and that was it. Whether I was the right age or the songs struck the right chord with me I don't know, but that day I knew I wanted to be in a band.

It wasn't a surprise to me that Cold Chisel would be so influenced by American music. Some of us liked British bands and British musicians, but the core of the music that moved us as a band came from the United States. Not just any American music, but black music. In reality it could all be traced back to blues music. Even the British stuff. I don't think we set out to be a blues band but that's what we became. A blues band that was influenced by everything that caught our ears on the radio. Pop, soul, hard rock, even punk. We took it all in and it came back out as some kind of rock fusion, moulded into shape by the gigs we were playing and the people we were playing to. But it was always blues based.

For years, when it seemed that no one in Australia was getting us, we thought that at some point we would go to the States. They would get us. We were confident of it. But by the time we got around to going there, we were pulling huge crowds here in Australia and were being deeply affected by the places we were playing. Australia became an integral part of the chemistry of the band. So we didn't really want to leave these shores.

But for the band to grow we knew deep down that we would have to leave home and try our luck overseas. America was calling us, calling us like sirens, whispering to us to come crashing to our deaths.

In June 1981 we jumped on a plane and headed for Los Angeles, California. The deal that we had signed to WEA in Australia gave them first claim to the band overseas. So we were signed to Elektra Records, a part of WEA International.

Things started going wrong from day one. We began falling apart at the airport in Sydney. Steve bought himself a huge ghetto blaster from the duty free shop. It was a Sharp twin-cassette deck. Anyway he filled it with enough batteries to power a small village and commenced playing music so loud the whole airport could hear it. People were scowling at him but he didn't care. Steve had started drinking as soon as he reached the airport, and by the time we went through passport control he was half drunk.

We got on the plane for Los Angeles via Honolulu and sat in our seats. The women serving on the American carrier didn't realise how pissed Steve was and continued to feed him full of drinks, much to the dismay of the passengers. Gerry Georgettis, our sound guy, had been selected by the band to sit with Steve and keep him reasonably together. He didn't succeed.

About halfway through the flight, one of the hostesses decided it was time to calm Steve down, as he was getting a little rowdy and insisted on trying to place his hand down the front of her blouse every time she served him. So she offered him a pill that would quiet him down, which he took before he even knew what he was doing. It wasn't long until Steve was weaving up and down the aisles, with his after-show Liverpudlian swagger, looking for trouble or chicks. He didn't care. Whatever he came across first.

Gerry tried his best to keep him in his seat, playing New Orleans funk music to him through his headphones. The mixture of the pill, the booze and The Meters seemed to work and he was starting to nod off when the pilot announced, 'Please fasten your seatbelts and set your seat to the upright position for landing at Honolulu International Airport. We will be touching down in about twenty minutes.'

Gerry didn't have long to get Steve to fill in his arrival forms. 'Come on, Steve. Sit still and we'll fill in our forms together.'

'Fuck off. I'm not filling in any fucking thing,' Steve slurred.

'Come on, brother. Don't fuck around here. We have to fill these in or we won't get into the country.' Gerry was becoming a little desperate.

'Shove them fucking forms straight up your fucking Greek arse, mate.'

'Hey, that's uncool man. Just fill in the fucking forms, would you?'

'Why the fuck would I want to fucking fill in any fucking thing?'

I could hear Steve's voice from six rows away over the roaring of the jet engines as the 747 slowed down to landing speed.

'All right. All right. I'll fill them in for you and you can sign them.' Gerry was panicking. It was illegal to fill in another person's forms, but he did it anyway.

'Okay man. Come on, just sign your name on the line here, would you?' Gerry said, sliding the forms in front of Steve.

'Yeah man, I'll fucking give you my autograph if you want it, you fucking twat.' Steve laughed and scribbled his name across half the form, missing the place where he was supposed to write it by a mile.

'Shall I add a couple of fucking kisses?' He reached for the form again, but Gerry snatched it away just in time.

'Shit man, that's so uncool.'

Gerry knew that it would have to do and that he had failed miserably at his job of babysitting Steve. We would be lucky if we got through customs at all.

We queued up to go through immigration in Honolulu. We were all in the same line, shuffling around, looking guilty even though we hadn't done anything. Suddenly music started blaring out from Steve's ghetto blaster.

'Hey man, turn it off or you'll not get into America,' Gerry pleaded, but Steve wasn't listening. He was too smashed to hear him and the music was too loud. He was starting to dance. That always meant trouble.

We all looked at one another. This was not good. I could see the officer at the top of the queue look down his glasses towards Steve.

'Fuck man. Turn it off!' Gerry was really starting to panic. 'You're going to get us all thrown out of the place. You idiot!' And he quickly turned off Steve's music.

Steve turned white with anger, and lifted the ghetto blaster up over his head. 'I don't want to go into their fucking stupid fucking country anyway,' he shouted at the top of his voice and smashed the cassette player, as hard as he could, onto the ground. The noise was deafening. The whole arrivals hall went silent and turned to us and stared. Myself, the rest of the band and our management immediately moved to different queues, leaving Gerry and Steve alone. They were next to be assessed.

Gerry grabbed the cassette player – which was miraculously still in one piece – and fumbled around the floor picking up the ten or so batteries that were rolling all over the ground. He shoved them into the machine just in time to hand it to Steve as he walked up to the counter.

Steve gave his slightly crumpled form to the officer and stood, swaying. The officer looked at the form and then at Steve. Then back at the form again. You could tell he was trying to work out what the scribble across the middle was.

'Ahem.' He cleared his throat nervously before he spoke to Steve. 'Sir, did you, er, did you fill in this form yourself, Mr Prestwick?'

'That's Prestwich.'

'Pardon me, sir?'

'That's Prestwich.'

'Ah, sorry Mr Prestwich.' He spoke slowly and purposefully. 'Did you fill in this form yourself?' he asked a second time.

'Nope. Not me. I never filled in anything. He fucking did.'

'But, er, is this your writing, sir?' The officer couldn't believe the guy in front of him

'No. I just told you I didn't fill in anything. He did.' Steve stood with a glazed look on his face and motioned towards Gerry, who by this point didn't know where to look, so he looked at his feet.

The officer shook his head and ran his fingers through his already thinning hair. He didn't need this. He had a look on his face like he wished he'd stayed at home for the day. He thought for a brief second and then, *bang!* He stamped Steve's passport. 'Have a nice day, sir.'

And he waved Steve on. We couldn't believe it. I can only assume that Steve appeared too difficult to deal with and the officer felt it was easier to let him go. Each of us was scrutinised a little but let through without too much trouble, except for Rod Willis. I think they worked out that we were all together and he might be the boss. So they set about giving Rod a right royal grilling.

In the meantime the rest of us assembled near the duty free shop. Steve swayed and turned the music back on. His ghetto blaster still played as loud as ever. I immediately went into the duty free shop and bought myself the exact same deck. This was a music player that could stand up to the rigours of life on the road.

We were on American soil, ready to start our US tour.

OUR FIRST AND ONLY tour of the States was a mismatch of gigs. I don't think there was really a lot of thought put into it by our American agent, our record company or even our management. Rod had done no work as a manager over there, so, like the band, he was learning the ropes on the fly. America was and still is a very tough nut to crack. It takes patience, time and a lot of luck. All of which we never really had.

Going from being a successful band in Australia, back to the bottom of the heap in the US, was enough to make me feel sick. I had spent years running away from having nothing at all. I'd been treated like shit for most of my life and I had only just started to gain some confidence. So going from being a big fish in a small pond to being a small fish in a big sewer did not fill me with hope. I only prayed I could keep my head above water.

Rod was inexperienced but the American agents just didn't get us or didn't care. I should have been thankful that we got to play to anyone but I wasn't happy with the shows they had set up for us. I could almost hear them talking about us in my head. I was sure they'd have said something like, 'Let's just throw a few shows together for these guys. They wouldn't know a good gig from a bad one. They'll play anywhere. They're just a little Australian band. What the fuck will they know?'

In hindsight the agents probably did their best. It wasn't easy to get a small band from Australia onto shows opening up for big bands in America. But they managed to get us on a few. We should have been grateful. But here we were playing supports again.

CHAPTER TWENTY

good evening, Red Rocks

USA, 1981

OUR FIRST US SHOW was in San Diego. Our agent, John Marx, swore to us that we would be treated well on this bill. John wasn't a bad guy. He loved music but he was smooth, almost a yuppie compared to us. He liked us but I think we were a bit wild for him.

Anyway, our first show was with a Canadian band called Loverboy. They didn't sound like our kind of band but we decided to take the agent's word and set off for San Diego with an open mind. The bill was Loverboy, headlining, followed by Heart as 'special guests', and us in writing so small that you would have had to crash your car into the wall the poster was plastered on to see our name. We arrived backstage at some big baseball stadium a few hours before we were due to go on. Our gear had been sent ahead with our crew. We'd done a million big shows in Australia so we knew how it all worked. We expected to get a little caravan for a dressing room, and not much room on stage to play, but we were ready for it.

When we found our crew, they were standing near the parked trucks with our gear, sitting in the sun. 'They wouldn't let us put our gear on the stage to do a line check. They told us to wait over here until they're ready for us. That was two hours ago.'

It wasn't an ideal start but we tried to stay calm.

'Where's our dressing room?' I asked, wanting to get out of the burning sun.

'You'll have to ask their production manager. They haven't told us anything. They're not very helpful.'

We went to find the production manager. He was sitting in an air-conditioned hut with a few girls in very short skirts, laughing and drinking a beer.

'Hi, we're the support band, Cold Chisel. Sorry to interrupt, but if you could just point the way to our dressing room, we'll get out of your hair.'

He had a lot of hair to get out of, now that I think about it. Anyway he didn't look happy to see us. We were obviously cramping his style with the girls, so he put his beer down and said, 'You're not the support. You're the fucking opener. You don't get a room. Now go and stand under the stage and wait until I tell you to play.'

'Sorry, I must have misheard you.'

'No, you heard me fine. Just fuck off until we need you.'

Now on any other day I would have busted his jaw, but this was the first gig in America. I thought I'd control myself and smash his face in after we played.

So there we were, standing under the stage, trying to stay calm in the shade. We were told we would be on stage in half an hour and we were in various stages of getting dressed when someone yelled at us, 'Okay. You fucking Aussies are on.'

'But our gear isn't even finished being set up yet,' one of our crew protested.

'Well you've been here all day. You should have been ready.'

Next thing we knew the MC on the stage announces, 'Would you give a big San Diego welcome to the first band here to play for you. All the way from Australia, Cold Chisel!'

I had no shoes on and hadn't put on my shirt. Mossy was still in shorts and none of the guitars had been tuned. We ran up the stairs and onto the stage. I tied my headband around my head as I ran. I was looking for something to drink on the way but there was nothing for us.

The gear wasn't ready. We were standing in front of thirty thousand people and we had no leads in our guitars. Our crew ran around frantically, trying to get us ready.

'Come on guys, play some fucking music,' one of the Canadian stage techs yelled at us. The light on our amps came on so we thought we were ready. But nothing had any microphone on it. No one would hear us. Then the power went off again.

'Play something you fucking guys, would ya?' someone from the side of stage shouted at us.

I went up to my mic. It worked. 'Good afternoon. We're Cold Chisel and as soon as we have power we'll play for you.'

We stood there for ten or fifteen minutes with no power for our guitar amps. The crowd were getting restless and started shouting and booing us. I looked around the stage, trying to work out which one of the crew I was going to kill first.

After about twenty minutes we had noise coming from the amps. It wasn't a good noise but we started playing anyway. Halfway through the first song all the power went out again. It seemed to be out forever, but eventually it came back on and we started our next song. We might get a show going after all. Then one of the stage crew called me over and shouted in my ear. I thought I'd heard him wrong.

'What did you say?' I yelled.

'Your time is up. You guys have to get off.'

We had only completed one song and even then not everything had worked. We finished the second song and they started playing music through the PA and roadies started tearing our gear down in a hurry.

I came off stage ready to kill someone. It was then that John Marx pulled into the backstage area. He was driving a Porsche, and he had a girl who looked like a model draped over his arm. He jumped out of the car and walked over carrying a bottle of Champagne, smiling at us. 'Hey. How did you go, guys? I hear you were great. Sorry I missed it.'

I ran at him, grabbed him by the throat and rammed his head into the side of his sports car.

'Where the fuck were you when we needed you? We've been treated like shit here.'

He was stunned. 'Hey man, it's not my fault. They promised they'd look after you.'

Rod, our manager, dragged me off him before I could do any real damage.

And so our doomed American tour had started. I was ready to quit and go home after the first gig.

'Come on, guys. Hang in there. It has to get better. We've got some great gigs coming up. Trust me.' Rod tried to lift our spirits as we drove away. He had asked us to trust him before and most of the time he came through. So we stuck with it. But it didn't get better.

WE DID A LOT of what were politely called the 'secondary markets', small towns that really weren't going to help break us into the bigger markets. It was like the booking agency and record company had something against us. I've heard stories as to why that might have been but I don't know anything first hand so I'll keep it to myself. Let's just say a few things might have gone down that fucked up our careers before the band ever got to the States.

We had our faithful crew, Gerry on sound, Harry on foldback, Mark Keegan on lights and Mark Pope the tour manager with us. They tried to make it work but it was hard. Every town felt like we were in Butt Fuck Idaho. No, I take that back, not every town. There were a few good shows. Austin, Texas, with Joe Ely, The Fabulous Thunderbirds and a young Stevie Ray Vaughan, was one of the highlights of the tour. I remember having a few drinks with them all before the show. They were wild people and I liked them. They loosened me up so much that I climbed the PA stacks. Mark Pope shadowed me in case I fell. He was just below me, feeding me the lead to the microphone. I got to the top and opened my mouth to scream and a huge Texan moth dived into it. I was about forty feet off the ground and I nearly keeled over. My automatic reaction was to spit it out as fast as I could. Unfortunately for Mark, I spat it straight onto him. Along with vodka and anything else I heaved up. I didn't even know he was there and just kept singing.

The show ended in a big jam session and I was on stage with Joe Ely, who became a good mate of mine, Stevie Ray and Jimmie Vaughan and a twelve-year-old kid who played fantastic guitar called Charlie Sexton. Charlie also ended up being a good friend and still is to this day. He now plays with Bob Dylan and I try to catch up with him whenever he tours. So we had a good time in Texas. Austin was the only town in America that reminded me of Australia. The people were down to earth, easy-going and liked to rock. We tore the place down that night and the audience got us. This didn't happen a lot in America. A couple of times.

We did a few good shows with Joe Walsh, who went on to play much later with The Eagles. But even back then he was unbelievable. A great guy and a great guitar player. His crowd liked us but really couldn't wait until we got off so they could see him play. One of the shows we did with him was at the famous Colorado venue called Red Rocks. This was a place that we'd read about in magazines like *Rolling Stone*. Word was it was one of the best places to play in the world. I think that we only managed to get onto the show because of an American agent called Chuck Morris. Chuck was partners in an agency called Feyline with a guy called Barry Fey. He was a bigtime agent and he wanted to manage Cold Chisel. I think he was good mates with Rod Willis for a while but we never took his offer any further. We didn't want to have an American manager for Chisel and neither did Rod. He wanted to keep us close to him. But Chuck did run Red Rocks, along with a few other people. When I first heard about this guy I thought someone said that Chuck Norris wanted to manage us. Now that would have been entertainment.

We got to the stage ten minutes before we were due to go on. I couldn't help but notice the dark clouds gathering overhead. As we walked on the heavens opened up. Joe Walsh's crew immediately started trying to get us off. We ignored them. We had travelled from Australia to play this venue and we weren't going to stop because of a little rain.

But it got heavier and heavier. By halfway through our set it was like a tornado. The wind was howling and the rain was coming in sideways. Joe's crew were panicking, calling me to the side of the stage. 'This rain is ridiculous. You guys better get off the fucking stage. One of you will get killed if you don't.'

I wiped the water from my eyes, smiled and said as casually as I could, 'This isn't rain. It's just a sun shower. We'll be fine. We play in weather like this all the time.' And I ran back out into the deluge. We were on fire. The band played the best show of the whole tour that day. Maybe the best gig of our lives when I think about it. We knew we were playing well too.

I was thinking, 'No American band would walk on stage in rain like this. The crowd love us for being out here, taking our lives into our own hands, to deliver for them. We'll be done and Joe will refuse to play and we'll be heroes.'

I could see it all. I could see the headlines in the local papers. 'Aussie band slays audience in horrendous storm'. But it didn't quite go that way. The crowd did love us and they were duly impressed by our tenacity. But as soon as we finished playing – in fact the minute we walked off the stage – the storm disappeared. It was gone as quickly as it had arrived. Apparently this sort of thing happened all the time in Colorado. Who knew?

Joe walked out to a warm, clear, starry night and the lights came up. 'Good evening, Red Rocks. What a beautiful night to play a concert for you. How lucky are we?'

The crowd went crazy. We could hear them screaming as we drove off to our next gig.

CHAPTER TWENTY-ONE

love your single

NEW YORK CITY AND LOS ANGELES, 1981

W E ENDED UP IN New York for about ten days, without any work. We were a sad, sad band. In the city that never sleeps, with nothing to do but sleep. Because the shows we were supposed to play had been cancelled – maybe they were never booked, we never knew – none of us had much money. As ever, I hated not having enough money to get by. It was the first time in a while that I had been in this situation and Jane was meeting me here too. This only made me angrier and harder to get along with. The band had no idea why it was such a big deal, and just laughed at me. They were happy just to be travelling around, playing music.

We were staying in a hotel called the Gramercy Park Hotel. Now, readers who have been to New York may know that the Gramercy Park is a pretty flash hotel, nowadays. But back then it wasn't. It was a nice building but a bit of a rundown fleapit – not quite to the Plaza's standard back home, but a fleapit all the same, so the rest of the guys were quite comfortable there.

So Jane and I were in New York together, with no money whatsoever. Times were very lean. We couldn't see the city the way either of us expected to. We could hardly afford to buy meals, never mind see the sights. I was struggling. I wanted to show Jane everything. She didn't want anything. She was happy to be with me.

Jane and I made the most of it anyway. We found a little bar around the corner from the hotel that was cheap and served reasonable food. I can't remember the name of the place but it was an Irish bar and was very pro IRA. There were photos of Bobby Sands all over the walls. Bobby Sands was a member of the Provisional Irish Republican Army who was locked up in the brutal Maze Prison and led and died from a hunger strike, along with nine other fighters. So this was a bar for real people. They served real food, not American food, and they made great drinks. Jane and I quickly became regulars, insulting the English, eating chips and drinking a drink called a Kamikaze. As the name suggests, it was extremely strong. So I really liked it. Jane and I worked out that for very little money we could sit and get completely smashed, without having to deal with the pushy, hustling, crazy New Yorkers who walked the streets around our hotel.

But we went too far. And on the last night before the band was due to go back on tour we really tied one on. I can't remember how many drinks we had but let's just say, for argument's sake, a lot. Jane had been slowly worn down by the lack of money and my aggression towards the other members of the band. Not to mention, she was sick of the drunks that lined the streets between the hotel and the bar. There was a lunatic on every corner. One guy in particular annoyed her. We saw him almost every night lying on the footpath, trying to start fights with passersby. On the last night he was lying with his trousers down around his ankles, playing with himself, and it really annoyed her. So we started arguing at the bar and it escalated from there and by the time we got back to the hotel we were out of control. Jane and I both had a bad habit of storming off when we fought, which isn't good, but we had got away with it at home. Every time Jane went, I thought I had lost her forever. But now we were in New York, where storming off around the streets drunk was not a good thing for a young lady, or a young man really, to be doing.

But that's what happened. We both left the hotel to go home to Australia alone. Jane was walking off in one direction and I was heading in the other. My plan was to hitchhike to Australia without my passport. You can see I had really thought it through. Whenever we did this, I would normally get a hundred yards down the road and then come to my senses and start to worry about Jane. More than once I had run to find her just as she was tearing into some unsuspecting bloke who thought she might be an easy pickup target. And then he would have both of us swinging at him. But this night I couldn't find her. I was in a state of panic. I wasn't sure what direction she had gone. Mark Pope had heard the fight outside the hotel and came running out just in time to see me leaving. He followed me and not Jane. I think he was more scared of her than me. Anyway, I made Mark hunt the streets with me, looking for her.

Jane in the meantime had walked past a park alone and a guy had jumped out of the bushes with a knife to rob her. He got more than he bargained for.

'Give me your money, bitch. Now, or I'll cut you up,' he shouted in his most intimidating voice.

'Ahhhhhhhhh!' Jane screamed at him. 'I don't care what you do. Kill me, rape me, stab me. Do what you want, I don't care anymore. Ahhhhhhhhh!'

This obviously caught the young guy off guard. 'Hey, wait a minute lady. What's wrong with you?'

'I don't care what you do, just kill me and go!' Jane was ready to kill him by this point.

'Hey, come on now. It's not that bad. What's wrong with you? Can I help you?' The thief had become the counsellor. 'What's happened to you, baby? Tell me.'

'This place is fucked. This town is a hole. There is shit all over the streets and people are drunk everywhere. It's fucked.' Jane started telling him everything she had seen that night. 'My husband is an arsehole and there's a guy lying on the street with his pants around his ankles and he's playing with himself. And you're robbing me! It's all fucked up!'

'Hey, calm down girl. It's not that bad. I know that guy who lays on the street. He just does that for attention. He's not that bad. I'm only doing this because I got no money, that's all. And where is this husband of yours? You want me to fix him up for you?'

He looked at his knife and then at Jane. By this point the situation was coming into focus and she realised that this was not a good place to be.

'No, I'll be all right. He's gone anyway.'

The guy was looking up and down the street trying to spot me. Jane in her haste had grabbed my Walkman. For those of you who don't know what that is, a Walkman was like an iPod for cavemen. It was a chunky-looking cassette player with headphones that you carried around. Jane was not good with technology and had put the batteries in back to front.

'I don't have any money but here, you can sell my Walkman and buy some food if you like.' By this point Jane just wanted to get away from him.

He tried to turn the Walkman on but had no success. 'Shit. This thing don't work anyway, baby. So why don't you just go home before you get yourself hurt? This is a dangerous town for a little girl like you.'

He handed it back to her. Jane turned and walked quickly back to the hotel with the guy still following behind her, saying,

'What does your husband look like? Me and my knife can fix him right up for you.'

'No, it's fine. But thanks for offering.' And she sped up and was soon back at the hotel.

WE WERE BOTH BACK in the room. Anger turned to tears and then laughter as Jane told me about her adventure. By the morning Jane was in the bathroom throwing up continuously. I had to get a doctor for her. The hotel organised one who came to the room. The doctor took one look at her and asked what we had been doing. I told him about the Kamikazes and he quickly came to the conclusion that Jane was suffering from extreme alcohol poisoning. He gave her an injection to stop the nausea and told me to keep her in bed and give her plenty of fluids.

But there was a problem. We were supposed to go back on tour that day. We had to fly to Dayton, Ohio, to start a tour with Ted Nugent.

I couldn't believe we were touring through the Midwest supporting this guy. I can just imagine the genius who came up with that idea. Some thick LA agent who didn't even know the band he was booking. 'Yeah, Ted Nugent will be good for these guys. They have a lot in common. Both bands have guitars and drums. Yeah, they both have hair. Yeah. It's a perfect match.'

But that was where the similarities ended. I didn't want to go. Ten days with no money, not to mention copious amounts of alcohol, had worn me down and I wanted to leave the band, again. So I rang Mark. 'I've had enough of this fucking band. I'm finished.'

I was in no mood for any of them. I'd been poor before. I didn't need to be in the biggest band in Australia and still be living like a pauper.

'Come on, Jim. It'll be better now we're back on the road. Meet you downstairs.' Mark was trying to be the voice of reason.

'Fuck it. I'm done. I'm not going.' I hung up on him. Jane was in no state to travel. Even with the shot, she was still throwing up every few minutes.

Bang. Bang. Bang.

It wasn't long until I heard a knock at the door. I ignored it.

Bang. Bang. Bang.

Whoever it was would not go away.

'Fuck off,' I yelled from the bed. I was sitting holding Jane's hand and didn't want to let anyone in.

Bang. Bang. Bang.

'Are you there, Jim? Come on mate, let me in. We need to talk.' It was Don. The last person I wanted to see. Don could talk sense to me and I wasn't in the mood.

'Fuck off!'

He didn't get the message. 'Come on, Jim. We're all in this together. Surely we can be civilised about this. Let me in and we'll talk.'

'Shit.' I sighed as I got up from the bed and went to the door. The curtains were all closed tight and the room was dark. It must have smelled like a brewery when Don walked in. One lonely light was shining from the bathroom.

Jane whispered to me, 'I need some water.'

Don responded before I could get up. 'I'll get it for you.' And went into the bathroom. He came back out looking pale. Holding the rubbish bin. Staring down at it, he said, 'What's going on, guys? Do you need to talk to me about something?'

There in the bin was the needle that the doctor had given Jane. Don looked at us like we were Sid and Nancy. His face was worried and scared. Suddenly Jane jumped out of bed, naked, and ran to the bathroom and vomited. This confirmed his worst fears.

'Are you guys doing hard drugs? You can tell me. I'm here to help.'

Jane slipped back into bed as I tried to get Don to leave us alone. 'Look mate. We're not doing hard drugs. The doctor gave Jane a needle.'

Don had his foot against the door so I couldn't shut it. 'Jim, we have to leave to catch a plane in fifteen minutes or we'll miss the show tonight. And if we fuck this up we'll never work in this country again.'

'Good. I don't want to work in this fucking country again. You guys go. Ian can sing. I'm staying with Jane. Now get out of here and leave us alone.' I slammed the door and went back to Jane's bedside and once again Jane managed to talk me down.

'You need to go, baby. The band need you. You go and leave me here and I'll make my way home.'

Now this was never going to happen.

'I'm not going anywhere. I'm staying with you.' I was probably getting hysterical by this point. 'I don't care about the band. I want to be with you, so I'm not going.'

The idea of being separated from Jane again made me feel sick. I couldn't lose her. If I let her go now I might never see her again. I always had the feeling that I would end up alone. I didn't deserve her. I couldn't let go.

'Go on, Jimmy. I'll be all right and I'll call you as soon as I get home.'

'No. I'm not going. I want to stay here with you. I don't want to go without you.' I was definitely hysterical now. I was crying.

Jane sat quiet for a while and then said quietly, 'I'll get dressed and we'll go together. The band needs you.'

So Jane got out of bed and got dressed while I packed. We grabbed the bucket from the bottom of a humidifier, just in case Jane threw up, and headed down to the lobby.

The band was waiting. We jumped into a minibus and headed to JFK Airport. We definitely didn't look good as we almost carried Jane through one of the busiest airports in the world, stopping every twenty yards or so, so she could throw up.

'Leave me here and I'll get a plane home,' she pleaded with me, but I wasn't going anywhere without her.

We got onto the plane and much to our horror we found out that US President Ronald Reagan had sacked all the air traffic controllers that morning and the military was in the process of taking over their jobs. We were stuck in the middle of the tarmac for three hours, with the smell of overcooked American airplane food wafting through the plane. Jane threw up continuously.

EVENTUALLY WE GOT INTO the air and on our way to Dayton, Ohio. I remember arriving there, in no state to start a tour. We dropped Jane at the hotel to recover and the band and myself jumped into the Holiday Inn's limousine to go to the first gig. We arrived backstage and the sun was burning hot. Ted's crew and a few of his band were sitting on road cases out the back of the venue, working on their tans, as the limo pulled up. We were all wanting to make a good impression on them. This was the start of the tour. If we impressed them enough they would respect us and help us do a good show. It wasn't easy. I wasn't far behind Jane as far as being sick went and the boys were all stressed from worrying about us. But we jumped out of the limo into the sunshine, acting like hardened rock veterans. I was leaning on the door of the car, looking around, when Mossy suddenly slammed the door shut. My hand was still inside the door. The car slowly moved off, with me still attached. I quickly opened the door of the moving vehicle, removed my crushed and bleeding hand and shoved it inside my leather jacket to stop the flow of blood. It was about ninety degrees in the shade so I must have looked ridiculous in a leather jacket anyway, never mind with my hand placed inside it, like some sort of Napoleon impersonator. We walked inside the venue, past the crew.

'Afternoon, gentlemen. You guys must be Cold Chisel,' one of the roadies said.

'Yeah. That's right,' I snarled back at him. I must have had tears in my eyes by this point. 'We are Cold Chisel.'

I was trying to act tough until we got inside our dressing room. Then I let out a scream that must have been heard outside. The pain was incredible. Eventually we got a doctor to stitch me up and we managed to do the first gig.

We got on stage and the crowd didn't get us at all. The bandaged hand and the grimaces of pain didn't help. I think we were a bit serious for them. I tell you how I knew this. Because we finished our set to silence, or almost. And then Ted opened his set by swinging across the stage dressed only in a loincloth. He received thunderous applause and the crowd was howling with laughter. That's what we needed, a gimmick. I wondered if we could talk Don into wearing a loincloth? I'm only kidding here, of course. We couldn't have found a band further away from what we were doing than Ted Nugent. Or so you'd think. But the agency found a few more.

We did a show in Detroit. The motor city. The home of Motown Records. A town with one of the largest percentages of black people in America. We thought, 'Great. These guys will get what we are trying to do.' We loved soul music. We loved the blues. But the agency had us playing not with a soul band, or a blues band for that matter. In fact, they put us on with the whitest band in America, The Marshall Tucker Band. The audience was full of good old boys and gals, with trucker hats and cowboy boots. There was not one black person in the crowd. They hated us as much as Ted's mob did.

Steve nearly got us killed in the bar of the hotel after the show. I walked in to find him chatting with some young black girls. Luckily, Steve had been drinking a lot, so they didn't understand a word he said.

'I fuckin' love black people. You got rhythm. You know what I mean? You can fuckin' dance. Fuck yeah. And you're not really black, are you? Well you are but you're so, so black you're almost purple, aren't you?' This was what I heard him say as I walked up to him at the bar.

The girls looked puzzled. They turned to me and asked, 'What did he say? He is so cute and that accent is adorable.'

I thought quickly to myself and translated for them. 'He said he thinks that you girls look fabulous and he'd like to buy you all a drink.'

They smiled. 'Oh, that would be wonderful. He's so nice.'

Steve stood, drunk as a skunk, next to them, trying to bust out a few Four Tops dance moves. We bought the girls a drink and I managed to get Steve to leave before they learned to understand his Liverpudlian accent and killed us.

'You fucking chicks are fucking hot, aren't ya? Let's go and get it on in my fuckin' pad.'

'What did he say that time?' they smiled and asked.

'He said goodnight ladies and it was lovely to meet you.' I grabbed Steve by the scruff of the neck and dragged him towards the door. All the while Steve was trying to dance like someone he'd seen on *Soul Train*, looking back at the girls, smiling and gesturing to them to follow him.

THE LAST SHOW OF the tour was in Los Angeles, the home of Elektra Records. This could very well have been the most important show of our careers. We arrived in town the day before and walked into the record company to meet all the big nobs. As we walked down the main corridor there were secretaries sitting answering phones outside the offices of various A&R people. By the way, A&R is short for Artists and Repertoire. This is the guy who signs and looks after bands within the label.

Each door we passed, some guy would lean out and say something like, 'Hey Chisel, yeah. Love your single,' then disappear back into the safety of their office before we got to say anything. It didn't feel right. In fact, I got the distinct impression that they might have been scared of us.

'Hey, you Aussies rock. Yeah baby.' And another one was gone, behind the closed door of his room. I'm sure I heard the door lock this time.

Finally, we got to the office of the man who was in charge of promotions for the band for all of North America. His name was Marty Schwartz. Marty's secretary greeted us.

'Hey guys. How are you all doing today?' She was smiling way too much for this time of day.

'Yeah, we're all good. Listen, is Marty in?' said Rod, trying to sound businesslike.

'He's on an important call, but if you take a seat I'll let him know you're here. He's very excited to finally meet you.'

She smiled again. I figured if he was that excited to see us he wouldn't mind if we went in. So that's what I did. Walked in and sat down opposite him.

'Ah. Yeah. Yeah. Look, ah, do you mind if I call you back? I'm in a, ah, a meeting. Yeah, cool, love your single by the way.' And he hung up. He sat looking at me. The boys followed me in and we stood around in silence for a second.

He gulped. 'You guys must be, ah, Cold Chisel.' He spoke nervously as he straightened out his desk.

'Yeah. I'm Jimmy. And this is Don, Ian, Phil and Steve. Oh yeah, and you've met Rod our manager before.'

Marty obviously couldn't remember Rod but he smiled and shook hands with him anyway. Marty was a typical American record company guy. Satin tour jackets and photos of himself with famous people adorned the walls of his office. He seemed nervous around us. I think he had heard that we were wild and he didn't feel safe in our company. I noticed he'd left his office door open after we walked in. Maybe so he could make a quick exit if he had to. We were the wild colonial boys he had heard about in our songs and he was right to be afraid of us. Beads of sweat broke out on his lip and brow.

'Hey, is it hot in here? Mary, turn up the air conditioning, would you. It's like an oven in here,' he shouted to his secretary. It wasn't that hot. 'Take a seat. Can I get you a drink? Beer, scotch, anything? Anything at all.'

We were too busy looking at the record wrapped in a nappy behind his desk. 'What's that behind you there?' I asked him.

He spun around and picked it up, his smile beaming from ear to ear.

'This is the promo first single,' he said and passed it over to Don. His smile seemed a little smug, as if he was showing us little country boys how they do it in the real world. 'Pretty impressive, don't you think?'

Don didn't look at him. Instead he stared in disbelief at the record he held in his hand. It was a copy of 'My Baby', the song they had chosen to be our lead single in America, and it was wrapped in a baby's nappy.

'Why is this single wrapped up like this?' Don's lips tightened as he spoke.

'It's a little promo gimmick I came up with,' Marty said. 'I didn't have time to run it by you, but it's great, isn't it? We sent it to every radio station in America like that.'

'Fuck man, that's my song you've sent out in nappies. Can you get them back?' Phil was worried. He had written 'My Baby' and was very proud of how well it had been received in Australia. He didn't want the Yanks to fuck it up for him. 'I'm a serious songwriter. I don't want to look as stupid as you do.'

Marty looked at the floor. I guess he wanted to sink into it. 'All of them. It's great. We love it. They won't forget your first record in a hurry, will they?'

Don threw it onto the desk and walked out. The band followed. Rod signalled to me to stay. He obviously wanted me to go into damage control with him. I watched as Don walked back down the corridor, past the secretaries. At each door some dweeby little guy in a satin tour jacket leaned out for a second time. 'Yeah. Rock'n'roll. Love you guys.'

Meanwhile Rod and I sat in the office with Marty, in complete silence. After what seemed like an eternity he spoke again. 'So, you guys have your big LA show tomorrow night. Should be great, eh? This is LA. The home of rock.'

It was hard to talk but I figured I'd better break the ice so I said, 'Yeah. Of course you're coming? It's your only chance to see the band and since you're doing our promotions it's important you get a sense of what the band's about.' I stared again at the single lying on his desk. 'You know what I'm talking about, don't you?'

He drew a deep breath and I couldn't help but notice a single drop of sweat form on his forehead and run down his face. 'Look, everybody liked that idea. We workshopped it around the office and they all loved it.' He was desperate.

'Don't do shit like that without asking the band. We're not a gimmicky sort of band, okay? But you are coming to the gig, right?'

I could see him squirm in his chair. He was obviously uncomfortable.

'Ah, ah, no actually. You see it's a, ahh, it's a very big DJ's party tomorrow and I can't come to see you.'

'You are doing all our promotion and it's the only show we are doing in your town and you're not coming because it's a DJ's birthday?' I was stunned.

'Well, it's not *his* birthday. It's his dog's birthday. But he loves that dog like it's his child and it's very important that I go.'

That was it. I wanted to kill him. I got up and left the office before I punched him in his face. As we walked away Rod tried to calm me down. 'I tried to warn him you guys wouldn't like it.'

'You knew? For fuck sake, is he serious?'

Rod was as pissed off as any of us. He looked down and kept walking.

'This place is fucked,' I yelled as I left the office.

The door to the next office opened up. 'Love your single.'

'Shut the fuck up.' I walked faster. I had to get away before I exploded.

THE NEXT DAY WE played at the Country Club in the Valley and it was a great show. We walked off stage covered in sweat and gasping for air. After a minute or so the backstage door opened and in walked Marty Schwartz.

'Hey guys. How are you all doing tonight?'

It seemed I had misjudged him. He was here after all.

'Marty, you made it. How did you like the show?'

Marty stopped smiling. 'Oh, ah. Well, I didn't see it. I just got here. The party went longer than I expected. But my friend the DJ told me to tell you guys that he loves your single.'

Covered in sweat and red-faced, it was hard to hide my disappointment, so I didn't try. 'You fucking didn't see any of it then?'

Marty grabbed my shoulder and pulled me to a corner of the room. I shot a look at his hand and he removed it from my shoulder. 'Hey Jimmy. I hear you're a wild boy, do you do any of this stuff?' And without letting the rest of the band see, he showed me a large bottle of white powder. Cocaine.

'Here, why don't you have a little? But keep it quiet, we don't want everyone in the room to know about it.'

The band were the only other people in the room so I could tell he didn't want to give them any. They didn't do drugs that much anyway, but he had grated me the wrong way now. I snatched the bottle out of his sweaty little hand, pushed him out of the way and walked through the door that led to the stage. Marty was close behind me, trying to get his cocaine back. There were a bunch of young guys still leaning on the front of the stage. I tipped the bottle over and poured out the lot in one long line and shouted over the house music, 'Any of you guys do this shit?'

Then I walked back into the dressing room. A very pale Marty Schwartz followed me back in. I threw his empty bottle in his face, grabbed his shirt and pulled him close to me and whispered in his ear, 'You're a dick. Fuck off before I beat the shit out of you.'

And then I proceeded to push him out the door and yell at the top of my voice at him as he walked away. 'Bye. Fuck off. Love your single. Don't call us, we'll call you.'

A FEW MONTHS LATER, in Paradise Studios in Sydney, I wrote a song about Marty. I'd had an idea for the words since leaving Los Angeles but the rest came to me in a flash. I sang the ideas I had for the guitar to Ian and he helped me with the guitar riffs. It was called 'You've Got Nothing I Want'. I wanted nothing from anybody. I now know this was all to do with my childhood, but at the time I was just angry. I needed to spit some venom. So I spat it at Marty. I sent it to him with a note telling him it was all about him. If Cold Chisel's career in America wasn't over before then, it certainly was when he got my note.

CHAPTER TWENTY-TWO

we weren't young boys singing for free drinks and chicks anymore

PARADISE STUDIOS, SYDNEY, 1981–82

TOWARDS THE END OF 1981, Jane told me that we were going to have ourselves a baby. I was excited and terrified at the same time. Excited because the idea of having a family with Jane was beautiful but terrified because of the way I had been brought up. What if I wasn't a good father? What if I couldn't provide? I wanted my kids to have everything. All the things that I never had. I started losing sleep wondering how I was going to support them.

SINCE THE AMERICAN TOUR I think that the band had started to see the writing on the wall. We had done it all. America was such a disappointment to us. The home of rock'n'roll was nothing like we had hoped. Nothing lived up to what we had dreamed. We were told to compromise what we were doing or we couldn't go any further. A little bit of the band died on that tour. It was only a matter of time until the rest died too. We fought even more with each other. We still played great shows but it felt to me like we were at the end of a ride.

Back in Australia we tried to reignite the flame that had been snuffed out by the politics of the music industry. Everything we had learned making *East* and touring Australia and America was useless to us, so we threw it all out. The way we dealt with crowds, the way we played music, the way we thought about life. It was like backburning. We started making *Circus Animals*. Everyone was pushing us to make a follow up to *East*. Keep the same formulas, the same sounds, just give us more of the same. They wanted *East* part two and we didn't want to give it to them.

At one band meeting Don came up with a new idea. 'Hey guys. I don't want to play the same thing night after night. Every night we play the same songs the same way. I think we should throw away all those song arrangements now. They've served us well but it's time to think outside the box.'

Don was always trying to breathe life into the band. Ian and myself sat scratching our heads, wondering what Don had in mind.

I think Steve probably caught on quicker than us. 'Are you saying we change the arrangements of the songs? If you are, I'm in, because I'm sick of playing the same fucking shit every night.' Steve was excited, so his accent got thicker.

But Don had more to offer us. 'I'm not saying change the arrangements. I'm saying throw the arrangements out the window. We don't need them. Start the song and if Steve wants to change the feel of the song then he can. Jim can sing when he wants, not always come in after just four bars like we've been doing every night. And if Ian gets an idea he can jump in and play it. No waiting for the solo, just step up and play. Push Jim out the way and play until Jim pushes him back and takes over again.'

I'd been pushing them around for years. How was this different? 'But won't we be playing all over each other then? It could get very messy.' I hadn't quite grasped the whole concept yet.

'At the moment we're going through the motions. We all know what's coming up and we play like we're on automatic pilot. If we do things this way, it will only work if we're all listening to each other very carefully. We each need to know what the others are playing and going to play before they play it. Or it will all fall apart.' Don was breaking down years of training here. It was a great idea but could we pull it off?

'I'll give it a fucking go,' Steve proclaimed.

'Yeah, all right then. I follow Steve,' Phil said quietly. 'That's really what I do anyway. I never know what I'm going to play until it starts. Sometimes even after I've started I don't know what I'm playing.' He laughed out loud.

I could see Ian thinking things over. Ian loved to jam but jamming was self-centred and boring. This was different to jamming. This was feeling what the others were going to do before it happened.

'I'm in. I always do what I want anyway,' I laughed.

Ian joined in. 'Yeah, yeah all right, I'm in too.'

THE BAND CHANGED. WE grew up. We weren't young boys singing for free drinks and chicks anymore. We had stories to tell and axes to grind. Our worlds had been turned upside down. And life had started to wear us down.

We had learned all we could from *East*, digested it and then spat out what we didn't need. Music would never be the same for us. We reinvented the band. We started playing songs that weren't straight four on the floor grooves. The rhythms of the band got a lot more interesting. If you listen to *Circus Animals*, which was released in March 1982, it is really obvious. The album opens with me spitting venom at the American record company in 'You Got Nothing I Want'. Ian wrote 'Bow River', a song that a lot of people to this day think sums up the sound of Cold Chisel. Don's songs in particular got more interesting. 'Wild Colonial Boy', 'Numbers Fall' and 'Taipan' became the sort of songs that only Cold Chisel played. No one else could play like that. Loose, rumbling feels that were laidback and menacing at the same time. We turned into a different kind of animal. 'Letter to Alan' was a song about lost friends. And 'Houndog' was the story of our lives together, dragging ourselves up and down the east coast of Australia, screaming at people until they couldn't ignore us any longer.

Steve hit his stride as a songwriter too. 'Forever Now' was commercial but different from anything else on the radio at the time. He wrote haunting melodies for me to sing and he even wrote the basis of the guitar hook that Ian plays throughout the song. Ian made it beautiful but the note choice came from Steve's head. And to this day 'When the War is Over', a beautiful song written by Steve for that album, still haunts me. Some nights, I have to stop myself breaking down as I sing it. The loss of Steve is still a raw nerve.

WE WERE STILL IN a tailspin that would ultimately break up the band. We fought more often and I in particular stormed off whenever I could. I drank more and drugs became more available to us, well to me anyway. I never wanted to be alone with myself. I hated it. I hated me. So I was taking more and more. All I wanted from life was not to feel anything. I was consuming ridiculous amounts of booze and cocaine. It was getting to the point where I was never doing a show unless I had lots of hard drugs.

My drinking had slowly gotten worse and worse as the years went on. I started to take more speed so I could remain standing up. The speed would counteract the booze and then I would have to drink to counteract the speed. Once cocaine became readily available in this country, things got a lot more expensive. Speed had been cheap. Most people couldn't give it away, unless I was around. But over the course of a few tours and a few recording sessions, I developed a preference for cocaine. My spending increased overnight. Soon, I needed to find more money to keep up with my lifestyle. Everyone would give you drugs while they were with you but if you wanted to hold onto them for yourself, you had to buy them.

I wanted to get away from the city. I needed to get off the merry-go-round, so that when I wasn't working I could clean up my act. Jane had no idea how bad my habits were getting. This of course only fuelled my already ridiculous feelings of shame and guilt. I started making more and more mistakes when I was away on tour, getting totally mindless and then waking up to find a trail of destruction in my wake. I would get up and empty my room of anyone who happened to be there and then sit and try to remember what I had done. Unfortunately, my memory was pretty good. It all always came back to me. I couldn't run from it. Everything was right there for me to see. So I started drinking earlier so I would stop thinking about it, and then I would need to take more drugs to keep me upright. Then I would go too far and repeat my mistakes from the night before. It was a vicious circle.

I needed to get home to Jane, where I had to behave responsibly, before I lost all that I had, including my Jane. She must never know what was going on on the road. Without even planning it I created another problem. I was only in control when Jane was there. When she wasn't there, I was out of control. This placed all responsibility for my own behaviour on Jane's shoulders. She didn't even know this was happening. It was fucked. I was fucked. We were fucked. Everything was fucked.

CHAPTER TWENTY-THREE

we've got a lot of very sick people in here

CHILDBIRTH, 1982

W E WERE SO HAPPY to be having a baby and made plans to build a better life. In July 1982, about eight weeks from Jane's due date, I wanted to take us on a little holiday. Somewhere warm and sunny.

'Why don't we go to Thailand?' was my bright idea.

'They won't let me fly with only eight weeks to go. And if anything went wrong we wouldn't be near our doctor.' Jane was always the voice of reason. I hadn't thought of that, of course.

'Why don't we just drive up the coast then? It'll be nice and slow and safe.'

Jane wasn't sure about it. 'How far do you want to drive? I don't know. I'm not sure it's a good idea, Jimmy.'

'Come on. It'll be fun. I'll sing to you and make billy tea. We can take our time and drive as far as is good for you. Come on.

I'll make up cassettes with great music to listen to. You'll love it.'

I was getting excited. Jane loved my mix cassettes. Well, not really. I liked rock music and Jane liked nice music. James Taylor, Carole King and of course the Carpenters. I would have to make a cassette with them all on it for her or I'd drive her nuts with hard rock.

'Well, all right. If you really want to we can do it.'

We set off for our short drive and after three days we reached Rockhampton. I can see now how tough a drive that must have been for Jane, but at the time I thought it was nothing. The band drove overnight, thousands of miles, all the time. Maybe that's why I wanted to do it. Because that's what we did.

I talked Jane into going straight onto a boat, out to stay at Great Keppel Island. Not the best destination on the Barrier Reef but I didn't know any others. We arrived and I couldn't wait to get out to the beach. 'Come on, baby. I'll set you up in the sand. It'll be so great. You'll love it.'

Jane wasn't too happy but she agreed. I can see now she only wanted to make me happy. 'All right, but not for too long. I'm very tired. That drive was so long and I feel a bit funny.'

'Yeah, I know. It was a bit far. I'm sorry, baby. But we're here now. Let's just take it easy and relax.'

So out to the beach we went. I had towels and an umbrella and water and it was going to be fantastic. As soon as we sat down, I dug a big hole in the sand.

'Here you go, baby. Just lie down with your stomach in the hole and you can sunbake. I saw this on television. You'll love it.'

Jane grudgingly went along with me. No sooner had she lain down than she looked at me and said, 'I think you'd better help me up. Something is happening.'

She had to be kidding me. 'Come on, baby, just give it a go. You'll be fine.'

Jane looked at me. I could tell she wasn't happy. 'Jimmy,' she said firmly. 'My waters have broken. Get me a doctor. Now.'

'What, are you serious? You're kidding, aren't you?'

'No, I'm not kidding. I need a doctor!'

I helped Jane up and ran to find a doctor. We were told that Jane's waters had broken, just as she had said, and that we had to get off the island as quickly as possible. The island was not equipped to deal with a birth, never mind a premature birth.

There were two ways off the island. By plane or by boat. Both were a worry but we had to go. No plane was available so it was decided we would get to shore on the last boat leaving the island.

It was rough and bumpy and Jane held her stomach the whole way. I sat panicking, all the while thinking, 'This is my fault. What an idiot. Who drives a pregnant woman for three days to an island?'

But it was too late. We had to hope for the best. We made it, jumped into a car and drove to the Rockhampton Base Hospital. The whole way Jane kept saying, 'I'm not staying here. I don't want to have the baby in Rockhampton.'

She had nothing against Rockhampton but it was miles from our friends and family. Jane knew that in a week Cold Chisel would be touring again and if she gave birth now she would be in Rockhampton by herself.

On the way to the hospital I suddenly became very hungry. I think it was the stress. 'I'm starving. Do you think that you can hold on long enough for me to grab something to eat? I'll eat anything.' I don't know why I was suddenly hungry but Jane was fine.

'Relax, Jimmy, we have plenty of time. Why don't you stop and get something?'

I pulled the car into a Kentucky Fried Chicken place, bought a bucket of chicken and sped on down the highway. 'I got a bucket in case you were hungry too,' I said to Jane.

'I'm not hungry but thanks for thinking of me.'

I had to own up. I had an ulterior motive. 'I didn't really think you would be. But I could be at that hospital for a few days, so I thought I'd stock up.'

Jane laughed as we pulled into the hospital carpark. She had thought I was an idiot before that day, but this proved it.

The hospital confirmed our worst fears. The baby was on the way. 'It might not be today but it will be very soon.' They advised Jane to settle in for a long stay in Central Queensland.

'I'm not staying here. Get me home to Sydney or I'll find a way of getting there myself,' Jane told me in no uncertain terms. I had to find a way to get her home. 'You're going to be on tour and I'll be stuck here for six weeks. Just me and the baby. I want to be near my family.'

The doctors advised against it, telling me, 'Look, the best thing to do is to stay right here. We'll be able to watch the baby and it will be fine. But if you leave we can't promise anything.'

I was in a spin. I wanted Jane near her sisters and nearer to me. One of the nurses took me aside. 'Look, Mr Barnes —'

'Call me Jimmy.'

'Sorry, Jimmy. We're not so sure that the baby will come straightaway. You might have time to get to Sydney. The only problem is the airlines won't let you fly once this whole process has started.'

'Well, what if they don't know it's started?' I suggested. 'Could I hire a nurse or two to travel with us, in civilian clothes of course, just in case anything happens?'

The nurses were not against this, I could tell. I think they wanted to be in Sydney too. 'Well, you'll need a nurse and a midwife. We could carry a few things. Space blankets and so on, in case the baby arrives midflight.'

I agreed before they had a chance to think twice about it. 'Right then, that's what we'll do. You guys find a midwife and one of you will travel with us.'

It was decided. Jane was happy to take the chance. 'I can tell the baby isn't going to come. It's my body, I can feel it.' I was scared but had to trust Jane. She was calm and knew what to do. 'Don't worry my love, everything will be all right.'

We left the hospital. I had made bookings for Jane, myself, a nurse and a midwife to travel on the next flight to Sydney. It was a stressful flight. With every bump and dip of the plane, I could feel the blood draining from my face. Jane was cool as a cucumber.

We arrived in Sydney and headed straight to the hospital where Jane was booked in. At eight o'clock that night Jane was in bed, but she wasn't happy. 'Excuse me nurse, I would like a private room. That's what I was told I would have here.'

The nurse was rude. 'This is all we have. You're lucky to get a room at all.'

Jane was getting rubbed the wrong way. She didn't like rude people. 'Well if I'm staying here, I want a room. This isn't even a proper room.'

Jane was sitting up in bed in an old balcony that looked like it had been enclosed in the fifties. It was cold and not very nice at all.

I took the nurse aside. 'Can I speak to you, please? My wife is going to be in here a long time and it would be better if she had her own room.'

The nurse couldn't care less. 'Look, we've got a lot of very sick people in here. Just because you're a rock star doesn't mean you get any special treatment.'

'I'm not a rock star, I'm a singer and I'm not asking for special treatment. I'd like a comfortable room for my wife. That's all.' I tried to be firm.

'Well, just toughen up. This is the best we can do. You'd better settle her down and then go home.'

I hadn't planned on leaving. I was going to stay by Jane's side as long as she needed me. But the cranky old nurse made it clear she wanted me out. And soon.

I told Jane about my progress, or lack of progress. She flipped. 'I'm not staying in here with these old spinsters without you. I am going home!'

I pleaded with Jane to let me try one more time. I grabbed the nurse, who by this time was scowling at me for wasting her time. 'I don't think my wife will stay here if you don't get her a room where I can stay with her.'

'Well, it's up to you two, but if she leaves now the baby will die.'

My jaw dropped.

'That's right. You two spoilt brats. Get her to stay here or you'll kill your baby.'

I ran back to Jane, who by this time was dressed and packed and heading to the door. I pleaded, 'Don't go. We'll kill the baby.'

'Who told you that rubbish?'

'The nurse told me that if you move we'll kill our child.'

Jane was furious. She had already rung the midwife who travelled from Rockhampton with us, who told her she knew a doctor at Royal North Shore Hospital. She would be waiting outside to take us straight to the maternity ward there. Jane stopped at the nurse's station as she was storming out to give them one last serve. 'You are nasty and mean and I would not have my baby born here with people like you if you paid me.' She walked out the door with me running behind her, picking up bits and pieces she was dropping from her bag.

'Goodnight,' I said as I left.

'Goodnight, Mr Barnes.'

'It's Jimmy.'

And we were gone. We didn't go straight to Royal North Shore. We went home until everything was confirmed. Jane was not going to another hospital until she knew everything was organised. Finally, after a few hours, we went to Royal North Shore where we were greeted by friendly, caring nursing staff. Things were much better.

'Maybe you should go home for a while and pack me a bag. I'm all good here. Have a shower and then come back. There's no rush.'

Jane was so much calmer. I quickly smelled myself. Did I stink? Jane just smiled at me. I did stink. Oh my God. So I headed home to have a shower and get a few things I thought she might need.

I arrived back and Jane was resting comfortably in her own private room, with a view out across the trees to the highway. I snuck in, trying not to wake her, but she was still wide awake.

'I wasn't sure what you needed so I grabbed things that I thought I would need if I was in here. I hope that's okay.'

Jane smiled at me. I placed the bag next to her bed, and we waited for the doctors to let us know what was happening.

'I'm afraid we will have to take the baby out, as it is stressed. The baby will be a little early but everything will be fine. We will induce it and it will be over in a few hours.' The doctor was calm and self-assured, so we were calm too. Well, Jane was calm. I hadn't slept for days. What with driving up to Queensland and flying back and fighting with the other hospital and then finally getting Jane home and then back out to Royal North Shore.

I sat down and my eyes began to close. Suddenly the doors opened. They were ready for Jane. I was panicking again. What if anything went wrong? I was up and following her as she was wheeled up the corridor towards the delivery suites.

Jane had decided long before that she was going to have the baby naturally. No drugs.

'I'll have her drugs,' I joked with the nurses as we walked.

They all laughed but I was serious. I needed something to calm me down. In the suite the contractions became more frequent and more painful. Jane was screaming, 'Give me some fucking drugs now.' Her voice sounded like the kid in *The Exorcist* movie. 'Get me an epidural now or I will die.' I was expecting her head to turn one hundred and eighty degrees but it didn't. She didn't even see me standing near her.

'Stay calm, Mrs Barnes, the doctor is on his way. We will organise an epidural for you and you will feel no pain,' one of the nurses said.

'Get her something quick. Do something,' I urged, holding her hand and stroking her face, trying to calm her down.

One of the nurses was looking at the monitor that measured the baby's heartbeat. 'The baby's heart rate is dropping, we should watch it closely,' she said quietly to the other nurse, thinking no one else was listening. But I could hear her.

'What do you mean the heart rate is dropping? Do something. What's happening here? Get a doctor in here right now.' I was completely hysterical by this point.

The doctor arrived and immediately said, 'Right. Calm down, Mr Barnes.'

'It's Jimmy.'

'Right. Calm down, Jimmy. This is a normal reaction. Nothing to worry about. I think it would be better if you went outside and got yourself a cup of coffee and took a break. We have everything under control.'

Then the calm voice and gentle hand of a nurse guided me out the door and pointed to the waiting room. 'Just take a small break and then come back in. Everything is fine.'

I sighed. 'Yeah, I'm just getting worked up because I'm exhausted. I'll make myself a coffee and sit down for a minute.'

I walked into the family waiting room, where I found another stressed-out father, making coffee and talking to himself.

'How are you going?' I asked to break the ice and let him know I was in the room and could hear him talking to himself.

'I'm fine. All good now.' He breathed in deeply.

'What happened to you? You look even more stressed than me.'

He went on to tell me a quick story. 'I was standing in the delivery suite holding my wife's hand when I noticed that the baby's heart rate was going up and down. All over the place.'

My ears pricked up. Was I hearing this guy right? It sounded exactly like what was happening in our suite.

'Anyway, luckily I'm a trained nurse and I knew this wasn't normal. The doctors took some quick action or we would've lost the baby.'

Smash! Before he could finish the sentence, my coffee cup had dropped to the ground and I was running back down the corridor and into the room. I burst in yelling, but everyone was calm and quiet. I quickly explained what I had just heard.

The doctor took me by the hand and led me out of the room and explained that the circumstances were different and that if I didn't slow down I would have a heart attack.

Mahalia, our first baby, was born a few hours later, without any real complications. She was a little premature but everything was perfect. Even as a child we called Mahalia 'the boss of everything', as she was constantly organising everything around her. She's grown up to be one of the most organised people I know, and I have her as my tour manager. When she had her first child, Ruby, we called her 'the new boss of everything'.

Jane was brought back to her room and the nurse helped her unpack her bag. The one I had packed.

'Not a lot in here really, Mrs Barnes. Very sorry. No pyjamas or toiletries. There is a cassette player and a pile of cassettes. And a leather jacket in case you need one. Did Mr Barnes pack this bag for you?'

Jane was used to my packing and she just laughed to herself. I walked into the room in time to catch the end of the conversation.

'It's Jimmy,' I said under my breath. 'And yes, I did pack it.'

And I collapsed into a chair.

CHAPTER TWENTY-FOUR

they'll fucking miss me when I'm gone

LEAVING, 1982–83

AT THE RIPE OLD age of twenty-six, after being in the band for nearly ten years, I was still making next to no money, had nothing in the bank and, at the same time, was playing to the biggest crowds in the country every night of the week. It didn't make any sense to me.

I was fighting more and more with the guys in the band. I wasn't sure if I could ever leave them, although I was beginning to feel I might have to. Eventually the time came to face up to the truth. I was going to have to leave.

Leaving Cold Chisel was like leaving my brothers and sisters behind. I felt like I was deserting them. Surely they couldn't live without me? More importantly, surely I couldn't live without them. I'd spent years letting the band know, in no uncertain terms: 'I'm fucking sick of you guys and the sooner I'm out of here the fucking better.' I would slam the door behind me telling myself that I was never coming back. Only to be crushed by a profound sense of emptiness. Even as I stormed away I would feel the fear of being alone swallowing me up. And it was always someone else's fault. Never mine. 'They'll fucking miss me when I'm gone.'

This pain was the same pain that I had felt over and over as a child when my parents walked out the door. I can only look back now and wonder why, if it hurt so much, did I keep on recreating the same scenario over and over? I did it with the band, my girlfriends and eventually my wife and family.

I think that like my mother, who became so uncomfortable when there was nothing to fear or no one to fight, I had become so conditioned to dealing with abandonment that I forced people to abandon me. If that didn't work, I walked out the door myself, because that pain had become my comfort zone. It is the same way that a four-year-old deals with life, and here I am fighting to stop doing the same thing at sixty years old. They call it arrested development. I stopped growing emotionally at four. I might be giving myself too much credit there; it might have been earlier.

Anyway, eventually I walked out of Cold Chisel, for a number of reasons. Some I'll tell you about and some, well, they just aren't anybody else's business.

THE SOUTHERN HIGHLANDS, just one hundred kilometres from Sydney, is a place that became special to me. Even in the height of summer it cools down and you can sleep at night. The place has four distinct seasons. The winter, cold and wet, is my favourite. I'm not sure if it's something to do with where I was born. Let's face it, Glasgow is very cold and wet and, like I have said in the past, that's in the summer. Or maybe it's the name itself,

The Highlands, that reminds me of Scotland. Whatever it is, it has been my home and favourite place on earth since I happened to stop by one day.

I'd driven through the area many times but always at high speed and always in a hurry to get somewhere else. That is until one day just after Mahalia was born. We had been visiting Jane's family in Canberra and we stopped in Bowral on the way home to see an old friend of Jane's. Steve Hill had worked in banking. He was the short-term money manager for the notorious Nugan Hand Bank. This was the bank that Jane's Thai father used to distribute money to his children living in Australia. The head of the bank, Frank Nugan, was her guardian. Jane would visit his office and be sent to see Steve, who was in charge of paying her allowance.

Steve was a mysterious Irishman with ties to the CIA. He was also ex-British SAS. Unusual qualifications for a banker, I thought. And he looked even tougher than he probably was. He had a long scar that ran from his forehead across his eye and down his cheek. It scared a lot of people but not me. A lot of my parents' friends had scars on their faces from knife fights. I'd seen bigger, but it was impressive all the same. Steve never told me how he got it because I never asked. But many years later I overheard Michael Gudinski, head of Mushroom Records, ask him about it while they were doing a deal. I could tell it worried Michael from the day they met.

'So how did you get, eh, how did you cut, ah, ah, that mark on your face. How did you −'

Steve interrupted. 'Are you asking me about this scar across my face?'

Michael squirmed a little. 'Yeah ah, is that too personal? You, ah. You don't have to tell me.'

Steve cut him off mid-sentence. 'It is personal but I'll tell you anyway.'

Steve leaned in close to Michael's face, very close, and said, 'I fell off my bike. Okay?' His Irish accent was broad and his voice sounded hard.

Michael swallowed. 'Yeah, that's fine. I was just asking.'

STEVE HAD LIVED IN Bowral since the collapse of the bank. I guess he thought it was a good time to retire and get out of banking. I'm pretty sure he wasn't allowed to work in that field of business anymore and he seemed to have a lot of spare time on his hands. He had obviously done well from banking and appeared to be reasonably well off. We spent the afternoon with Steve and his family.

How had I driven through this place so many times and not noticed how beautiful it was? Well, I had driven all over Australia and hardly seen anywhere. I would sleep in the back of the car, recovering so I could do the next show. But now that I'd opened my eyes and actually seen this place, I loved it.

'This must be a great place to live. Especially with a young family,' I said to Steve as we were out walking his dogs.

'You should move down here too. Fresh, clean air and space. No one watching you. That's what kids need. Space.' He looked around as he spoke.

I had been daydreaming about living in the country since I'd got there. 'Must cost a fortune for houses down here. Anyway, if I was going to live down here I'd want to be on some land.'

Steve smiled at me. 'How much land did you have in mind?'

He took us for a drive across town and up a hill called Mount Gibraltar. He pulled into the driveway of an old farm and said, 'What about this place?'

Jane and I looked at each other and then got out of his car. We were on the crest of a hill, looking down a valley. There was a small wooden cottage at the end of the driveway. I looked at

Jane. 'This is the sort of place I want to live. It's beautiful.' But once again I was dreaming. 'I have to work in Sydney all the time. I couldn't live down here.'

Steve looked at me. 'It's only an hour and a half to Sydney, Jim. You can commute. A lot of people do, in fact.'

I loved the place. 'Is it for sale?'

Steve laughed. 'Everything's for sale, Jimmy. Everything's got a price.'

I presumed he knew who owned it. 'Do you know what they want for it?'

'I do actually. It's mine. I'll sell it to you for what I got it for. It's a steal. You need a place like this. You've worked hard for it. You deserve it.'

I didn't need convincing. As usual I turned to Jane. 'Can we get it? I love it.'

Jane didn't even think twice. 'We'd have to work out the money but we should be able to. You guys earn a lot of money you know, Jimmy.'

Steve was next to talk. 'Get the bank to give you the money, Jim. They've got way too much and they're dying to give it all away. Believe me, I know, I used to work for one of them.'

COLD CHISEL HAD GONE from success to success, sold-out tour to sold out tour, but we were still making very little money. We had a huge live album in *Swingshift* and an amazing studio album and tour in *Circus Animals*. For this tour we once again took risks. Most bands at the time would have gone out and played stadiums or even big pubs. But we decided that in keeping with the name of the record, we'd play in a circus tent. The name, by the way, came from Don. He thought that playing in a rock'n'roll band was a lot like being in a circus. You roll into towns and do the show and roll out. We were freaks, misfits, drifters. And people came to stare at us and see what we looked like up close and then went home to the safety of their normal homes.

We liked the idea. We joined the circus and every night we performed under the big top. 'Ladies and gentlemen, for your viewing pleasure tonight in the big top, we bring you Cold Chisel!' The band would start playing as the fumes and the noise from the wheel of death died away. The wheel of death was two motor bikes racing at high speed around and around inside a small cage, missing each other by millimetres. The crowd would roar. This was entertainment. Sitting, eating their popcorn, waiting for someone to die.

By the end of every show I would be singing and drinking vodka straight from the bottle as I balanced on a trapeze underneath a motorbike as it sped up a tightrope over the heads of the audience. Fire eaters and camels and jugglers scattered throughout the crowd, who sat with their mouths wide open, mesmerised, waiting for me to fall. But I never did. I had found my calling. This was where I belonged. In a circus. In a cage. I was an animal.

But even with all this going on our wages had hardly gone up. Not since we signed our record deal four years earlier. Jane got more money a week for pocket money from her dad. I was embarrassed. I knew something was wrong. The only way I could front up to the band and ask for more was to get angry and start a fight. I didn't want to do that.

Cold Chisel held their monthly meeting in the Cross. The meetings were always the same. I would turn up and sit recovering with sunglasses on, not saying much. There wasn't much point in talking. It was always the same discussion. Rod would tell us how well he was working the record company and we would ask where we were touring next. But I wanted to ask about money. It didn't go well.

'I need some money for a down payment for a house.'

Rod was quick off the mark. 'Yeah. Don't we all. I need a new fucking Ferrari but I'm not getting one am I. Can you guys give me the money for one? I don't fucking think so.'

So I snapped back, 'I'm fucking serious. I have a family now and I don't want to be renting some shithole for the rest of our lives.'

The rest of the guys were quiet. They always were when I asked for money.

'You can't just take money out of the business. If one of you takes it then you all take it. Do you guys need money?' Rod turned to the band. They all looked at the ground.

'Na.' Steve was never short of an opinion. 'What do I need it for? I've got enough. Maybe if you didn't drink and party so much you'd have some too.'

'Fuck off. It's my money and I'll do what I want with it. If you guys don't want or fucking need the money, that's fine. You can shove it in an account somewhere. I don't care where you shove it. Shove it up your fucking arses for all I care. But I want my money.'

Rod was trying to stay calm. 'Let me look into it and we'll see what we can do after the next tour. If you guys can keep the costs down, maybe, just maybe, we might be able to do something.'

But that wasn't good enough for me.

'I don't like the fact that we're the biggest-earning band in the country and I don't make enough money to look after my family properly. I don't want to live and support a family and survive on the road on what we earn. I can't do it anymore.'

But the band dug in. And Rod had made his mind up. 'Look, I have to go. You guys sort this shit out and someone tell me what you want me to do. See you.'

The meeting had got more and more heated as it went on. I had been talking with Steve Hill and a few other people. I had a few new ideas I wanted to share with the boys but I would have to wait.

Rod was halfway out the door when he turned around and walked back in. He waved at us all to quieten down. 'I nearly forgot to tell you. You guys have been asked to do a big tour of Germany with a guy called Roger Chapman.'

'Who the fuck's Roger Chapman?' Ian asked.

'He used to sing with a band called Family. They were a bit like Genesis. Now listen, I put a fucking lot of work into this so let me know if you think you're earning enough money to do it. Otherwise I can cancel the fucking thing. Right. I'm off now. One of you call me and let me know what you think.'

Rod shot a glance off at me and left. There always seemed to be something that distracted us from the problems we were having. It was as if Rod had been saving the announcement of the tour for a moment just like this.

The band jumped at the chance to tour overseas again. All other issues were put on the back burner, where they could stew away. Maybe we didn't need America after all. If we could break into Europe we could continue to tour without burning out our market at home. And we would be all right. So we all agreed to tour Germany.

THE TOUR WAS CALLED Man Go Crazy, named after Roger Chapman's new album. He had been big in Europe a few years before we toured with him, and he still pulled a few people. So we were to play fifteen hundred to two thousand seaters across Germany. And we were booked to play a lot of shows. Maybe twenty-five or more.

Rod informed us a week or so later, 'Listen guys, we'll be travelling in a tour bus with Roger's band. There'll be no room for families, especially kids.'

Everyone looked at me.

'Roger doesn't want any kids on his bus. He doesn't like them.'

I didn't like him and I hadn't met him yet.

'Why don't we get our own bus then?' I was quick to say.

'Yeah, right. Great idea. We're made of money. We can't afford a fucking tour bus.' Rod had all the answers. 'If you want to do this tour then this is the only way it is going to work. So you'd better get used to the idea.'

There was no way I was going without Jane and Mahalia. 'I don't want to go on his fucking bus. I'll make my own way around. Hire a car or catch a train. I'll get there somehow.'

Nobody liked the idea of me being separate from the band. They were probably thinking that I wouldn't make it to the shows, but I'd made up my mind. 'Don't you guys worry. I'll be there every night. Jane and I will have fun touring on our own.'

That was the plan. Jane and I would find our way around Germany and turn up on time to play every day. What could go wrong?

I WAS DETERMINED TO buy the house before I left, and with a lot of help from Jane's father, a little from the band and some advice from Steve Hill, I managed it. The house was only small but it was the first home that any of my family had owned. It made me feel proud. I would stay away from the city, keep it together and try to have a normal life. But this would only happen when I was home in Bowral. Unfortunately, I had to go to work. We were doing shows all over the country before the European tour started and as soon as I left home the old me came out. I was a different person to the man I was at home. At home I was quiet and loving. When I was away I was an absolute lunatic. Drinking, drugging and jumping into bed with women wherever we ended up. All that would have been fine if I was single, but I had a family and every time something happened I hated myself even more. I could no longer look at myself in the mirror without feeling ashamed. Not of where I came from anymore, but ashamed of what I'd become. I no longer could blame my family. This was all my fault. I tried to stop but I couldn't. I couldn't stop drinking or getting smashed either. It all went hand in hand. I had made myself into a monster and I could see no way back.

BY THE TIME THE band got to Europe in May 1983, we were fighting every night. Night after night, we would all be screaming at Steve, urging him to play faster, but he didn't listen.

'Play the fucking song faster,' I'd shout in his ear, over the sound of the band. Steve would just look away and ignore me. This had never happened before. He always listened eventually, but not on this tour. It felt like Steve had given up. He fought with me, he fought with Ian and Phil too and eventually even Don and he nearly came to blows. I was tired and fighting with Jane too. My whole life was crumbling around me. The band was falling apart. I was drinking way too much and taking too many drugs. Nothing sounded good. Every night we came off stage disappointed in ourselves. We had never been like this.

On the last show of the German tour, Steve was having a particularly bad night and I gave in. I kept pouring vodka down my throat as fast as I could. If he wanted to play like shit, so would I. That was when Don snapped. His piano, which was held in a big iron frame that allowed me to climb all over it, came crashing over on the stage, nearly killing me. The band came to an abrupt halt. He walked off. We were over.

Steve didn't defend his playing, he just ignored us. We wanted to sack him there and then. This band were brothers. One for all and all that shit. But we couldn't play with him anymore. We still had shows booked to do back in Australia. How the fuck were we going to get through them like this? We would have to work it out when we got home.

We returned to Australia with our tails between our legs. One more place that didn't get us. But this time we knew why. We had played like shit.

WE MET IN THE Cross like we always did. By this time Steve was on his way out of the band and we all knew it. Not only that, I didn't like the way our business was being run and I had to tell the guys what I was feeling. We had a lot of things going wrong and our management arrangement was one of them. Not the only thing, but we could fix this, surely.

'I don't think it's right that Rod takes his money off the gross. We should all be paying the costs. It should be off an adjusted gross. Why does he not pay for phones and offices and all the other shit that we have to pay for? We pay for everything. It's not right.'

I should have been talking about the state of the band but it was all too raw and too soon. So I picked on what I thought was a less sensitive area, the management. Twenty per cent off the gross meant that Rod quite often made more money than the band did. Especially if all our money was being sunk back into the bottomless hole we called a business. We paid for the office, the travel, the hotels, the crew, the truck, the support bands, the lights, the sound systems and all the advertising. There wasn't a lot left over after that and I was sure Rod was making more than us. It didn't seem right to me and it wasn't a good way to run a business. That and the fact that I needed more money as usual.

Don could tell I hadn't come up with this alone. 'Who's been in your ear then, Jim? We've always paid management off the gross. That's the way it's always been done.'

But I didn't listen. It wasn't right, no matter how long we had done it. I had talked this over with Jane and I had got some advice from Steve Hill. This was just basic business stuff. 'I don't care. I don't want to pay it like that anymore. I think we have to change the way we do business.'

The rest of the band didn't want to change a thing. That just made me angrier.

'Look, this is a democracy. We can vote on it but I don't think anything is going to get changed today.' Don was the spokesperson. The others said nothing. They always went along with Don. No matter what we were fighting about, Don had to do the dirty work. He must have hated it.

By this time, I was feeling completely out of my comfort zone. I was feeling sick, asking for money. I was back as an eight-year-old, begging for money because I was hungry. I snapped, 'If you guys want to pay twenty per cent of the gross to Rod but don't want to help me support my fucking family, well you can do it without me. I'm fucking finished.'

The band never budged. They'd seen me threaten to leave before but this time it was different. I had changed. I wasn't begging. I was telling them what I wanted and how I felt.

I got up, looked at them sitting around the table and said, 'I'm finished. You guys do what you like but I'm leaving the band. And I won't be fucking coming back.'

I walked out. I was furious. Getting angry was the only way I could show them how I felt. But as I stormed down the road it almost felt like my life was flashing before my eyes. I was drowning. Drowning in fear. The band had given me the only security I had ever felt. These guys were my brothers. We had gone from being a bunch of spotty kids, afraid of looking at an audience, to having all of Australia eating out of our hands. We had grown up in a very tough world together and I was walking away from them. Could I do this on my own?

I needed them. But I had walked out and this time there was no turning back.

There was no talking for a while. They thought this was normal. Usually, I would ignore any messages from them and then, in my own time, I would come around and start thinking straight and we would settle back down to work. The difference was that this time, none of us wanted to get back together. I was sure the guys were as worried about their futures as I was, but we all needed to get away from each other. It was time to grow up. Stand on our own, like men. We weren't boys anymore.

Management and record companies and friends and fans of the band all tried to talk us into staying together, but it was over. We decided that we would make one last album. We had already recorded a few things. Then we'd do one last tour for the fans and call it quits.

TWENTIETH CENTURY WAS TO be the band's swan song. But we had died long before we got to the studio. Steve was gone, and in his place was Ray Arnott. Ray had filled in for Steve a couple of times when Steve was sick. He played simple, straight, four-on-the-floor, rock'n'roll drums. Nothing fancy, nothing that wasn't needed. We had all been fans of Ray's since we'd seen him play with The Dingoes back in Adelaide in the old days. But as good as he was, he wasn't Steve. Steve was inventive and he knew how to swing a track like no one else. Steve was our brother and he thought the same way we did. Ray was up against it from day one in the studio. We were fractured and falling apart. The songs were works in progress. If we hadn't been breaking up, we would have kept writing for another year or until we were ready. But suddenly here we were without our drummer, making the record we didn't want to make. Our last.

One of the songs that was written before Steve left turned out to be one of the best songs the band ever recorded. We used the demo version with Steve playing drums. 'Flame Trees', written by Don and Steve, was a song about going back to your hometown and looking at the life you used to live, the people you hung around with and the places you used to go. This song has taken on a lot of different meanings for me over the years. I left a lot of things behind. Maybe more than most people have. And sometimes driving in a car or drinking with mates in a bar can take me back to places I never want to revisit. When I think about going back to Adelaide, I think about nothing but pain and have nothing but bad memories. As the years have gone by, more and more bad memories have surfaced and the song has been even more painful to sing. Some nights, it's all I can do to make it through without breaking down, but it has remained one of my favourite Cold Chisel songs to this day.

Every place I left behind me held ghosts of my past, and as I ran away from them I created new memories and new ghosts that I wanted to leave behind. More people I could never look in the eye again. More people who I hurt or who hurt me. I spent ten years on the road with Cold Chisel during our first life and we never stayed still long enough for anything, let alone the past, to catch up to us. Life on the road saved me. I could fall into the car and drive away from anything or anyone. If I was lucky I might never have to face up to anything. But Australia is a small place really. We always had to go back to places that held memories I preferred to leave behind. So I started drinking and taking so many drugs that I didn't feel anything, and I certainly had trouble remembering anything I had done on previous visits. I went around the country, running in ever shrinking circles, waiting for the world to come crashing down on me. It would eventually, but not for a while. But who needs that sentimental bullshit anyway? Not me.

'SATURDAY NIGHT' WAS A song that came from left field. It took us all by surprise. Don has written a lot of good songs but this one captured a snapshot of Sydney like no other. It oozes with the smells and sounds of Sydney in the 1980s. If you listen closely enough you can almost get a bit of dirt from the Cross on you. And the film clip captures it all. The band walking aimlessly, lost, not knowing where we were heading. Ian and I stumbling into the Mardi Gras parade. The parade is a celebration of Sydney's gay community but even more, it is a defiant stand against oppression. Even while people judged and scorned this community, its members walked the streets with heads held high, celebrating freedom. Celebrating life. We were welcomed into the parade with open arms on that night and I can feel that spirit every time I watch the clip. Ian and I were just two more lost souls who found some peace in the crowd that walked the streets of Darlinghurst. Many years later I would be asked to play at the Mardi Gras party. It was an amazing honour for me. I have so many great friends within the gay community. I spoke with strangers at that party who broke down in tears, telling me that the only record of friends they'd lost to AIDS was in the film clip that we made that night. Dressed bright as butterflies, proudly dancing on a balmy Sydney night. We didn't have the keys to the city, but for one night we kicked the doors down.

Some of the songs on the album could have been written a little better or produced a little better, but we worked with what we had. This was the end and we were all heartbroken to be leaving each other behind.

THE LAST STAND WAS the name we gave our final tour. It would be a massacre and we would be the cavalry who were led to the slaughter, running head on into the fight, night after night. This would not be an easy tour to complete. Every single show we played was to a crowd who had shared a life with us, even if we hadn't met them all personally. We had been at their parties. We had sung at their weddings. We had played at their funerals. We were all members of the same family. Every town wanted to give us a send-off. I hardly slept for the first half of the tour, finishing each show and then drinking with friends we had made as we travelled around the country. By the end of the shows in Adelaide, our old hometown, I couldn't speak. I was spitting blood out while I sang for the last three shows, cauterising the wounds with straight vodka and then screaming again until my throat bled even more. After Adelaide, we had to reschedule the rest of the dates until I could sing. I have always joked that my voice is like a Mack truck, hard to start but once it gets going nothing can stop it. But Adelaide stopped it in its tracks. I wasn't sure if I was going to be able to sing ever again after that part of the tour. I'm not sure now whether I ever wanted to sing again. I was finished. Ready to lay down and die.

But my voice came back. In December 1983 we hit Sydney for the final shows at the Entertainment Centre. Each night we came off wrung out, feeling nothing but empty. I remember singing and the feeling of fear coming over me. 'Will I ever get to be in such a great band again? Why am I leaving?'

But I would just take a long drink from one of the many bottles of booze I had on the stage and dive headlong into the crowd and those thoughts were gone. As I crashed to the floor, dragging countless fans down with me, I could only think about surviving, nothing else.

PART 2

THE BEGINNING OF THE END

CHAPTER TWENTY-FIVE

this is not a song

BOWRAL, 1984

*K*ARAANG *KARAANG KARAANG*
Fuck. This guitar sounds out of tune again. I only just tuned it.

Karaang Karaang Karaang

It looks right when I play through the guitar tuner but shit, it's out again when I try to play a song. What song? This is a joke. This is not a song. 'Khe Sanh' was a song. This is three chords played by an amateur. What am I going to do?

Karaang Karaang Karaang

It's not getting any better. It must be the cold. Fucking thing. I don't care about writing songs. Fuck it, I won't make a record. It was stupid to think I could do this on my own. I've got no talent. I'm fucked.

Karaang Karaang Karaang

I want to throw the guitar against the wall. Calm down. Put the guitar down for a second and breathe. I close my eyes and lift my head up. A slight breeze brushes across my face. It's cool and calming. I open my eyes. I can see the stars between the top of the wall and the ceiling, where the wind sneaks through every now and again. I'm in my little farmhouse in the Southern Highlands. It's not a mansion but I love it here. This is the first place that I have felt at home in my whole life. It's mine, no one can take it from me. It's my home.

In the next room the fire is roaring and it is warm and dark. Jane is asleep in front of the fire with Mahalia in her arms. Every time I take off the headphones I can hear her breathe, deep and slow.

I'm in the front bedroom. The room is really too small to be a bedroom so I claimed it for my studio. It might have been part of the front porch at one time but someone decided long before I got here that a house with three bedrooms would sell for more money than a house with two, so they put up a couple of badly constructed walls, and there it was, a third bedroom. I have a four-track cassette recorder in front of me and I'm playing a Fender Telecaster, the first guitar I ever owned. It's black and white and loud and I love it. I'm desperately trying to write songs for my first solo record. If I am to have a life in the music business I have to make a good record and I have to make it soon.

'Take your time, Jimmy. You've just left the biggest band in the country. You deserve a break.' That's what I've been told, but I know, I can feel in my gut, that if I don't make a record, and make it fast, it will all be over. The longer I wait, the closer everyone will look at what I'm doing, the more it will be compared to Cold Chisel. Even the thought of being compared to Chisel scares the shit out of me. Over the ten years that we were together, I wrote a handful of songs for the band, not all of them good ones either. Suddenly I am on my own and people are going to listen to what I can do without Don writing for me. I was lucky. I was the singer in the band with one of the best songwriters Australia has ever produced. And believe me, I am grateful for that. But now I have to go it alone and I wish I'd never heard of Cold Chisel. Fuck. I pick up my guitar again and put the headphones back on.

Karaang Karaang Karaang

It's not getting any better. I'll just have to write a song that doesn't need the guitar to be in tune. I turn up the preamp until the guitar is screaming. My eardrums nearly burst. That sounds better. This is a battle, a street fight, it's a war. I'm fighting against the voice in my head that's screaming at me, 'You're not good enough. You don't deserve any of this. You belong back in the gutter.' It's always there, always shouting unless I'm so drunk I can't hear it.

Karaang Karaang Karaang

Fuck it. So it's a war, is it? I hit the guitar even harder. The strings bend across the neck, on the verge of breaking. They vibrate, they howl, until something happens that feels like a miracle to me – they begin to sing.

Karaang Karaang Karaang

The opening chords of what would become 'No Second Prize' ring out in my ears. I refuse to lie down. Fuck Cold Chisel. Fuck the music industry. If I'm going down, I'm going down fighting.

I'VE HEARD THAT SOME of the Chisel boys thought I was lured away by promises of more money and more fame, made by Michael Gudinski. Nothing could be further from the truth. Michael had become a friend of mine. I liked the way he worked. He was a bit wild – no wilder than me – and he was passionate about music, unlike the multinational companies I had dealt with in the past. Over the years I had watched Michael pour his own money, not the company's, back into Australian music. He lived and breathed it.

Whenever I was in Melbourne we would get together and talk about bands that we loved. Michael even put up with me moaning about the way things were falling apart in Chisel. He always told me to hang in there, that the music is its own reward. 'Every band makes mistakes, Jimmy. But this is a great band and it's where you belong,' he told me night after night.

When I did finally leave, Michael didn't know I was going to do it. I rang him from the farm and told him, 'This is it. I've told the guys that I'm not coming back. We're making one last record and doing one last tour then it's over. Finished.'

Michael was quiet at the other end of the phone. Then he said, 'What are you going to do now? And do you need some help? Someone to talk to?'

I told him yes and he and his wife Sue were on the next plane to Sydney to see Jane and me. We sat around the fire and laughed and cried together. After a while I told Michael that I wanted to be on an Australian label. Not any Australian label. His label. I liked the way he stuck by bands. I'd seen lots of bands signed up, chewed up and spat out by big labels. It was a case of deliver or pack your bags and shut the door on your way out of the building. This sort of treatment could finish a young band off. But with Michael they were nurtured and given time to find their feet. He stuck with the bands he believed in and I needed him to believe in me. From that day we have worked together, through good times and bad. He has made mistakes and so have I, but we have always been there for each other.

I had left the biggest band in the country to go solo. I wanted to be good at what I did but I also wanted to be the biggest singer in the country, even bigger than Cold Chisel, and that's what I told Michael. I needed people to like me. I wanted to like me.

'Don't you worry. That's exactly what I want too. I want you to be huge. We can do this together,' he promised.

We shook hands and went about figuring out the fine details of how we would work together. Michael had his lawyers talk to my lawyers and I would have my new manager talk to him, once I found one.

I NEEDED A MANAGER. I wasn't capable of managing myself, so I looked around. I could see no one that appealed to me. No one I trusted with my family's future. One day I sat in Steve Hill's car, driving down to Bowral for a game of golf, a sport I'd never thought I would play. It was never a good idea to give me a stick to hit things with.

'There has to be someone you trust, Jimmy. You've been in this business for a long time.' Steve tried to get his head around it.

'Managers are a rare breed, Steve. All the good ones have people they're looking after and I don't want to play second fiddle to anyone.'

We sat in silence, Steve thinking about slowing his backswing down and me thinking about my career going down the gurgler. Then it came to me. 'Why don't you do it, Steve?' Steve had been sidelined, either by himself or the bank, since its collapse. I could tell he was bored out of his mind. He was razor sharp and I knew he was honest, so it seemed like a good idea.

Steve snapped back to reality. 'What? Manage you? You have to be kidding. I don't know a thing about music. I own one cassette, *Little Feat Live*, and you gave that to me. No mate, you need a manager who knows the music business.'

I thought about it for a while. 'I know the music side of things. You know about business. We can do it together. Business is business. You were good at it, weren't you?'

Steve was a hard businessman and his entrance to the music industry scared a lot of people. The first person he had to deal with was Michael Gudinski. Michael never knew how to take him and Steve liked to keep him guessing.

My lawyer was as good as it gets. Peter Thompson worked for Tress Cocks & Maddox (now TressCox), a big Sydney law firm. He was tough and very smart. We have remained friends and I still ask for his advice whenever I need it. Peter drew up the contract, Michael's lawyers said their bit and we had it all ready to sign. As we sat down, Steve turned up and said, 'Can I see that contract before you sign it?'

Michael slid it over to him. Steve picked it up, laid it in front of himself and started writing on it in pen.

'What? You're amending the contract right now? You can't do that,' said Michael.

Steve looked up at him and said, 'I just did.' And slid it back to Michael. In pen at the bottom of the last page, Steve had written:

Michael Gudinski agrees to pay Jimmy Barnes $25,000 cash on this date every year for the length of the contract as a sign of good will.

Michael picked it up and gasped. 'Aw. This is bullshit. You can't do that. My lawyers have agreed to everything you wanted. You just can't add shit in pen for the sake of it.'

Steve stood up. 'If you don't want to sign it, well, we can all go home and I'll find someone who wants to sign Jimmy. There are a lot of people out there bidding, you know.'

Michael was pale and breaking out in a sweat. 'Wait a fucking minute here. I never said I wasn't going to sign it. I was just saying.'

Steve kept putting the pressure on. 'Well, I've got some things to do.' He was walking towards the door.

'Yeah, all right, all right. Here you go.'

Michael signed the deal that would see him and me working together for nearly all of my recording career, through good times and bad. It was good business but we were great friends and will stay that way until the end. Which, I might add, is a long way off. I still have a lot I want to do and so does he.

MARK POPE, WHO HAD been tour manager for Cold Chisel for a long time, had teamed up with a guy called Richard MacDonald. They had started Bottom Line Touring and Agency after the demise of Cold Chisel. Richard had been the booking agent for Dirty Pool, Cold Chisel's management. So they weren't happy when he quit to start his own business with Mark, and lawsuits followed.

Mark and Richard were my agents once I left Chisel, which meant they booked all my live gigs. I trusted and liked Mark. He was a creative thinker. Richard was a great agent. Both were passionate and ready to tackle the industry with me.

JANE AND I WERE spending as little time as we could in Sydney. In the country, we would cook and spend time with Mahalia, doing things that normal people did, even though I was far from normal. I tried to keep off drugs and stay sober as much as I could. I did smoke a little pot, something I never did much on the road. When I was touring, I didn't want anything to slow me down. I preferred uppers. But I found that the pot calmed me down at home somewhat.

Life was blissful. We would walk in the country with our baby, up through the forest at the end of the road, through the volcano crater and up to the lookout. I had found out that Mount Gibraltar was in fact an extinct volcano. I liked the idea of there being something else that might once have exploded, just at the end of the street. But it was extinct, whereas I just lay dormant. Calm on the surface but ready to blow everything to pieces when I could take no more. I hoped that the longer I spent there, the less chance there was of me exploding, just like the volcano.

I WAS WRITING AND finishing up songs for the album I had to make. I had never written more than two songs an album with Chisel, so the idea of writing a whole album on my own scared me to death. I had 'No Second Prize' and a couple of others, and I had a few ideas that I thought were not bad, but I still worried whether they were good enough.

A couple of songs I had presented to Cold Chisel at one time or another. 'Promise Me You'll Call' and 'Daylight' had been done as demos by Chisel, but not that well. Cold Chisel didn't like big distorted guitars. I liked them doubled and tripled, layered until they roared out of the speakers, but I'd found that whenever I wrote a song, I couldn't get the band to give it the treatment that I was hearing. Cold Chisel had one guitar, and a lot of the time the band would only want to put one guitar on the record. If I really fought, I might get two, but never as distorted as I wanted. I couldn't get my ideas across, and the band nearly always knocked them back. In the end, this was part of the reason I left.

It was always hard to write for Chisel. Who could write for that band better than Don? It was intimidating to say the least. But even though Chisel rejected them, I thought, with a bit of reworking, my songs could be good. 'Promise Me You'll Call' was a song I wrote for Mahalia. A little message in a time capsule. If she grew up and was anything like me, she would leave home and I would never see her. That's what I did when I left home. I was never going back, and the less contact I had with my past, the better I was. I had to force myself to call home. And I thought she might hear this song and call me.

'Daylight' came about after an all-night recording session in Paradise with Chisel. I had gone home to the apartment Jane and I were renting. This place had no block-out curtains. As I lay awake, trying desperately to sleep, the sun was burning my eyes. I only write songs about things that happen to me. 'Daylight' was all I was thinking about.

Another night I had left the Paradise studio rattling from copious amounts of speed, coke and vodka, every cell in my body vibrating, and I wanted to write a song about it. All I could come up with was something that moved as fast as my heart was pounding. I would either write a rock song or have a heart attack, one of the two. A song jumped out of me the same way my heart was jumping out of my chest. 'Paradise' was that song.

Jane tried to inspire and educate me. She would find books that she thought I should read, a list of what she thought was required reading – a selection of classics that I would have read at school if I had stayed or paid attention. There was a whole world of literature out there that I had missed, lost in the trauma and fear I felt as a child and then drowned in booze and speed as I ran away from my past. By the time I left school I couldn't sit still long enough to read a book.

Jane looked for titles that might get my attention. She tried to give me Shakespeare but I couldn't make head or tail of it. Eventually she found me *Tales from Shakespeare*, a book for children by Charles and Mary Lamb, and I started to get it. She gave me *Kidnapped* by Robert Louis Stevenson in an attempt to appeal to the Scotsman in me. I loved it, but the first book that really grabbed my attention was *Lord of the Flies* by William Golding. It was about society breaking down and violence taking over. I could relate to that easily enough. I'd lived it, so I devoured it, read it in a couple of days. I remember as soon as I finished it I went into my studio and wrote 'Boys Cry Out for War'. I was angry and wanted a guitar riff that showed how angry I was. The song was a simple grinding assault on the senses. I could hear how the band would play it live, intense and loud like a battering ram. This was the sort of music I wanted to make.

I had spent years fighting with Cold Chisel, pushing them to play louder. Now I had a chance to play as fast and as loud as I wanted. That's what I would do.

When I pulled all these songs together I felt I was almost ready to record. Now I needed a band.

LEAVING THE SECURITY OF Cold Chisel was tough but putting a band together was even tougher. Chisel was still right there, The Last Stand still ringing in my ears. We had only finished the tour two months before. But I wanted to hit the ground running. This was what I did best.

I needed players I felt safe with. Players who, like the guys in Cold Chisel, had been around. Players I'd worked with before. Ray Arnott, the drummer, was the first to join. Ray and I had become good friends since he'd worked with Chisel. As I mentioned before, he had played with The Dingoes, one of the few Australian bands that Cold Chisel looked up to, and also Mighty Kong, a band that formed after the breakdown of Daddy Cool, one of the greatest bands Australia has ever produced. So Ray had the credentials.

He had also recently been through the same wringer that I was caught in. He had given up drugs and drinking. In the old days, Ray could put it away with the best of them, so if he could give up, maybe there was a chance for me. But I wasn't ready to give up yet. I just needed some steadying influences in my band. Ray was the first.

The second player I approached was probably the most influential musician in my life besides Don Walker. Bruce Howe was the bass player from Fraternity. He had a style like no one else I've worked with. As far as I could tell, Bruce only played upstrokes on his bass, so his sound was very aggressive. His playing was very pushy but still in the pocket.

As I said earlier, when I joined Fraternity for six months in 1975 I learned more about singing from Bruce than I have from anyone else. He was tough and demanding but he encouraged me to drag more out of myself. And now, just like in the days when I was in Fraternity, he would lean on me when I sang, listening to every note and every inflection in my voice and hitting the back of my head with his bass if he thought I wasn't giving enough. Bruce always wanted me to sing harder and louder. He wanted my pitch to be perfect and he wanted me to use as little vibrato as possible. Vibrato was for pussies.

I can't thank Bruce enough for working with me after I left Chisel. He was the one musician I needed around me at that crucial time in my life. In years to come, my kids called him 'Big Old Bruce'. He was mean and tough and a bit scary but as soft as a marshmallow once you gained his trust.

I spoke about Stars earlier, the band that Michael Gudinski signed rather than Chisel way back. Not long after Stars signed to Mushroom, a bloke called Andy Durant joined their band. Andy wrote a new batch of songs for them, songs about love and Australian history instead of guns and horses. They lost the hats and stars, and seemed to grow up as a band. The Stars guitar player was a guy called Mal Eastick. Mal had always been a reasonable guitar player but when Andy joined the band he seemed to find his stride. His playing got better every time I saw him.

Tragically, Andy passed away in 1980. Mal and his band put on The Andy Durant Memorial Concert in Melbourne and they asked a bunch of musicians to join them in celebrating Andy's life. I was honoured to be asked to join them for a few songs. The concert was moving and heartfelt but the thing I noticed most was Mal Eastick. The loss of his dear friend made him dig very deep inside himself, and instead of finding just a hole full of grief, he found himself as a guitar player. Andy would have been so proud of him. Anyway, I left St Kilda that night amazed at Mal's guitar playing. He was the next person I asked to join my band.

Like Bruce and Ray, Mal was a steadying influence on me. He was a passionate guitar player and he cared about music. I had surrounded myself with three very similar characters. All three were different musically but all three were like big brothers to me. I thought at this point about getting a piano player but I knew the comparisons to Chisel would come too thick and fast. But I did need another instrument to fill the sound I heard for these songs; they were loud and guitar driven so I knew I needed another guitar player.

I had worked with the best guitarist in the world in Ian, so I didn't just want a gunslinger, hotshot guitar player. I wanted someone who could bring some depth to the band. I had a feeling that I would need a lot of volume to cover up what was missing in my songs.

I thought long and hard about it and then I had an idea. The Dingoes' guitar player, Chris Stockley, played rock, old-style rock, like Little Richard and Gene Vincent. I had watched him night after night as a young fellow. I had spoken with him after shows. He was a wild guy but a very serious musician. I wasn't sure he was hard rock enough for what I was doing but I thought he could bring a lot to the table as far as songs and arrangements were concerned. He agreed to play and my band was formed.

BEFORE RECORDING, I WANTED to get out and play some music live, but I didn't want to play in the big cities. I was afraid of living in the shadow of Chisel. So I bought the guitar players the biggest amps I could find and we headed to North Queensland and worked our way down the coast. We didn't spend a lot of time rehearsing. Most of our rehearsals were done during the first few shows in front of an audience. This was a tough way to pull things together. Every night we laid our heads on the chopping block and only the experience of the players, the volume of the band and the sheer brutality of the treatment of the songs got us through. We played every song at breakneck speed. There were no ballads. We were relentless and we wouldn't stop to let people think.

I went from filling stadiums with Cold Chisel to playing to half-empty pubs and clubs as a solo performer. It was hard but at least I was playing. Not everyone knew who I was and not everyone cared. Some people hated me because Cold Chisel had ended and nothing any of us did would ever be as good. A few people would come along to see how bad I was. They'd stay for a few songs and then I'd watch them leave halfway through our show, shaking their heads and unblocking their ears. They didn't know if they had enjoyed us or if they had been violated. But, by the end of a show, the people who stayed definitely knew they had seen a rock'n'roll band. We sweated and bled for every song. We played mostly my songs but we needed a few covers to fill out the set. I didn't have enough material. We played 'Mercury Blues' and 'Resurrection Shuffle', a song that has made it through to this day, still getting a spot most nights in my set, and 'Piece of My Heart', the Janis Joplin song that made it onto the first album.

The songs, like the band, got more polished as we got more and more shows under our belts. But the better the band got, the more I wanted from them. I wanted them to be harder still. I wanted the show to be wilder. I would stand right at the front of the stage, staring into the eyes of doubting punters, all the while pushing the band to play faster and louder. A lot of people left because of that, thinking I was going to attack them. But I didn't care. If they didn't like it, they could fuck off. I was crazed. I was consuming more speed than ever and a few of the band started joining me in an attempt to keep up. We drank too much, played too hard, and slept too little to stand a chance of getting ready to record. I would have to worry about the album when I came to it. We would have work to do in the studio.

By the time we got back to Sydney we were red-eyed but match fit and we wanted to get into the studio as fast as possible. But I still had the same nagging doubts. How would people take my music? This definitely wasn't Chisel. I lost a lot of sleep.

CHAPTER TWENTY-SIX

rock is dead

ON MY OWN, 1984

LONG BEFORE I LEFT Cold Chisel, I had talked to Mark Opitz about doing a solo record, so he was the first and only person I approached to make the album. Mark had a track record as long as your arm. He had worked with The Angels on *Face to Face*, an amazing record. He had produced Cold Chisel, INXS, The Divinyls and many others.

We went into a new Sydney studio called Rhinoceros and set about finding a sound. We didn't stray far from what we did in the shows. The sound was hard and loud and not very polished.

I was back in the recording studio less than four months after finishing with Cold Chisel. All I could think about was being compared to my old band. I didn't have Don's songs. I didn't have Mossy. I would be laughed at. I couldn't do this on my own. So I did what I always did in this sort of situation, I drank and I got smashed. If I didn't care, it wouldn't matter if no one liked it.

Every morning I would wake up and walk to the studio panicking, wondering how long until it was all over. But Mark and the band would be there waiting, excited about the record. This gave me a little confidence but it would disappear as each day went on. By the end of every night I would be mindless and broken, staggering home to Jane, smelling of booze and shaking from too much speed and coke. I would toss and turn and hardly sleep, then get up and go straight back into the studio to beat my head against the wall.

WE DID HAVE A few laughs at Rhinoceros. Michael Gudinski came up at the end of one week for his first listen to my new material. So we spent a few hours recording one or two cheesy country songs. When he arrived, we all sat straight-faced as I explained my plan. 'Michael, you know that a lot of people are waiting on this new album. I'm going to be compared to Cold Chisel. You know that, right?'

'Yeah, yeah, I know, but we'll worry about that later, just play the songs.' He was chomping at the bit.

'But Michael,' I went on, 'I don't want to be compared to anyone.'

He started to look concerned.

'I want to do something completely different. So this new material is taking me off in a new direction. Are you ready?'

I could guess what he was thinking: 'Just play the fucking things, would you? I'm sure it's good.'

I pressed play. A cover of Johnny Cash's 'I Walk the Line' filled the studio. Michael sat motionless, never lifting his head, which rested in the sweaty palms of his hands.

I played 'Jackson' next. I could see beads of sweat forming on his brow. I stopped the tape. 'Listen Michael, before you hear any more or say a word, I've spent a lot of time in America and country music is the new big thing. Rock is dead. This is what I want to do now, okay?'

Michael looked around the room, coughed and cleared his throat to speak. But I cut him off. 'You fucking idiot! Of course I'm not playing country music. It's a joke!'

The band laughed. Mark laughed. Michael laughed, but he wasn't happy. He had almost had a heart attack. 'Yeah, yeah, yeah. Very fucking funny. I knew you were kidding. I was just playing along with you.'

I think if I had decided to make a country record, Michael would have backed me all the way. That's why I love him. Luckily for both of us, I wasn't making a country record. I played Michael some of the real songs and I could see excitement in his eyes. I wasn't as scared anymore.

We finished *Bodyswerve*. It came out in September 1984 and entered the charts at number one. I was back on the merry-go-round. It would be the first of seven records in a row that entered at the number one spot. More than Chisel ever had. We were up and running, but Cold Chisel was always there in the background, the yardstick, the measure I was trying to live up to. Driving me harder, making me fight.

ELIZA-JANE WAS THE NEXT baby to come along. She didn't arrive without a few dramas though. One day early in the pregnancy, Jane started to bleed. I rushed her to the hospital to get things checked out, and we were told that she was miscarrying. We were shattered. The doctor told us that it would be best if Jane stayed in hospital for a curette. The baby was dead. We sat crying, waiting for a room to become available for the procedure.

While we waited a young doctor came in to console Jane. He said out of the blue, 'Why don't we have a quick look on the ultrasound while we're waiting?'

We followed him into a room and he turned on the machine. It was all very sad until he spoke. 'I suggest you look at this.' There was a baby jumping around on the screen. 'Who told you the baby was dead? There's nothing wrong with this baby.'

If he had not asked us to have that ultrasound, we would have lost Eliza-Jane. I can't begin to think what life would have been like without her. I wanted to belt the other doctor but we were so happy that we let him off the hook.

Eliza-Jane arrived in December 1984. She was early, so early in fact that we weren't expecting her for another six weeks. This, as you'll remember, was the same as Mahalia. She arrived six weeks early too. Our girls have always been a bit impatient it seems, so we should have guessed it might happen. I had meant to be in Sydney for the birth but with the baby's sudden change of plans, I was caught out. I was waiting to go on stage at the Playroom on the Gold Coast when I got the news that Jane was in hospital.

There was nothing I could do. We had spent a small fortune setting up to film two shows. We would film one show, then have a day off and then film the second show. But Eliza-Jane was coming and there was no stopping her. I had to resign myself to the fact that I would miss her birth. I hated it. I wanted to cancel but of course I couldn't. The shows were all set up, ready to go, not just the band's gear but the cameras and sound recording equipment. We had about twenty people working flat out on getting it all in place, so I was trapped.

As fate would have it, Eliza-Jane didn't come that night after all, so I jumped on a plane in the morning. I was so relieved that I would be there. I got to the hospital and waited for her arrival, but still she didn't come.

We tried to encourage her to come out, singing into Jane's stomach and pleading with her. 'Come on, baby. I'm here waiting for you. Come now, because your dad's got to go back to work and record the second show.'

But it didn't happen. She obviously wasn't listening to me. Reluctantly I left the next day to continue filming. While I was on stage that night, Eliza-Jane came into our lives. And what a blessing she has been. Always a bit of a rebel, but sweet and soft and beautiful. She was named after my granny, the woman who delivered me into this world. They used to call my granny Liza, short for Elizabeth, but later in life she was known as Betty. Our little Eliza-Jane would be known as EJ. As she got older we noticed a wicked streak in her. When it comes out we call her Evil J. Just for fun. There's really nothing evil about her, she is an angel.

THE BAND WENT FROM strength to strength and it wasn't long until we were playing to full houses. Everybody was happy. But Michael Gudinski had one wish – he wanted a big album in the States.

'All I fucking want, Jimmy, is for you and me to get to number one in the States. That's all I want. Well, that and St Kilda to win the premiership. Come to think of it, there's a few other fucking things too, but that will do for starters.' Michael always got animated when he talked about success. His hands would fly around the place, because that success would mean a lot of money. He set about working on an overseas deal for me.

One day I got a call from Michael, who was in New York. 'We are not fucking around. I just want you to know that I am working my arse off here for you.' I could hear laughter and the tinkling of cutlery.

'The A-team is onto it. My good mate Paul Schindler is the best lawyer in New York and he's all over it. We're looking good, son.' I listened as Michael told me about the who's and why's of the American music industry. It seemed everybody was in my corner. Well, they were according to Michael anyway. 'Geffen Records are very interested. There's a guy called Gary Gersh who's the A&R man there and he loves what you've done. I think you should come over and meet him.'

I wasn't keen on going back to America but I didn't tell anyone. America was still the home of music. It was the biggest market in the world. If you could sell records in America, you had it made. So in autumn 1985 I headed off to meet the company that might handle my career in the States.

I hardly slept on the plane, worried about what might or might not happen. This was compounded by a feeling of impending doom. Why did I have to be separated from Jane? The only time I felt secure was when Jane and I were together, probably because when we were apart I went into a crazed state, drinking and taking drugs, and this always led to me needing female company. Then of course, I felt guilty. I knew it was wrong.

But here I was on the plane, drinking the bar dry. It was the beginning of the downward spiral. And I knew this spiral so well. I knew that drinking was the start, and here I was practically mindless on the plane, staring at the small pile of miniature vodkas I had drunk. Why did I do this?

Los Angeles looked like it needed a coat of paint. It was grey and dirty. The sun was shining and the sky was blue but it was hard to see it through the pollution. I felt a cough coming on as I landed at LAX. This was one of those times when I was so glad I had my sunglasses with me. I put them on and left the plane. Bleary-eyed and still half-drunk from the trip, I walked out to find a limousine driver looking at me, holding up a card with a name on it. It said 'JAMIE BARNES' in big letters. I presumed it was for me.

'Do you mean Jimmy Barnes?' I asked sheepishly.

'Hey, sorry about that. The company must have heard wrong. So how are you doing anyway? Let me carry that bag.'

He seemed a little too keen. 'It's fine. I've got it. Who sent you? I never ordered a car.'

He smiled at me in that insincere way that only someone working as a limo driver in LA can, and said, 'Compliments of Geffen Records, sir. I'm at your service. Anything you need, just let me know. Come on, give me the bag. I've got to earn my money somehow.' His speaking voice was high and annoying. He looked like Ronnie James Dio in a suit and tie that didn't quite fit him properly.

I followed him to a waiting stretch limo. 'It's only me, you know that, don't you? Could you bring a bigger car next time?' I laughed as he opened the door.

'Well, you never know who you might have met in first class.' He winked and closed the door. I didn't have the heart to tell him I'd flown economy.

I thought about closing the window between the driver's seat and me but it was too late. He spoke. 'So. You in the music business then, are you?'

I struggled to hear him properly. It seemed like he was a hundred yards away.

'Yeah. I am. I'm a rock'n'roll sing –'

He cut me off. 'Yeah. I'm in the entertainment business too. I'm only driving this car until I get a break. Here, have my CD and bio. I play guitar and I sing. I'm an actor too and I can work a bar if you're having a party. I do it all.'

I took the press kit and told him I'd listen later.

'Thanks man, appreciate it, you know,' he squeaked. I couldn't get 'Man on the Silver Mountain' out of my head. I think I might have even called him Ronnie, I can't be sure.

I was staying at the Sunset Marquis Hotel. Everyone seemed too nice, I didn't trust them. The porters, the front desk, the driver. They had to be up to something. No one was that nice all the time. I was drunk when I arrived, drunk the whole time I was there, and drunker when I left.

I HAD A SHOWER and went to see Gary Gersh at Geffen Records on Sunset Boulevard. Gary was as much of a rock star as the people he signed. Before he joined Geffen he was vice president of A&R at EMI America and had been responsible for signing David Bowie, Stray Cats, J. Geils Band and George Thorogood to mention a few. He was a smooth-talking, fast-operating powerhouse of a record company guy.

My first meeting with Gary went well, I think, although I was a bit worried when he said, 'So we'll have to redo most of this record. It's a little underproduced, I think.'

I knew it was underproduced. It was under everything. I was underfunded. I was underprepared. I was under pressure. I was probably living under a rock but I didn't need him to tell me I was under anything.

'I thought I was here because you liked the record and wanted to release it,' I said. I have a feeling I might have glared at him a little. I was tired.

'Hey, don't get me wrong. I do like the record but for this market things have to be done a certain way. We like things a bit more polished, if you know what I mean.'

I knew what he meant but he was beginning to offend me. Which could end up putting him in danger, if you know what I mean.

'I'd like to get you together with some great songwriters and producers and see if we can make this record a little more suitable for the States. But hey, stay cool, we're jumping ahead of ourselves here. Let's go and get some lunch and talk over some of the plans I have for you.'

I didn't have much of an appetite but I thought at least I could get a drink. He took me to The Ivy, Beverly Hills. I wasn't really dressed for it. Everyone was in white linen shirts with shorts and shoes without socks. They were unshaven and wore expensive-looking sunglasses. Nearly every single person in the place looked like they were in a TV show of some sort.

'Is that someone famous over there? I'm sure I've seen him in a sitcom or something,' I whispered across the table.

Gary had a look. 'You know, I think you're right. I think he might have been in a sitcom. But he's our waiter now.'

Then the young, jaded-looking guy with the perfectly chiselled profile and too many muscles walked over to our table and offered us menus. 'The crab cakes are great here. You have to try them. Can I get you some water? Perrier, perhaps?'

I could hardly stop myself from laughing. 'I'll have a vodka soda, thanks.'

Gary looked at me and smiled. 'Just a spring water for me, thanks. With a twist of lemon.'

'Yeah, yeah, I'll have a twist too,' I quickly added.

Gary was a funny, decent bloke. He had a lot of good ideas, and he seemed to know what he was talking about. I liked him, I just had to get over the initial shock of someone telling me what to do. We finished lunch and then headed back to his office to meet the guys who would work on my record if I signed with Geffen.

I met the PR guy. Marco was full of beans and didn't even have a seat in his office. His wraparound desk was chest high, and he walked between one of his many phones and the fax machine, yelling at his secretary to bring him another coffee.

'Hey, let's catch up tonight for a drink and a chat.'

I had no better offers so I said, 'Sure, I'm staying at the –'

He interrupted me. 'Yeah, I know where you're staying. Fuck man, I booked it. That hotel has the best bar in town, man. Wait until you see the girls that get in there. Woo! See you tonight. Love your record, by the way.'

We met the accountant who would pay all the bills. Gary told me, 'That's his secretary, Darlene. Be nice to Darlene because if she doesn't like you we are all fucked.'

I smiled nervously at her. We both laughed but I got the feeling he was serious.

Gary pulled out a few tapes and played them for me. 'I think I can get a few great guys to write with you. Do you know a guy called Chas Sandford?'

I had no idea who he was talking about but I pretended I did.

'Chas wrote "Missing You" for John Waite. You'll love him. I'm going to hook you two guys up next time you're in town.'

Gary had told me he wanted to get Bob Clearmountain to remix everything. Bob was the best in the business at that time. Gary was talking a lot but I would reserve my judgement until something real happened. Talk was cheap.

THE NEXT LEG OF my journey, on my way to New York, was a bit of a secret stop. Gudinski didn't know about it. Steve Hill had organised a side trip to Virginia Beach – the home of the CIA I later found out – to talk with a lawyer friend of his.

I got off the plane and was met by a middle-aged black limo driver who looked like he played in a blues band. He was dressed casually, no tie, and his jacket was over his arm.

'You must be Jimmy.' He walked straight up to me. The plane was full but he picked me from the crowd.

'How did you know?'

He laughed. 'It's my job to know, young man.'

He led me to the car. It was another car that you could have fitted a short par three golf hole in the back of.

'So, Jimmy. My name is George and I am here to make your trip easy. I will take you to your hotel and drop you but I will be back at eight-thirty a.m. sharp for you. Mr Colby likes to be on time. So be ready. Now in the meantime if you need anything – anything at all – let me know.'

I looked at him in the rear-view mirror. He nodded at me. 'I'm doing this as a favour for Mr Hill, I normally only drive VIPs. So I am connected, young man. I can get you anything you want. Do you want some weed or coke? Shit, I can get you heroin if you need it. I know a couple of fine young black girls who will wear you out, son. But you better be up and ready first thing in the morning. Mr Colby don't like to wait.'

I thought this might be some sort of test so I said to him, 'I was thinking about getting an early night.' I knew I smelled like a brewery.

He smiled at me. 'Whatever you want to do.'

He dropped me at my hotel. I rang Steve to report in.

'So tomorrow you're going to be signing your deal with Geffen but I wanted you to go over the contract with our lawyers first. I don't want those bastards thinking they have anything over you.' Steve was in business mode and his Irish accent sounded thicker to me. 'Sorry I couldn't be there with you. But you're in good hands. William Colby, your new lawyer, used to be the director of the CIA.

'You'll meet with these guys in the morning and then fly to New York in the afternoon to sign. George will look after you. Did you meet George by the way? He's a good man.'

I went to sleep worrying about the next day's work. The hotel phone woke me at seven-thirty.

'It's George here. I thought I'd call just in case you found your own trouble last night. Best get up now and get yourself ready.'

'I'm already up and I've been to the gym,' I lied.

The meeting was like nothing I'd ever been to before, or since really. I sat in a chair at the head of a table. William Colby walked around me while five or six different lawyers shot off questions at me about the deal.

'I'm here to make you look like you know this deal back to front. I know you don't, but we are going to tell you things to say and ask that will make them think you do. These guys don't normally deal with anyone who really knows their shit, but they are going to think that you do, even if you don't. So just listen to us and try to take in a few of these points, all right Mr Barnes? Do you understand?'

I breathed deep. 'I think I do, sir. I think I do.'

'Good. Let's get started. We've got a lot to cover.'

I sat in the office with William Colby and his team for about three hours. Then I was taken to the airport by George and sent on my way.

'Here's my card, Jimmy. If you get back this way some time give me a call and I'll send over those young ladies I was talking about. Good luck.'

In New York, I was taken straight to Geffen's office. There, Paul Schindler, Michael Gudinski and David Geffen waited for me to sign the deal.

I asked a few questions. 'The changes Steven asked for have been made, haven't they?'

I quoted one of the points that my new friends in Virginia Beach had outlined. Everyone in the room was shocked. I shouldn't have known about this, never mind asked about it. Worried looks were shot from one to another.

'Yes, they're all done as asked.'

Michael coughed and we went on with the signing. I was now a Geffen recording artist. Things were looking up for the time being.

CHAPTER TWENTY-SEVEN

it'll sound better when
I sing it properly

AMERICA AGAIN, 1985

So I was signed to a big American record company. I wasn't sure I liked the idea. I wanted to break into new markets but I didn't feel safe in America. It felt like the place was out of control and as I was always out of control too, it was hard to feel safe at all. But I had to make this work. Michael Gudinski had gone out on a limb for me. He had a lot of faith in me. I didn't want to let him down. I had let a lot of people down already by this point, Jane especially, and I wanted to make it all better. The only way I could see to do that was to make things work in America, become so big I could give her anything she wanted. And in the meantime, I could buy myself enough time to get myself together once and for all.

After a short time at home, the family and I went back to Los Angeles. I would see Gary Gersh and make my record good enough for the American market. This rubbed me the wrong way. I knew what Gary was talking about but it was a fine line between listening to advice and losing sight of myself, and I was already fighting to have some say in my own life. But this was a country that I knew nothing about, so I had to take some advice from Gary, even if it didn't always ring true to me. I was in a state of panic. My gut told me to tell him to shove his opinions, but my head said, 'For once in your fucking life, just listen.' I would fight this battle the whole time I was away from home.

GARY HAD SET UP all sorts of people for me to meet and work with. This was a new world for me and I would come home after writing all day with songwriters and just be frazzled. I couldn't tell if I had written something good or not. Jane was my sounding board.

'What do you think of this, baby?' I would ask, turning the music up too loud and waking the babies.

'Shhhh. I can listen later. Why don't you have a shower and we can go out and eat.'

Jane was the only one who would give me an honest opinion. If something was good she could tell, even before me. She is still like that. But if something wasn't quite right, she hated it.

'It's not finished yet. It'll sound better when I sing it properly.'

But she would already have left the room. 'I don't think it will.'

So, I stopped playing things unless I was sure they were ready and good enough to be listened to.

THE FIRST PERSON THAT Gary set me up with was Chas Sandford. Chas and I sat around a studio at his house for most of the first day, trying to get something started. I was uncomfortable. Chas was like a big kid, and for a minute I thought he might be on something. He seemed distracted, running in and out of the room. Eventually I had to say firmly, 'Shall we try and finish this song now, Chas?'

'Hang on a minute. Let me play you a song or two that I've been writing lately,' he said, bouncing around the room. I think he'd had too much sugar. We spent the next hour listening to parts of songs he had written for other people. Big acts. Much bigger than me. And not whole songs, just bits of songs. It was driving me nuts.

'Why don't you just write one like that for me?' I asked as he changed tapes for the tenth time.

'It's not that easy, Jimmy. I have to know your sound.'

I sat and thought for a minute. 'I'll leave you a record and then you can listen to it and hear what I sound like.' It made sense to me. At least I could get to fuck out of there for a while.

'Just let me play you a few more things.' Chas was manic by this point and proceeded to play me song after song, all earmarked for someone else. There was one for Stevie Nicks, one for Don Henley, and some for other great singers. Then he played me a song that seemed not to be for anyone. I liked it better than all the songs he'd played so far. It was the kind of song I wanted to sing.

'What's this song?'

'Oh. I didn't mean to play this one. It's for my solo record. Forget I played it.'

I sat on the edge of my chair. 'But wait a minute, you did play it, Chas, and I like it. What's it called?' I asked.

'Don Henley wanted this one too. But I'm saving it. I knew I shouldn't have played it for you.' He looked at the ground. I could tell he was nervous.

'What's it called?'

'I'd Die to Be with You Tonight,' he mumbled under his breath.

'I like it. I think you should give it to me,' I said. 'When are you recording your record?' I was cornering him and he knew it.

'As soon as I get time. Soon. Very soon. Maybe this year. But I got a lot of songs to write for people.'

This was what I thought. He had plenty of time to write for himself.

'Just give that one to me. Surely a talented guy like you can write another one for yourself whenever you need it.'

He picked up the guitar and started working again. 'I'll write you another one. Better than that one, okay?'

It took a few days but eventually, with the help of Gary Gersh, Chas parted with the song and I had a new track for my album.

NEXT GARY SENT ME to work with a couple of big songwriters. Tom Kelly and Billy Steinberg had written 'Like a Virgin' for Madonna. So off I went, not knowing what to expect. I arrived at a nice house in the Valley somewhere and was met by Billy. We sat and talked for a while and then Billy said, 'You know, Jimmy, I really like your voice but unfortunately we don't have a lot of time. Maybe if you could leave me a few songs you've started, we could finish them off for you. That's about the best I can do.'

So that's what I did. I had a couple of songs I'd started writing with a friend in Germany and never finished. They were tough, German-sounding rock songs. I gave him a tape of them and left. 'I'll come back on Monday and see how it's going,' I said as I jumped into my hire car. 'See you then.'

When Monday came around I was surprisingly excited. 'Like a Virgin' wasn't my favourite song but it appeared these guys

were very good at what they did. I arrived, and again, Billy was
the only one there.

'We finished off two of them. We made some new demos.
Hope you like them.' He handed me a tape. I think he had
someone in the studio already so I didn't even go inside.

I thanked him and drove back over the hills. On the way I
played the cassette in the car. My tough rock songs now sounded
like German cabaret songs sung by a cantor, with the slightest
hint of Madonna thrown in for good measure. I never played
them again. I wanted to throw the tape out the window but I
drove to Gary's office and gave it to him.

He agreed they were not for me. 'Too bad. You know, it
might have worked. These guys are great but it's just not the
sound we're looking for, is it?'

I tried not to laugh. This was certainly not the sound I was
looking for. I was glad he agreed with me. It could have been a
deal breaker.

He went on, 'So, take a seat a minute. I want to play you
something.' Gary sat at his desk. I lay on his couch.

'I called in a few favours. I asked my friend Little Steven for a
song for you and he sent me this. Do you know who he is?'

Of course I did. I loved Bruce Springsteen, everybody did.
And everybody in music knew Stevie played with him. Gary then
proceeded to play a demo of a song that was obviously recorded
on a dictaphone, with an acoustic guitar and what sounded like
someone beating time on a couch, but it still sounded really
great. That song was 'Ride the Night Away', written by Stevie
van Zandt and Steve Jordan.

'I really like it. Who will produce it? Will they do it?'

I got the feeling Gary couldn't deliver either Steve to produce.
He said, 'I want to keep the Australian flavour of the record alive
so why don't we get your friend Mark Opitz to come over here
and do it? I can keep an eye on him then.'

I knew Mark would hate that but at least he'd be involved. 'Yeah. Good idea. I'll ask him.' The album was taking shape.

'I've asked another songwriter to come and meet us today. A guy called Jonathan Cain. Do you know him at all? He used to be in The Babys and now he's in a band called Journey.'

I loved The Babys and had heard of Journey. They were massive in the States but hadn't really worked in Australia.

'I'm going to play you a song of his I want you to do. My idea is to get this guy to produce you.'

He played me a song called 'American Heartbeat'.

'It's okay but it's not really for me. I'm an Australian singer, not American. I'm Scottish too – but "American Heartbeat", I don't think so,' I said.

But Gary had a plan. 'This is America. It's a different market to Australia. I know this market so you have to listen to me. When he comes just tell him you love it and see what happens. I'm asking you to trust me on this one.'

Now Gary had set up a couple of good things already so I felt that I should listen to what he had in mind, even though my instincts were telling me to run home. I was feeling out of my depth and I was trying not to lash out at him, not yet anyway.

An hour later Jonathan turned up at the office. He was dressed in spandex tights and the loudest, tightest-fitting T-shirt I'd ever seen. His hair was perfect, not a hair out of place, and I could have sworn he was wearing makeup. Maybe I imagined the makeup.

We spoke for a while. He obviously loved music and he knew what he was talking about. And even though I wasn't completely convinced, I told him, 'I'll record this song if you'll produce it.'

He agreed. That was one of the best deals I did in America. Jon was a great songwriter and a great guy and it was the start of a beautiful collaboration. I thought in the back of my head that in the end I would leave the track off the record, but when it came down to the final choice I listened to Gary and I left it on. I feel that ultimately that was a mistake. I should always trust my instincts, full stop.

Jon called me a few days after our meeting. He was excited; I could hear it in his voice. 'Hey, Jimmy. You know how we were talking about your audiences? How they're blue-collar folk and salt of the earth and loyal and all that?'

I wondered where this was going. Again I was worried. 'Yeah. I remember, Jon.'

'I've written you a song about them. It's called "Working Class Man". I think it's a smash hit myself. I'll send it to you.'

What was this going to be like? Another 'American Heartbeat'? I was panicked until the song arrived. Jon was right. From the minute I heard the song I knew it was for me. There were a few lines that were too American – 'Across the wild Midwestern sky' for instance – but I would sing it differently when I got the song home. I would make it Australian. I would sing it from an Australian perspective with an Australian attitude. A good song is a good song after all.

So Jon and I went into the studio and cut two songs. The band he put together consisted of Jon on keyboards; Tony Brock, a drummer I loved, who would end up playing in my live band for the next ten years; Randy Jackson, a bass player who played with Aretha Franklin and Keith Richards; and Dave Amato, a great LA guitar player who played with a lot of different bands. The sessions went really well and this became the basis of the band I would use for a few albums.

The next thing I had to do was cut the song I had wrangled out of Chas. Chas wanted to produce it himself and I'm sure he could have done a great job but Gary had another idea. 'Jimmy, I want to get Waddy Wachtel and a few of the guys from Little Feat to play on this with you. I'll get Thom Panunzio to engineer it.'

Thom had a pedigree as long as my arm. Bruce Springsteen, Patti Smith, The Rolling Stones, and I loved Little Feat even though we'd had a run-in with them many years before. So this was exciting. I ended up in the studio with Bill Payne, Kenny Gradney and Sam Clayton, along with Waddy Wachtel and Kim Carnes. I couldn't have been happier. When that was done, I was sent to work with Mark Opitz and Mick Fleetwood and a few friends, Billy Burnette and Charlie Sexton and Kenny Gradney again, and cut 'Ride the Night Away'.

I was in heaven. These were players I had read about since I was a kid. This was as good as it gets. I just had to keep it together. I tried but I'm not sure I did that good a job. Cocaine was easily available in Los Angeles. And I was always ready to drink too much. It was too easy to forget why I was there and just have a good time. But somehow I got things done. Sitting in the studio, with my heart pounding from way too much coke, while trying to speak to these musicians about real music was a challenge. But I did it. Only just.

ONE DAY, AFTER FINISHING recording, I got home and Jane was waiting to go out. 'I just want to catch the shops before they close. The children are asleep. Can you keep an eye on them for a little while?'

I was hardly in the door and Jane had her shoes on and was halfway out. She was obviously in a hurry. On the way out she turned to me. 'Oh yes. Eddie Van Halen called for you. Bye!'

Did I hear her right? 'Wait a minute. What did you say?'

Jane barely stopped. 'Eddie Van Halen called for you and he left his number. It's on the desk. He asked if you would call him back.' And she was gone.

I looked on the desk and there was a number and Eddie's name written down next to it. I called the number and waited for an answer. It must be a joke.

'Hello.' The voice was soft and sweet. It wasn't Eddie. It was a woman.

'Er, yeah. Hi. It's Jimmy Barnes here. I was asked to call this number and talk to Eddie.'

There was a short silence. 'Hi Jimmy, it's Valerie Bertinelli here. Eddie's wife. How are you doing?'

I was confused but I answered, 'I'm fine. Yeah. Fine. And you?' It was a joke. Who was this?

'I'm great. Just hang on and I'll get Eddie.'

I heard her put the phone down and I waited. After about two minutes Eddie came to the phone. 'Hello Jimmy. Thank you for calling. I was wondering if you could come over to my house, I'd like to talk to you about something important.'

Jane was gone. I couldn't drive anywhere because the kids were sleeping. Besides, I'd had a few drinks and I didn't want to risk driving.

'Sorry. Do you mean now?' I said politely.

'Yeah. It would be good if you are available.'

I explained that I was home babysitting and couldn't go anywhere.

Eddie quickly spoke again. 'Well, where are you? I'll come to see you if that's cool.'

I gave him the address. What could this be about? I knew that David Lee Roth was out of his band so I thought maybe he needed a singer for something. I sat and waited. It wasn't long until there was a knock at the door. I opened it and there was Eddie Van Halen and another guy. Eddie mumbled a few introductions that I didn't quite catch. But I think it was himself and Ted Templeman, his producer. We sat down.

'We were wondering if you would be interested in trying out for the band. We need a singer and you come highly recommended.'

They both sat looking at me. I was flattered but a bit rattled at the same time. I had just started my record.

'Listen, I've just left a band after ten years and I'm not really sure I want to join another one, to tell you the truth.' I tried to be as polite as possible. 'But I do love Van Halen and I would love to sing with you. I just started recording my first record for America and I –'

Eddie cut me off. He was a bit erratic and rushed. 'The new band is nothing like Van Halen. We're going to do mainly ballads,' he said, almost under his breath. I got the feeling he wasn't sure what he wanted at that time.

I had to be sure I heard right. 'If you're just doing ballads, I might not be the best man for the job. But I do love your band.'

He stood up as quickly as he'd sat down and headed for the door.

'Hey, but Eddie, if you need someone to scream all over your record, I'm available,' I joked, but he was already halfway out the door and then was gone. What was that? It was like a whirlwind. It was definitely Eddie Van Halen. I knew that because I was a big fan. I sat and tried to digest it all. Eventually Jane came home and I told her the story.

She wasn't that impressed. 'Shall we go out for dinner now?' she said. My Eddie Van Halen story seemed to mean nothing to her. I'm not that sure she knew who he was.

'Sure. What do you want to eat?' I said. We went to dinner. But I couldn't help but wonder if I had imagined the whole thing. I should at least have gone for a sing but it all happened too fast.

THE RECORD WAS READY to be mixed. Gary came through with his promise to get Bob Clearmountain to do it and I travelled to New York to meet him.

Staying at the Ritz Carlton was scary and amazing at the same time. Suddenly having a suite overlooking Central Park blew my mind. The city that never sleeps. Did I need to be here?

I never slept anyway. I had a room full of booze and cocaine and I went crazy. By the time I got to the studio I was almost falling apart. But all I had to do was sit and watch Bob work. It would be easy. Or so I thought. I got to the studio and Bob was waiting, ready to go.

'Hi Jimmy. I've been listening to your stuff and I hear it much different to the way it's been done. I want you to sing it all again.'

I swallowed hard. Was I in a state to sing? I wasn't sure.

'Cool. Whatever you want. I'm ready,' I lied.

Bob wanted me to sing in the control room right next to him. We set up and I thought, since we were going to spend a lot of time together, I should lay it all on the table.

'I like to drink and take the odd bit of drugs while I sing, Bob. Is that cool with you?'

Bob smiled. 'Whatever it takes, Jimmy.'

I emptied my pockets. An ounce of weed and a big bag of coke. I picked up my bag and pulled out a bottle of Stolichnaya, then rubbed my hands together. 'I'm ready when you are,' I announced.

We went about singing the first four songs. Bob couldn't believe how well I sang, especially when he saw what I was consuming. I would roll a joint and light it up, then pour a drink and lay out about a gram of cocaine – smoking, snorting and drinking all at the same time. Bob did none of this stuff. He was dead straight. I'd sing one song and then Bob would chop up the multitrack tape and rearrange the song on the spot. He was like a surgeon. It was amazing. I'd never seen an engineer work like this. In Australia, we used razor blades for chopping other things, not the master tapes.

By the end of the first night we had completed four songs. Bob turned to me and smiled. 'I don't know how you did that. I've worked with a lot of great singers but none have worked as fast as you. I just finished an album with David Bowie and he took a month to sing one song. You just did four in a night. That's unbelievable. Get some sleep and I'll see you tomorrow.'

I bounced off the walls as I left the studio, looking for my hotel suite and any trouble I could find along the way.

Next day Bob looked worried. He asked me, 'Could you take drugs in a different room? They really affected me, I don't know why. I couldn't sleep.' He had bags under his eyes.

'No worries, mate.'

The album was finished in five days and I headed back to Australia to await the outcome. Would Gary like it, or would it all be too wild for him? Would Michael think we had a chance or had I missed the mark? And would Jane think I had done well and see how hard I had worked for us? I'd have to wait and see.

The album *For the Working Class Man* came out in Australia in May 1985 and entered the charts at number one. Mark Pope and I came up with the ideas for the 'Working Class Man' film clip and the tour that followed. He helped me fight with Mushroom to bring the record out at the right discount price. Because most of the material had been out already on *Bodyswerve*, we wanted it kept below thirteen dollars. This was a big deal for a double album at that time. The whole concept of giving something back to the punters was a big part of its success.

Unfortunately, things didn't go as well in America. In the end, the album was too Australian; we hadn't changed it enough to make it suit the US market. But what we had done was kick my career in Australia into the next gear.

------

CHAPTER TWENTY-EIGHT

this business is full of crooks

A NOTE ON MONEY

Music is a business. Don't let anyone tell you it's not. If you don't want to be in the business, then get a little band and play in your garage. If you want someone to sink money into what you're doing, then be prepared to work. It's hard work, but like any hard work if you do it right it will pay off. Now I say that with reservations. Paying off might not mean fame and money. Paying off will mean you will get good at what you do. And if you love what you are doing enough to stick with it, you will be happy. There are a lot of bands and musicians who never make a cent and are perfectly happy.

Back in Australia, things kept getting bigger and bigger. Record sales, concert ticket sales. The family was growing, the house needed to be bigger. My drug use was slowly becoming more of a problem, as was my drinking. But the thing I noticed most was my debts were growing. The more I earned the more I spent. Our little country house was becoming too small for my growing family. We were spending a lot of time down in the country although we were still renting a house in Sydney. We didn't want to be in the city that much and we both knew more babies were on the way.

Fred Legg had been married to Millie, a friend of Jane's, for many years. He was an excellent builder and we decided that he would help us with our extensions. Fred was a top-quality operator and we knew that what we wanted would not come cheap. But after all, this was our home. I wanted it to be perfect, although the idea of finding enough money for the extensions was making me lose sleep. I would have to work harder.

I was already away far too much. Jane and the kids stayed at home while I worked. This was causing problems. My dual personality was running wild. It got harder to come back to being a loving father and husband after coming off the road. I was damaging our lives.

FRED DID A MAGNIFICENT job and we moved back into stage two of our little country home. It wasn't quite as small anymore but it still had all its charm. The family was happy to be home. I toured and worked all over the country. Along the way I found I had to change management. Steve decided he'd been in the music business long enough and retired back to the country. Even with Steve's history of wild investment banking and the CIA, the music industry had worn him down.

'This business is full of crooks with no morals, Jimmy. I'm finished with it,' he said one day. I thanked him. If it hadn't been for Steve I'm not sure I would have been ready to get back into the swing of things. He gave me confidence. Especially with money.

Money had always been a source of pain for me. Not having it reminded me of my childhood. I could still feel the shame of begging for money from the neighbours so that my brothers and sisters and I could eat. Or my mum crying every day, scratching to find enough money to put clothes on our backs. But having money opened up another can of worms. I didn't know how to manage it. The more money I had, the more trouble I got into.

I remember one day when I was stressing about the finance for my house, Steve pointed out, 'You know, Jimmy, these guys in the bank just work there. It's not their fucking money. They are paid to be there for you, so in reality they work for you. That's the attitude you have to have when you deal with these bastards.'

I wasn't sure, but I trusted him. He was confident and calm about all the things that stressed me out. Particularly money. I think it's easier to be confident when you have money or you're used to having money. But I of course was always expecting it all to disappear, leaving me with nothing. This reappearing theme ran throughout my life.

'How much do you need? Half a million? Fuck them, just ask for a million. They'll give it to you without a fight.'

He was right. The house was financed and I was up to my ears in debt before I could say, help! But Steve left and I had to fill the hole in my management. Steve had got on well with my agents, Mark Pope and Richard MacDonald, and he thought Mark was capable of taking over the job. Mark liked Steve and had worked closely with him, helping him with things he didn't know about the music industry. Mark became my manager.

I remember overhearing them talk one day. Mark was trying to dig into Steve's somewhat mysterious past.

'So what exactly was your business before managing Jimmy again, Steve?' he casually asked, waiting for Steve to give away his darkest secrets.

'If you must know, I was in the iron and steel business.'

Mark was shocked. 'You were in mining? I thought it was banking.' Steve was even more mysterious than Mark thought.

'Yeah, that's right. My wife stays home and irons and I go out and steal. Are you satisfied now?'

CHAPTER TWENTY-NINE

harder than Chinese algebra

TOURING, 1986

M Y BAD HABITS WERE getting worse. Everything I was consuming was taking a toll on me. I was slow out of the gates. The shows lacked impact. It took me half the show to get over my hangover, and then in the second half I was too pissed to really fire up. I needed to do something to keep fit.

I had met a lot of guys who did martial arts over the years, working backstage and so on, but there was one guy who I thought was the best. His name was Noel Watson. All his mates called him Crazy Horse, because he was completely crazy when he lost it. Noel was harder than Chinese algebra, but I had never seen him lose it. I rang him and asked him if he would come on the road and train me. I thought that getting fit would help me straighten myself up a bit, and I needed someone tough to make me do it. And Noel was about the toughest guy I had ever come across. He worked the doors at the clubs around Perth. I had seen him fight but it was always measured. He only used whatever force was completely necessary. I had seen a lot of guys who just went nuts and beat people half to death. Noel wasn't like that at all, he was vicious but fair.

I used to ask him about working doors. 'How do you deal with these big guys that come through here? Doesn't it worry you?'

He just looked at me and smiled. 'The bigger they are, the easier they are to hit.' I got the feeling he liked the challenge.

'There are certain places nobody can build muscle, Jimmy. You just got to know where they are and belt them where it hurts. Then it's just like chopping down trees. *Bang-bang-bang* and they all fall.'

I thought Noel could be security at night and train me during the day. Noel took his job very seriously. No one, and I mean no one, got near me unless Noel cleared it with me first. I came out of shows to find record company people standing outside in the rain. I would ask Noel, 'Hey mate, why are these people outside the gig? They're my record company and my mates.'

He would look me in the eye and calmly say, 'You said no one backstage so I threw them out.'

So I had to be very specific with what I asked of Noel. He ended up being my best mate on the road. We would get up in the morning and no matter how hungover I was, he would make me run for miles and miles. Then we started to train, kicking bags until I felt my legs were going to snap. Punching pads until I could no longer lift my arms. Then we would go for lunch. He made me eat healthy and kept me in line. Well, at least until night-time, and then I did whatever I wanted. Night-time was my time. Noel would walk behind me, cleaning up the mayhem I left in my wake. When it got too wild for him he'd say, 'I reckon we should call it a night now, Jim, or we'll all get killed.'

I would go home with him and then sneak out after he had gone to bed and continue on my rampage. But I got fit, regardless of how much I drank or snorted. I was doing hundreds of push-ups and running for miles and throwing thousands of kicks. But I needed to be more than fit. I needed to meditate, not medicate.

IN ORDER TO MAKE things work in America, Gary Gersh needed to get me under control. My manager Mark Pope didn't know the American market. Besides, Geffen felt he was a liability. He couldn't get me on track. Then again, they thought that anybody they didn't control was a liability. Gary looked for US management that would be tough and that knew how to sell records in the States.

He came up with a couple of Canadian guys who were connected and happening in America. Bruce Allen had managed Bachman-Turner Overdrive. But he didn't have time to manage me on his own so he recruited another Canadian manager to help him, Lou Blair. Lou was a big likeable guy who managed Loverboy. He was the size of a fridge and tough as nails but a teddy bear inside. They both liked my singing and wanted to be involved if they could get me under control. Better men have tried and failed, might I add. No one could control me. Never could and never will. The only one who had a chance of controlling me was me. And I wasn't equipped emotionally or mentally to do it yet. These guys didn't stand a chance.

They secured me a number of dates throughout America supporting ZZ Top, starting January 1986. The promoter was a guy named Don Fox. He owned Beaver Productions and was very close to Bruce and Lou. Don had started out in the music business as a doorman in clubs around Chicago. He was a tough guy. So between Bruce, Lou and Don Fox, I think Gary had the toughest guys in North America ready to set me out on the right path, if I would listen.

The management wanted the band to be clean and together and they didn't want to pay them a lot of money. This would cause problems for me from the start. I had become very close with Tony Brock, who drummed on *For the Working Class Man*, and with Randy Jackson, who played bass. Both of these guys wanted to play the songs live because they liked the record we made. But the management didn't want a bar of them. Tony liked to party with me, so they weren't having him anywhere near the tour, or me for that matter. Randy, they said, was a liability in middle America because he was black. When I heard this I wanted to sack them on the spot. I had never heard people talk like this before in my life. I was furious. Gary calmed me down by telling me I had heard them wrong and besides, Randy was doing other things and wasn't available. I knew what I'd heard but I didn't want to fight with Gary. I should have sacked them then and there and I regret that I didn't. They wanted to put together a band out of Vancouver, guys they could control and trust to set me straight. I didn't like it. I wanted to bring my live band from Australia but this was out of the question.

I was touring in Australia until just before the ZZ tour started, so the band they hired started rehearsing even before I met them. I had never hired a band sight unseen before, or since come to think of it, so I was deeply concerned. But the management insisted. This was the only chance I had to get *For the Working Class Man* out to the people who would buy it. I knew that Geffen was on the verge of dropping the ball, so I agreed.

I arrived in Vancouver with Noel. Noel was my safety net. He was as straight as they come, didn't take any drugs, so I knew they couldn't say no to him being there.

We went into Bruce Allen's office to say hello. 'Hi Bruce. I'm ready to start touring. Oh, by the way, this is Noel, my karate instructor.'

Bruce was behind his desk. There a heavy punching bag swinging behind him. I believe that when he wanted to intimidate people at meetings, he got up and punched it. He didn't move when we walked in.

'Hey Barnes.'

Canadians tend to call people by their last names.

'Hey Barnes. Let me talk to you alone for a minute.'

He looked at me and then at Noel and then looked down at his desk.

'Yeah, no worries mate. I'll wait outside,' Noel piped up and walked out, never taking his eyes off Bruce for a second.

'What the fuck is this supposed to be? You're here to tour, not fuck around punching things.'

I was surprisingly calm. 'Look Bruce, if you want me out on the road with a bunch of strangers, this is how I'm going to do it. Noel and I can train every day and keep it together for the shows, okay?'

Bruce didn't like it, but he agreed and motioned for Noel to come back in. 'Listen here, karate boy. You better fucking do your job or I'll come out there and show you how real men fucking fight. Do you understand?' Bruce stood up and started punching his bag.

Noel's face went red. 'You listen, motherfucker. You speak to me that way again and I'll shove that heavy bag up your fucking arse. Do you understand?' Noel leaned on the desk.

'Settle down. I know you'll do a good job. I was just setting the ground rules.' Bruce was backpedalling as fast as he could without losing face and I knew it, so I jumped in to help.

I grabbed Noel's arm, which was rigid. He was ready to jump the desk and kill my new manager. 'Thanks Bruce. Noel and I appreciate your concern and you don't have to worry about us, okay?' I slowly pulled Noel back from the desk and from certain death for Bruce and my career in America. At the very least, Bruce came very close to losing his teeth that day.

'If that motherfucker ever talks to me like that again, I will rip him apart,' Noel said as we walked out of the office.

'I know, man. I know.'

THE BAND WERE ALL great players but they played a lot lighter than I was accustomed to, so for three days I screamed like a banshee at them. 'If you guys play like a bunch of pussies out there on stage with me, I will kill you.'

They got the message. By the time we hit the road they were a lot tougher. Still not like my Australian band, but I liked the guys and they worked really hard to get things together.

I remember they were styled by Big Lou. Now Lou was a good guy but I'm not sure he was known for his style, so it took a bit of fighting until they looked okay. Jeff Neill, the guitar player, wore the same thing every night. Jeans and a cut-off black T-shirt. I could deal with that. He looked and played like a rock musician. It was him and me up front and we became good friends. Jeff went on to move to Australia for many years, playing with me and writing songs. He played hard and loud. Every night on stage he put it all out there, leaving nothing in the tank for later. That's why Jeff was the only one from the Canadian band who I kept on.

But on tour things didn't go that easy. The rest of the band played very well but there was something missing. They had all the moves and sounds but they didn't hit hard enough. I thought that like most North American bands I'd seen, they had more front than grunt. And I needed more. I felt naked out there. I was alone.

ZZ's crowd were a lot like Cold Chisel's crowd, or my crowd at home. They were there for one reason and one reason only. To see ZZ. I could understand that but I wasn't used to it. Plus, like I said, I was training four hours a day and drinking heavily and using coke most nights. So I was a tad aggressive.

We were playing a lot of shows in ice-skating rinks in towns like Bismarck, North Dakota. They would cover the ice with wood and set up on top. It was midwinter so the shows were freezing cold. The temperature didn't get above freezing and the wind chill outside was twenty below. ZZ's crowd were hoons. I know this because most of my crowd were the same, wild bastards out for a good time. After one or two songs they didn't recognise, they got bored and started throwing coins at the band. One night I had had enough.

'Throw them again and I'll jump off this stage and fucking smash you,' I yelled at the audience. The crowd let out a roar and *bang!* I was hit by about thirty coins. I was about to jump when the Canadian tour manager grabbed me, trying desperately to keep me on stage and out of jail. I wanted to kill them but bit my lip and kept singing. When I came off stage one of ZZ's crew took me aside and tried to console me. He had a Southern drawl and was a good guy.

'You know, Jimmy, here in America people are just like that. They will throw shit at you if they don't know you. We all have to go through it. So relax man, and have a drink and sit up here side of stage with me and watch the show.'

I went to the bus and snorted about two grams of coke and grabbed a large vodka and went side of stage ready to look for the arseholes that were throwing shit. But I got sidetracked by Billy Gibbons. He played guitar so well I couldn't take my eyes off him. I got over it, until next time.

WE HARDLY EVER HAD hotel rooms. The management were saving money by keeping us on the tour bus. This meant we would do a show, travel all night to the next town and then hang around all day in the backstage area, waiting to play again. This went on for months. I would have gone crazy had Noel not been there.

Every day we would wake up and look out the window and try to work out where the fuck we were. We'd go inside to the backstage and shower and then Noel would crack the whip.

'Right, boy. Let's run.'

And out into the snow we would go. Running five to ten miles a day, the wind cutting through the scarf I had wrapped around my face and biting at my skin.

'Keep up. If you stop now, you'll fucking die out here,' Noel would shout over the wind. Then we would sprint back to the gig and find a space somewhere in the backstage area to train. Next Noel would make me go through my katas, a series of movements strung together into a sort of dance – only this dance, when done properly, was the choreography to a deadly attack or a way to repel multiple attackers. Each movement took different stances that I had to hold until my legs burned. Each stance held the secret to a way to disarm an opponent. Then *snap!* A combination of punches and kicks would bring you back to the centre, ready for the next assault. I loved it. I loved having some sort of discipline in my life. I had to focus or else Noel would work me over. He never beat me up, but he made me feel a lot of pain just by the workload he put on me. I can look back at those times and see that Noel kept me alive. No one else on the road had any control over me. Especially myself. But Noel got me up and kicked my arse every day. I wish I'd had a better attitude when I was learning all of this. It could have been more useful to me. But I didn't.

We would eat lunch and then take it easy for a while. Around three o'clock Noel would get me into another session. 'Come on, Jim. You can't be a ninja if you don't train hard.'

We used to go at it for about four hours a day. Every day. Lifting weights, punching focus pads and kicking for hours. The roadies from ZZ would wander over to check us out. 'What are you crazy Australian fuckers doing over here?'

Noel would turn to them. 'Fuck off or we'll use you as the punching bag, fat boy. Okay?'

They never bothered us again. Dusty, the bass player, came over wanting to train but we scared him off. I remember he was watching and every time I took my eyes off what Noel was trying to teach me, Noel made me do fifty push-ups.

'Get down and give me fifty, motherfucker.'

I dropped to the ground and struggled through them.

'Don't you look at these other guys. I'm the one teaching you. You concentrate on what we're doing. Understand?'

I would be dragging myself up. 'Yeah, I got it,' I would say under my breath.

'Hey, look at me. Do you understand?' He was very serious about this.

'Yes, sensei,' I would shout. And we would be back into class. No one wanted to train with us after a while. They all kept their distance.

By seven o'clock I was pumped and ready to perform. Noel had done his work and he would leave me to get ready. As soon as he was gone I would start drinking and snorting lashings of coke and by eight o'clock I was crazed.

I WAS MISSING MY family. Jane couldn't come out on tour with me straightaway as we were just about to have another baby. It was so hard to leave home and miss the birth but the US management had made it clear that I either started the tour when I was booked or I didn't do it at all. This was the only chance I had to take on America live. So I went. Bruce and Lou were old-school managers. Women didn't belong on the road anyway, as far as they were concerned. They wanted me working hard and chasing girls, all the things that rock singers were supposed to do. But I knew that I needed Jane and the family with me or I would fall apart. Being alone reminded me of being a kid. That feeling of emptiness was back and I drank more to try to drown it out. I needed my Jane with me.

Jackie was born in February 1986. Jackie was a big baby. He weighed eight-pounds-ten. Not big by my standards – I weighed fourteen pounds. So, no one was big compared to me. But he was our biggest baby. He came on tour at the age of two weeks. From the safety of home straight out into the Chicago winter with a wind chill temperature of thirty below. Maybe that's why Jackie still loves playing shows in new places every night.

He is soft and gentle. Growing up with three sisters taught him how to be respectful of girls, and besides, his sisters were much tougher than he was and would have killed him if he wasn't. Everybody loves Jackie. He is a good boy, smart and very, very talented. Jackie is over six feet tall – by the time he was fifteen he towered over me. He doesn't get his size from me or my side of the family. I don't know many tall Glaswegians. We are all well below six feet. We think it comes from Jane's Chinese grandfather, who was six-feet-four. So, Jackie looks like a tall, Asian version of me.

I HAD TO FIGHT with the management to get Jane and the kids out to the US. For it to work with Jane, and the three kids, and Anne Maree the nanny from Jindabyne, and Noel all with me, we needed another tour bus. It would cost at least another thirty thousand dollars. I didn't care, I wanted them with me. The management weren't happy.

Towards the end of the tour they tried to get me to send Jane home again, rather than rehire the extra bus. But I insisted they stay. One day I was in a limousine with Lou Blair, on the way from one of the few hotels we stayed at to a show, when we started fighting.

'Barnes, it's time to send your wife home and get down to some real work,' Lou said to me in as strict a voice as he could manage.

'It's Jimmy.'

Lou stopped talking and looked at me. 'What?'

I said again, 'It's Jimmy.'

He acted like nothing had happened. 'So, Barnes. What's it going to be? Are you going to send her home or what?'

I looked him straight in the eye. 'It's Jimmy, and no I'm not.'

Lou's blood pressure was rising. I could see his face reddening. 'What is this, Barnes? Some kind of fucking Yoko Ono thing?'

He had crossed the line. I'd had enough. I already felt bad about letting them talk shit about Randy Jackson. I would not put up with them talking about my wife.

'Driver. Stop the fucking car. You, get out of here. We're finished. This is over. I will have my new manager contact you guys and sort out the details later. Get out. And it's Jimmy by the way, not fucking Barnes, okay?'

I didn't have a new manager, but I wasn't going to tell him that. Without the clout of Bruce and Lou, Geffen gave up on the tour support and this album was over. They didn't drop me from the label – for some reason they wanted me to stay – but it would never be the same after this.

CHAPTER THIRTY

chemicals can do strange and wonderful things

HELL, 1986–87

Mark Pope and Chris Murphy, the manager of INXS, came up with the idea for a tour called Australian Made. The concept came from the widespread misconception that overseas bands were better at filling halls than Australian bands. Mark and Chris thought differently. They knew I was filling every stadium I played in, as were INXS. So they put together a bill to prove their point. Australian Made featured myself, INXS, Divinyls, Mental as Anything, The Saints, Models, I'm Talking and The Triffids. It was a great bill and marked a change in attitudes towards Australian acts. The tour, which ran from December 1986 to January 1987, didn't sell as many tickets as the promoters would have liked. Does any tour sell as many tickets as the promoter would like? But music in this country was viewed in a different light from then on.

INXS and myself decided to record a song to promote the tour. We booked ourselves into Rhinoceros Studios in Sydney and started to look for a song. Glenn A. Baker, the well-known rock historian and uber music fan, came up with the idea of 'Good Times'. The song had been written by The Easybeats and recorded in England. It featured Steve Marriott on backing vocals. As soon as I heard it I knew it was the one. We all did. This was the perfect song to celebrate the good times we all were having, although in reality I wasn't having a good time at all.

We spent a day and a half in the studio recording the song, writing the B-side and mixing the tracks. Michael Hutchence and myself didn't sleep the whole time we were there. It was a booze- and drug-fuelled couple of days. On the last day we made a film clip for the song. The clip features us playing live in the studio and generally going crazy, smashing the place up a bit.

When I see that clip now, I know at that time I could see over the edge of the precipice. I was standing right on the edge of a cliff with no way out but down. Success, excess and addiction were staring me in the face. They had been for a long time, but now they were calling me to take that final step. I was afraid but I didn't want to stop and think. There was too much to answer for. There was no going back. So I didn't just step, I jumped in head first without a second thought.

Fame can be tough. I made so many decisions before I even thought about consequences. If the world was screaming out my name I would be all right. But things were beginning to unravel. I was falling apart. I could see it every time I looked into my eyes in the mirror. So I stopped looking. I just went for it. This was a pivotal time in my life. I wonder if Hutch felt like this too? He must have. But I wasn't going to ask him. I wasn't going to talk to anyone about any of this stuff for a long, long time. If I never had to talk to anyone about any of it, I'd be happy. It was best kept hidden away deep inside of me. Festering.

BACK IN AMERICA, GEFFEN had big ideas for my next record. They felt they'd started behind the eight ball with the first record because I did most of it in Australia. That would all be rectified this time round. Gary Gersh wanted me to record in the States under his supervision. Gary was still waiting on that big album that would secure his position at Geffen Records, so money was no object. He was willing to pay whatever it took.

I was being introduced to the cream of the North American songwriting crop, so I had to be on top of my game. I was worried. What was the top of my game? Had I ever been on top of my game? I don't think that happened until many years later.

Gary Gersh had started the ball rolling with Jonathan Cain on the *For The Working Class Man* album and now it was time for his plan to come to fruition. Jon would write or at least cowrite and produce the next album. Gary had organised all this without talking to me that much. I didn't mind because I thought that Jon and I would work well together.

I started writing with Jon in San Francisco. I stayed in a hotel not too far from him. He lived on the outskirts of what I think was the Napa Valley, at a place called Novato. Every morning I would fall out of bed, work out where the fuck I was and then drive over to Jon's house to write. We would spend the early part of the day writing and then, later in the afternoon, drive over the bridge to Oakland. There we would go into a studio owned by Neal Schon, who played guitar with Journey, and work up whatever song we had come up with that morning with the band that Jon had put together. The band consisted of Tony Brock on drums, Randy Jackson on bass, Neal Schon on guitar and Jon on keys. Now this was a smoking band. I couldn't believe how great these players were. They took every song we wrote and within minutes had it sounding polished. Jon's playing was impeccable, and then there was Neal. I hadn't heard a guitar player with so much raw talent in a long time. Everything he played was exceptional. I knew that the record was going to be great.

Each morning Jon would meet me at the door of his house, dressed in spandex tights, like the pants that bike riders wear. Only Jon didn't ride a bike. He always had his German shepherd next to him and he held a large, and I mean very large, cup of coffee in his hand. I got the feeling that it wasn't his first cup for the day either. The dog looked like it had been drinking coffee too, eyes darting from Jon to me and then back to Jon. He would bring me in and offer me a coffee so I could catch up to him and then *bang!* We would start work.

He was a creature of habit. So was I, but his habits seemed slightly healthier than mine. Each day on the drive to Oakland he would stop his sports car at the Burger King drive-thru and order the same thing. Six mini hamburgers for him. Six for me whether I wanted them or not, and six for the dog, who was sitting on the back seat that was too small for a human being, right behind my head. The dog by this time was practically drooling on me. If I couldn't face the burgers, the dog always wanted more.

'You know, Jimmy, there's something about the chemicals in junk food that really get the creative juices flowing. Have you noticed that?' Jon would say.

I had similar theories. 'Yeah, chemicals can do strange and wonderful things, all right.'

On one of these drives Jon was grilling me, wanting a title for our next song. 'Come on, Jimmy. We need something to write about tomorrow. If you can come up with something, I can work on it overnight. Come on, give me an idea, man.'

The car was very small and the highway was full of big trucks. I was stressed by all the traffic, looking around and punching my foot to the floor on the brake pedal that wasn't there. 'What about a truck-driving song?' I suggested, as the sixteen wheels from a passing truck almost killed us. 'Shit, did you see the size of those wheels?'

Jon slowed down. 'Good idea. Truck driving. Big wheels. Rolling wheels. Driving wheels. I'm onto it, Jim.' He patted the dog, smiled at me and planted his foot to the floor.

After about a week we had enough songs for an album. But Gary wanted me to write with a few other guys too. So I said bye to California and headed up to Canada to write with Bryan Adams and Jim Vallance. As it happened, Bryan had been called away on tour and I was left with Jim. Jim was the quiet one of the songwriting team but he was very good at his craft. We started a few songs. One of them became 'I'm Still on your Side', a song that gave me the title of the album. 'Sometimes I feel like shoutin', Feels like a freight train in my heart.' My heart pounded most nights as I tried to sleep and kept on pounding when I wished it would stop. I was on track for a disaster and I knew it, but I couldn't stop. These lines in this song defined me as a person for a long time.

The other song we wrote for the album was 'Lessons in Love'. But the songs weren't finished by the time I left, so I had to finish them with Jon when I saw him next. Jon dragged lyrics out of me that I would have been scared to write by myself. He could see me and wanted me to write the truth.

FROM SAN FRANCISCO I went home, where Gary had organised for me to hook up with one of the biggest writers they had to offer. Desmond Child had started his career as a singer in the band Desmond Child and Rouge, but he had really found his feet as a writer. He had written for a lot of bands by the time I met him: Aerosmith's 'Dude (Looks Like a Lady)', Bon Jovi's 'Livin' on a Prayer' and Kiss's 'I Was Made for Lovin' You' were all huge hits. Desmond's songs were being sung in pubs and clubs all over the world, and as far as writers went, he was on top of the pile.

Desmond came out to Australia to write with a few people, and it was organised for him to meet me in Bowral. I spoke to Desmond and he seemed very quiet but nice.

'How are you getting down to my place?' I finally asked him.

'Oh, don't worry about me. I'll catch the train. It'll give me time to clear my head,' he very calmly said.

'Okay, I'll pick you up,' I offered.

'Oh thanks, that's very nice of you.'

I had never met Desmond before so I said, 'Hey Desmond. What do you look like? I don't know you.'

He laughed and said, 'Oh yeah, of course you don't. I'll be wearing purple. See you at the station.'

He gave me the time and hung up. He'd be wearing purple. Purple what? Shirt? Pants? A jumper? What? I guessed I would have to wait until he got there. I arrived at the station in Bowral just before the train.

There were a few country blokes standing around. 'Gudday, Barnesy. What are you doing in this neck of the woods?' one said.

I didn't want to get into a conversation. I said, 'Just picking up a mate from Sydney.'

He kept talking. 'Is it anybody I know? A rock star or something? Ha ha ha.'

I had to laugh. 'No mate, it's a songwriter from America, if you really want to know.'

He looked interested. 'Hmm. A songwriter, eh?' The train pulled in, cutting the conversation short. 'Right, see ya later then, Barnesy.'

I nodded. By this time, I was looking for Desmond. There was a bloke in moleskin pants who looked like he was being met by a horse. That definitely wasn't him. There was an old lady. That wasn't him. I was about to give up when at the end of the platform I spotted him. He didn't walk like the other people on the platform. He walked with a Los Angeles gait, light and careful where he trod. He was wearing purple. Purple shorts. Purple socks. Purple shoes and a purple shirt. Oh, and a purple beret.

'You must be Desmond,' I said as I walked up.

'Yes I am. How did you know?'

I smiled. 'Just a guess.'

I picked up Desmond's purple bag and we headed for the car. In the carpark the bloke from the platform was loading his mate with the moleskin pants into his car.

'Songwriter, eh?' He grinned. Desmond had hit the Southern Highlands.

Desmond was an unusual character to say the least, but a sweet man. He was immediately taken in by my family. Desmond taught Jane how to make red beans and rice, a Cuban speciality he had learned from his mother. Then we got stuck into writing. We wrote the song 'Waiting for the Heartache'. Then he played me 'Walk On', a song he had written with Joe Lynn Turner. Both songs sounded great, but I knew there would be problems because Desmond made it clear that he only wrote songs for people if he produced them too, and Jon had told me he was producing the whole album. I would work this out with Gary later.

THE ALBUM WOULD BE recorded in two places: upstate New York at Bearsville Studios near Woodstock with Desmond, and the Record Plant in Sausalito, California, with Jon. Desmond wanted to make the entire record and so did Jon. But I managed to keep them both happy. Each recorded the songs they wrote with me. It wasn't ideal but it worked. I started in Sausalito with Jon. The Record Plant had a history. Fleetwood Mac, Santana, The Grateful Dead, Sly and the Family Stone had all recorded in the room we used. Jim Gaines was the engineer. Jim had worked for

Stax and with all sorts of amazing artists including Otis Redding. He had a million stories to tell me. He didn't mind that I got wasted.

'Hell, Jimmy, I've seen the best of them get smashed while they work. For a while this studio used to have nitrous oxide tanks outside, with pipes running the stuff straight into the control room. There were masks hanging from the ceiling and you could just grab one and float away. You ain't that bad, let me tell you.'

Mid-recording with Jon, we took a break and headed to New York to work with Desmond. Bearsville Studios had been built by Bob Dylan's old manager, Albert Grossman. It had a great history too. Everyone from Dylan to The Band, Alice Cooper, 10CC and even Divinyls recorded there.

Jane and I flew to New York and then had a car drive us up to Woodstock. I was expecting to see hippies everywhere. There was definitely still a bit of counterculture within the community but it had been softened by time. They now drove cars instead of riding bikes, and the peace and love had been replaced by commercialism. You could still buy peace signs in the shops but they were very expensive, and the tofu served in the Chinese restaurant we ate at was perfectly carved in the shape of a fish and cost much more than any vegetable dish on the menu. The hippies had grown up, and instead of handing out flowers, they wanted their fair share of what was there to be had. But I could still feel the underlying history. For that weekend of the festival, the town must have been amazing.

Jane and I stayed in the accommodation at Bearsville Studios, which according to everyone who worked there was haunted. There were marks on the door of our room. We were told to leave it open, otherwise the local ghost would come and stab the door with a kitchen knife. I slept with one eye open. I'm scared of the dark at the best of times but knife-wielding ghosts only make me worse. If Jane hadn't been there with me I would have got no sleep at all. Not just because of the ghosts, but because I never slept a lot when Jane wasn't there.

The studio was isolated, which worked out for the better. I could not buy cocaine. Desmond didn't drink or take any drugs so the sessions went really well. I was a little edgy but we got through it. After all, vodka was easy to find.

I remember one night doing vocals, Desmond trying to pull more emotion out of my performance. He stood two feet in front of me while I was singing, pulling broken faces and staring at me with his sad Cuban eyes.

'Hey Desmond. I really appreciate what you're trying to do, but I can't sing with you looking at me like that.'

Desmond smiled at me. 'If you sing it properly I'll leave you alone.'

I sang it the way he wanted and Desmond kept his word and left me alone in the vocal booth. 'If you need help I'll come back in, okay?'

I think that I was a bit wilder than a lot of the singers he'd worked with before, but we hit it off. He liked me and I liked him.

So then it was back to finish the album in San Francisco. Jon was a little touchy about me working with another producer but he got over it.

While I was away things had taken a turn in the studio. He'd done most of the overdubs that we had left and was pretty well ready to start vocals. We were recording the vocals for 'Too Much Ain't Enough' when I noticed a new gadget in the control room.

'What's that box, Jon?' I asked.

'It's the singing machine.' I think that's what he called it. 'Steve Perry and I use this when we record. You'll love it.'

I sang a few takes of 'Too Much' and then Jon spoke to me through the headphones. 'Yeah. That's good. Now go away for a few hours and I'll make you sound great.'

What did he mean? Either he liked my vocal or he didn't. You can't make a bad vocal sound great. I left in a huff and returned four hours later. Jon was sitting in the control room with a big smile on his face.

'Hey. Wait until you hear this.'

He played the song. When I'd left I'd had a vocal that sounded rough and heartfelt, like Otis Redding or something. What he played sounded like Barry Manilow.

'What did you do to my vocal?' I asked.

'This baby here fixed it. The old singing machine.'

The singing machine, I found out, was a little mixer that you sent the vocal through. It gave you the capability to make every syllable perfectly in tune.

'I don't like it. All the character is gone.' I was worried and slowly working myself into a frenzy.

'Well, you'll have to learn to like it because this is how we're doing your vocals, Jimmy. I think it's much better this way.'

I sat and thought for a second, my blood boiling. 'You're not doing that to my singing. I'm taking the album somewhere else to finish.' And as usual I stormed off out of the building. I rang Gary Gersh and told him what was happening.

Gary reassured me. 'Just come down and I'll find someone else to do the work for us. It'll all be all right.'

I got on the first plane to LA. Things didn't work out. When I got there Gary told me, 'I've got a great engineer coming in, a guy called Terry Manning. But I need you to come in first so we can talk over a few things.'

So into Gary's office I went.

Gary sat in his office, with a slightly worried look on his face. 'You know, Jimmy, the record is going great but there are a couple of songs that I think you should get rid of.'

I was shocked. I thought all the songs were good.

'Just hear me out. "Lessons in Love" and "Still on Your Side" aren't good enough.'

I was beginning to boil again.

'But don't stress. We'll talk about it when Terry comes in. He's waiting outside right now.'

Terry Manning came in and we were introduced. I could hardly concentrate. I was furious. Terry was the first to speak. 'I listened to the material and I have to say there are a few great songs here.'

Gary smiled at me, trying to cheer me up. 'Which songs do you like the most?' he asked.

Terry looked at me, smiling, and said, 'I think "Lessons in Love" is a smash.'

Gary turned to me and said, 'I was just saying that to Jimmy before you came in.'

The room went into slow motion. Did I hear him right? What the fuck was he talking about? Gary and Terry went on talking but I didn't hear a word.

I stood up. 'You're a lying bastard,' I screamed at Gary. 'Fuck you and your company. I'm taking this record back to Australia to finish.' And I left. Stormed back to the hotel and rounded up Jane, the kids and Jane's mum and we jumped on the first plane back to Sydney.

I DO FEEL BAD it didn't work out. Gary Gersh put a lot of hard work into me and for that alone I wish we'd done better. Getting the chance to work with him was a big opportunity, and I can look back now and say I wish I had done more with that chance. But he introduced me to the cream of the music industry and I owe a lot of what I have today to our work together. Even though he had signed big acts, in America, you are only as good as your last record. Gary, in signing me, put his career on the line and I really appreciate that. But I couldn't stay with that label. They didn't know me or get me.

Wipe the slate clean and start again. I felt the need to do this over and over again. Don't ask me why. When too much bad blood builds up – be it with management, agents, record companies, bands, songwriters, girls or friends – it's time to walk away.

Gary didn't panic when I stormed off. He waited for me to finish the album at home. I had the feeling it was already over but they had spent too much money just to throw the record away. Gary was still under pressure.

I hired a great mix engineer called Mike Stone out of England and with the help of a few friends – including Mark Lizotte, who I will talk about a little later on, and the amazing Brewster brothers from The Angels – I finished the album. *Freight Train Heart* hit the top of the Australian charts the week it came out, late in 1987. I was flying. In every way. I was riding high on the charts as an artist and I was personally as high as a kite.

CHAPTER THIRTY-ONE

what's it going to take

AND BACK, MOSTLY 1988

'I'M HOMICIDAL, NOT SUICIDAL,' I used to joke whenever I would hear about some poor soul ending it all. 'Why would I want to hurt myself? What have I done wrong? Nothing.'

I've never felt so bad about anything that I'd want to end it all. Life is good. Well. I do remember sitting by the sea, thinking about swimming out as far as I could swim. I hadn't really thought about getting back. But that doesn't count. I was a kid, for fuck sake. Kids do stupid things. Anyway, I never did it. I was too scared. So that doesn't count.

I must admit that when I climbed out the window at night when I was little, I knew there was a chance that someone could hurt me, even kill me, but I didn't care. What did I have to lose then? Nothing. No one would have cared if I had died anyway. No, I was all right.

I once sat on cliffs at the South Head of Sydney Harbour, drinking whisky. It was late at night and I was alone. But my friends were at a party across the road. They knew where I was. I was sure I'd mentioned it to them. 'I'm just going across the road to look at the sea. I'll be back.' I was sure I said that.

It was dark and I couldn't see anything but I could feel the waves crashing onto the rocks below me. They came in sets. I liked sitting there alone, counting them. Then there would be nothing, just for a second. And then *crash*. Another set would begin. I liked that sound. *Crash*. Another. *Crash*. And then another. It was calming. The noise of the waves shut out the sound of my own voice in my head talking shit to me. Why was it always the same story? Why did I always feel like a fake? Like I was running out of time. Like at any minute I would be found out. I heard that voice in my head even when I was a kid. I remember it on the beach.

Another wave brought me back to the moment. I looked down into the darkness. It looked so black and empty. But I liked it. I'd better get back to the party before I did something bad.

But that was just the booze. I wasn't suicidal. Far from it. Everyone had drunk themselves into oblivion at some time or other. I knew I tended to do it a lot, but hey, I liked it. What was it that I liked about it? Maybe it was because I didn't feel. Maybe it was because I didn't care what happened. I used to drink for fun. Didn't I? I always drank more than my mates. More than anyone really. But I was just showing off. Surely. Or was I? I never wanted to stop. I never wanted to sober up. Even as a kid. Shit. I'd never thought of this before. Now I was getting worried. I'd always thought it was just the booze talking when I sat and looked in the mirror. No one else was around so no one would think that I was crazy. But I never got any answers.

'What's it going to take, eh?' I would look into my own eyes, trying to see something. 'What will it take to kill you?'

There were never any answers. My eyes were empty. Like the rest of me.

I needed a drink. I hated feeling like this. Maybe that's why I smashed so many mirrors over the years. In dressing rooms, in cars, in hotel rooms. Shit, I remember diving off my go-cart onto one in Scotland when I was four. There was a whole yard to jump off in and I jumped just where there was a mirror lying on the ground.

I didn't want to see me. But I was always there, looking straight back at me.

'I'm suicidal, not homicidal. Fuck, what am I going to do?'

TOURING HAD GONE FROM big to bigger each year. Every tour I took out more lighting, more sound gear. My band had more amplifiers on stage and I hired more roadies to help us run the beast. I hired backing singers to make the whole thing sound sweeter and then another guitar player because it was getting too nice. It was like a wildfire, swallowing everything that came in its path, including any money I earned. But it didn't matter, I was on a one-way ride to the top. No stopping and no passing go. I couldn't put a foot wrong. Yet I was losing the battle with my past. As fast as I ran, it wasn't fast enough. I could always see my past in my peripheral vision. I could feel it snapping at my heels, waiting for me to fall.

But I didn't fall. Fuelled by musical success and the love of a beautiful family, not to mention copious amounts of uppers, I didn't show any signs of slowing down. Even the ghost of Cold Chisel couldn't catch me. I had number one album after number one album. I had already sold more records than the band ever did. I was winning awards and I could do pretty well what I liked. I thought I had beaten the curse of Chisel. Every now and then, though, someone would write something in the paper. One sentence in a long article, mentioning that maybe, just maybe, my songs weren't as good as Chisel's, and I would start to panic and throw more money into the fire, trying to compensate. It seemed that the harder I worked to get out of the shadow of Cold Chisel, the longer that shadow grew. I was playing to packed stadiums every night, screaming 'Khe Sanh' at the top of my lungs, and every night someone would go home and say, 'Man, Cold Chisel had some good songs. I must buy them and listen to them again.'

Cold Chisel grew at the same time as I did. The band's music was played at every backyard barbecue in Australia at some time. Our songs became part of peoples' lives. We were always connected to our audience, partly because I was out there playing those songs every night, but there were other reasons too. The most important reason was our songs. I guess they touched people even when we couldn't. No other band in Australia has seen that sort of growth after they were gone. Cold Chisel doubled their sales post-Last Stand. The band never really went away. They were just waiting in the wings. They were always going to be a part of my life, but for a long time I could not come to terms with that simple fact.

'Let's bring in some of those great players from America to play live with me,' I regularly suggested to my management.

'You don't need them, mate. Your band is as good as any in the world,' Mark Pope or Michael Gudinski would tell me, wondering what was going through my head.

'But I want it to be even better. I need the players that were on the record. I want them. The crowd needs more.'

I always seemed to be able to convince anyone that I was right. 'If you think you need it, then that's what we'll do.'

I remember dragging guitar players down from the States to tour with me. They were in over their depth. These guys, as good as they were, couldn't play as hard or as fast as I had pushed my own band into playing. Charlie Sexton, a young guy I first met with Cold Chisel in Texas, came down for a while. Charlie was and still is one of the great guitar players, but he is a blues player, slow in hand and slow on his feet. I brought him out and immediately wanted what I had been getting from my last guitar player, before I burnt him out. Charlie wasn't up for that sort of pressure. Luckily he knew what he wanted to play and moved on to do his own thing. Now he plays with Bob Dylan and not some hopped-up maniac who is trying to beat the land speed record in music, but we are still friends.

Some guitar players did well, some fell by the wayside. Others were tossed. Dave Amato played on 'Working Class Man'. He was a great studio guitar player and he had played with some supposedly hard rock'n'roll bands – like Ted Nugent. My grandmother is harder than Ted Nugent. Poor Dave didn't realise what he was in for. But he came up with the goods. He played nice guitar night after night in front of thousands of people. He would get dressed for the stage as if he was going out with REO Speedwagon, another band that he played with for a long time. He would put on makeup and wear feather earrings and shiny clothes that he had spent a lot of money on, only to have me jump all over him, throwing him to the front of the stage while I turned his amps up to deafening volume. But the Australian audiences liked him. His heart was in it.

Dave joined the band just after the *Freight Train Heart* album. He was one of two guitar players I had on stage with me. The other guitar player in the band at the time was a young guy from Perth. He made it hard for Dave to sound good. This guy was phenomenal.

When I'd come home from recording that album I had needed to find a great guitar player to help me finish it. The rest of the album was full of blisteringly good guitar playing by Neal Schon, so I knew I needed someone exceptional to finish the parts that were left. All the guitar players I knew were out of town. Even the ones I knew, though, probably weren't going to sound great next to Neal. Neal had been playing unbelievable guitar since he was about fourteen years old, and had played with John Lee Hooker and Santana.

I was in the studio wondering who to get, when Jane said, 'There must be some good guitar players playing around Sydney. It's Saturday night. I'll go out and see a few bands and see what I can find.'

Now Jane, I knew, was a remarkable girl, capable of anything she put her mind to. But finding a world class guitar player in one night was a big ask for anyone. Out she went, full of optimism. She came back to the studio a few hours later with a big smile on her face.

'I found one.'

I was sceptical. 'Really, eh? Just like that?'

But Jane was confident. 'I went to Sydney Cove Tavern and saw a band called Johnny Diesel and the Injectors. This guy is fantastic. Good looking too.'

I was going to have to check him out. I might see if he could play guitar too.

Mark Lizotte (aka Diesel) was unbelievable and this was who was in my band with Dave Amato. Dave and Mark played off one another for the whole tour. But even with Dave's years of experience recording and touring in America, Mark stole the show every night. I doubt whether anybody could have played with more fire and taste than Mark at that time. Mark was, and still is, a force to be reckoned with.

WHEN MARK LIZOTTE AGREED to record and tour with my band he would not leave his mates behind, so I hired his band as the opening act and Mark played with both bands. From the day we started working together, I liked him. He was a real musician. He loved what he did and he worked hard. He was always learning and always trying out new things.

Every girl I knew pointed out how handsome he was and I knew how good a guy he was. Jane's young sister was single.

Jeppy was a strikingly beautiful young woman and, like Jane, she was beautiful inside and out. Mark was the same. Jane and I started thinking, 'Wouldn't it be good if these two got together?'

At first it was just a bit of a joke, then we noticed that they liked each other. 'Imagine what beautiful babies they would make,' I said, half-joking. I started matchmaking. I hired Jep as the wardrobe mistress for the tour. Anyone who has seen my band would agree that we needed a wardrobe mistress, but nobody wore what Jep suggested so she had a lot of spare time. Every night when we checked into our hotel I would make sure that Mark and Jep had rooms next door to each other. Adjoining, if I could organise it.

I also started calling band dinners. Everyone had to attend. Then none of us would turn up and Mark and Jep would be left to have dinner alone. This went on for a while. Eventually they started dating. They have now been married for many years and have absolutely beautiful children. I was right. But all jokes aside, they are two of my favourite people in the world and I am so glad that fate, with a bit of help from me, brought them together.

I REMEMBER PLAYING ON the oval on the closing night of the Royal Easter Show in Sydney. Thousands of punters were standing in the rain on a balmy Sydney evening. It rained just hard enough to make the whole night look surreal. The lights sparkled through the mist.

It's funny but no matter what had happened in the past or what was going on in the world or in my life, I knew I would find peace in the most chaotic and unlikely place. The stage. My world could be crumbling and falling around my feet but it was like being in the eye of a cyclone. I would get on stage after fighting with my record company or screaming at my management, storming out on Jane or wrestling with my own personal demons. After drinking and snorting and smoking and panicking, the lights would go down and the drummer would count 1–2–3–4 and I would feel a sense of peace that I felt nowhere else in my life. I could feel my feet on the stage, firmly planted, my heart would start to settle and, if all was going well, I would find peace. In those moments, I was in control of my life. It was all up to me to do what I knew best and the show would soar. It was like meditation. Effortlessly I would sail through the next few hours, bending the band, the music and the audience to suit my will and lift them up high. It wasn't the drugs, it wasn't the volume. It was that connection to the world through my audience. I knew I belonged. This was what I longed for in my life. To belong to something. I could do things that I didn't know I was capable of doing, the crowd giving me a leg up. Then the show would finish and the eye of the cyclone would pass and I would feel the full force of life again. I would be tossed around like a ship lost at sea – until the next show.

That night at the Easter Show, Mark and Dave played soaring guitar solos that echoed around the stands and out into the dark night. The neighbours must have been up until we finished. The band was loud and we played late but no one seemed to mind. I could see the police, who were supposed to be keeping people in line, watching the band, singing along with the fathers with their children on their shoulders. It was a beautiful night and luckily we were filming the whole show. No one was starting trouble, they had nothing to do but enjoy the music. I walked through the sideshow alley afterwards in a daze, the lights still shining and spinning on the attractions as workers swept away the rubbish and prepared the showground for whatever it was hosting next. Even the cleaners were smiling. It was one of those nights when everything goes the way it is supposed to.

I had to go back to my life and wait until I could stand in the eye of the storm again. Some shows it didn't happen but most it did. Maybe not for the whole show, but there were always moments. Precious and needed.

THERE WERE A FEW guitar players who failed miserably. There was one guy who played on my next album, *Two Fires*, who shall remain nameless but let's just say he had played with a lot of big names overseas. He came out to tour with me and never made it through the warm-ups. He was one of these guys from California who had more front than grunt. He had a lot of issues. Weight issues, so he was on all sorts of wonder diets. He talked about his colon and what came out of it. He had drug issues so he was always on the lookout for Narcotics Anonymous meetings, which was fine, but he talked about them all day. He drove my Australian band nuts. Of course, we could have all done with NA meetings too, but we didn't want to go anywhere near one. In fact, we avoided them at any cost.

We had done one or two little shows before heading to the big cities, when one day he turned to me in the car. 'Hey Jimmy, I want to talk to you.'

I remember thinking, 'Fuck, what has he eaten now?'

But he didn't want to talk about that this time. 'Listen, Jimmy. I want us to look like we're all having a good time up there on the stage. But I don't want you near me. Don't touch me. I don't want any sweat on me, okay? I'm happy to rock out and I'll make all the right moves and all that. But fuck, we're only pretending up there, okay? It's just a show.'

There was silence in the car. The band were waiting for me to kill him. It wasn't just a show. This was our lives. Every night for years we laid it all on the line. I had bled for shows like this. These shows were the only thing that kept me sane. And this guy thought it was just a show? I was speechless. Was he serious? Is that what he thought I wanted from him? To pretend? I watched the road and he went back to talking about how happy he was since he had gotten his divorce and married that young girl.

For the rest of the trip I thought carefully about what he had said. Was I taking him the wrong way? Maybe I had missed something. We drove into Warrnambool not long before we were due to go on. I kept my distance as I went through my warm-up, which in those days consisted of drinking half a bottle of vodka, snorting a gram of coke and screaming for an hour. By the time I hit the stage I was pumped. I had brushed off what he'd said and wanted to concentrate on doing a great show. About a third of the way through I walked to his side of the stage. I wanted him to know I didn't hold a grudge. I stood next to him and immediately he went into a stance which I can only describe as Los Angeles Rock Guitar Player Stance Number Seven. But he made sure I was out of his reach. The rest of the band, including myself, were saturated with sweat. This gig was one of those old-style, boiling hot pub shows that we used to do with no air conditioning because the publican had turned it off to make the punters drink more. The rest of the band looked like drowned rats. This guy didn't have a bead of sweat on him. He'd had the crew set up a small fan just beside him and I could see the creases he'd ironed into his jeans. Now he was pouting and posturing away in front of me. I snapped. I grabbed him by the back of the neck and the seat of his pants and threw him into the crowd. He landed a few rows from the stage. I felt better already. He tried to get back on stage but I blocked the way and shouted over the screaming of the band, 'Fuck off back to America. Now. You don't belong here.'

By the time we finished he had packed his guitars and was back at the hotel. Then one of the crew took me aside and told me, 'Listen Jim, he wants to have a word with you. He says you were out of line and acted totally unprofessionally but he's willing to forgive you and give you a chance.'

I sent the roadie to pick him up and drive him back to Melbourne and put him on a plane home. He didn't get it. He never would. I haven't spoken to him or seen him since. We don't mix in the same circles.

CHAPTER THIRTY-TWO

this was a racing car and
I was a lousy driver

THE WHITE HOUSE, 1988–89

I NSTEAD OF BUILDING A family home that would bring us closer together, Jane and I built the White House – a home that had everything I had dreamed about or seen on television growing up. Every single thing my parents never bought us kids, and a whole lot more. I could buy whatever we needed, so this wasn't a problem – I was the biggest touring and recording star in the country. Money grew on trees. Well, if it did, I would have bought a few money trees too.

What we really needed was for me to be at home, sorting myself out, stopping the drinking and whatever else I got up to on the road. But I wasn't ready for normal family life. Everything I did was exaggerated. Our home was a normal family home on steroids.

Jane wanted me to have everything I wanted. She was used to having everything she wanted, so this didn't feel strange to her. In fact, I was still trying to live up to what I thought she wanted from a husband, in every way except the things that mattered most. She needed a husband who was faithful and loving.

I didn't know how to be normal. I had never seen a normal family. The families I knew were all fucked up, full of abuse and deception and violence and more. So I was trying to fake it until I knew how to be a good husband, and what I lacked I tried to make up for by buying Jane anything she wanted. I was running out of money, but more importantly I was running out of time, fast.

Even the extension wasn't big enough. The house was beautiful and we had rooms for ourselves and the children. We had five bedrooms in all and a huge kitchen and lounge room but we needed more. We should have stopped then but we kept on building. Looking back, I don't know why. Maybe I needed more places to hide my face and Jane needed some distance between us. We never consciously wanted to be apart but the house ended up so big we needed an intercom system to speak to each other.

Fred the builder came back and this time we added a new wing, with a study and a formal lounge that doubled as a theatre room. We extended the kitchen to include an old baker's oven. It had been used about one hundred years earlier in Yackandandah, a town down near the Victorian border. We had it dismantled brick by brick and transported to our house and then carefully reconstructed in our kitchen. It was a work of art but unfortunately you had to burn a whole tree to get it up to a temperature that was operational. Once it was running you could have cooked an entire cow in it, it was so big. We used it once. We didn't cook a cow, just bread.

We had a Japanese teppanyaki table so I could cook and throw food at the kids at the same time. We found a ten-burner antique

Kookaburra stove that we had restored and installed and we also put in a complete indoor barbecue. The kitchen was so big we could cater for parties and often did. A typical family Sunday dinner could be as large as thirty people. Downstairs we built a full recording studio so I could make albums without leaving the house, and a billiard room that had a fireplace so big you could walk into it, complete with a 1930s Art Deco corrugated glass bar. We bought the bar and a container full of other stuff while we were shopping one day on Melrose Avenue in Los Angeles.

We only bought things we needed though. Like the three full-size fibreglass cows that we stood outside on the grass. When people drove along the road at the end of the hill they looked real. We used to stand them up in trees to confuse the neighbours. We also bought a 1950s jukebox, complete with a catalogue of original singles, and a handmade leather and sterling silver Bohlin saddle. This was a beautiful piece that had been used in the movies and I really loved it, but unfortunately it was a Western saddle and my horse would only use an English saddle. The rest of the container was filled with stuff that wasn't as useful.

We added a guesthouse above the five-car garage we built to house the Ferrari 246 Dino, circa 1975, the 1960 Mercedes sports car and the 1962 Chevrolet Corvette Stingray that I hotted up so much Jane refused to travel in it. This was a racing car and I was a lousy driver. I hardly drove any of them. I drove a 6.9 litre Mercedes-Benz that was way too fast for Australia; consequently I lost my licence a few times.

Oh yeah, and we built an indoor swimming pool. You could swim to the outdoors and back inside, so you didn't have to get out of the water outside. I had seen this at a hotel in Canada, somewhere where it snowed. The pool had ozone filters, one of the first in the country to use this system. Swimming in this water was like swimming in a mountain creek. When the gas heaters were turned on, the pool was so warm you could have cooked lobsters in it if you wanted to. Next to the pool we built a gym and a steam room.

To finish all this off we also bought two angels carved in the 1600s for a Baroque church somewhere in Germany. Then we had to build a pond in the middle of the driveway to mount them beside. The angels were an accidental acquisition. An antique dealer begged us to buy them because someone with too much money and no taste wanted to buy them and have them sandblasted or painted to make them look newer. We bought them and left them with the four hundred years of history that was covering them intact. They looked beautiful. Dark and mysterious, they welcomed people to the house.

All these things and this building work cost a fortune and I thought I had a fortune but it kept disappearing. We all flew first class. The kids were two feet high and they slept in first class on airplane seats that could have fitted three of them on one seat. They ate caviar and foie gras. I didn't know any other children who ate caviar. We stayed at the best hotels in the world, in the best suites, with butlers and maids. So did anybody who travelled with us. We threw our money around to anyone we thought needed it. We could always find more. I borrowed more and more money to pay for everything. I soon found myself in massive debt. To make things worse, interest rates started rising and they didn't stop. I had to work more than ever, just to pay the interest on my loans. Interest rates got to 26 per cent and I found myself running uphill. I had bought all of these things to make up for my mistakes as a husband. I should have been staying home and working on our relationship but instead I was on the road more and more, making more mistakes and getting further away from the ones I loved.

But good things happened to us too. We had the most beautiful children in the world and we both adored them. We were blessed. I was a million miles from where I'd started out.

I'VE ALWAYS THOUGHT BEING poor is like having a disease. It eats away at you slowly. It knocks you down and you have to pick yourself up, only to be knocked down when the next bill comes in. My mum and dad's disease was incurable. It was passed down from their parents, who contracted the disease from their parents, and so on and so on. There seemed to be no cure and if there was one, we couldn't afford the treatment. There was no way that things were ever going to get better. I watched as Mum got her hopes up, only to have them torn down or punched out of her every single day of her life. Just like a disease, there are secondary infections too – alcoholism, violence and shame, to mention a few. Every one of them can kill you on its own, but put them all together and the prognosis is bad. You won't die fast but you will die. Slowly, painfully, without any hope. Eventually it will bury you. If you are lucky enough to get by for a while, you will be racked with pain and fear and guilt. I know my mum and dad felt it and I watched them suffer. They thought we deserved better, even if they didn't. They felt they must have done something terribly wrong to be struck down by such an evil disease.

I used to walk through the shops with my mum and she could never look people in the eye. I wondered why. Now I know. She thought everybody knew she was sick. They knew she was poor. She wasn't worth anything. The only time she did look people in the eye was to spit venom at them. 'What are you fuckin' looking at, eh? Come on kids, don't worry about these people. They don't know what it's like te struggle. Get oot o' my fuckin' way.'

Mum would pull us quickly past some poor unsuspecting person she thought had more than us. More anything. Just more. Straightening our clothes and sticking my hair down with her own spit, acting like she didn't care at all. But she did. I could feel it. Her disease was bad and I could feel it in my bones too. I knew I had it.

'Don't worry, son. One day you'll leave aw this shit behind ye,' she'd say as we walked away. 'You wait. The whole world will be yours. You're lucky. You're no like me. You'll get away from here. I know it.'

When I did get away, it was as if I had turned against my mum. She hated that I had anything. I tried to share all I had with her but she wouldn't have a bar of it. In fact, she threw it back in my face. 'I don't want yer money. I don't need anything from you. You think you're so good. You wait. When it's all gone you'll be back here with us where you belong. Mister high and bloody mighty.'

So I was convinced it wouldn't last. I'd end up back in the gutter where I belonged, just like Mum said. For years that's what I was expecting, and when it didn't happen, I did my best to make it happen. That's where I belonged, in the gutter like the rest of my kind. The disease was still lingering in me. It was strong. I drank. I drank way too much. I could feel the shame even when I had nothing to be ashamed of. The same shame my mother and father felt. I could hear that familiar voice. It screamed inside me, 'Who do you think you are? Get back where you came from. You're not fooling anyone.'

EVERYTHING I TRIED TO do for Mum wasn't enough.

'Mum, I've bought you a beautiful house. It's right next door to me so you can see the kids.'

The house was on ten acres on a property adjoining us, with four bedrooms and a view that looked straight down the valley. It was a beautiful home. I thought she'd finally be happy.

'Well I don't need a hoose. I'm happy in Elizabeth. I'm no livin' in a fancy hoose, surrounded by snobby bloody neighbours. Looking over the fence doon their fuckin' noses at me. And I suppose you think I'm gonna be yer babysitter, do ye? Well, I'm no.'

Eventually she and her husband Ray moved into the house but she never came near us. She lived less than one hundred yards from her grandchildren. We were hoping she would spend time with them. She never visited once. When I took the kids over to see her, it was as if we were putting her out. I tried to include her in the life we were living but she wasn't comfortable with any of it.

One day we took her for lunch at a dear friend's house. She lived in a big old house, filled with beautiful art and antiques. Mum sat there scowling at everyone, with her lips pursed, as if she'd been forced into something horrible. Our friend was warm and friendly, going out of her way to make my mum as comfortable as possible.

Halfway through lunch as our friend went out to get the next course of the meal, Mum looked around the room and then turned to me and said with a voice full of poison, 'Ye'd think with all this fuckin' money she could buy some new furniture, eh?'

Then she sat back with a smug look on her face, as if she'd let me know, in no uncertain terms, that she wasn't impressed by any of it. Lunch was lovely but the shine was gone out of the day. I couldn't wait to take her home.

A few months later she called me up and announced in her usual acid tone, 'This hoose is too fuckin' cold for me. I've got arthritis. Ye should have thought of that, shouldn't ye. Anyway, I want to go and live back in Elizabeth with ma real friends.'

'Mum, the house isn't cold. There's central heating and an open fireplace.'

'Ye think I can afford wood, do ye? We're no all millionaires, ye know.'

'But Mum, you don't have to buy wood. I pay all the bills. You just have to relax and enjoy it. It's all for you.'

'How can I relax in this toffy bloody place? I know naebody here. And I don't want tae know any of 'em. It's lonely for us here. We want tae go back where we belong.' Mum always spoke for her and Ray. I hardly heard Ray speak, come to think of it. Ray was either a listener or an idiot. Probably a good thing considering he was living with Mum.

She never thought of spending time with her grandkids. That's when I realised that Mum didn't have a maternal bone in her body. She never had. She wasn't cut out to be a parent. I just wish she had of thought of this before she had six children. But we all live and learn.

I was starting to learn too. After about six months I rang Mum.

'Hi Mum. Why don't you come back to your house? It's sitting here empty. Waiting for you.'

'It's no ma hoose. I don't own it.'

'Mum, I bought it for you.'

'Well I don't want it. You can fuckin' sell it as far as I'm concerned. I'm never coming back tae that cold miserable place.'

I was hurt but I was angry too. Nothing ever made her happy and I swore to stay away from her if I could. I put the house on the market but I asked one more time before I sold it. 'Mum, are you sure you don't want to come back up here with us?'

'No. I'm happy right where I am.'

I sold the house the next week.

Months later I heard that Mum had told my brothers and sisters that we had thrown her out. 'They threw me oot on the street. Right on ma arse. I loved that hoose. It was that bloody dragon woman. I know it.'

Mum apparently had a new name for Jane. I was furious but Jane couldn't care less. My mum could never hurt her. Not like she could me.

JANE TOLD ME SHE was pregnant again with our fourth child. This was the best news we'd had in a long time. Our babies were a source of joy to us. No matter how much we fought or how bad I felt, the babies made us smile.

We couldn't wait for our new baby to arrive. As it happened, we didn't have to wait that long. The baby arrived very early. At twenty-five weeks, Jane was showing signs of going into labour, so the doctors insisted that she be near a hospital that could cope with such an early birth. The baby would need intensive care if and when she arrived. Westmead Children's Hospital was miles from our house so we moved into the new Travelodge hotel in Parramatta. We had a huge suite that was about ten minutes from the hospital. I had a songwriter coming out from America to write for the upcoming album, so I set about building a makeshift recording studio in the suite. We could write songs and I would still be able to reach the hospital quickly if an emergency arose. We never wrote anything worth using.

Jane went into labour and moved into the hospital. Elly-May was born in May 1989, fourteen weeks premature. She weighed 750 grams. Like a little lump of butter. This was very early and was a dangerous time for our beautiful little baby. She was so tiny and fragile. We used to bathe her in a kidney dish. She spent most of her time in a humidicrib, attached to all sorts of machines that helped her breath and measured her vital signs. The machines would make loud noises to warn the nurses when something was wrong. They'd spring into action.

'Out of the way,' one of them would call as she ran across the room.

'Can I help?' Jane would ask.

'Better if you just stand back, please.'

The nurses were used to bad things happening, we could tell, and they wanted us to stand back and let them deal with things. But Jane stayed right by Elly-May's side. She never left. We would wait with our hearts pounding in our chests, saying nothing to each other. Most of the time it was okay but we couldn't be sure.

I spent my time between the hospital and the hotel, supposedly writing songs with the American songwriter. This guy thought that writing songs with him should have been my first priority. He was so wrong, and in the end I sent him away. Songwriting was really the last thing on my mind. I had set the studio up for nothing. I couldn't concentrate on songwriting at all. Although in saying that, there was one day that was different. I had been visiting Elly and was sitting in the waiting room when suddenly, out of the blue, I had an idea for a song. I grabbed a pen and paper from one of the nurses and began to write. I wrote a whole set of lyrics. This was good. Then suddenly I had another idea, and another. Songs were pouring out of me. I thought I was truly inspired.

Nurses were running around, in and out of the ward. It was very busy, there was something going on, but I was too busy writing to take notice.

Suddenly one of the nurses stopped and yelled, 'Quick, grab a baby. We're evacuating the ward.'

I looked up, dazed. 'Er, what do you want?' I didn't expect her to be talking to me.

'Get up and help us move the babies. Now!'

I threw down my pen and sprang into action.

'Get them all out. There's some kind of poisonous gas coming through the air conditioning.'

We managed to get the babies out, humidicribs and all, and they were set up in the hallway outside of intensive care with drips and machines going beep. It was like an episode of M*A*S*H.

We found out that someone had accidently painted the room where the ward's air compressor was, and paint fumes had been filling the room. This was why I was so inspired. I was sniffing paint fumes. They moved the compressor and all the babies were brought back into the ward safely. The words I had written were lousy.

EVERY DAY WAS AN emergency in this ward. Every day I would arrive to find another empty humidicrib and another little life changed. Sometimes the babies went home but sometimes they died. It was a hard place to work. The nurses would be in tears with grieving parents one minute and celebrating with gaunt but happy parents the next. How they did this job was beyond me. Every day I would stand next to Elly with my hand inside the crib, singing as softly as I could to her and reassuring her that I would always be there for her.

One day, some parents stopped us in the hallway. 'We thought you should know that there are some bad bugs going around the wards. Staph infections and even worse. If it's possible you should get your baby out of here.'

The nurses at Westmead had been incredible. They had saved our baby's life. We didn't know for sure that she was in danger, but we'd heard of a couple of poor little babies falling foul to infections, so we took drastic steps. I bought a humidicrib and all the machines we needed, hired three nurses to work around the clock, and moved Elly-May home to our house. We set up the study as the hospital ward. This was the only time that room was useful.

Elly-May made it through, but due to a small brain bleed she'd had in hospital she would have cerebral palsy. Elly's life would never be easy but she was special. She was a fighter and she has fought every day of her life. She spent a lot of her young life visiting the rehab centre at Westmead, where they helped her with her struggle with CP. We still have friends there and to this day support them however we can. I think, after seeing these kids and all that they go through, I always will.

CHAPTER THIRTY-THREE

out of control like a bushfire

THE VALLEY, LA, 1990

I'D BEEN CAUGHT BETWEEN two fires for a long time. One was the inferno that I had built with my success and addictions, which by this time had just about consumed me and everyone I came in contact with. I was out of control like a bush fire and I continued to throw petrol on the flames every single night. I was a fire starter and now the flames were licking at my heels as I ran from the heat. The other was the fire that burned for my family. I would trade the inferno that was fame for love in a second. Love, peace and quiet was all I really wanted. But then how would I look after my family? I never wanted them to struggle like I had. Now they were struggling with me and what I was becoming. This was going to be the death of me if I didn't sort it out.

MICHAEL GUDINSKI HAD TAKEN over as my manager. Mark Pope worked with him for a while but not long. Michael now ran the booking agency, the record company and the management. He was firing. All the number one albums were good for business and for his confidence. It was like he couldn't put a foot wrong, not as long as I didn't, anyway. We were a good team.

He set about securing a new American deal for me. He still wanted a number one album in the States, probably even more than me. I was over the place. Like I've said, I never felt good there. Whether that was my own fault or not, I'm not sure, but I would have been happy to concentrate on working at home.

Michael and his New York contacts soon had me talking to the legendary Atlantic Records. Ahmet Ertegun was one of the greats of the music business. He had worked with Ben E. King, Solomon Burke, Otis Redding, Sam & Dave, Percy Sledge, Aretha Franklin and Wilson Pickett, to name a few. Every great singer in the world wanted to be around Ahmet. Every singer I looked up to. These were the people who inspired me and they had got their start because of Ahmet Ertegun. This was my chance to get together with him. I went to his office in New York.

He said to me, 'You know, Jimmy, I heard that song you did with INXS and I thought, great. How come I didn't hear this singer with them before? When I found out you weren't in the band I wasn't happy. I was even more unhappy when I found out you were signed to another label. So I'm glad that they're gone and you're here talking to us. This is where you belong, right here on Atlantic.'

I couldn't have been happier. I signed to Atlantic Records. Maybe things would work out better this time around. But Ahmet, I found out after I signed, was only the figurehead of the company by then. Doug Morris ran the place. I hoped Doug liked me as much as Ahmet had and I hoped he knew the business half as well as Ahmet did. I would have to wait and see.

It was time to find an American producer to work with me to find songs and make a great record. The name that was being thrown around was a guy called Don Gehman. Now Don had worked in the music business for a long time, starting out as a live sound guy and moving on to engineering and finally production. Most recently he had produced work for John Mellencamp. 'Jack & Diane' was a game changer and a massive record. I'd also heard Don's work on REM's *Life's Rich Pageant*. On paper he seemed like a good choice. In saying that, let me just clear up something. I didn't like John Mellencamp at all. He sang badly and the lyrics were a bit naff but he had resonated with the Midwest of America and that's what the record companies seemed to target. So they were keen as mustard. Back in LA, a meeting was organised at a place called Jerry's Diner, in the Valley somewhere. It appeared Don didn't want to move too far from his house.

We sat down and Don proceeded to order half the menu without looking at it. I sort of knew he ate at the same place every day.

'So. Hi Jimmy. Glad you could find the place. The food is very good here if you're hungry at all.' Don spoke like a Mennonite farmer, slow and measured and with a strange hint of an accent. He could have been from anywhere, I guess. But there was something calming about his tone.

'No thanks, Don, I ate before I came.' I didn't lie. I did eat before I went to America. Since arriving in LA though, I hadn't eaten much at all. Coke was too easy to get in LA and I could never eat once I got into the same town as good coke.

'All right then. Please yourself. I hope you don't mind if I eat.'

I nodded. 'Please, go for it.'

By the time I'd said a word, Don was tearing into a whole chicken. Was he really going to eat everything? I thought he'd ordered for both of us. I was obviously wrong.

'You know, Jimmy, I have listened to your demos and you're a good singer. But here's the thing. I think your songs suck.'

I sat opposite Don and tried to plant my feet firmly on the ground. Just so I wouldn't jump the table and belt him.

'I think if you write some more songs and let me hear them, maybe we could do something together.'

Slowly the veil of red over my eyes lifted and I calmed down. Everybody else I'd met in the States bullshitted their way through meetings like this, telling me how much they loved me and how they couldn't wait to get started. Even if I didn't like what Don was saying, he at least was being honest.

So I said, 'Well, what do you think I should do next then?'

Don sat quiet for a minute, while he ate the other half of the chicken. Then he spoke. 'Well, I don't know.' This guy was full of good ideas. 'Maybe I could put you with a few writers and we can keep meeting until we are both happy.'

That was the best offer I had had all day. I stood up and shook his hand, which was still somewhat greasy from the chicken, grabbed my car keys and walked out of Jerry's.

There were a number of meetings before we agreed to make a record, all of them in the Valley and all of them in Jerry's Diner. At one of these meetings I noticed Don wasn't as calm as usual. And he wasn't eating.

So I asked, 'Are you okay? You're not sick, are you?'

He looked at me as if I was his best friend and said, 'No Jimmy. I just had a colonic irrigation and I'm feeling a little weak.'

I was almost stuck for words. 'Get to fuck out of here. They'd have to kiss me before they tried that on me.'

Don blinked his pale eyes and said calmly, 'You should really try it. You wouldn't believe what comes out of there.'

I cancelled my order.

Don was trying a lot of alternative treatments and diets and I never knew how he would be until we were face to face.

Some days he was bright-eyed and upbeat and other days he was drained and tired looking.

'Hey Don, how are you today?'

'Oh, I'm okay. I've been living on potato juice for the last week and I'm feeling a little lightheaded.'

I had never heard of such shit. 'What? You fucking what?' I wanted to joke but this wasn't funny.

EVENTUALLY DON THOUGHT THE songs were good enough and we booked into Chapel Studios, owned by Dave Stewart from the Eurythmics. The studio was, by the way, in the Valley and just walking distance to Jerry's. Jane and the kids and I settled into the house at the studio for the next six weeks. We were making a record that would be called *Two Fires*, and besides Don's ups and downs we had a good time making it. Don was an odd person but I liked him a lot. He was very clever and funny and he knew how to make a record. But living in LA was not good for me, especially with it being so easy to buy cocaine. You could get it delivered. It was quicker than pizza.

Noel had stayed back in Australia, so I wasn't training as much as I should have been. One afternoon, one of his karate mates came to the studio for a visit. He brought a famous American martial artist named Bill 'Superfoot' Wallace with him. I had heard of this guy. He was in movies and magazines, and well known in the karate community. He sat quietly and watched as we recorded and then, towards sunset, as we sat outside chatting, he said, 'I hear you do a bit of training.'

I acted casual, mainly because I hadn't been training that hard. 'Yeah, I've done a little but not lately.'

He looked at me with his predator eyes. I've seen these eyes on a lot of martial artists. 'Well, why don't you come down to the gym and work out with us tomorrow. If you aren't too scared.'

I could feel his glove being slapped across my face. 'No man, I'm recording here. I'm not sure I can get away.' I was as polite as possible.

'Typical fucking musician. They all pretend they train, but when it comes down to the hard work they bail out.' He looked at his mate and sniggered.

'Yeah. All right then. What time do you start, smart-arse? I'll come down.' As soon as I spoke I could feel the hook in my mouth. I had taken the bait. He gave me a time and went home to rest for the next day. It was about eight o'clock at night at this time.

As fate would have it Don wanted to work late. I was in the studio singing and drinking and snorting coke until four in the morning. I headed to the gym at eight-thirty. I was a bit dusty. I arrived at the Jet Centre, a famous landmark in the martial arts world. The gym was owned by Benny 'The Jet' Urquidez, probably the best fighter of his time.

'Guess I got you all wrong, Jimmy. You ready to go for it?' Bill smiled at me.

'I was born ready,' I lied.

Bill 'Superfoot' Wallace took me through what felt like the kind of workout you might do if you were training for a world title fight. He was a world champion. But I didn't stop. I couldn't. Every now and then I would excuse myself to go to the bathroom and throw up, but I wouldn't stop. By the end we stood looking at each other, drenched in sweat.

'You know, Jimmy, I'm really sorry I misjudged you. You are the real deal. We're here every day if you want to train with us. You're always welcome.'

I walked around the corner to my car and threw up again before I drove to the studio. I could hardly walk for a week, but I wasn't going to let some smart-arsed American think he could push me around. Anyway, I wondered if he would have been that tough if I'd met him on the street in Elizabeth with a baseball

1. **Poor Mark Pope** used to have to share a room with me on the road. Both of us obviously think this headline is about the rest of the band. (BARNES FAMILY COLLECTION) 2. **Me and Big Ole Bruce (Howe)** having a good ole sing together. (BOB KING) 3. **Here's me with the musicians** from my first album, *Bodyswerve*, in 1984, after being presented with gold records by Michael Gudinski. This would be the first of seven number one albums in a row with Mushroom Records. (BARNES FAMILY COLLECTION)

1. Randy Jackson, Tony Brock, me, Jonathan Cain and Neal Schon. These amazing musicians played on many of my recordings in 1986–87. (BARNES FAMILY COLLECTION) **2. Me with Prime Minister Bob Hawke,** presenting the Street Beat campaign, which aimed to stop young guys dying from drink driving. (NEWS LTD, NEWSPIX) **3. With Michael Gudinski** at a Double Platinum Record presentation for *For the Working Class Man.* (COURTESY OF SUE GUDINSKI) **4. Me, Michael Hutchence, Chrissy Amphlett and Sean Kelly** on the Australian Made Tour in 1986. I'm glad I dressed up for the shot. (BOB KING)

1. **Me and my mates in a limo,** around the time of the Australian Made Tour. (**Bob King**)
2. **My Canadian band** with ZZ Top and a few of the road crew, on tour somewhere in America, 1986. (**Tom Lang**) 3. **Can somebody get me some louder pants please?** Stage designer Patrick Woodroffe came up with the set design, light show and colour scheme for the Barnestorming tour in 1988. (**Bob King**) 4. **Our second daughter, Eliza-Jane,** is in very safe hands here with Noel Watson, my martial arts trainer and her uncle 'Crazy Horse'. (**Barnes Family Collection**) 5. **I've always enjoyed escaping to Thailand,** and for many years we'd go to the beachhouse where Jane's family had always taken their holidays. With us here is producer Mark Opitz. (**Barnes Family Collection**)

1. **Starting work** on our house near Mount Gibraltar and the town of Bowral in the Southern Highlands of New South Wales. Our little country home gradually became a mansion. 2. **The indoor–outdoor pool** adjoined a gym and steam room. 3. **The completed 'White House'** viewed from on high. That's the way I liked to look at it. 4. **Jane bought me a Ferrari 246 Dino, circa 1975.** It was a shame was such a bad driver. (ALL IMAGES: BARNES FAMILY COLLECTION)

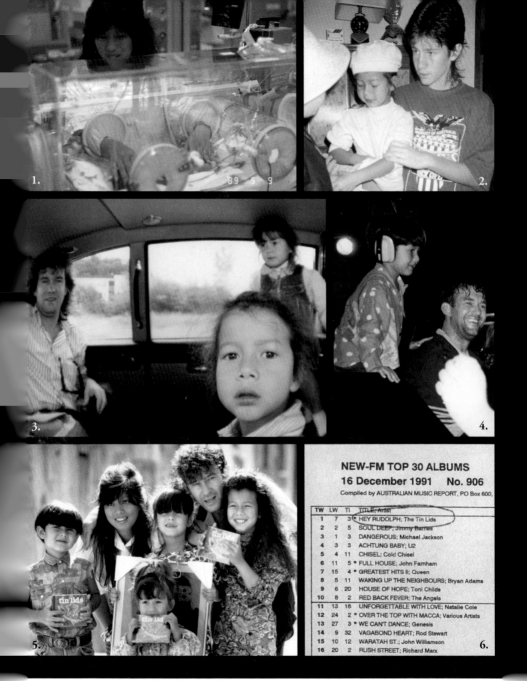

NEW-FM TOP 30 ALBUMS
16 December 1991   No. 906
Compiled by AUSTRALIAN MUSIC REPORT, PO Box 600,

TW	LW	TI	TITLE; Artist
1	7	3	HEY RUDOLPH; The Tin Lids
2	2	5	SOUL DEEP; Jimmy Barnes
3	1	3	DANGEROUS; Michael Jackson
4	3	3	ACHTUNG BABY; U2
5	4	11	CHISEL; Cold Chisel
6	11	5	FULL HOUSE; John Farnham
7	15	4	GREATEST HITS II; Queen
8	5	11	WAKING UP THE NEIGHBOURS; Bryan Adams
9	6	20	HOUSE OF HOPE; Toni Childs
10	8	2	RED BACK FEVER; The Angels
11	13	18	UNFORGETTABLE WITH LOVE; Natalie Cole
12	24	2	OVER THE TOP WITH MACCA; Various Artists
13	27	3	WE CAN'T DANCE; Genesis
14	9	32	VAGABOND HEART; Rod Stewart
15	10	12	WARATAH ST.; John Williamson
16	20	2	RUSH STREET; Richard Marx

1. Jane in the neonatal intensive care ward at Westmead Children's Hospital with our baby Elly-May, who was born on 3 May 1989, fourteen weeks premature, and weighed just 750 grams. **2. A very young David Campbell,** with an even younger Mahalia at the White House. **3. Myself, EJ and a very inquisitive Mahalia** driving through the Scottish countryside. **4. Our boy, Jackie, loved touring** and was always ready to get on stage. **5. The kids got in on the act,** forming their own band, The Tin Lids, and making a number one album, *Hey Rudolph!* **6. A top 30 chart** showing The Tin Lids at number one, with yours truly and a host of big names below them. (ALL IMAGES: BARNES FAMILY COLLECTION)

1. With my band and Stray Cat Brian Setzer (third from left) while promoting *Two Fires*. Who knew that one of these guys would not make it through the tour? (BARNES FAMILY COLLECTION) **2. A country-looking Don Gehman** in the studio in California. Don produced *Two Fires* and became a regular collaborator. (BARNES FAMILY COLLECTION) **3. On stage during the Soul Deep tour.** Taking such a big band on tour was not cheap. (BOB KING) **4. I was lucky to sing with this legend, John Farnham.** Here we are sitting around having a few drinks and laughs during the filming of the 'When Something Is Wrong With My Baby' video. (PIERRE BARONI) **5. Celebrating the 1992 ARIA award** for Best Male Artist, for *Soul Deep*, with Jane and Sue and Michael Gudinski. (COURTESY OF SUE GUDINSKI) **6. Working with another legend, Tina Turner,** on the 'Simply the Best' single for the NRL. How lucky was I? (COLIN WHELAN/NRL)

1. **I've been blessed enough** to have played with the some of the best guitar players in the world. My brother-in-law Mark Lizotte is right up there. (**Barnes Family Collection**) 2. **During the** *Heat* **sessions** I had a Buddhist monk from the Sunnataram Forest Monastery near Bundanoon come to Festival Records in Sydney to bless the studio. (**Barnes Family collection**) 3. **Ross Wilson and myself** performing a song from *Flesh and Wood*. I feel honoured to have worked with Ross often over the years; he's one of the best. My friend Michael Hegerty is in the background. (**Bob King**) 4. **Jeff Neill and I** played together for a long time, and he's another guitarist who became a good mate. (**Mick Hutson, Getty**)

1. **Our home in the south of France**, at Les Granettes, near Aix-en-Provence. **2. Painting Mont Sainte-Victoire from the backyard.** My French friends said my painting was very naive. I think that meant really bad. **3. The Cours Mirabeau in Aix-en-Provence.** Jane and the kids and I walked this street all through the summer, eating ice cream. **4. Jackie, EJ and Elly-May** in the fields next to the house. (ALL IMAGES: BARNES FAMILY COLLECTION)

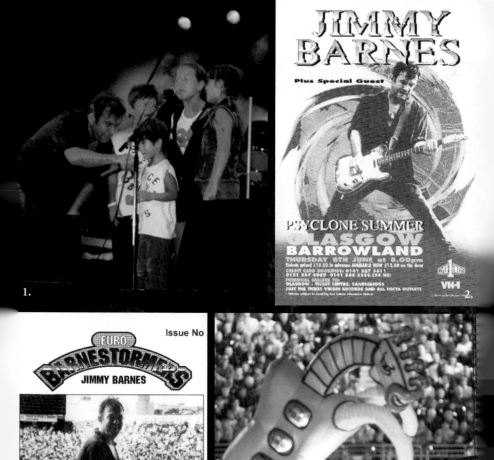

1. **Often the kids would get up on stage** and join me in a number like 'When Your Love Is Gone'. (BARNES FAMILY COLLECTION) 2. **After making** *Psyclone* I did some shows in Europe, including one at the Glasgow Barrowland. This was a sort of homecoming, playing the hall where my mum and dad used to dance. (BARNES FAMILY COLLECTION) 3. **The cover of my European fan magazine.** We had fans all over Europe but especially in Germany. They really liked to rock there. (BARNES FAMILY COLLECTION) 4. **Singing at the 2000 Olympics.** It wasn't one of my happiest shows, but it brought me my biggest ever live audiences: 8 million watched in Australia and more than 1 billion worldwide. (SARAH REED, NEWSPIX)

1. Singing on the Soul Deeper tour. I lined up a great band for this tour, packed with seasoned soul players like James Gadson, Larry Fulcher and Johnny Lee Schell. They taught me to slow things down a bit. On stage at least. (STEVE POHLNER, NEWSPIX) **2. Australia Post produced a 'Khe Sanh' stamp.** This photo looks like somebody stamped on my head. (JOHN HARGEST, NEWSPIX) **3. Singing with Jon Bon Jovi** at the Raw concert at the Colonial Stadium in Melbourne in 2001. The show was organised to raise money for emergency services. (MARTIN PHILBEY, GETTY) **4. I really enjoyed the *Live at the Chapel* show** and was delighted with the recording. (MARTIN PHILBEY)

1. **In 2004, our family got to travel across Australia** on the annual Indian Pacific 'Christmas Express', singing at remote communities and helping to raise money for the Royal Flying Doctor Service. (**Barnes Family Collection**) 2. **Backstage with Jane and Deepak Chopra.** Jane and I went to India with Deepak to learn to meditate. (**Barnes Family Collection**) 3. **They say you look like your dog**, but I think Oliver looks better than me. (**Peter Morris, Fairfax**) 4. **In 2005 I was honoured** to be inducted into the ARIA Hall of Fame for the second time, on this occasion as a solo artist. (**Bob King**) 5. **Jane's mum** trying to keep out of the sun as we travel up the Mekong River on our way to visit and meditate with Buddhist monks. (**Barnes Family Collection**)

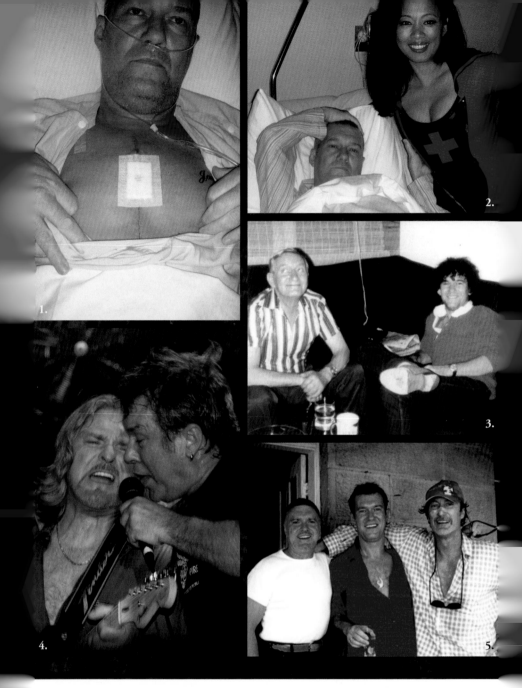

1. Just out of heart surgery in 2007. I don't look too happy. (BARNES FAMILY COLLECTION) **2. Jane tried to cheer me up** with her nurse's uniform. It nearly killed me. (BARNES FAMILY COLLECTION) **3. My dad passed away the same year I had heart surgery.** Fortunately we had worked through some of our issues before he died, and were closer at the end. (BARNES FAMILY COLLECTION) **4. As I recovered from surgery,** I was devastated to hear that one of my heroes, Billy Thorpe, had died of a heart attack. (SAMM HALL) **5. One day I spent with Billy in 1998** was the most Aussie day I've ever had. At a barbecue at Bryan Brown's house in Sydney I sang 'Waltzing Matilda' with Billy, looking out over the harbour to the Harbour Bridge. (LYNN THORPE)

1. I screamed till I was blue in the face, and my mate Richard Bailey kept taking photographs – the photo shoot for *Out in the Blue*. (RICHARD BAILEY) **2. Here I am with my great mate and producer Kevin Shirley,** my son David and beautiful grandson Leo. (BARNES FAMILY COLLECTION) **3. In 2014, for my *30:30 Hindsight* album,** I got to sing with one of the greatest rock'n'roll bands that Australia has produced, The Living End. (BARNES FAMILY COLLECTION) **4. At home with Little Steven,** aka Steven van Zandt from Bruce Springsteen's legendary E Street Band. He had a day off from the Springsteen Tour and came to record with me for *30:30 Hindsight*. (BARNES FAMILY COLLECTION) **5. In my flash red suit,** on the 2016 Soul Searching tour. (BARNES FAMILY COLLECTION)

1. Here I am with the A Team, my dear friends Frank Stivala, Michael Gudinski and Warren Costello. (Courtesy of Frank Stivala) **2. Music industry legends** Eric Robinson and Ian 'Smithy' Smith. I miss them both. (Barnes Family Collection) **3. Whenever I go on tour,** Snoop Dog and Oliver jump in my suitcase and try to come with me. (Barnes Family Collection) **4. Singing with Elly-May and David,** at the Emerald Ball, Westmead Children's Hospital's annual charity gala. (Pat Brunet) **5. Our gang of good friends** (clockwise from left): Erica Gregan, Jep Lizotte, Paul Clarke, Jenny Morris, Neil and Sharon Finn, Jane and me. (Barnes Family Collection)

1. **Sam Neill and me looking dapper** under an umbrella at Elly-May's wedding to Liam Conboy in 2015. (TED O'DONNELL) 2. **This beautiful family shot** was taken in our garden at Elly-May's wedding. (TED O'DONNELL) 3. **Sitting back and being entertained** at my sixtieth birthday party at our Berrima home, Riverbend. (BARNES FAMILY COLLECTION) 4. **My granddaughter Ruby sang and grandson Dylan danced.** They were part of an all-star cast that evening. (BARNES FAMILY COLLECTION) 5. **At home with our newest grandchildren,** Zoey and Rosetta. (BARNES FAMILY COLLECTION) 6. **My grandchildren** sitting on my couch like angels during my sixtieth birthday celebrations. (TED O'DONNELL) 7. **My beautiful daughters** Amanda and Megan. (TED O'DONNELL)

1. Performing the *Working Class Boy* stage show in 2016. (BOB KING) 2. Mahalia and Jackie were part of my band for the show and for the Sydney Opera House performance we were joined by Elly-May and David Campbell (at left) and Mark Lizotte (second right). **(STEPHANIE BARNES) 3. What better way to start the show** than to have my mate Anthony Field join me on stage with a bunch of pipers. **(STEPHANIE BARNES) 4. With Jane's parents, Kusumphorn and John Mahoney,** at Government House, Sydney, for my Order of Australia medal ceremony, in 2017. **(BARNES FAMILY COLLECTION) 5. It was another proud day for my manager John Watson and myself** when I received the 2017 ABIA (Australian Book Industry Award) for the year's Best Biography for *Working Class Boy*. **(BARNES FAMILY COLLECTION)**

bat. Maybe he would have been. We'll never know. I went back to recording.

TWO FIRES GAVE ME the chance to work with some great musicians, including Brian Setzer from the Stray Cats. I had been a fan of his for a long time. He joined me on two songs, 'Little Darling' and 'Lay Down Your Guns.' He played fantastic guitar and I think he was one of the highlights of that album.

The Stray Cats were a great band. They gave me hope for American music. These guys could play hard and fast and with conviction. They were the real deal. Most of the bands I saw in America didn't have any edge. No danger. There is something about growing up playing in Australian pubs that makes a band play a certain way that I like. It must be the thought of playing in front of a thousand Australians who will kill you if they don't like you that sharpens up a band's chops. Our bands sounded tougher than the rest.

The Stray Cats would end up opening for me on the JB2F tour of Australia and New Zealand. Noel came along too, to keep an eye on things. We were all drinking in a club after the Auckland show when things got a little out of hand. Now, coke was a rare commodity in New Zealand, so instead the locals liked to get a head full of speed and go out for the night. Well, when in Rome. I was wired to the max, and of course when you take speed you can consume copious amounts of booze, so I was like a time bomb. Lee Rocker, the Stray Cats bass player, said the wrong thing at the wrong time and I had him by the throat ready to kill him. I think the people that Lee hung around with in America were a bit nicer than me and Noel. The tour was nearly cancelled on the spot.

Noel grabbed my arm. 'Hey, Jimmy, cool it or you'll get us all arrested. Let's put the bass player down and step away from him. That's it.'

I dropped Lee and backed away. 'Sorry mate,' I said to Noel.

My blood was pumping and I was ready to rock. Noel marched me out of the building. After a short while things settled down and we went back into the bar and got on with drinking. I reluctantly apologised to Lee and both bands went back to having a good time. Lee was just a little wary of me from then on. I don't blame him.

The Stray Cats hired Noel to travel the world with them from that night on, just in case they ran into other people like me. I think they were in good hands. I wouldn't fuck with him.

NOEL HAD MADE ME fit and deadly. But all it did was keep me standing longer and make me harder to deal with. I became a machine. I knew I had to either stop martial arts or stop drinking and taking drugs. I couldn't give up the latter so martial arts had to go. If I was going to be deadly then I had to be in control of my temper. This became obvious to me when Jane and I had an argument after a gig at the Sydney Cove Tavern. Jane stormed off on me. I was probably being a jerk, I can't remember now. But anyway, as usual, I followed her at a distance just to make sure she was all right. As she walked past two guys leaning on a pole, one of them stuck out his foot to trip her up and she fell over.

I got to him just as he was shouting down at her, laughing, 'Fucking gook.'

Bang! I hit him way too fast and way too hard. His teeth smashed and he crumpled into a heap on the ground. I was over him, waiting for him to get up or his friend to move. He looked at me, smiled and said, 'Barnsey. I've travelled five hundred miles to see you sing tonight.'

I glared at him and his mate. 'One more move and you're going home in a box.'

I helped Jane up and we left. But I'd hit him too hard. It was an automatic reflex. My body had done what it was trained to do.

I had a bad attitude. A bad temper. A bad coke habit. So I stopped training until I had some control. It would take years. The harder I tried, the closer to the edge I got.

RELENTLESS TOURING WAS WEARING us down. Jane and I loved each other but we were seeing each other less and less. We weren't making any headway with our finances either. I was working more than ever and struggling to pay interest on loans, never mind paying the ever-increasing tax bill. A tax bill would come in and I would have to work to pay it. Then that meant I needed more money because I'd made more money so the tax bill kept getting bigger. The wheels kept turning and I couldn't get off. Running, constantly running, and never getting anywhere.

I was playing big tours to big houses. The huge, state of the art sound systems I needed to ensure that we sounded better than anyone else in the country were costing more every tour. I was happy to pay as long as my sound was great and the people were getting their money's worth. I had The Rolling Stones' lighting guy, Patrick Woodroffe, design a massive light show with moving trusses and a million lights for a tour that was the size of a Rolling Stones warm-up show. Patrick was a nice guy and charged me a fraction of what he was charging anyone else in the world, but it was still more than I could afford. I knew I was never going to make money like this, but I felt this was an investment in my future touring. If I kept spending more each time, then the tours would get bigger each time too. I was still selling a truckload of records. *Two Fires* sold over 400,000 albums. It went six times platinum. It was my fifth consecutive number one album. The tour was massive. It seemed I could do no wrong, but bad money management on my behalf was dragging me down. I tried not to think about it. I could always make more money.

CHAPTER THIRTY-FOUR

higher and higher

IN MY STUDIO, 1990–93

CHRISTMAS 1990 WAS GOING to be spent in our home. I would tour right up to Christmas and then take a short break. My band would stay with us over the holidays and then continue touring through the New Year. Don Gehman, who had produced *Two Fires*, loved my family and wanted to spend Christmas with us. We were going to have a house full of people. In reality, Jane and I probably needed to spend time together, just us and the kids, but that never seemed to happen. There was always somebody; most of the time a lot of people.

A few of my band were travelling from North America every time we toured. Tony Brock and Jeff Neill had become regulars, Tony coming from Los Angeles and Jeff travelling from Canada whenever I needed them. Jeff eventually moved to the Southern Highlands to be nearby in case I needed him and to help me with the costs, but Tony wanted to stay in Los Angeles even though he only played for me. Tony's airfares and the wages were adding up. I was paying him in US dollars. A lot of US dollars. It was a lot of money to be taken out of the pot. I tried to talk him into moving. 'It'll be better for both of us, Tony, if you move over here. You'll save me a fortune in airfares and you'll get to see your family more often.'

'Na mate. You see I moved to LA from England to make it in the big time. I got me green card and things are going well. I want to be famous in America, you know what I mean, so I'm staying there.'

I never understood this. With the money he was making from me he could have been set up for life in Australia, yet he preferred to live in a small apartment in LA. I thought he was crazy.

But at the time Tony wanted his wife and two kids to come over and stay for Christmas. Don brought his wife too. Then there was Jeff and the rest of the band, all staying with us. The White House was big but it wasn't big enough for all this. Still, it was easier and cheaper to keep all my band in Australia than send them home for Christmas and then fly them back immediately after to tour. So I decided that rather than have everyone sitting around the house getting under each other's feet, I would make an album over the Christmas break. This of course didn't really make things easier. Now we needed roadies and an engineer.

I discussed it with Don and the band. We would make an album for fun. It didn't matter if we never released it. We decided to record all the songs I'd liked as a young guy. Songs I heard on the radio. Songs I sang at parties or at soundchecks. We started making a list. It became apparent that most of the songs were soul songs, so we decided to make a soul record. Don had a lot of ideas. Budget restrictions and the unavailability of good horn players meant we wouldn't use real horns on the record. Anyway, we would make it sound more modern by using samples. Tony by this time had a definite idea of the sounds he liked for his drums too, and they were modern, with drum samples as well, so the record would not sound like a traditional soul record at all. It would be either really good or it would stink.

Don had gotten even stranger by the time he arrived in Australia. He was constantly fasting and on radical cleansing diets. This made him moody and he could at times be difficult to be around. But he was a great guy, dry and funny and full of great stories about the music industry. Don had done it all, from building Elvis's concert sound system to helping record some of the Bee Gees' biggest albums. He had lived a hard fast life. But he'd had to change his ways or die by the time I met him. He no longer drank or took drugs. Making records was the only thing besides his family that brought him joy.

I would sometimes walk into the control room and there would be Don holding court with the rest of the band. 'You know if you only eat raw food and nothing else your bowels start to –'

'Enough Don!' I would cut him off

Anyway, Don wanted to make the record his way. But this was my record, so we fought each other to get it done our own way. It wasn't that we had big fights. It was a bit like arm wrestling. I'd lean on him until he bent a little and did something the way I wanted and then he'd lean on me until I let him do his thing. But even when he was at his most difficult, Don knew what he was doing. And as strange as he could be sometimes, I liked Don a lot and I trusted him. I put my career in his hands.

WE FINISHED THE RECORD and sent it to Mushroom. There was an obvious silence from Michael. I'm not sure he got it. In fact, I know he didn't like it at the time.

Eventually he called. 'What are you doing, mate? Your fans won't know what the fuck you're doing singing this shit.'

I had to convince him. 'For a start, this isn't shit. It's soul music, Michael.'

'I fucking know that. It's not bad, it's –'

I interrupted him. 'It's better than not bad, Michael. I think it's pretty good.'

I could almost see Michael pacing as he spoke on the phone. 'Yeah, all right. It's good, but can we just wait until *Two Fires* is gone before we confuse the fuck out of your audience? I know what I'm doing, trust me. We wait until *Two Fires* is off the charts and then we slip this one out without too much fanfare. We'll see what happens.'

As we got closer to a release date for *Soul Deep*, which is what I called the record, Michael was even more unsure. 'Listen. Why don't we just shelve this fucking thing for a while and make a rock'n'fucking roll record?'

It was a battle. Michael was sure that my audience would hear the record and think that I had lost my mind. I wasn't sure that they wouldn't either. And to be fair, some of them did.

We had to wait a long time, nearly a year. *Two Fires* would not die. It just kept selling. This was a good problem to have, but during that time the soundtrack of the movie *The Commitments* came out. It was all soul music. When we finally released *Soul Deep* at the end of 1991, some people thought we were jumping on the soul bandwagon. Luckily for us it entered the charts at number one, making it six number one albums in a row for Mushroom and myself. It also went on to become one of the biggest albums in Australian music history, going more than nine times platinum and making Michael Gudinski a fortune. To be fair to Michael, as soon as he got it, he went into action. And when Michael gets something, he knows how to sell it better than anybody else in the business. I used to hear Michael on the radio, taking the credit for the record. 'Yeah. It was a gamble but that's what Jimmy and I do. We take risks. This one paid off and I'm glad I got him to make it.'

MY KIDS THOUGHT THAT everybody played music. Our house was always full of musicians and singers and producers, so why would they think any different? It was only a matter of time before they asked me if they could make some music too. As parents, Jane and I always thought that there weren't enough albums of kids singing for kids. It was always adults singing to kids, acting like kids. We decided to let them try. There was never any pressure to make anything great. It was all just fun.

David Froggatt was a friend of the family and, besides playing great guitar, he knew his way around a studio. David loved the kids and volunteered to take on the job of producing the band, which we called The Tin Lids, after the rhyming slang for 'kids'. It was great to watch. You can't force a five- or a six-year-old to do anything they don't want to do. Dave would sit and wait for that moment when they were ready and hit the record button. Then as quickly as they were ready to record, they would be finished and running out the door to play again. He was extremely patient.

We decided that a Christmas album would be fun and David came up with some arrangements for a few classic carols. The album, *Hey Rudolph*, worked. It had a sense of fun and seemed to connect with a whole bunch of children out there, who wanted to sing songs with other children. The album was released for Christmas 1991 and tore up the charts, hitting the number one spot in a few markets around the country. And the kids had a great time. They even went on tour. But we never made them do anything they didn't want to do. Music had to be fun for them or they wouldn't be a part of it.

Our kids made a couple of records, did a few tours, and then lost interest until they got a little older. Now I can't keep any of them out of my studio. In fact, I have to book to get time to record myself. I'm often asked if I was worried about bringing my children into the music business. I know it can be hard and cut–throat. But the way I see it, they're in a business where their job is to bring joy to people's lives. That's not a bad thing.

WITH *SOUL DEEP* SMASHING records all over the place, we prepared to go out on tour, which not surprisingly ended up being a bit of a costly exercise. To play this stuff well, we needed a big band. Bigger than usual. We needed a horn section and three backing singers. It wouldn't be an arena type of show so we planned to use smaller theatres, like the State in Sydney and the Palais in Melbourne. These venues fitted fewer people and cost loads to hire, so it was more expensive all across the board. I soon found out that touring with a large soul band was not the best way to make money. Just like the title of one of my singles off the album, the costs kept getting higher and higher, and so did I. But it kept the album in the charts and selling, which was why we were doing it.

Every show for a long time was a soul show. They were quieter and less aggressive. It wasn't long until I wished I had never made a soul record. I wanted to get out and scream and pin people to the back wall but that wouldn't happen for about a year. By that time, I was chomping at the bit. I would go on to revisit my soul roots quite a few times over the years and every time I did I learned more about singing and how to pace a show. I made *Soul Deeper* (2000), an imaginative title if I don't say so myself, then *The Rhythm and the Blues* (2009) and lastly *Soul Searching* (2016), each time working with amazing musicians from Memphis to Nashville. Every time I did it was an education that was invaluable to me as a singer. Eventually the shows would morph into one where I could play soul songs and rock songs in the same set. But that would take time.

TINA TURNER HAS ALWAYS been one of the great singers for me. Since I first heard 'River Deep, Mountain High' as a single back in 1966, I was hooked. Even as a young boy I could feel the electricity. I could feel the heat. I didn't know what was generating that heat. I was too young to understand the raw sexual power of

Tina and her look. But I knew I liked it. Nearly ten years later, I heard that Ike and Tina Turner were coming to Adelaide and I wanted to be there. By this point I knew exactly why I liked it. It was more than the sound.

Myself and a few of my mates drove to Kingston Avenue in Richmond and kicked in the back doors at the Apollo Stadium so we could see her. Nothing was going to stop me. That night was more than a concert, it was part of my education. I watched, mesmerised by the singing and dancing and energy of Tina and the Ikettes. I had made my way down to the very front row. I stood right in front of Tina, eyes wide open as she danced in front of me. In fact, it was as if she was dancing just for me, sweat dripping from her brow as she screamed and moaned her way through her set.

Behind Tina, I noticed something else going on. There was someone else driving the whole thing along like a steam train. Ike, her husband, was in the background, pushing and shoving the band until they played better than they thought they were capable of playing, pushing them to the very edge and beyond their playing ability. This, in combination with the sexual energy generated by Tina, made me sit up and take notice like never before. I watched as Tina poured her heart and everything she had out on the stage and as Ike drove the band harder and harder as every song started. By the end of the night the band, the singer and the crowd were ready to explode.

So, imagine how I felt when I was asked to join her in a campaign promoting rugby league. This campaign was one of the greatest collaborations of music, sport and advertising I had ever seen. Since 1989, Tina had taken rugby league, a game strictly for blokes and blokes alone, and made it accessible to women and families. To the masses. The game went from strength to strength. The whole idea was absolute genius. In 1992, the NRL asked me if I would consider joining Tina in the TV ads. This meant I would have to travel to Holland to record and make a film clip with her. They would pay me a fortune. I had to bite my lip to stop myself from laughing. I would have paid them to let me sing with her. It was one of the great moments in my life to stand next to Tina as she sang in the studio.

Everything I remembered from being that ten-year-old kid listening to her sing on the radio was right there in front of me. She was strong, beautiful, emotional, sexy, warm, loving and incredibly powerful. Tina was the real deal. I stayed in touch with her for a while after that, jumping up to sing with her whenever she asked.

Tina and I shared more than music. I had watched as my mother was beaten at home by her husband, just like Tina had been. But Tina escaped from that pain. She never let the violence define who she was. I often wished my mum had done the same, but everyone deals with things in their own way, I guess. Tina took that pain and it made her stronger. She took everything life had thrown at her and tossed it straight back, proud, strong and defiant. No matter how old she got, she never changed. She was committed to her life and her art. She shared her soul and her pain every night with her audience. The hairs on the back of my neck still stand up when I hear her sing. Just like they did in 1966.

AFTER A YEAR OR so of soul music, I decided to make a hard-sounding record. Grunge had taken hold, with new bands like Nirvana and Soundgarden playing louder and heavier. I don't try to follow trends, in case you haven't noticed. All I knew was that rock'n'roll was getting played on the radio again and I liked it.

I set about writing songs that I could record. I think it was Jeff Neill who showed me G tuning on my guitar. This was an old blues tuning that was made popular by Keith Richards. I loved it, and as soon as I picked up my guitar, new songs started pouring out of me. The songs I was writing with Tony and Jeff were heavy. The guys were practically living at my house by this point. All Jeff wanted to do was work all the time. Tony and I liked to work but we also wanted to have fun. A lot of my writing time involved consuming lots of booze and cocaine, which as I have said was becoming more and more readily available in Australia. It wasn't cheap. Tony would laugh and call it 'Dandruff of the Gods'. The price of coke was obscene. I hate to guess how much I spent in those days but – spoiler alert here – it was nothing compared to the ridiculous amounts I would spend later. I'll tell you more about that when we get there. Tony seemed happy to stay and write with me.

THE SONGS WE WROTE had potential. Some were hard and political, others were trippy and twisted. But I still needed more songs for my record. Something was missing. I reached out to Don Walker for the first time since the Cold Chisel break-up.

Now, let me clarify that it wasn't exactly the first time. I had asked Don for help in the past but he hadn't responded. I probably made it sound like I didn't really want his help that much. Anyway, I was brushed off. Don was happy to help Ian with his career but was reluctant to help me. I'm not sure if he was still angry that I'd left the band or if he thought I was doing well enough without him. I think it might have been a bit of both. Anyway, much to my surprise, this time Don responded positively.

'Yeah. All right, Jim. Let me have a look and I'll see what I can do,' he said in that Queensland drawl that I knew so well.

What he did was write the best song on the album. 'Stone Cold' sounded to me like a classic Don Walker song. Bluesy and soulful and full of great melodies for me to sing. It felt great to be singing one of his songs again. We recorded the song, with

Ian Moss playing guitar. I can see now that this moment was the start of the big thaw for us. For all the reasons you know and some that even we don't know, the break-up hurt each one of us in a lot of ways. Wounded, we scattered, trying not to think too much about the mistakes we had made. But from this recording on, we got along better.

Don even joked with me, 'I really like this album, Jim. I'm not sure I liked the others but I like this one. I think you'll find that this one won't sell that well.'

Don was joking but there was a bit of truth in there too. My other records were too commercial for his tastes. I tried not to take it personally. Don just didn't like straightforward songs. His tastes were a bit darker than mine. But I did take it personally. I hated that the Chisel boys didn't like what I was doing without them. I needed their approval. I tried not to show that it affected me, but I was always sure they could see it did.

Steve had told me a hundred times, 'That fucking rubbish you call music is shit compared to what we could be making.' I remember him saying, after twenty-five drinks at a party somewhere, spitting on me the whole time, 'It's the fucking songs, Jim. They're shit, you see. What can you do?'

I did want to punch him sometimes, but when he was drunk he was just funny.

Phil would pretend he hadn't heard my music. 'Yeah, yeah, Jim, I hear your record's good, but yeah, na, I haven't heard it yet. But don't worry, I'm going out to buy it soon.' Phil would never want to hurt my feelings. Ian just never mentioned it.

Don was right though. *Heat*, my sixth studio album, released in March 1993, failed miserably compared to the others. It stiffed. The album only reached number two on the charts, and fell away quickly, selling a fraction of what my previous albums had done. Anyone else in the world would be happy with that result, but for me the writing was on the wall. I was a failure. The behaviour, the drinking, the drug taking had dragged me back towards the place I belonged. The gutter.

THINGS HADN'T WORKED OUT for me in America. I'd been dropped by Atlantic, but Mushroom Records had set up an office in London with the aim of taking on some new territories. So I travelled to Europe about six times in as many months, trying to break into new markets. I had *Heat* under my arm and I'd bounce happily into radio stations, expecting them to play it, only to be met with, 'Hey, can you do a song or two unplugged?'

To start with, I didn't know what they were talking about. Apparently the new big thing was playing songs live on the radio, accompanied by an acoustic guitar or the like. Everyone was playing unplugged. I sent for Jeff Neill and we started playing songs from *Heat* unplugged. Now *Heat* was probably the most plugged album I had ever made. Most of the songs didn't lend themselves to this treatment. But I didn't let it stop me. 'Yeah, absolutely. Unplugged. I can do unplugged.' And we would tear into versions of my songs that sounded nothing like the originals. We were never going to sell any records this way.

I decided after being asked to play unplugged for the fiftieth time to make my next record a bunch of songs I could play with an acoustic guitar. I was basically behind the eight ball from then on, following trends instead of setting them.

I CAME BACK TO Australia and put together an album I could play unplugged. I was beginning to hate that word. Up until then I had been one of the most plugged-in singers, from one of the most plugged-in bands in the country. The music world was changing rapidly. A lot of it had to do with MTV and their bloody *Unplugged* series, but there were changes going on everywhere.

I didn't like a lot of them. I had a way of doing things. My system. Even though that system involved me getting fucked up, it was a system I knew. It was hard to make music in the state that I was in when everything was so bare and stark around me. I had nowhere to hide. All of my faults were uncovered – dare I say unplugged – for the world to see. I couldn't get away with them in this new acoustic world I was being dragged into.

The resulting album was called *Flesh and Wood* and, regardless of all my worrying, it ended up being a great album to sing and make. Don Gehman was at the helm again. I really loved Don, but he was getting stranger as our time together went on. He decided that not only would this album be acoustic but he wouldn't use any real drumkits as such. Every day we would put together various bits and pieces from the kitchen and hit them in front of microphones, trying to get a sound out of them. Pots, pans, frying pans; you name it, we hit it. Cardboard boxes instead of bass drums, jars filled with rice and used as shakers. I think a few good drumkits would have made the record even better, but considering we didn't use any I think we did a great job. The album hit the charts at number two in December 1993, despite having great songs and a bunch of great singers involved in the project. After so many number one albums, now I had two in a row at number two. I felt like I had lost all my momentum. I was a failure.

CHAPTER THIRTY-FIVE

we're not getting any fucking younger

MY BIRTHDAY, 1993

*C*RACK.

Suddenly I can see bright lights flashing inside my head. This is what they mean when they say you're seeing stars. Steve Prestwich just head-butted me while I wasn't looking.

'Hey you!'

Crack.

There he is again. I'm not trying to ignore him, I'm just busy talking.

'Are you listening to me, you bloody twat?' Steve interrupts me. He's had a few drinks, obviously, and he wants to talk shit with me. We're standing in the front room of my house, the White House, up on Mount Gibraltar. It's my birthday and everyone in the place is starting to get warmed up. There are at least another hundred people Steve could terrorise but he wants to get stuck into me.

'I'm just having a word with my wife if you don't mind, "Our Steve".' That's what his brothers call him when they talk about him. 'Our Steve'. I think it might placate him for a minute and I go back to my conversation.

Crack.

He won't take no for an answer. He wants to talk to me and he wants to talk now. 'Come on, Jim. Fuck. I need to talk to you, all right?'

I apologise to Jane. She laughs and walks away. Jane knows how Steve and I get after a few.

'What do you fucking want, you stupid fucking Scouse git?'

I know that sounds harsh but I am speaking from a place of love. Steve often calls me a fucking twat because I act like one sometimes. And I, more often than not, call him a fucking Scouse git, because he comes from Liverpool and he can be a right git when he gets pissed.

'You know what I'm going to say, don't you?' He's smiling at me now and trying to cuddle me.

'No, I don't. Come on, what? You tell me what I'm supposed to know.'

I look him straight in the eye. I have to, otherwise he'll head-butt me again. Every time he does it, it gets a little harder. Like he's trying to make a point.

'We –' He looks around the room to make sure no one's listening. 'We should get the fucking band back together. And soon,' he tries to whisper in that way that only a drunken Liverpudlian can. The whole room can hear him. I can see his eyes are starting to water a little. He's getting sentimental now. 'We're not getting any fucking younger, you know. And I want to play some music with my mates. Fuck all the bullshit. Let's just play fucking music, man.'

I look at him and I can tell that even though he's drunk too much and he probably won't remember this tomorrow, he is deadly serious. I give him a cuddle. 'Well, you talk to the others. If they are in, I'm in. I've been working hard since we stopped. You guys are the lazy bastards.'

THE BOYS HAD BEEN anything but lazy and I knew it. It was strange. What we thought of each other and what we said to each other were never the same thing. We would say the harshest things to one another in public, even though we thought the world of each other. Cold Chisel was a very complex beast.

So Steve knew I was kidding. Ian had made a career for himself. He had some very big records and toured relentlessly, just like me. Don had formed the band Catfish and would go on to make some great records with Tex, Don and Charlie. Phil had taken a break and spent time with his family, something that we all yearned for but couldn't quite bring ourselves to do. He kept up his chops playing bass with Ian's band and with me occasionally. And Steve, of course, wrote beautiful songs. He'd joined the Little River Band for a short time and even played drums with John Farnham before he'd finally made a record of his own and toured a little with his own band. So we had all been busy.

Whenever Steve put shit on me or the music I made, I reminded him how many records I had made and sold, just to shut him up a bit.

I LAUGH AND START to walk away. Steve calls me back in close. 'Hey you!'

I turn back towards him, thinking he wants another cuddle.
Crack.

He hits me with another head butt. 'I am gonna fucking talk to them, you bloody twat. But you'd better be ready to sing well this time. None of that shit you sing in your solo fucking band. Working Class rubbish. Real fucking rock songs mate, all right?'

Steve turns away and spots one of the many girls at the party. He starts to dance, the way he always does when he's drunk and happy. He may be a git but I do love the guy.

BUT WE DIDN'T GET back together, not straightaway. I heard soon after my party that Steve was having troubles with bad headaches. Blinding pain behind his eyes.

'I think he's got that headache from head-butting me so many times,' I joked with Jane.

Steve had a benign brain tumour removed in 1993. It was nothing to do with him head-butting me. When we found out we were all stunned. I thought we would live forever, so this news about Steve rocked me. Cold Chisel would always be there. They were my first family. When I left home and joined them, it was the first time I felt safe, the first time that I was a part of something positive and good. My family before that was never safe, was never positive. It was dark, and thinking about them made me feel some sort of pain. My family never knew what a family really was. But Chisel was different. We fought, laughed and cried together. I still looked back on my years with them as the good times. They were the family I had always wanted. Now there was a chance that we would lose Steve. Lose a brother. I couldn't think about it.

Steve had surgery not long after. Everything went well but everything changed too. Steve had realised that life was short and he wanted to have a good time. He was no longer angry or aggressive. He was a peaceful, happy, loving father and friend. The thought of leaving his family behind, including us, had made Steve realise how lucky he was.

'We're not here for a long time, Jim, we're here for a good time. We shouldn't take each other for granted. Let's make some music before one of us dies, for fuck sake,' he said to me, next time I saw him. He was very serious and had tears in his eyes.

No one but Steve ever wanted to make the first move. He was always trying to get us in a room and play music. 'Come on, guys. Just fucking give it a go. What have we got to lose?'

But it never happened. We all stood back, protecting ourselves. I for one didn't want to get hurt again, although I would have to risk it to get over the feeling that I was no good without Cold Chisel to prop me up. And it was more than just personal. Musically we still had work to do. We all knew it. The band had imploded for a lot of reasons but the heart of it, the music, was not one of them.

BEFORE LONG I WAS told by my accountants that things were really bad, and getting worse by the minute.

'How bad can it be? I can make more money,' I laughed.

They weren't laughing with me. 'We are going to have to make arrangements. Settle with all your debtors, and you will probably be bankrupt in a month. You have over-capitalised, Jimmy. There is no more money.'

My world was crumbling around me. What was I going to do? That day had come. The whole world was going to see that I was a loser. I deserved this. I should never have been successful. I went into a dark place. A state of depression. That voice that I had heard in my head was screaming now. 'You'll end up back in the gutter where you belong. You thought you were better than us. Well, now we know you're not.'

I could hear it going round and round. I tried not to let the family see that I was so down, but I'm not good at hiding these sorts of things. We were going to have to sell the house. My home. I had worked my whole life for this. This made me different from the family I had left behind when I joined the band. I was the first person in my family to buy a house of their own. This was the home my children were supposed to grow up in. I had buried our old dog Theo in the grounds of this house. I couldn't sell it. They couldn't take it from me. But they were going to, along with all the stuff I had collected over the years that made me feel like I meant something. Statues, saddles, paintings, furniture, all of it was being ripped from me.

As far as I could tell, Jane took it well. She didn't seem to mind. 'It's just things, Jimmy. We don't need things. We can make a better home. We still have each other.'

She was right. Somehow I still had my Jane.

ONE DAY, JANE MADE a suggestion. 'Jimmy, you've spent the last six months in and out of Europe. Why don't we pack up and move there for a while? You can work on building a new audience and we can have fun. The children will love it.'

This sounded good to me. We could run away and I wouldn't have to see everything I had lost. I thought that if I stayed in Australia I would have it rubbed in my face. I had to get away.

I sort of believed what Jane had told me. I had all I needed. My children and my wife. I didn't need all this stuff and I could make more money. I was free. But it was still weighing heavy in the back of my mind. I tried to keep a brave face, but alone I would break down and cry. I had fucked it all up.

PART 3

A NEW BEGINNING

CHAPTER THIRTY-SIX

wipe the slate clean

AIX-EN-PROVENCE, 1994 TO 1996

W E HAD TO DECIDE exactly where we would live. Jane was excited about the prospect and me, well, I just wanted to hide my face. So, to distract myself, I did what I did best, the only thing I knew how to do. I worked. I carried on doing promotion around Europe, trying to sell records and maybe break some new territories so that I could rebuild.

Jane travelled around France looking for the right town for us to live in. We had decided we couldn't live in England. It was cold and wet. Hamburg was a good place but then we'd still have the Northern European winter to deal with. Italy sounded great. The food, the people, the sun and sea. It was beautiful but everything ran on Italian time. Airplanes and trains didn't get away on schedule. If I suddenly had to be somewhere, I might not make it. Then there was Scotland. It was colder than England and nothing was going on there musically at the time. So through a process of elimination we ended up with France. France had

great food, fantastic people, the sea, the sun and even the snow in
winter. And if we stayed in the south, we could be anywhere
in a matter of hours.

I was in Germany somewhere when I got the call. 'I found
a place. It's perfect for us. There are nice schools and good food
and it is just so beautiful, Jimmy. You'll love it. It's called Aix-
en-Provence. It's not far from Marseille, only thirty miles, and
there's an international airport there. We can fly in and out for
work as we need to. I'm going back to Australia now to finish
things up. Can you go down and take a look at it? I don't want
you living somewhere you don't like.'

Jane never ceased to amaze me. Our whole world had come
crumbling down and here she was, as excited as ever. More than
ever. It was as if she was happy to leave everything that we had built
behind. Looking back, maybe she was. I wondered if Jane knew
everything I had been up to. Was this an opportunity to wipe the
slate clean, start fresh for me? I hoped so. This is what my mum
must have felt whenever she ran away from everything, trying to
keep one step ahead of the past. If she could run far enough away,
everything would be left behind and no one would be wise to her.
But it never worked for Mum, so how could it possibly work for
me? I didn't deserve another chance but I had to try.

I HAD A PLAN. I was working all week but I had the weekend off.
Jeff Neill and myself would jump on a plane and fly to Marseille,
rent a car and drive to Aix and see what my new hometown was
like. I knew we were moving there regardless of what I thought.
Jane loved it, and if she loved it I was sure I would be all right.

We booked into the Hôtel des Augustins, right in the centre
of town. The hotel was hundreds of years old and looked haunted
to me. Maybe there were enough ghosts around here that my
ghosts could disappear into the crowd? The whole town looked

old, but it was old and beautiful. The main street was wide, cobblestoned and lined with tall trees. Paul Cézanne and Ernest Hemingway drank coffee in this street while contemplating their next move. I could do the same.

This was a long way from Elizabeth. Some of the buildings were falling down, just like in Elizabeth, but the difference was they had been standing for centuries. And they weren't being torn down by people like me. It was also a long way from the Australian rock'n'roll scene. No one knew me here and I felt I might be able to relax for a while. I wasn't going to be in the spotlight. I thought that was a good thing. But I had gotten used to being in the spotlight. I knew how to hide there. When everybody is focused on the big picture, small things go unnoticed. It would take a little getting used to.

The Cours Mirabeau would become a second home to me. Plane trees lined the streets, which were filled with tourists and locals drinking in the bars and coffee shops. It stretched from the enormous Fontaine de la Rotonde at one end to the markets at the other end. The town looked like a postcard. In fact, I've bought a few postcards since with that very street on them. At night you could walk the length of the street taking in the sights. There were artists painting portraits of passing foreigners and musicians playing classical music for tips. Occasionally I would hear an Australian accent cutting through the crowd, but I would just lower my head and keep walking. There were ice-cream stalls in the summer and in the winter, street vendors selling roasted chestnuts. All year round you could buy crepes smothered in Nutella. My kids would grow to love this place. But Jeff and I would have to get a feel for it. We went out into the street, set ourselves up outside a particularly busy bar on one of the corners, and started playing music. Tables filled with people were scattered across the footpath. Pretty soon they were clapping their hands and dropping money into Jeff's guitar case. If worst came to worst, we could almost make a living doing this. Not the living we had become used to though. Locals kept bringing drinks out to us from inside the bar. Pastis was the drink of choice. It tasted like ouzo and had a kick like a mule. The more we drank, the more we played.

We were having a break when I heard a familiar-sounding voice. 'Fuck me. You're Jimmy Barnes. What are you doing busking on this street?'

The voice was croaky and hoarse and obviously Australian. It belonged to a scrawny-looking young guy, dressed like a hippy, who I soon found out was attending university in town. 'This is how I pay my rent. I busk on the Cours.' He could speak French but with a hard Australian accent. Even I knew it didn't sound good. I thought maybe we had taken his spot.

'We can move if you normally work here. We're just fucking around. I'm thinking of moving to Aix for a while and we thought we'd test out the vibe of the town.'

He stood with us and drank one of the many free drinks we had lined up, and went on to tell me his life story. He was studying in Aix, but he was doing it tough. He was nearly flat broke, and he hadn't been able to sing for a week because of a bad throat. He was hungry and needed some help.

'I tell you what we can do. Why don't you walk around with your hat while we sing and we'll give you a commission at the end?' I suggested. This seemed to make him happy. By the time we had finished we had made a lot of money, more than he could fit into his hat. He had already folded quite a lot away and put it in his pockets. He pulled it all out and handed it over to me. I looked at Jeff. We didn't really need the money. This guy did, so we gave it to him.

'Here you go, mate. You look like you need this more than us. Maybe you could finish these drinks too.'

Jeff packed up his guitar and we started to leave.

'Thanks guys, this is a great help. I would have been fucking starving this week if it wasn't for you bastards.'

Then we walked back to our hotel. This town was all right. It was happening. The people seemed nice enough. I thought that the family would be fine here.

AIX WOULD BECOME OUR home for a few years. We rented a few different places. One in the foothills, set back against a hill. It was rustic and surrounded by lavender. It was like a painting. Late afternoon we would see men smoking cigarettes as they walked into the bush carrying guns. They were hunting rabbits. I could hear the sound of rifles firing in the distance as I sat out in the garden. But eventually Jane found a house she loved that was for sale. We rang Australia and asked Michael Gudinski to buy it and then rent it to us. We told him it was a good investment, and Michael was our friend. He was happy to help.

The house was a two-hundred-year-old *bergerie*, a shepherd's house, surrounded on all sides by grapevines and wheatfields, with red poppies growing all through the wheat. It was breathtaking. It was like we were surrounded by living art. The wheatfields changed thoughout the year, from bright green to brown to golden yellow, each season offering something new and more beautiful.

Somehow we had managed to set up a new life that was perfect for us. Despite the damage I had done in Australia, Jane had found this home. It had a room that I converted into a studio so I could start to write music again. The smaller children attended the local French school, and within a few months they were all speaking perfect French. Mahalia was starting high school, and this was a little more difficult. We couldn't find a place that was right for her. Jane's Thai father, Khun Suvit, wanted her to go to a great school, and he let us know he was happy to pay for it. We found an amazing one on the shores of Lake Geneva in Switzerland, called Le Rosey, one of the best and most expensive schools in the world. John Lennon's son Sean had gone there. Mahalia was happy, the little ones were happy and Jane was happy.

I was sort of happy too. Life was perfect when we were home. On warm summer mornings we would set up easels outside the house to paint Mont Sainte-Victoire, which stood in the distance, a few miles from our backyard. This was the mountain Paul Cézanne had painted so many times. After dropping the kids to school, Jane and I would walk through the town to the markets and buy fresh produce, stopping to drink hot coffee and eat baguette with jam, with me trying to talk to people in broken French as Jane blended in with the locals. I was the only member of the family who hadn't mastered the language. The people of Aix-en-Provence were friendly and warm and were quick to excuse my broken French. We made beautiful friendships that have lasted until this day.

For anyone else and for me at any other time, this would have been the perfect life. But, like I've said, I was troubled. Troubled by my past. I had issues to deal with before I could settle down to enjoy a life as idyllic as this. I didn't belong in the South of France. I belonged in the gutters of Adelaide. I didn't deserve to be wandering around the marketplace like I was. I deserved nothing. I was good for nothing and I knew it.

I felt like it was all happening again. I'd watched Mum start to get ahead, only to be dragged back by Dad's drinking and bad behaviour. This seemed to be the cycle that my family were all doomed to. I didn't know how to get off this merry-go-round. I would start to get on top and then the rug was pulled out from under me. I can see now that it was me pulling the rug from under myself. It was self-destruction. But at the time, I only knew I was afraid. I tried to hide my fears, but it was affecting my moods.

Plus, in the back of my head was a nagging sense of loss. I had failed in Australia. I hadn't been able to look after my family properly. I'd lost my home and all the things we had surrounded ourselves with. I had nothing. And I felt useless. I was in a strange country and not making money yet, living on handouts from Jane's father and from my friends at home. I couldn't enjoy this. How could I?

I tried to ignore all these thoughts that were eating away at me. Every day I would get up and try to relax. But I couldn't make money here. The longer I was away from Australia the less chance I had of making it back to the top of my business. The family loved it, but I was different here. There was no rock'n'roll, and none of the trappings that go with it. I couldn't get smashed and go crazy because no one did that in this town. Our friends would come for dinner and sip wine with their meal and that was it. I never saw any of them drunk. They didn't take drugs. They liked jazz music, not rock. And God help me, I started liking jazz too. The sound of Miles and Coltrane began to fill my home. I'd never thought it would happen but it was calming to me. To Jane, jazz was like fingernails on a blackboard. She couldn't take it at all. She would turn off my records and play The Carpenters. I was starting to like them too. What was happening to me? Jazz and The Carpenters. Fuck me. I'd gone soft. I met a lot of musicians but not one rock'n'roll musician.

Some of our friends would have music nights. A few of them even had a band. Drums, upright bass and piano.

'Hey, Gimmy. Why don't you sing a song with us?' they would ask, but I would say I didn't know the songs.

'You must know this one.'

But I knew nothing. I started sneaking out and buying albums by jazz singers like Sarah Vaughan and Ella Fitzgerald and Frank Sinatra, but I didn't really like them that much. I would occasionally get up and sing 'Georgia on My Mind'. I sort of knew that. It was Ian's song really, I'd heard him sing it a million times with Cold Chisel. But he would never know.

My French friends loved it when I got up with them. 'Oh Gimmy, you sing so loud. It's like you 'ave a, a, how you say, a speaker system built in or something.'

They would all laugh. These people were happy, well-balanced human beings. I wasn't used to people like that. At home in Australia I had spent my life surrounded by people like me, who were going crazy trying to fit into a world where they didn't belong. And as much as I loved being in France with my family and our newfound friends, I knew I didn't belong here either. Not now anyway.

I WAS GOING AWAY on tour a lot and getting more and more wasted while I was doing it. Jane could feel it and so could I. I didn't plan it. It just happened. Like I was waiting for a chance to break loose. Just a little at first, but slowly I got worse and worse. It was as if I wanted to fuck up all the peace of our new lives. I had these problems before I left Australia but I'd never even admitted that they were problems. If anybody suggested I get help or anything of the kind, I just wiped them. They didn't exist.

I remember flying to London for a recording session and going out with a few mates and going ballistic. This was around the time that house music and hallucinogenic drugs were all the rage in England. Raves were popping up in disused factories all over the country. My friends took me to a rave. I swallowed a handful of ecstasy tablets and went to an old rundown factory that had been cleaned up for the night. Whoever did it up knew what they were doing because when we got there the place looked like a spaceship. I had never heard anything like the music they were playing there. How did musicians come up with this stuff?

By the end of the night we found ourselves in a little house near the factory and the drugs got harder. Sheets of blotting paper infused with LSD were handed around like lollies. And of course, I had pockets full of cocaine too.

At five in the morning I came to my senses a little. 'Shit, I've got to get back to London and check out of my hotel. I have a plane to catch back to France this afternoon,' I pleaded with the mate who'd brought me.

'Fuck man. I can't help you. I won't be able to drive for about three weeks, I think.'

I looked at him. He was right. His eyes were like saucers. He wasn't going anywhere. I wasn't any better.

'Well, how the fuck do I get back to London then?' I asked.

'You can get the Tube. The fucking train goes right to your hotel door, Jim.'

I was worried. 'I can't go in this state. Look at me. How am I going to get there by myself?' I was having trouble standing up by this point.

'Here you go. Take these. They'll help you keep it together. Have a fucking line too.' And he pushed a sheet of LSD into my top pocket. I snorted another half gram and walked to the door.

I stepped out of the house. It was dead quiet and snow was falling. *Crunch crunch crunch.* I could hear my feet breaking through the fresh snow as I walked. Everything looked like a dream. The cold on my face made me feel alive for a second. I walked down the street with my head tilted back and fresh white snow falling on my equally white face. How would I get out of this?

Somehow I managed to find the station and got on a train. I hoped it was the right one. I was standing on a busy train absolutely shitfaced and I could still hear the rave music rolling around in my brain. I was trying to take my mind off the journey by going through the music in my head, to work out how they had come up with music like this. The big album of the day was by a band called Leftfield. All I could hear in my head was Leftfield. Then the music started drifting, blending into the clicking of the tracks as the train cut through the snow, heading for central London. The rhythms were the same. That was what they were writing. Urban rhythms. The sounds of the city. The sounds of the Underground. I was happy I had got it, but it wouldn't help me get to my hotel and then out to the airport and back to France in the state I was in.

I made it to the hotel and rang my mate. 'I fucking can't do this. I'm fucked,' I begged him.

But there was nothing he could do. 'In your top pocket are some of those acid tabs. Take one or two and you'll be right, mate,' he said to me. He didn't have to walk through Customs and travel internationally like I did.

I packed, snorted a line and headed to the airport. I made it onto the plane and was feeling closer to human when I remembered the acid in the top pocket of my jacket. I would get busted for sure. How did I get through customs in England? I went to the bathroom and flushed the acid and any cocaine I had left down the toilet. All except one line and one piece of blotting paper, which I thought I'd better swallow to help me walk through Marseille Airport. Jane wanted me to come straight to a friend's house for dinner. I couldn't face it. I decided I would call from home, saying I was sick.

I arrived and walked straight though the whole airport without any problem. Outside, I was looking for cab when I heard a voice I knew. The thick French accent trying to speak English was unmistakable. It was Gerard, our friend.

'Hey Gimmy. It is me, Gerard. I 'ave come to pick you up for dinner. Jane said to bring you straight to the soiree.'

I was in trouble. Gerard laughed at me in the car. 'You are a crazy person, Gimmy. I want to be like you too.'

We got to the house and I couldn't eat or drink. I sat and tried not to look anyone in the eye.

I MADE ONE RECORD while I was in France, *Psyclone*. The name said it all. My life was like a cyclone and I needed psychiatric help.

We recorded most of the album in Chateau Miraval in the south of France, a beautiful place with its own winery and chef. This was one of the most beautiful studios I had ever seen. Pink Floyd had recorded tracks for *The Wall* there. It was state of the art. We hired a Southern boy from Memphis called Joe Hardy to produce the record with me. Joe was great. He had at one time, years earlier, contemplated becoming a priest, but decided to make rock'n'roll instead. I think the choice still haunted him. He was wild and clever and troubled and had made a few of my favourite records. *Psyclone* wasn't my best work but I had begun to write songs about the real issues I faced. At this time I was staring into the abyss, not sure if I could make it through life in one piece, and the lyrics reflect this. Maybe this was the start of a change, but it would take a lot of work and time to get my head above the water. Time until I could just breathe. I didn't start working on myself for a long time after making *Psyclone*, but I do see this record as the start of peeling away the layers that would reveal the real me. The me that in the end would either sink or swim. Some nights I prayed to God, even though I'd stopped believing a long time before, that I would eventually learn to swim.

WHILE I WAS LIVING in the south of France, I started to get messages from Rod Willis and the band. It seemed enough water had flowed under the bridge to wash away any bad feelings we had about our falling out. The music was calling out to each of us. I was happy making music alone but it wasn't the same as Chisel. Even the success felt empty in some way. I had it all and couldn't keep hold of it.

MY LIFE SHOULD HAVE been full and satisfying. A change of scene. A brand-new life in a new country with new friends. I had peace and I had time to think. But that time to think only made me afraid. Afraid of what I had become. All the drugs and all the music, nothing could stop the noises in my head. Screaming at me, telling me I was no good. I knew it.

Leaving Australia the way I did had hurt me. I would speak about it in interviews, saying, 'Oh yes, when the tax man took my house I realised that I didn't need it. I didn't need things. I didn't need possessions. I have all I need right here with me.'

But I was fooling myself. I felt like a failure. Inside, where no one but me could see it, I knew I was fucked, and it was eating me away. I wanted to go back and prove something to everyone in Australia, but more importantly to myself. I wasn't only worth something if I was successful, if I owned a lot of stuff, if people threw themselves at me. But secretly, that was how I measured my own self-worth. It was shallow and I knew it. I wasn't that stupid, was I?

In 1996 we made plans to move back to Australia, away from the peace and quiet of rural France and back into the firing line of the music business. Jane didn't want to leave, I think she knew what was ahead of us. I convinced myself that I was going back to make music.

CHAPTER THIRTY-SEVEN

love songs don't sell anymore

AUSTRALIA, 1996–98

I RETURNED FROM FRANCE determined to get everything back on track and before long it all was – I was back on the same track I had tried to jump off. Only now it was worse. I was drinking more than ever and taking more drugs than ever before. In 1996 I released *Hits*, a greatest hits anthology that came in at number one. I had a single at number one on the radio charts as well, so I should have been on top of the world, but I was falling apart again. Jane and I were fighting more and more, mainly because I was fucking up in every way possible. To make things worse, Jane was starting to party too. I was tearing down everything we had tried to rebuild. It was one step forward and ten steps back. Cocaine was easy to find in Australia by now and I found it all the time. I would be on tour and come home smelling of booze and women. Smashed and not even capable of making excuses for myself anymore. Instead, I would just storm out of the house and find more of everything.

WHILE WE WERE IN Europe, I had recorded a song that Jane and I wrote. I remember reading the lyrics and squirming in my chair. Was Jane trying to let me know something? I had to stop myself from thinking about it. The song was called 'Lover Lover'. It was poppy and catchy. I felt it was something that people might get to like.

When Jane decided she wanted to write songs I was surprised. She started walking around the house with a clipboard, counting to herself, deep in thought.

'What are you doing, baby?' I asked her after a few days of this.

'I'm writing a song. I think I've worked out how to do it.'

Great. I hoped she would tell me once she'd figured it all out. 'That's good. But what are you counting?' I was curious. It was like she was doing a maths problem.

'I'm counting out the number of syllables I need for this verse. I'm doing research. This is like an assignment at school and I want to get an A+.'

I laughed quietly to myself. 'That's not how you write songs. You don't have to count like that.' She had obviously got the whole thing wrong.

'You do it your way and leave me to do it my way.' She walked away. I thought I'd let her do it her way, then I'd help her at the end. But she didn't need my help. When she had finished she played it to me.

'It's really good. How did you do that?' I asked her.

'I have my own way of doing things. Music is like maths to me. It's a language of its own. When I was little and living in a lot of different countries, the only common language was maths. So I saw maths as a language. Music is the same.'

I had no idea what she was talking about but she was obviously right because the song was a cracker. I played it to Mushroom, who had their song specialist look at it. He rang us up and said, 'Listen. I'm not sure it will work. You should write something else.'

I was gobsmacked. 'What don't you get? It's hooky and it has a great melody. This is a good love song.'

The songsmith thought for a second and then replied, 'Love songs don't sell anymore.'

I hung up. He had no idea what he was talking about. I told the record company to put it out as it was. They did and the song hit the top of the charts late in 1996. Apparently people did still like love songs. Who knew? Not the songsmith from Mushroom anyway. 'Lover Lover' was my first number one airplay hit as a solo artist. If I had to write a report for Jane it would have gone like this: 'Jane Barnes has been very attentive in class and has done all her homework. For songwriting I have given her an A+.'

But having a number one just made things harder for us. The song was everywhere, so I was away more often and I was suddenly back in the public eye. I didn't cope well. I was falling apart. I was crumbling. Cold Chisel was looming on the horizon and I wasn't ready for it.

ENOUGH TIME HAD PASSED for us all to forget why Cold Chisel had broken up. Besides, when we looked back, it wasn't that important anyway. We just needed some space to grow up a bit. I wasn't sure how much I had grown up but I knew that I wanted to play with the band again. I missed the feeling of belonging to something bigger than just my own band. I needed to reconnect with my brothers. I think I needed them more than ever.

I was happy that I had a big album with *Hits*, so I wasn't walking back with my tail between my legs. I was rejoining my mates, with a full head of steam. My bad habits had become worse and my sanity was on the line. I needed to belong.

We started writing and rehearsing for the making of an album and, if all went well, a big tour. I started singing with the band but most of what I could see was through the bottom of a bottle. I knew they were worried, but we ploughed on through. Some days I was bad, and others I was worse.

MICHAEL HUTCHENCE CAME INTO Sydney looking tired and flustered. I remember seeing him on TV and thinking he needed to rest. I thought I knew how he was feeling. I needed a rest too, and Hutch's life was a million times more hectic than mine.

I spoke to him on the phone. 'Yeah, yeah, let's catch up. I'm busy and I know you're busy. You're here for a while, we can catch up soon,' I said. I was living around the corner from where he was staying. I might have walked by his hotel a few times. But you never expect to run out of time, do you? There is always later.

Everyone in Australia wanted a piece of Michael from the minute he stepped off the plane. I didn't want to be one of those people. Jane and I could wait. We'd find a moment when the madness died down to connect and say, 'So how are you holding up?'

Hutch was rehearsing. He was flat out. I was busy trying to keep my head above water. Then I heard the news. No. It wasn't true. Fucking press. They'd write anything for a headline. Of course Michael wasn't dead. They were always writing shit about him. But the reports kept coming in. Phone calls from hysterical mutual friends. It was true. He was gone. It was 22 November 1997. He had been found hanging in his room at the Ritz Carlton Hotel. Everybody wanted a piece of him but he died alone. I felt a shiver run down my spine.

This was a sad day, not just for his friends, or his millions of adoring fans. I could only think about his baby, Tiger Lily. She would not get to grow up with her dear, loving father. How could he have done this to her? How desperate had he been? I didn't notice how bad things were when I talked to him. He seemed fine, but he wasn't. What sort of friend was I?

I don't know what pushed him over the edge that day. I have stood on that same edge looking down but something always stopped me stepping off. I wish someone or something had stopped him. That moment of bad judgement was all it took. We can all be sad, and we can all be angry. We can all have an opinion, but we were not in his shoes that night. We were not lost in the dark like he was. If there was a way out I'm sure he would have taken it. But he just couldn't see any other way. Oh Michael.

Jane and I went to say goodbye at a funeral home in Bondi Junction. There was a body lying in the room but Michael wasn't there. I would not remember him like that. Michael was alive and vibrant. He loved life and he loved people. Michael could walk into a room and light it up. Jane wrote a poem for him and I slipped it into his pocket. He would never get to read it.

The funeral was a massive event. I'm not sure Michael would have wanted an event. I'm not sure Michael wanted any of this. The fame, the hurt, the loneliness. But the world wanted to say goodbye. There were fans scrambling to find a spot where they could pay their respects. Friends in dark sunglasses that couldn't cover the tears. And family, lost and confused. 'Into My Arms' floated across the church and out the doors, fading as it was blown by the wind down the streets of Sydney.

WHEN *THE LAST WAVE OF SUMMER* album was released in October 1998, it debuted at number one on the charts. But it didn't happen easily. Chisel started rehearsing new songs and I would roll up still drunk from the night before and the night before that. I was barely capable of standing up, but for some reason I could still sing. I was an animal. I would snort and drink my way through rehearsals and then go straight out to clubs, without going home, then turn up at rehearsals wearing the same clothes the next day.

Finally, we went into Festival Studios to make the record. Don had written a lot of great songs as usual, but for some reason they seemed to resonate even more than normal with me. It was as if Don had been reading my mail. Every song felt like it was telling the story of some part of my life falling apart. I would sing each one and feel the emotion overwhelm me as soon as I opened my mouth. So I drank more to calm the nerves. I never hid anything from the boys by this time. Cocaine and weed and bottles of vodka sat on the bench next to the mixing desk, and I would shovel them into myself throughout the day and night while we worked. Sometimes it seemed like the band wanted to test me, waiting to catch me falling apart. It would be three in the morning and we'd have been recording for twelve hours straight. My eyes would be almost crossing as I sat slumped in a chair in the corner of the control room, and Don would say, 'Hey, why don't we do Jimmy's guitar take now?'

The rest of the boys would look at me in disbelief, waiting for me to admit that I was too out of it. Don would look straight at me, 'What do you think, Jim? You up for it?' His eyes probing, testing my ability to cope.

I'd be having trouble focusing my eyes on him at all but I didn't let him know that. 'Fuck, yeah. I'm ready. Are you guys all too tired to work? Pussies. I'm fine. Let's do it.' And I'd stagger into the booth to try to tune my guitar.

'Hey Tony,' I would call through the talkback microphone, 'could you send Mossy in here to tune this fucking thing? I can play it but I can't tune it.' I was talking to Tony Cohen, the engineer. Tony disappeared a few years after this, and eventually turned up living in the country. Tony was a wild boy in his day too and his health was damaged. He died recently. Another great member of the music community gone.

I don't know how much of my playing they used on the record. I can hear it in a few places. Maybe Don just liked sloppy guitar playing? I got it done quickly and walked back into the control room. They were all staring at me.

'How the fuck did you do that?' Tony asked. He'd seen everything I had consumed.

'It's too easy,' I lied, trying to make it to a chair before I fell over. 'Anything else you want me to do?' And I sat down and poured out another gram of coke.

Many nights the sessions would end in fights, but not directly because of me. Don and Ian seemed to be fighting a lot. Maybe Don needed to take out his frustrations with me on someone who cared. I felt nothing. It would have done him no good to talk to me.

I remember singing 'The Things I Love in You'. That night we were overdubbing vocals and bits and pieces at Trafalgar Studios. This song was like a raw nerve for me. It's the story of a relationship breakdown. Whenever I sang it at rehearsals, it hurt. But the night I did the final vocal it nearly tore me apart. I was destroying my relationship with Jane, the girl I loved, and I knew it. She was the most important person in my life and I was hurting her. But I couldn't stop myself.

I sang the song with such fury and venom that when I finished it, my blood was boiling. I smashed up the studio booth. I took off my headphones and walked into the control room with tears in my eyes. 'There's your fucking vocal.'

I stormed off into the night alone. Every time I hear that vocal I get a knot in my stomach. I was a different person when I sang it. I don't know who I was or where I wanted to be, but I know that I was in pain and I wanted it to end.

When the album was finished we sent it to New York to be mixed by an engineer called Kevin Shirley. Kevin would play a huge role in the lives of Cold Chisel and myself for many years to follow, but it didn't start well. We all arrived in New York separately. I turned up to the studio once and spent the rest of the time in a drug-crazed haze, holed up in the Mercer Hotel in Soho. Why Kevin chose to work with us after that I'm not sure. Perhaps he could see something that I couldn't. Maybe it was because we'd made a hit record. Despite all the pain we felt while making it. Despite the wild way we recorded it and despite the state I was in as I sang it. We had made a great record and it entered the Australian charts at number one. Cold Chisel was back with a vengeance.

CHAPTER THIRTY-EIGHT

it's a gift from God

A NOTE ON SONGWRITING

S ONGWRITING COMES EASY TO some people but not all. Some folks spend months, even years, building the perfect set of lyrics. Others, like me, just don't have the time. I can't sit long enough to think about words in too much depth. Maybe I should, although the best songs I have written have come in a flurry: a title followed by the storyline, which steamrolls to a crashing conclusion. Probably exactly what is going to happen with this book you're reading. But they have a point or a meaning or even an emotion that I need to get across. Something I need to say and once I've said it I let it go and walk away. It's just the way I work.

No two writers are alike. I like people who tell stories. No matter how they go about it. I have worked with a lot of songwriters along the way, some who spend forever trying to express exactly what they mean. Don Walker is one of these people. Don has presented a set of words to me and then within days taken the song back. As far as I can tell he has given up on it, when out of the blue I will see a trace of the song I once heard written into a new story and it is perfect. He has waited patiently for the right vehicle to come along and then it finds a home. A good example of this was 'Four Walls' off *East*. When he first wrote it the chorus ended with the words, 'Four walls, washbasin, hotel bed'. The whole song was about being trapped in a sleazy hotel. I'd have left it at that but Don kept tinkering. A few months later he changed one word and that changed the whole song – 'Four walls, washbasin, prison bed'. Apparently patience could be a virtue. Who knew? I love the way Don writes. The pictures he paints. They sound like my stories. Things that I might have done or seen. I feel lucky to be the one who has had the chance to tell Don's stories, to sing his songs.

I have seen all sorts of writers. Most are quiet, deep-thinking, gentle souls but there are a few exceptions. Many years ago, a songwriter came out from America to write with me at home in Bowral at the White House. He had written beautiful, soulful songs and had won Grammys and a load of awards. But when he arrived he was not your usual sensitive songwriting type. In fact, if I had to sum him up, I'd say he was a redneck. He arrived at my house and started telling me how he did things.

'I know you have kids, Jimmy, but I don't want them down here in the studio with me. I don't like kids.'

My blood started to boil.

'And another thing, I don't eat that Oriental food I saw up there in your kitchen. I want American food. You know, just kill a beast and cook it. Plain and simple.'

By this point I wanted to take him out and put him on a spit and roast him, so I left the room and rang my record company. 'Get this guy out of here before I kill him,' I told them, but they begged me to give him time.

'He probably has jetlag. He'll settle down tomorrow. This guy is a great writer.'

So I gave him time. That night he went into my wine cellar and drank six bottles of pink Dom Pérignon Champagne. Not that that is so bad, but this guy drank it without asking me *and* he mixed it with orange juice. He was uncool, he had no manners and he had bad taste. I think he knew I was angry because the next morning when I walked into the studio and looked at the empty bottles, he asked where he could find a store to restock my cellar.

I thought maybe I had jumped to conclusions. One more thing I forgot to tell you is that when he arrived, I had to find him a jam jar to drink out of. He told me, 'You know, Jimmy, I'm a simple country boy and where we come from we drink out of fruit jars.'

Then he drank my vintage Champagne out of one. I wanted to smash a fruit jar over his head. But I showed him where the bottle shop was and I introduced him to the manager so he could get a good price. Everybody in town knew me and I wanted to help. He came home with two dozen bottles of pink Dom, which he proceeded to drink over the next few days.

Then he told me how he wrote songs. 'You see, Jimmy, I don't write them. It's a gift from God. He writes them and sends them to me. Of course, I keep the money.'

Now, I thought that if this was true then I had a new reason for disliking God. It appeared it was true. He sat and wrote beautiful melodies that sounded like angels should be singing them.

Every time I offered any help he would stop me and say, 'Just wait on there, Jimmy. This song ain't for you and if you help I would have to give you a share of it and I don't want to do that. This is my song. It's my money.'

I bit my lip instead of punching his and walked away, but after a few days of this I had had enough. I rang the record company again and told them, 'I'm going to Sydney for the day and he had better be gone by the time I get back or he will be dead.'

And I slammed the phone down. When I got home he was gone and my house was at peace again.

I don't think there are many people out there like him but I have met a few strange ones. Most songwriters have their own way of doing things. They are superstitious. They have lucky pens or a lucky coffee shop. Jonathan Cain used junk food for inspiration. Like I said, each one is different. Some are just weird. Not normal like me and Don.

CHAPTER THIRTY-NINE

let's ride

ON STAGE, 1998

THE LAST WAVE OF SUMMER tour was going to be bigger than Ben Hur. Chisel was going all out. We wanted a massive PA, big enough to pin the audience to the back wall, and lights enough to light up the whole town. We wanted props and dancing girls, all the bells and whistles. And that's what we got.

We had a twenty-five-foot-high wave built, to be unveiled halfway through the show, like a tsunami rolling over the stage. When it was revealed I felt like I was being turned inside out by the Bondi surf. The wave was like my life, about to come crashing down on me. It was ridiculous. It was built out of steel and weighed a ton. This prop wasn't made to be transported every night but that's what we did. It took three trucks to move the thing around. A friend of ours, Eric Robinson of the Jands production company, was running all the production, not because we hired him to do it, but because he was the best man in the world for the job. We had used Eric's equipment forever. It was the best. Eric shared a long history and friendship with the band, and he wanted to be on the road, sharing this tour with us. Eric was close to most bands that toured Australia. The biggest bands in the world refused to tour the country without him. He was the godfather to nearly every person working in a road crew in this country. Most of them had jobs or got their start thanks to Eric.

Eric had rushed me on and off that stage so many times. 'Are you guys going on tonight or shall I see if the hall's available tomorrow for you?' he would say while trying to get us all on. Then he met us with that same acid humour as we came off. 'Do you think you played enough songs? If you played any longer we would have to give out sleeping bags to the crowd.'

Anyway, half the budget of the tour was spent on the bloody wave. The other half, I felt I was spending on drugs and booze. Well, I wasn't really spending that much, but I did spend enough money to put a dent in what I would receive at the end of the tour.

Like I said, we wanted dancing girls, but not ordinary dancing girls. Our dancing girls had to have a certain something, to take the audience somewhere they didn't expect. Somewhere confronting and wild and scary. So we searched around for the right girls. The band hired a friend of ours, Gary Leeson, to find and produce our dancers. Gary hired a young guy called William Forsythe to do the choreography. Gary had worked with William on some big shows, including Mardi Gras – not the kind of shows that your average Cold Chisel audience would see, so it would be all new to them. Gary, William, Jane and myself and a few of the band started going to strip shows, to see if we could find the perfect dancers. They were hand-selected for maximum impact.

Once we had selected the right girls, Gary suggested that we give the crowd a little bonus. As well as the dancing girls, we would slip in a few drag queens, something they would never expect. We hired Anthony, who has become a friend of my family since that day, and his friend Anthony from New Zealand. Australian Anthony was a shy, handsome young fellow who transformed into a seven-foot-tall gregarious blond bombshell, stage-named 'Amelia Airhead'. Amelia was afraid of no one and could reduce most straight men to frightened, slightly effeminate slaves in seconds. New Zealand Anthony wasn't that big either and he too was a bit shy. But when he became 'Tess Tickle' he was larger than life and was trouble with a capital T, wrapped in sequins. I thought this would be the perfect combination. The wilder the show was, the more I liked it. The more distracted the audience were, the more places I had to hide, and the less chance of people noticing how out of it I was. But they did notice. I practically glowed in the dark by the time the tour started.

During the first few shows we got the dancers out for a few songs, the last one being 'Pretty Little Thing'. Now this song sounds like music to strip to. The girls would come out grinding and go through their routine until, at the climax of the song, they would line up along the front of the stage, ready for their big reveal. By this point it was more menacing than sexual. The music would come crashing to a halt and the girls would drop their gear and then, *bang!* The front row of guys, leering and drooling over the girls as they dropped their last tiny items of clothing, hands stretched out, touching the air in an attempt to get to them, would see that two of the girls they desired so much were actually boys. Their hands would snap back to their sides and the smiles would disappear from their faces as they turned to one another in shock. How could Cold Chisel do this to them? This was unfair. Chisel were a butch band. They shouldn't confuse their audience by making them lust over naked boys.

The dancers would exit the stage, leaving G-strings and feathers everywhere. Half the crowd would be cheering and the other half laughing. A few blokes would be looking down at their shoes uncomfortably, waiting until the lights went down so they could limp out of the auditorium. We loved this part of the show. I waited for it each night. But then something strange happened. We were at soundcheck one afternoon and we noticed that Steve had not arrived. The doors would open soon and there was no word from him. We were worried that something might have happened to him. Finally, we got a call. Steve was not going to do the show if the dancers were on with us. He thought it was disgusting for a band like us to have young naked girls out on the road. Not to mention boys too. What were we doing? We were taking advantage of them.

Had he missed the joke? He had appeared to be as amused as the rest of us over the first few nights.

'Tell Steve to grow up and get here before I kill him,' I joked to the tour manager.

'No Jim, this is serious. He said he won't do the show unless we stop the girls. He doesn't want them on the road and he won't play if the band is paying for something like this.'

I was furious. 'Tell him if he's not here soon we'll get someone else to play,' I screamed. The rest of the band and Rod grabbed me. Steve was serious. We needed Steve to play, but he was getting grief from his wife. It wasn't right. But that was it, the girls were taken out of the show.

The tour lost a lot of its sting that night and I lost interest. The band had folded to outside pressure. We had never done that before. No matter what anybody said, if we liked it, we did it. Full stop. Wives, record companies, managers and promoters had all tried to tone down the wildness of Cold Chisel live and we had told them to fuck off. Now here we were changing a major part of the production halfway through the tour because it was a bit risqué and offended someone who wasn't even a member of the band. I'd had enough. I loved this band; it was like my family. But now, like my family, they were making decisions about my future and I had no say in it. I was no longer in control of anything. I had lost control of my life, I had lost control of my sanity and now I was losing control of my career. I had to do something that was on my terms. I would not lay down.

So I did the only thing I could do. I paid out of my own money for the strippers and dancers and Gary to come on the road anyway. Every night, they would be standing side of stage as my guests. After every show I would hit whatever town we were in arm in arm with two seven-foot-tall drag queens as security. Steve was furious. At different times during the set I would walk out with a pink sequinned G-string and drape it over his drums and tell him they were coming out to dance in the next song. The blood would drain from his face. Fuck it if you can't take a joke, Steve.

Some shows were filmed. Cold Chisel likes to document things. We have a dear friend called Robert Hambling who went everywhere with us, filming and taking photos. So there is an unreleased film of the Last Wave from start to finish, the making of the album and the tour. When, after the dust from the tour had settled we watched the film back, we were stunned. I went from looking like a normal healthy singer at the start of the film to looking like Gollum, skinny and pale, with crazed eyes and fear written all over me. Over the recording of the album I had fallen so far that I looked like I was about to die. It hurts to see it now. The rest of the band don't like watching it either. We were all going through our own pain at the time, but none as obviously as me, I'm afraid.

I have a record of my fall from human to something I can't describe. I remember every night screaming 'Let's ride' and wanting the wave to crash down on me and end it all. But I kept standing and so did the band. It would take more than a few hiccups to stop us. In fact, it would take death itself to come knocking at our doors before we changed.

CHAPTER FORTY

---

read my lips

POINT PIPER, SYDNEY, 1999

I USED TO SEE blokes in bars with LOVE and FEAR tattooed on their knuckles. I thought they were just thugs, but around the turn of the millennium, I had those words tattooed on my psyche. To me, there were only two emotions. Love and fear. And depending on which one was strongest at the time, I would react accordingly. Unfortunately, fear seemed to rule over me most of the time. I had painted myself into a corner. Every step from the time I was a young man had taken me further and further from a place of love. I loved my children, I loved my darling Jane. But my conditioning and my behaviour had taken me to a place where I thought I was going to lose them, a fearful place. My reaction to fear was to fight. It's like I always put myself into the corner, where I felt most comfortable. With my back against the wall and nothing left to lose, I could lash out and spit venom at the world.

As I write this I sound like I am describing my mum. In fact, I think I might have used very similar words about her in my last book. But the difference is that my mum had nothing and still she was afraid of losing it. I had everything to lose.

I started writing songs for an album that I'd decided would be called *Love and Fear*. It was the perfect album title for me at that time. I could sit and come up with catchy phrases that summed up my state of mind at the drop of a hat. I just couldn't take it any further, and help myself. I came up with a name for my management company. ICU. Intensive Care Unit Management. This was exactly the kind of management I needed, but unfortunately the guy I chose to manage me was not qualified for the job. He couldn't manage to find a fuck in a brothel with a handful of fivers – an old saying, but sadly it was true. Instead of being a caring nurturing manager, which was what I needed at that time, he was more of an ambulance chaser. And I was always in the ambulance. Anyway, we didn't last long and he left. I think he took the ICU name, which was a shame because I thought it was quite funny.

I started writing songs while we were living in a house that we bought in Point Piper. By the sound of that address you would think I was doing all right. We lived in one of the best streets in one of the best suburbs in Sydney. But it wasn't me who got us into the house, it was Jane with some help from her Thai father. Once more I was being thrown help. By this time her father must have thought I was on my way out. He never made me feel bad about any of the help he gave us. He was just being a dad, doing whatever he could to help his children get ahead. But I was sabotaging us with every step I took.

THE SONGS ON THE album reflected the way I was at the time, jumping from angry battle cries one minute to mournful pleading for forgiveness the next. A couple of songs I had written a year or so earlier, on a writing trip to America. My favourite place. My publishers had set me up with a writer in Nashville, who according to them was very good. I could stay with an old friend, Rick, so the trip wouldn't cost me a fortune. Rick was the engineer Don Gehman had used for a few records we worked on. I had heard some of Rick's writing during that period, so I thought we could also write together while I was there. Rick had married Maja, a girl I had known since she was a child. Her mum was like part of Jane's extended family.

I turned up at Rick's house and immediately met a few of his wilder mates, who could help me find drugs. I scored enough to keep me going for a few days, got myself wired, and then headed off to the big Nashville writer's house. To say I was uncomfortable going to a stranger's house in the shape I was in would be an understatement.

The taxi was almost there when the cab driver announced in some sort of Southern drawl, 'The house you are looking for is right down this street, sir.' I looked for the number. I hoped the songwriter would be a nice quiet guy, not some loud-mouth with a huge ego who I would have to put up with for the next few days.

'Yes siree. If I'm not mistaken that is the house right there.'

Ahead, in this small suburban street, was a house with a huge banner outside, displaying a picture of a guy I presumed was my writing partner and the words 'NASHVILLE'S NUMBER ONE SONGWRITER' in letters big enough to see from space. I leaned towards the driver and said, 'Don't slow down, just keep moving,' and then I ducked down in case the songwriter was waiting outside.

'I beg your pardon, sir. Is this where you asked to go?' The driver was confused and was still slowing down.

'Just keep moving. Don't stop. In fact, put your foot down.'

We sped off. There was silence in the car for a minute, then the driver asked, 'Can I drop you somewhere else, sir?'

I didn't know anywhere to go, except for the place I'd scored the coke. Rick had told me that these guys were crackheads but they were good musicians. So that's where I went. To write with a bunch of crackheads instead of, according to his banner, Nashville's number one songwriter. I hung out with these guys all day and went back to Rick's apartment a little later. Me and the crackhead guys didn't write anything memorable. Funny that.

Rick was in trouble with his wife by the time I got to his place. Probably because we had partied too hard. He was sitting upright in his chair, waiting for me.

'I got a little studio set up in the spare room. And I got an idea for a song. Let's go,' he barked at me. We went into this small room in a small apartment and wrote a wild, fast, loud rock song called 'Sorry'. It was basically both of us saying sorry to the world for being fuck-ups, but it was sarcastic. Neither of us was sorry at all, although I had a lot to be sorry about.

I woke up next morning. Maja was sitting alone in the kitchen. Her eyes were red from crying.

'I'm sorry, Maja.' I offered my apology.

'Yeah. So I heard over and over the whole night, Jimmy. I'm sorry too. Sorry I had to be here.' She didn't even look at me.

I left and headed to LA to write with Tony Brock.

Tony and I had written a lot together but only when I was fucked up. I arrived and scored more coke and we started writing at about seven o'clock in the evening. By seven in the morning I was sprawled on the couch mindless while Tony sat obsessing over a drum loop that was way too dark and way too complicated to ever use again. No one but us would ever really get this song. I think it was the last thing I ever wrote with Tony. We aren't really friends anymore. We blew ourselves apart.

The song was called 'Blind Can't Lead the Blind'. The title says it all. It ended up sounding like a post-apocalyptic cry for help. Very hard to listen to right to this day.

I WENT HOME WITH next to nothing. Jane and I started fighting as soon as I got there. The drugs were doing so much damage. I remember storming out of the house one day after a fight. I intended to go to my studio above the garage and get smashed. As I walked down the garden path, a friend turned up. This friend was very nice but he was a hippy. He grabbed me and hugged me. I could smell the patchouli oil straightaway.

'I've come to read your Tarot cards, Jimmy.'

I was in no mood for a reading. I wasn't in the mood for anything. I took a step back and pushed him away. 'Read my lips. Fuck off.' And I continued storming off to the studio. But he followed me. I picked up my guitar and turned it up as loud as I could so he couldn't speak to me.

Karaang Karaang. It was deafening. But every time I stopped for a second, he was there.

'Jimmy, do you want to talk?'

Karaang Karaang. I drowned him out. I pretended to be recording and pushed the red button. *Karaang Karaang.*

'I'm here for y –'

Karaang Karaang. He wouldn't leave. He was very persistent.

'Let's talk, Jimmy.'

I wasn't ready to talk at all. I grabbed a pen and paper. 'You want to fucking talk, do you?' I screamed.

'Talk about hate. Talk about fear. Talk about trust. Talk about you. Talk about me.' I was yelling as I wrote what I thought were a nasty set of lyrics about Jane. I continued with my rant and by the time I looked up again, he was gone. I had calmed down. I read the diatribe I had scribbled on the page. In front of me were a great set of lyrics. But they weren't about Jane at all. They were about me. It was the best song I had written in years, 'Love and Hate'.

Then there was 'Time Will Tell'. This was me with my back against the wall. Nowhere to turn and no one to turn to. Even my friends would tell me to just let go. 'You've done the wrong thing, Jimmy. Take your punishment like a man.'

But I wouldn't.

'Fuck you. You might take it on the chin but not me. I won't lie down like a dog.'

I started to write the song.

I will not lay down with just a whimper
I will not be strong because it's simpler ...
I will not be told because I'm not waiting
No sacrifice can take away the hating.

This was what my mother would have sounded like on performance-enhancing drugs. If I was going down, I was taking the whole world with me. I was angry with myself and so drug crazed I couldn't see a way to back down. And if I was going to burn in hell I would take everything I treasured with me. This was a bitter, cold place.

'Thankful For the Rain' was me accepting that I had lost everything. And I was going to be noble and learn from the experience. I was thankful for all the pain I was feeling. It was a chance to grow.

But I wasn't thankful, and it wasn't a chance to grow as far as I could see. I jumped from writing that song to writing 'Temptation', a song about obsession and addiction and poison.

JUST AS MY ALBUMS were selling less and less, I was playing to smaller and smaller crowds. I was becoming a joke. Well, that's the way I saw it. I would walk on stage having not slept for days, or weeks sometimes, my eyes hanging out of my head and my nose red raw from shoving handfuls of anything that was available up it as fast as I could. I was sure that people were coming to see me fall. I tried not to. I tried so hard.

Most times, I would struggle to find a voice. Most nights I did it, but there were a few I find painful to remember. I remember a show in Melbourne, in some small club that I would never have played a few years earlier. Here I was, trying unsuccessfully to fill it. My guest list was bigger than the audience I was pulling at this time.

Jane and I had been fighting even more than normal and I was more out of it than I had ever been. I walked on stage and opened my mouth to sing. Nothing came out. My voice had always worked. But there I was, in front of an audience that wanted me to fire it up and there was nothing. I drank more vodka. Nothing. I drank hot water and honey. Nothing. Even at my worst shows in the old days I could always use sheer willpower to get through. This time I had none. I had nothing to give. My tank was empty. All that had got me this far had been the will to be liked and now I didn't care. I hated myself and I was sure that the world hated me too. I stopped trying to sing and stood at the mic, alone.

'I can't do this. You deserve better. Go to the front desk and get your money back. I'll try to come back when I can sing,' I croaked with my head slumped. Maybe I should have been making this speech to Jane and my kids. But they couldn't go to the door. There were no refunds in real life. The band were looking at each other. I was always the one who never gave up. I used to threaten them if they thought about lying down. And here I was on my knees.

I walked off. Shattered. Ashamed. I had done this to myself. I deserved to feel ashamed.

I crawled out of the show and into the car. I went back to my hotel and tried to drink myself to death. I didn't even have the balls to kill myself. I wanted the booze to do it. I woke up and it was another day. It hadn't ended. I would have to go out and try again.

THE ALBUM WAS ALL like this. Jane wrote songs with me. Sweet and hopeful. My songs were crying one minute and lashing out the next. It was a painful record to make. But when I hear it now, I can see that my songwriting had improved in a lot of ways. Once again I had written lyrics about the real me, the pain I was feeling, and although I had found no real answers to my problems, I could see those problems a lot more clearly by the time I finished it. I should have had those words tattooed on my forehead. LOVE and FEAR.

The album entered the charts at number three. This was the worst chart position of my career. I had filled stadiums and football grounds. I had been bigger than anyone in the country. Overseas bands that could have toured on their own came out to play support for my tours. If I wanted more lights, they were there. If I needed more sound, I got it. If I needed anything at all, it was always there. And I had gone from all that, from having the world at my feet, to being on my knees in front of my own family, with nothing to give.

CHAPTER FORTY-ONE

world record time

OLYMPIC STADIUM, 2000

EVEN BEFORE THE SYDNEY 2000 Olympics I was running on empty. If they had drug-tested me when I sang at the closing ceremony, they would have thought I was in the Bulgarian weightlifting team. Uppers, downers, all-rounders. You name it, I had it in my system. I was on a downhill slide that just kept going down. I was shaking and sweating as I walked to the stage. I had been smoking hashish and snorting coke in the dressing room. A dressing room that I shared, by the way, with three great Australians. Slim Dusty, Greg Norman and Paul Hogan had no idea what was going on in that room or they would have run a mile in world record time. This made me feel even worse about the state I was in. I couldn't look at them when we were introduced to each other.

I needed to warm up and, besides, I thought that my warm-up might keep people away. At the time, there were only myself and dear old Slim Dusty in the room. Slim was sitting on a bench, waiting to be asked to do something. He sat quietly with his hat on his lap, watching as I paced up and down.

'Hey Slim. This is going to get a bit loud. I have to warm my voice up,' I said to him before I started to scream. I was about to sing live to a billion people and I was having trouble talking, never mind singing.

'No worries, Jimmy. I've seen a few singers warm up in my time. Off you go.'

I wasn't sure he'd seen someone warm up the way I did, but I went on with it anyway.

'Ahhhhhhhhhhhhhhhhhhhhhhhhhhhhhh!' I let out a scream that started quite high and slid up until I reached the top of my range and my maximum volume. People have told me I sound like I'm in pain when I warm up.

Slim looked startled. A huge Maori security guard burst into the room. 'What's going on in here? Is everyone all right?'

He looked around the room, trying to find out what had happened. I quickly told him, 'It's all right. It was Slim. He's a troublemaker.'

The guard shot a stern look at Slim and left the room.

Slim looked at me and smiled. 'That was very funny, Jimmy. You know, I've been wanting to talk to you for a while. I'd really like to make a record with you sometime. A duet. You know that song you sing with your band, about Vietnam. I think it would be great.'

I was stunned. 'You mean "Khe Sanh", Slim?'

He smiled again. 'Yeah, that one. I reckon we could do a good version of it together.'

In the midst of all that was going on in my life, Slim Dusty was asking me to sing 'Khe Sanh' with him.

'I'd love to do that, Slim. Anytime you're ready. I'll contact you soon, shall I?'

He nodded and I went back to warming up. It was going to take me a while to find a sound that would work for this show. My voice was a little shredded. But somehow I managed to get away with it. I seemed to get away with a lot. I don't think that people, the police or the public in general, turned a blind eye. I just think that they all wanted the best from me. They liked me and didn't expect me to be such a fuck-up. That night was one of the highest points and also one of the lowest points in my public life. The whole of Australia, and a lot of the world, watched me as I struggled through my performance.

Not long after that Jane found a house to rent in Vaucluse. I think she was moving into it with or without me. But somehow I managed to stick with her and we moved in together. And things went from bad to worse.

SOON AFTERWARDS I MADE a second album in the soul series, in Los Angeles. *Soul Deeper* was a good record but I drank a lot during the making of it. Cocaine is always too easy to find in LA as I've said, so I spent weekends driving down to San Diego to visit my friend Deepak Chopra. Deepak and I had met when he was on tour in Australia. He loved music and I was looking for answers. He might have given me those answers back then but by the time he did I had forgotten the questions. Still, we did stay friends over the years. He is a very intelligent, caring man and I have a lot of time for him.

While making this second soul record, I would visit on the weekends and try to get myself together. I would turn up at his door like a lost dog, tail between my legs. All week I would be working ten hours a day, recording with some of the best musicians in the world, all the time taking copious amounts of coke and booze. By Friday night I was always nearly dead. Deepak would get me into his clinic and fill me full of supplements and fresh juices. He would get me massaged and doing yoga and generally dry me out. Come Sunday night he would give me a pep talk and send me back into the ring for the next round.

Once again, my mate Don Gehman helped me pull together some unbelievable players, and even though I was a complete basket case, coked to the eyeballs and drunk out of my mind, the album turned out pretty good. I sang well and managed to live through another American trip without dying or getting arrested.

I HIT ROCK BOTTOM, bounced back up and slammed down into it a few more times, every time inflicting potentially fatal wounds on myself and my marriage and everyone around us, before I found the courage to try to tackle the problem head on.

'Get some clarity and things will look a lot better, Jim. It'll be like a holiday. You'll love it,' one of my healthy, drug-free, sober, boring friends told me one day as he tried to drag me kicking and screaming to an AA meeting. 'It's not as bad as you think. You find you have a lot to be thankful for. I am thankful every day.'

I couldn't help think to myself, 'You should be thankful I don't smash you in the face.'

But I knew he was trying to help and I knew he wasn't that boring. I just thought that a world without drugs and booze would be the kind of world that would put me straight to sleep. Then again, was that such a bad thing? I could have done with a good sleep by this point in time.

When I did go, I decided to go not really for myself, which apparently is the only real reason to go, but in an attempt to save my marriage. Appease Jane. Show her I was trying. I also knew that if I didn't do something, I was going to die.

By the time I went away, I was drinking two, three bottles of vodka every day. The booze would stop me stressing out about the amount of cocaine I was consuming. I would buy ten grams of coke a day, sometimes more.

A mate of mine once told me, 'You know that buying coke is God's way of letting you know you have too much money, Jim. Way too much.'

It was obscene the amount of money I was wasting every single day. It makes me sick to think about it now. Even the drug dealers would tell me to take it a bit easy, and that wasn't in their best interest. I would share it with whoever was with me but I always took more than anybody else, lots more. I used most of it in fact.

My head hurt so much. My nose was swollen and throbbed and bled all the time. I thought I was going to die from a brain bleed. I would wake up and I couldn't breathe through my nose at all. My chest was wheezing and I sounded like I had pneumonia.

The first thing I would do when I woke up, no matter what time it was, was to swallow a handful of Nurofen Cold & Flu tablets with a few Aspro Clear in a glass of water. That was breakfast. This would take down the swelling enough to allow me to shove the first line of coke up the passages of my nose, which by this time, along with my liver and kidneys, were pleading for mercy. As soon as my nose cleared I would chop out a line. Not just a little line like a normal drug addict, but a massive one. Half a gram of coke at least. And then, *bang*, the world would light up. My eyes would weep as the coke, which was normally cut with all sorts of shit – speed, sugar, even crushed glass – would hit me like a hammer. I would have to sit for a moment, to make sure I wasn't going to die right then and there. Then I would shake my head and fall out of bed.

Jane would be up and about. She wasn't feeling much better than me but she could somehow still function. It was Jane who was looking after the kids, not me. I tried but most of the time I just fell apart. I had trouble facing the world. I could do nothing. I had trouble getting up. When I did I would just sit and think, 'What did I do last night?' And then it would all come rushing back to me. I had destroyed any hope of salvaging my life with my family and the girl I loved. There was no turning back. It was over.

I didn't want to feel at all when they walked out the door. If Jane was going to leave me, I didn't want to be able to see it. I wanted to stay drunk and smashed for as long as I would stay alive. And I hoped that wouldn't be for long. But I would always make it through to lunchtime, Jane ignoring me and me trying to stay out of her way.

By most lunchtimes I would have to track down my mate who sold me this horrible shit and make sure I had enough for the next day or so. I never wanted to run out, even for a minute. I would meet my dealer and start drinking again. Maybe a beer or three with lunch. I didn't eat much, I normally moved the food around the plate so it looked like I'd eaten, but I hadn't. The whole circus was back in town. Another drink, another line. 'That one felt good.' I wasn't thinking about last night. Maybe I'd have another drink and another line. By mid-afternoon I was mindless and no longer cared about anything or anyone. I was in this world alone. And I was glad about it. My world was a horrible place and I didn't want anyone I cared about to see it. Ever. I would disappear. By the evening, a lot of nights, I had swallowed two or three ecstasy pills on top of everything else.

'That'll stop the pain for sure.' But it didn't. More booze, more coke. 'Maybe I'll smoke some weed to mellow out a bit.' Then I would need another massive line to pick me up. Unfortunately, I would be out and about by this point so this was happening in public. I would be bouncing off the walls in some bar somewhere, doing drugs on the table right where I sat. Not even hiding them. Sometimes I attracted attention too. But no one seemed to care; in fact, they seemed to want to join me. Girls would sit at my table and tell me I was crazy to behave like this in public. Why didn't I go back to their place, where it would be safer? This was a typical day's running amok. I would stagger home and Jane would be there, not really waiting for me anymore. The house would be full of people and the party would continue. More coke, ecstasy and a lot of ketamine thrown in for good luck. If you don't know what ketamine is, it's basically an animal tranquiliser that comes in different strengths. Some batches might be for small animals, and if you took them it would feel like your consciousness hit a little speed bump. Other batches were for much larger animals. Much larger than humans. Then it would feel as if your whole mind had stepped into outer space for a rest, the universe hurtling past at breakneck speed while you were left clinging to the floor, hoping you weren't going to die this time. We did this for fun.

It was only a matter of time until my mind never came back from one of its little excursions and I was left staring blankly into space while a nurse spoonfed me with food that had been mashed so I didn't have to chew it. This went on for years. I was always amazed how much of a beating a body can actually take. Mine just didn't give up.

Quite often during this time, I would be working five nights a week. I would arrive backstage at a show after not sleeping for days on end, my body shaking and my eyes darting from one member of the band to the next, looking for one of them to assure me I was going to be all right. But I wasn't all right. In a state of panic, I would shovel a gram or two of coke into me before I went on stage. By this time, I would be completely crazed, jumping out of my skin again and ready to throw punches at anyone I thought looked sideways at me. I don't know how I did these shows. They couldn't have been good. I wonder if people used to come along, waiting to see me drop. But I kept standing. I think the longest I ever went without sleep was seven or eight days. I lost count. It was on a tour to Perth towards the end of my rampage. I was taking eight or ten ecstasy pills a day. I would take one before I went on stage and another halfway through the show, snorting as much cocaine as I could get my hands on and drinking. At my hotel I had booked myself into three different rooms and I had parties going on in each room with different people. I would excuse myself from one and stagger to another floor and another party full of strangers, stay for a while then move to the next. If I got bored with these parties I would nip out to a club and fill another room in another hotel with more people I had never met before.

CHAPTER FORTY-TWO

keep your nose out of trouble, son

IN TRANSIT, 2003

B<small>Y THE TIME</small> I did go to rehab in 2003, it didn't matter why I was going, I just needed to get some help. Any help might save my life. Jane had tried to save me but she couldn't, no one could, so she tried to save herself by going to a rehab centre in the States. She left while I was away on one of my binges. I was mortally wounded. I thought I'd lost Jane and it hurt so badly. I thought she had given up on me. I can see now of course that I had given up on me years before and Jane trying to get herself together was the best thing she could do. Nonetheless, I was wounded. I went even crazier for a while. If I could make myself feel I didn't need anyone, then I wouldn't be hurt. But it did hurt. More than my childhood. More than all the booze and drugs hurt me and more than I could ever hurt myself.

JANE CAME BACK, READY to get on with her life with or without me. So I booked myself into the same place she had gone to. It was in Arizona. This was it. I was going to try to get myself straight. I headed for the plane after a couple of days of binging. I would sleep on the plane. Well, that was the plan, but in case I didn't sleep I would take along some ecstasy and a few grams of coke. I was starting off with the wrong attitude. On the plane ride I went crazy, drinking bottles of Champagne and terrorising the guests in first class, every now and then disappearing into the bathroom to take another pill or snort more coke, then coming back out and jumping all over the seats. Thank God the crew liked me. They tried to keep me happy and out of the way of the other paying customers. At one point I sat on the top of a first class seat and it snapped and I crashed backwards onto the feet of the lady sitting behind me.

'I hope you don't mind me dropping in like this. You seemed so lonely back here by yourself,' I said. She just laughed and shook her head in disbelief.

ANYWAY, I MADE IT to Tucson, where I was met by a guy from the rehab centre. He was big and wasn't the slightest bit fazed by the state he found me in.

'I was a bit nervous so I had a few on the plane,' I sheepishly said. By this point the drugs were wearing off just a little.

'Don't worry sir, we've seen worse than you come through this place. It's going to be all right.'

He piled me into a van and drove off. I felt like this was the last day of my life. Like I was crossing the Bridge of Sighs. My eyes scanned the areas we drove through. I was thinking of where I could run to when, not if, I ran away from rehab. It was hot and dry and I felt like I was an extra in a western movie. I was definitely a desperado of the worst kind. This place had a reputation for being a very good rehabilitation centre. I knew it was going to take a great one to help me.

They checked me in, ignoring my funny, smart-arsed comments. They'd obviously heard them all before from people much funnier than me. Anyway, I wasn't feeling very funny by this point. They sedated me and I slept next to the office in a detox room. The room was like a cell inside a hospital. The door was bolted and the windows were barred. I slept for about three days. Every now and then someone would wake me and give me another pill and some water. I needed to sleep so badly. I don't remember dreaming. Just my eyes opening and seeing figures talking to me and about me, before they shut again and I was gone, back into the blackness.

AFTER THREE DAYS I woke up. I was hungry and refreshed. Maybe I could go home now. I felt much better. A doctor came in to talk to me. I immediately asked the obvious question. 'Will I be allowed to go home or at least have my things? I have some music and books in my bag. I thought they'd keep me busy while I wait to get out.' I didn't tell her that there might be some pills hidden there in case of emergencies.

'We think it would be better if you stayed with us. Let's not think about going home for a while. We have been through your bags, Jimmy, and there is nothing in there you will be needing. We will supply everything you need now.'

I was getting anxious. 'But I can't live without music. I play music all day, every day. I need it.' My voice sounded desperate and was slightly raised by now.

'Just stay calm and maybe you can ask your therapist about that when you meet.' Her voice was calm and sounded like she was singing a nursery rhyme to me.

I dug my heels in. 'I'm a fucking adult, you know. So don't fucking talk to me in that whiny tone of voice. I'm not a bloody kid. I want my music and I want it now!' I was shouting by this time.

'Jimmy.'

I stood up and started looking for my clothes.

'Jimmy, calm down.'

But I didn't hear her. 'Somebody better get my music or I'll smash this place up. Right now.'

I suddenly noticed the other person in the room. He had moved a little closer while I spoke. He was very big and didn't look like he had a sense of humour.

'Why don't you sit down and we can talk about this?' His voice was deep and stern and he laid his hand on my shoulder. It was the size of a leg of lamb. I wanted to smash him but I had no strength and I was suddenly dizzy. I sat down. What had I done? I was trapped.

After I calmed down a little they took me out to the main area where all the other residents were milling around. I found out later that they were collecting their meds. I immediately started calling them inmates but the big male nurse escorting me made it clear I should stop, and quick.

I felt like I had gone to sleep and woken up as an extra in *One Flew Over the Cuckoo's Nest*. Some of the patients looked worse than I felt. The centre was mixed, filled with both guys and girls. I was surprised we were all in the same area. Apparently some volunteered to be there; others were sent by the courts as a last stop before jail. I could tell who was who just by looking. 'He's a junkie. Look at his eyes. That one without the teeth is definitely a speed freak.'

They were probably doing the same thing to me. We all looked strung out. I was taken to a hut. There were eight men to a hut. This was where I would stay for the next twenty-eight days, and I was told I would not be alone for a minute while I was there.

'This is Les. He's going to be your buddy for the next few days. Just until you get used to the place.'

I looked at Les. He was somewhere in his mid to late seventies as far as I could tell, and he wasn't happy to be stuck with me. What the fuck could a guy his age be in here for?

'Just throw your fucking bags down over there and come here. I'll tell you the fucking rules,' he snapped at me. I didn't care how old he was, he'd better watch his tone of voice when he spoke to me or else. He ran me through everything I would need to know to survive my stay. As he spoke his tone softened. I could tell he didn't want to be in there anymore than I did. And he certainly didn't want to have to hold my hand while I whined and cried like a baby for the next few days.

'Just man up and keep your nose out of trouble, son. And believe me, there is trouble to be found in here.' He didn't come across like a very happy person.

'What are you in for?' I asked him as he walked away from me.

'What? What did you say?' He turned towards me again.

'I said what are you in here for? What's your poison?'

He didn't get what I was saying.

'What's your drug of choice? Why are you in here?'

I knew straightaway he didn't want to talk about it but he did. I was surprised.

'I have anger issues. My wife said this is my last chance to sort it out or she'll leave me for good.' He looked at the ground. He was ashamed.

'I should have guessed,' I said off the cuff, trying to break the ice.

'Don't be a fucking smartass, because I haven't got them under control yet. I may be old but I could still give you a fucking hiding. Do you understand me?'

I tried not to smile. I could see it was going to be a long twenty-odd days until I got free from this hell.

DETOXING WAS DIFFICULT BUT dealing with everything sober, straight, and in that facility in America alone, was frightening. I would go for walks inside the wall that encircled the centre. There was a path called the Serenity Trail, a place to find some peace and calm within your heart. I would walk alone, occasionally joined by the odd rattlesnake basking in the sun or one of the many giant tarantulas, the size of dinner plates, that patrolled the perimeter of the compound, moving like death itself in search of company. My heart would pound hard in my chest as I snuck past, almost hoping one of them would wake up and put an end to it all. One bite and it could have been over. But it never happened. The heat made them slow to react and I guess, when it all came down to it, I didn't really want to die. I had a life of pain to make up for with my wife and children and I couldn't get away that easily. This was going to take work and I wanted nothing more than a chance to make it all better. Somehow.

CHAPTER FORTY-THREE

everybody in this place was crazy

REHAB, ARIZONA, 2003

IN REHAB I GOT clean but not really serene. My life had never been serene. It was always like being tossed and turned upside down by the ocean, hoping you would find which way was up. Fighting for breath, never knowing if you would ever make it through the storm. But in Arizona, there were times when the storm seemed to pass, at least for a little while. For the first time in longer than I could remember, I was clear headed. Still wounded, but present. The surface wounds had healed. I was sober and I knew there were still festering sores deep inside me. But I would have to deal with them at some point in the future.

I remember standing on the wall that surrounded the centre, scanning the horizon for Jane. Waiting for her to come and save me. Everybody in this place was crazy, and I was on the verge of insanity. It was a plague that ran through the whole rehab centre. And then to top things off, they wanted be put me in Trauma Group.

'Why would you possibly think I need to be in Trauma Group?' I asked the doctor. Were they fucking serious?

'I'm feeling a little aggression in your voice at the moment. Do you need a minute to breathe, Jimmy?'

All I could feel was a weight on my chest. Maybe I did need a minute to breathe.

'No, I don't need a fucking minute to breathe. I want to know why you think I've suffered trauma. I haven't. I'm a fucking drug addict. That's all.'

Their voices were all too condescending and far too musical. 'Everybody has suffered some trauma, Jimmy. Just relax. We're here to help.' They thought we were all the same.

'Fuck you.' I tried to hold it all together. But the more I tried the more I fell apart. The pain of looking at my life was unbearable. I did need Trauma Group.

'OKAY, LET'S START WITH Sally. Come on Sally, tell us your story.'

Sally had been taken captive by her plastic surgeon and locked in a dungeon for months. Every day he came down to the dungeon and injected her with heroin and then he raped her. When she was found she was covered in her own faeces. A dribbling mess. The plastic surgeon was gone, but until she came into the centre, he still found ways to contact her, threatening to kill her. Her story was gut-wrenching. This was fucking trauma.

'Okay, Donald, why don't you tell us all your story?' The therapist sounded like she was auditioning for *Play School*.

Donald's story was different. He was a young, well-dressed guy. Neat and well groomed. 'My dad hated me. At sixteen years old, when all my friends got automatic BMWs, my dad gave me a stick shift. I hated it. Why did he do that to me?' He broke down and cried.

'You fucking idiot.' I was up out of my seat, heading across the room towards Donald. 'Did you hear Sally? What the fuck are you talking about, you stupid fucking rich twat? I want to fucking punch you until you grow fucking up.'

I was dragged out of Trauma Group. I wanted to kill him. Maybe I did need help, but if I had got my hands on this guy he would have needed real help. Fuck. I was a basket case.

THE DOCTORS KEPT DIGGING deeper and deeper into my past, uncovering it as if they were removing bandages, and leaving the sores weeping. I had hypnotherapy. Group therapy. Private therapy. Craniosacral therapy. Electromagnetic pulse therapy. Gestalt therapy. I even had acu-detox therapy. I don't know if that's what they called it, but they sent us to a room where a guy who looked like he should have been a resident stuck acupuncture needles into our ears and then we sat for an hour and meditated. He played a cassette of Buddhist monks chanting 'Ohm'. This was the closest thing I got to music the whole time I was there, so I loved it. Eventually they stopped the acu-detox sessions because they found out the acupuncturist was on heroin. The chanting tape lasted for a whole hour. It probably gave him time to hit up and then get a little sleep. But at least, while it lasted, no one spoke to me. The room was quiet. No one asked, 'What are you feeling?' in their Mr Fucking Rogers voice.

'I'm fucking tired, that's what I'm feeling. Stop fucking asking me stupid fucking questions.' I sounded like a cross between Oscar the Grouch, Angry Anderson and Billy Connolly.

'No, not those feelings. Remember to go to your *core feelings*, Jimmy.'

I would look around the walls, searching for a chart or a sign that told me how to say, 'I feel alone, empty, helpless, hopeless, worthless, inadequate, insignificant. Oh yeah, and I feel like killing you,' without extending my stay. Signs reminding us of these feelings were plastered on every wall, in case we needed them at short notice.

I had done enough work to admit that I had major problems but I would have needed to stay there for another year to work through them. So by the end of the third week I would stand alone on the wall, whenever I could, waiting for the only one who had ever taken away my pain, even for a minute. My Jane.

THERE WERE MAFIA HIT men, models, rock stars and socialites mingling with jailbirds and desperadoes. It was weird. Some blokes in there should have been behind bars. I didn't know who to trust, so for a while I didn't trust any of them. I was alone.

Eventually I connected with some of the other crazy people I met in there. There were good souls struggling to get by and there were a few people who shone so bright that they were worn out by their own inner light that never dimmed and burned in their eyes like spotlights. I didn't like everybody in the place though. Some people are just fucked, with or without drugs. There were a few guys who kept bragging about nailing chicks out back on the basketball court. Not just girls, but fragile, wounded people who should have been safe inside these walls but were targets for predators. I heard them brag to each other over lunch and it made me ill. I wanted to kill them, fucking smash their faces to bits, but I would have been thrown out, and I needed to be in there.

LIKE I SAID, MUSIC wasn't allowed inside the centre, but I would walk around singing to myself wherever I went. Every day, someone would graduate. We would all stand around and cry, hugging whoever was leaving and promising to stay in touch. We had shared too much to be separated. I would sing 'I Can See

Clearly Now' to everyone who left. Don't ask me why. No one was supposed to know I was a singer. But they fucking did. And none of us, in reality, could see anything clearly. We could only just focus, for the first time in years, and most of the time what we were seeing wasn't pretty. But I didn't mind singing, that was all I had to give. Then they would leave and I never saw them again.

Some people sent messages back to those of us left behind. One of the carers would read them out to the group. 'Guys. Guys. Come on. Keep it down. Gather round. We have a letter from one of our dear alumni.'

> Dear family. That's what you guys are. My family. It's tough out here without you all. I can't seem to talk to people out here. They don't understand. But I am trying to keep it all together. I am attending meetings every day, sometimes twice a day. I must have said the serenity prayer a thousand times since I left you guys. Stay strong. I will see you on the outside.
> Peace and Love

Everyone would clap and cheer and say good things about whoever wrote the letter, even if we didn't like them. Maybe they would write again and tell us the truth about how hard life had become out in the real world? But they never did. We would hear nothing else. The silence was deafening. I know that a few people made it through, but even before I left we got notice that one of the graduates, a particularly fragile soul who we all loved, couldn't take it outside. Without the drugs to mask the pain, it was all too much to bear. He ended it by throwing himself under a train. No one spoke about it. A little of each of us died along with him.

I've said the serenity prayer a million times.

God grant me the serenity to accept the things I cannot
 change,
The courage to change the things I can,
And the wisdom to know the difference.

Sometimes it helps, I don't know why. Then there are other times
when nothing can help.

I would see the car coming through the gate and wipe away
the tears and try to look happy. I didn't want Jane to think I had
gone completely nuts and leave me there. But she didn't leave
me, even though there must have been times when she felt like
walking away.

I lasted twenty-eight days. Not a minute more or a minute
less.

TOWARDS THE END OF rehab, there was family week. This was
when the family got a chance to tell you how they felt. Mahalia,
EJ and Elly-May came over and had to sit in front of me and tell
me everything I'd done wrong. It hurt them as much as it hurt
me. We had a lot of work to do.

When we left Arizona, Jane and the girls told me they
wanted to go across the border from Los Angeles to Tijuana
in Mexico. This was the place Californians went to go crazy.
In Tijuana you could buy drugs, booze or anything that was
your poison or floated your boat on every street corner. I
thought this must be a test. My nerves were shot and I felt
like I was walking on broken glass with every step I took as
we crossed the border. At night the sound of cheap fireworks
echoed through the city, and as each one shattered the silence,
my heart pounded louder in my chest. Should I get up and just
fuck up like I was supposed to? No, I would fight the urges and
stay in bed and cry. I hated it. It was one of the seediest parts of

the world I had ever been in. But I must have passed the test. Jane took me home.

I CAME OUT OF rehab without my skin. That's what it felt like. David, my son, said this to Jane one day when I wasn't around. 'It's like he has no skin. He's raw and in pain all the time.' That was me. There was nothing between me and the world. I was the skinless guy who needed help.

My memories of the first few days back in Sydney are scattered. Fear and anxiety are all I remember. I was going back to the world I had left behind, only now I was sober and straight and every sight and sound reminded me of something else I had fucked up.

The first day home I was walking down the street and I bumped into someone I'd known in my old life. I was still fragile and lost. Before I knew what was happening, I was drunk, my head spinning from the drugs that had been pumped into me by this old friend. I didn't need friends like this anymore. I was ashamed.

I started to go to AA meetings and NA meetings, but even there I felt uncomfortable. The meetings seemed to be full of desperate people like me, trying to cling on to something, anything that might offer a second chance at life. There were good people there, people who genuinely wanted to help. But there were also people I knew from my old life, the life I had run around the world to distance myself from. And here they were, at the meetings, pretending to be something that they weren't. Maybe they weren't using drugs anymore but I knew they were still selling them. They offered them to me. They were there in the meetings looking for prey, young girls trying desperately to keep clean. I could see the girls being groomed for future use by these animals. I didn't like it at all. So I found meetings where the clientele were more like me, trying to make it in the world, one day at a time. There were a lot of them. Meetings and people. I just had to look for them. I know the meetings helped me, and I know they saved the lives of some good people with no one else to turn to.

'My name is Jimmy and I'm an addict. I've been straight for a month now and it's hard. Not to stay straight. It's hard to stay calm. I don't know how long I can do this. Sometimes I feel like I really do want to kill somebody. Sometimes I just want to kill me. I don't like who I am. I don't want to see the real me. I hate him. Thanks for letting me share.'

Then I would run from the meeting before anyone spoke to me. I didn't want their help. Except for that first day home, I managed to stay straight for years. For a long time, I tried to be strong. I tried to be someone else. But, except for a few meetings, I didn't get any help. I tried to deal with a lifetime of trauma, sober and straight, all by myself. I was too ashamed to tell anybody about the things I had seen and that had been done to me. Or the person I had become. It was just a matter of time before it all fell apart.

CHAPTER FORTY-FOUR

I'd been nobbling myself for years

SOBER, 2003

W ALKING BACK ON STAGE for the first time since rehab was scary. I had done only a handful of shows in my life sober or straight. Never both. I didn't think I could do it. I walked around backstage, even more nervous than when I was having trouble standing up in the past. I found a space to be ALONE and sat down and tried to settle myself.

I said the serenity prayer. I didn't know if it would help. It had worked while I was in rehab, maybe it would help outside too? I hadn't suddenly taken to believing in God by the way. It was just meditation. I was asking anyone or anything that was out there to give me help. I wasn't fussy. I just needed all the help I could get. There was something about looking inside for strength that I liked too. I had always told people I could do anything I put my mind to, even when I didn't really believe it myself. If I said it enough times, someone would believe it. Hopefully it would be me. I needed it to be true.

I walked on stage. It was a small pub in Melbourne and the first thing I noticed was how close the audience was. The stage was only about one-foot high so I was looking straight into their eyes. How did I let things go so far downhill? Now I was sober, I could see that I had driven my career into the ground. I was playing in a pub with a few hundred people in it. I was glad I was sober now. I had work to do. No matter what state I was in, I would have to dig deep and work my way back up into the light. I knew how to work, it didn't scare me.

'Yeah, fucking Barnesy! You twat. Let's go!'

I could smell the booze on their collective breath and the sweat dripping down their backs. I tried not to gag but I did at first. I was off to a great start because I hadn't really smelled anything for years. It was a good sign. But I could see how pissed they were and it worried me.

'It's a pub show for fuck sake, that's exactly why people go to them. They can get pissed and see the band,' I told myself. I didn't look into any one person's eyes for the first half of the show. I kept mine shut and tried to feel what I was doing. The first thing I noticed was that it was easier to breathe, which meant it was easier to sing. I had done a thousand gigs with a head full of coke, struggling to get air into my lungs. With all this newfound air coming past my vocal cords they worked the way they were designed to. I could sing really well. I was getting a spring in my step. I would not throw in the towel again. Things slipped into automatic pilot. I didn't have to worry. I could stop panicking and allow myself to be in the moment and just sing. It was easy. The show finished and I walked off with a towel over my head and I sat in the corner of my dressing room. I wasn't worn out. I wasn't gasping for air like I had been lately. What was happening? My sound guy ran into the dressing room.

'Fuck me, Jimmy. I've mixed you for years and that was the loudest you've ever sung. I had to turn your microphone down by at least a third or you were going to blow up the fucking PA system. Your pitch was good too. Welcome back, you fucking idiot. You should have done this years ago.'

I thought for a second. I felt like I could do another show right away. That's when I knew that I'd been nobbling myself for years. I couldn't have made my job any harder if I'd tried. So now I knew I could sing straight. But I would have to get used to seeing my audience this way too. There were people absolutely mindless in the front row, watching the band. Well, I think they were watching the band. I had seen one guy, his eyes rolling back and booze spilt all down the front of his shirt, with his arm around a girl who was blowing kisses at me. Lucky his eyes were rolling, I guess. I had been told I would need to keep my distance from drinkers for a little while. That's what they told me at AA as well. If the people you hang around with drink or take drugs, change the people you hang around with or you will relapse so quickly you won't even see it coming.

But I wasn't going to be one of those guys. I had met guys like that in the States. 'Hey man, I don't mind you having a good time but could you not do it around me,' they'd say.

I didn't know what the fuck they meant. 'What, you want me to have a good time by myself and a shitty time around you? I fucking do that anyway. You are as boring as batshit,' I used to joke, but they never laughed. Now I knew why. I told myself that no matter how hard it got, I would never stop my friends from getting smashed. I could take it. It was my problem, not theirs. And that's what I did. Some nights it was hard, other nights it was harder, but I had to be strong. This went on for years.

BEFORE REHAB I HAD tried to write a book. Somehow I wanted to purge myself. Spilling everything out and onto paper might help me get through it. But as I have said before, I was so out of it

I could only make light of the state I was in. I didn't understand what I was up against. In fact, if the truth be known, I think that I'm only just starting to see it all now, and it still scares me. It did occur to me to write again now that I was clear-headed and fresh from rehab but I really didn't have any answers yet. I had spread all the pieces of my life out on the table, like pieces of a jigsaw. But I had lost the box, so I didn't know what the picture was supposed to look like.

I had been a lunatic and I had almost gotten whiplash from slowing down so quickly. Every night I would fight the urge to deal with things the old way. I knew that model was broken so I took all the shit that was running through my head and I shoved it as far back as I could. Hopefully I would never see it again. Everyone kept telling me how well I looked and how well I was singing. How proud they were of me. How much nicer I was to be around. But inside it was a battle. All that shit that had been unlocked at rehab wanted out. It wanted to be dealt with. I just kept saying, 'No. I'm not ready to talk to anyone. I can do this alone.'

I was a stubborn bastard. Then, at night when no one was around, I would cry and look into the mirror. Just like I used to when I was smashed. I could see the other me, still there. The real me.

'Fuck off. You're not going to win. I can do this. I can do this.' Then I would try to stop myself from breaking down and crying. I would not be ready to write for another few years, if ever.

Tsh Tsh Tsh ...

Later, when I wrote my first book, *Working Class Boy*, I talked about my mum's life being like a pressure cooker, ready to explode. That feeling was back. Only this time, it wasn't my mum.

Tsh Tsh Tsh ...

Stop it. I don't want to hear it. I would turn the music up, do anything to distract myself – well, within reason now.

Tsh Tsh Tsh ...

This time it was me. I was the pressure cooker. I was the time bomb. I was ready to blow. I would knock myself out with a sleeper and hope that I wouldn't dream. I wanted peace. Nothing else. Just peace. I would wake up and the sound would be gone. I was all right. Every day started this way and then slowly as the day progressed ...

Tsh Tsh Tsh ...

... it would return. This was a battle I knew deep down I couldn't win, but I had to try.

IN THE MIDDLE OF 2003 Cold Chisel was back. Ringside was on the road. The band wanted to play again. I wanted to play with them. Even Cold Chisel had gone down a few rungs on the ladder. The tour before, we were doing Entertainment Centres, about 12,000 people a night. Now we were doing Hordern Pavilions, more like 5500 people. We told ourselves that it was because we wanted to do smaller venues, but no one really wants to do smaller venues, and don't believe them if they say they do. But we would do the best shows that we could. I had hardly ever sung straight with Chisel and I wanted to do it and do it well. It was so much easier this time. The band were relaxed and happy to be around me, although I could tell that they were still a little wary in case I fell apart.

Every day Steve would walk up to me. 'How's it going, our kid? Are you holding up all right?'

I was fine. It was always a bit of a battle but I had fought much worse. 'Yeah mate, I'm good. Thanks for asking. You just do your fucking job and I'll do mine.'

Steve laughed. 'You know, you are a bigger twat sober than you are pissed. I think I liked you better before.'

But I knew he was kidding and he knew I was only kidding too. It was our way of breaking the ice. I needed to know that the boys were all behind me and they were. Every night before the show I went through my little ritual. Remember I said I have compulsive tendencies? I just had to change what I was compulsive about. So instead of being compulsive about destroying myself, now I was compulsively moderate.

I would get to the gig at least an hour before the show. In the old days that gave me enough time to get drunk and consume all the drugs I needed to get through the night. But now that meant I could walk to the stage and get a feel for the place, then find a room backstage and put out my clothes and look at the set. Play a bit of music to calm me down. I used to play the whole *Highway to Hell* album every night for years before I went on. Now I only played some of it. Then I'd sit and try to meditate. I wasn't always successful, by the way. I would say the serenity prayer and I was ready to rock. But if that routine was broken I was at a loose end, unsettled, unfocused. I thought that as long as I stuck to my routine I would be all right. Simple. But the fact that when it was interrupted I was thrown so far out of whack was a big warning sign and I knew it.

The Ringside tour was difficult for all of us. We had never played in the round before. The audience was all around us, which meant we couldn't have our usual wall of amps and gear to hide behind. The guitar amps had been almost like security blankets for us. We could wind and wind them up until they were so loud that we would settle. All of us were like that, I soon found out, not just me. But for Ringside all our gear was under the stage. It was bare. It was as if we were standing naked up on the stage. That took a lot of getting used to. It was just one more thing to distract me from my real problems. I could worry about that instead of worrying about the drug dealer in the third row, who I hadn't seen in years, with the two hookers on his arms, motioning for me to join him after the show. In the old days I would have been obsessed with the idea of taking off with them for the rest of the show. Not now though. I had enough on my plate. I had to get this band to rock. And I was happy. I had a job to do. My friends needed me to be at the top of my game. I wasn't digging myself a hole anymore. I was getting on with it. Sure it was hard, but it had been so much harder before. And I didn't want to turn the heat up under the pressure cooker at any cost. If it blew again, the damage this time would be total devastation.

CHAPTER FORTY-FIVE

all roads seemed to lead to me

BACK IN THE STUDIO, 2005

IT WAS TIME TO get back on the bike and try to make a solo record. It was 2005, so it had been five years between records. In the old days I had sometimes made two records a year, so I had slowed down considerably. For me it was a long time between drinks. Figuratively and literally.

The new album would also be my first since signing to Michael Gudinski's new label, Liberation. About six years before, Michael had sold Mushroom to Rupert Murdoch. I never in a million years thought that my music would be owned by Rupert, and if I'd seen it coming I would have taken steps to avoid it. I have nothing personal against Rupert but I didn't like my music being owned by someone who didn't have a music background. When the change came it was swift and clean, like a slice from an open razor. It seemed Michael and Rupert both did business a lot like it used to be done in Glasgow. It was cut-throat. Someone would lose out on the whole deal, and at the time I thought I was going to be the one to bleed. I went from being signed to one of the best independent labels in the world to being owned by one of the biggest men in media. Thankfully Michael had organised my deals so I didn't have to be stuck there on my own. I eventually moved on. So now, in 2005, I was back to making independent music.

I hadn't made a record since *Soul Deeper*. This time everything was different. I was straight. It was time to get back in the game.

I started working closely with Warren Costello, who was running Michael's new label. Warren and I have worked to keep my recording career on track ever since. Sometimes I have been so off track that Warren has had to keep the whole thing in line without me. Warren is a gentleman, which in the music business is a rare thing. He says what he means and means what he says. There are no hidden agendas. We have fought but only about things we both think need to be done. We always come to an agreement and we have stayed friends. Michael was still in charge though and we settled back into our old rhythm. We eventually had more success and got our friendship back on track, but Liberation could never be the same as Mushroom for any of us.

I got a bunch of songs together for the new album. It soon became apparent that it would include a lot of collaborations. Maybe I should do all duets. The *Double Happiness* album was the result. Michael originally wanted a single disc, mostly of safe covers, but Warren and I had different ideas. We wanted to write and find new material as well. The finished product was somewhere in between. I recorded more than twenty songs and most of them made the album.

Double Happiness was a lot of things, including my way of saying thanks to the people who had helped me pick myself back up and start living again. Most importantly, my family. I wanted the record to be a celebration of friendship and family. I did songs with lots of friends, members of my extended family, and with my children. Diesel produced a few tracks and sang with me.

Mahalia wrote and sang a song with me. EJ wrote and sang with me. Jackie played drums on a lot of the album and sang a duet with me. Even Elly-May was confident enough to sing with me. I wanted my son David to be on the record, so we found a great old Jimmy Webb song to do. And then to round off the whole thing, I asked my big brother to sing with me. This was like going back to the start and wiping the slate clean. That's what I thought. I had started singing with my brother as a kid, so what better way to show that everything was all right than to sing with him again?

But singing with John brought back a whole set of problems. For a lot of reasons, whenever I'd got together with my brothers and sisters in the past, it had been uncomfortable. The past was always there, waiting to explode, unresolved, twisting our feelings for each other, making it almost impossible to relate to one another. We would be happy to see one another but always looking for a way out. A way to escape. This is how I felt, anyway. I loved them dearly and I wanted to be able to spend quality time with them but I just couldn't do it. I thought that now I was straight those feelings would be gone. But they weren't. As soon as I spoke with John, I felt the knots twisting in my stomach again. Once we were in the room together I was a nervous wreck and so was he. I wondered if John only felt like this around his siblings, the way I did? Or did he feel like this all the time? It was too hard to ask him these questions, so I stayed uncomfortable and waited for the session to end.

I knew then that stopping the drinking and the other self-destructive behaviour had only removed a big part of my coping mechanism. All the pain was still under the surface, waiting to be dealt with. I hadn't really dealt with anything. I had taken away the most obvious problem, the drinking and drug-taking, but what was left was just as dangerous, if not more dangerous, without help. It was only a matter of time until I broke down, relapsed or died. Looking at my childhood without booze to soften the memories was too painful. I pushed it away, back, way back into my subconscious, where I couldn't see it and might not have to deal with it. Not now anyway.

This record was a new start. I had replaced one obsession – drugs – with another – work. And booze, with fame. I didn't want it to be tarnished by the ghosts of my past coming back to haunt me. So I stuck my head in the sand and kept working.

The record came out in July 2005 and it entered the charts at number one. My first release with the Liberation label became my first number one album since *Soul Deep*, fourteen years earlier. I was back on track and powering up for another charge. But for how long? *Double Happiness* had some of the best singers in the world doing duets with me. Why did such good singers and people have time for a guy like me? I had wasted half of my life living in a haze. These people had seen me at my worst and they still liked me. It had me baffled.

Later that year I was inducted into the ARIA Awards Hall of Fame for a second time. Cold Chisel had been admitted back in 1993, but this time it was for my solo work. Not many artists had done this before me, so it was a big deal. But like all awards, for me it ran a close second to getting myself up and running again. I knew that my future was in my hands and the more I looked after my own career, the better it would be.

IN 2005, I WAS contacted by a young woman after a show in South Australia. A letter with my name on it was slipped to one of my crew. I get letters all the time, some thanking me for coming to town and others asking me never to come back, so I wasn't surprised. This was just another show and another letter. I put it in my bag and forgot about it. I got back to my hotel and came across it when I was emptying my bag. The letter was from a girl, who told me that she had been looking for her birth parents for quite a while. She had found her mother and all roads seemed to lead to me as her father. The letter was well written, with a gentle tone. It was obvious that the young woman was genuinely trying to find out where she came from. She went on to ask if I would be willing to take a paternity test. I knew I had been a wild boy in my younger days in Adelaide and I thought it could be possible. She sounded like a nice person and even if I wasn't her father, what could I do but help her?

I had heard stories when I was kid in Elizabeth that a girl might be pregnant somewhere. All the guys I hung around with heard this at some point and all any of us did was hope it would go away. But these things don't go away. We were too young to realise what it all meant. We were all just kids, sleeping with each other to make ourselves feel good about ourselves or feel wanted or even safe. We were wild but we were just learning about life, the hard way.

If I knew I had children out there, I would want to find them. But I didn't want to rush into things and have them fall apart, and I didn't know who I was communicating with. I asked for some help from a dear family friend, Richard Cobden. Richard was studying law in Canberra when Jane was at university there, so he knew Jane long before I met her. He has been a good friend of mine for many years too, so he had a history with the family. He is incredibly smart and absolutely trustworthy and I knew he would be a good person to ask for advice.

Richard was worried that I might be taken advantage of as well. He told me, 'You never know who you'll be dealing with, Jimmy. I think it would be best if you leave this to me.' From that day, he became the family consigliere. He deals with any personal legal problems the family comes up against.

The young woman's name was Amanda Harrison and all she wanted was to find out who her father was. I agreed to take a paternity test. Richard handled the delicate matter of getting the test done and checked swiftly and confidentially. And sure enough, it came back positive. I was Amanda's father. I spoke to her on the phone and organised to meet. I knew as soon as I saw her that she was my daughter. She looked like my mother, which meant she looked like me. Amanda had tried to get a message to me before, but it hadn't happened.

From the minute I told Jane, she was nothing but supportive. Just like when I told her about David, if I had another child in this world, she wanted her to be a part of our lives. I had married an amazing woman. Now, I had to get to know my new family. Amanda, her daughters Tabitha and Tyra, and her son Toby all looked like members of my family. There was no doubt about it. They were warm and friendly. I got the feeling that Amanda was hurting. Why wouldn't she be? She had been brought up not knowing who her real parents were. But she was intelligent and loving and warm and I am so happy to have her and her beautiful children as part of our lives now. Amanda was very cool and only wanted to feel part of something. A family, her family.

Even now we are still learning about each other. It hasn't been easy. When children grow up with you, you know how to communicate with them. You know how to show love and argue and fight and all the things that families do without even thinking about it. But my new daughter and my new grandchildren were strangers to me. We had to learn about one another before we could get close. It gets easier all the time.

David Campbell knew Amanda at school. They were in the same year, but didn't know they were brother and sister. They didn't get on that well. Amanda was a bit wild for him and David was a bit mild for her, which is a good thing because imagine if they had liked each other or gone steady or something. That never happened, thank God. Jane's and my children opened their arms with love to the new arrivals. The family was growing all the time.

TWO YEARS LATER, I heard that there was another daughter in Adelaide.

'Couldn't be. Could it?'

But of course, it could be. As a young man in Elizabeth, there were nights when I slept with two or three girls. Like me, most of the girls I knew thought that if someone slept with you, you were worth something. We were all trying to make our way through life in the hard, working-class suburbs of Elizabeth. And if we could find an escape that made us feel good, for even a short time, then we fell happily into each other's arms. But it didn't really work that way and we got into a lot of trouble.

I thought I'd better get to the bottom of this. If I had another child out there, I wanted to know. I wanted her to be a part of my life. I contacted the consigliere again. Whenever I call Richard now, the blood drains from his face. He approached this new girl.

Megan Torzyn is a beautiful, strong mother of two very handsome young boys, Luke and Lachlan. She lives with her husband, Nathan, a gentle, hardworking Aboriginal man with a great disposition. Megan never wanted anything from me. All she wanted was to have her father's name written on the line on her birth certificate that said 'father unknown'. She just wanted to be complete.

And of course, I was her father. Once again all it took was one look and I knew, but we had already done the tests to make sure. Richard didn't want anything to be done out of order. I adore her and her family. I did from the day I met them. They are a strong unit. Megan is a tough, fair mother who has brought up polite and decent children. Nathan loves her dearly, and once I had met them all, I could not think of them not being in our lives.

The world works in mysterious ways. I thought that all connection to my past only brought back bad memories, but these children have brought love to me from a place where I was lost and alone. And they make that place worthwhile. If they were conceived at that time then something beautiful was happening, I just didn't know it. I am so blessed to have them in my life. Luke, my grandson, recently got married and brought even more joy to the family. I now have a great-grandson, Lewis.

CHAPTER FORTY-SIX

I'll live forever

SYDNEY, 2006–07

MORE TOURING FOLLOWED, more work. I was rebuilding a career that I had stripped to the ground and laid waste. Every step I took up the ladder felt like I was taking that step for the first time. Each achievement was a milestone. I was clawing my way back up to the surface where I could breathe. The venues were getting bigger and the crowds were too. I was singing better than I had ever sung and my band could tell. It was as if they were happy for me and were lifting their game to support me. I'll never forget them for that. But the pressure was incredible. Every night I would end up in a hotel room somewhere, wondering if I could cope with all this again. I would sit on the end of the bed, where I could see the minibar, lined up next to the fridge. Waiting for me to reach out and ask for its help. But I fought the urge. I didn't want to let everybody down again. But I was waiting to fuck up. Some nights I even reached out and picked up one of the bottles. How much could one small bottle of scotch hurt? It would help me sleep. No. I would put it back. In fact, I'd grab them all and put them in the drawer where I couldn't see them. Then I would be safe. I still had a long way to go. I was fighting for my sanity and my life and I had too much to lose.

I DECIDED TO KEEP myself busy. I should get fit. That would help me. If I was healthier I wouldn't want to spoil it by getting wasted. So I started trying to work out a bit. Just little things. I would do a few sit-ups and push-ups each morning. It was hard. It was like my body had forgotten what fitness was. Everything was hard to do. Maybe I should walk first. Get out and walk around the oval. In our search for a new start we had moved to Botany, a suburb full of working-class people with working-class values. I felt more at home there.

I could step across the road to the oval and walk my dogs. That was bound to help. So out I went. My lungs and chest hurt. All that smoking and snorting things into my lungs had obviously damaged me. But I pushed through. The boys, my little schnauzers, needed to walk as much as I did. But it did hurt. The more I pushed, the stronger the pain got. It was tight, my chest felt like I couldn't take in enough air without pain. I thought I'd better go to see the doctor. Fuck, after all this, after all I'd been through, now I was going to die of lung cancer.

Early in 2007 I went to see my GP, who ordered a few tests. I was sent to do a stress test, running on a treadmill for twenty minutes or so to see how my lungs coped. I had finished and was sitting in the waiting room, gasping for air and trying to recover, when the doctor came in.

'As far as we can see your lungs are all right, Jimmy. But we think that you should go and see a heart specialist.'

A heart specialist? It wasn't my heart. One thing I thought that I'd inherited from my father was his ability to keep going. My dad used to say, 'You know, son, I've run so much in training that my heart beats slower than a normal human. It beats so slow that it will last longer than a normal heart. I'll live forever. Ha ha ha.'

Then he would break into a coughing fit. His heart might last forever but his lungs were going fast. We both knew he wouldn't live forever but it was a bit of a laugh. So I was convinced that I had inherited a big, slow-beating heart from my dad. I had a heart like Phar Lap. That's what I always said. That's why I could keep going for so long.

'I think it would be best if you went to see a cardiologist as soon as possible.'

What an idiot. There was nothing wrong with my heart. I wasn't going anywhere near a cardiologist. I left.

'What did the doctor say, Jimmy?' Jane asked as I stepped into the car.

'Oh, nothing really. My lungs are fine. It might be something else.'

Jane knew me well enough to know when I wasn't telling her something. 'What did he say?'

I had to tell her, even though I knew he was wrong. 'Look, I think he's completely wrong but he said I should see a heart specialist.'

There was silence in the car for a second.

'We'd better make an appointment now.' Jane didn't want to wait even though I assured her I was better.

I had a series of tests at St Vincent's Hospital. I was wired up to machines and blood was taken. The doctor listened to my heart and then got someone else to listen. I sat waiting for the all clear.

'Yes, Jimmy, come in. Sit down.'

I didn't feel like sitting. 'No, I'm all right. So how did we go? Can I go home now?'

The doctor and Jane insisted I sit down and listen.

'You have a congenital defect in your aorta. Most people have a tricuspid aortic valve. You have a bicuspid valve. We are going to have to operate.'

I could feel the blood drain from my face. Jane looked at me with tears welling in her eyes.

'What sort of surgery are we talking here, doctor?' I asked. Surely this would not be invasive. Minor surgery. I had a lot to do.

'I'm sorry to tell you it will mean open heart surgery.' It was like he said this in slow motion: 'II'mmmm sssooorrryyy bbuuuttt iiiiittt wwwiiilll meeeaan oopppeenn hhheeeaaarrrttt suuuurrrrggggeeeerrry.'

Was he fucking serious? I wasn't ready for this. I was going to have to put it off.

'So when do you think we'll have to do it?' I was expecting him to say in a year or two.

'You need to do this right now. The sooner the better. Your valve sounds like it's shot. If it stops working you'll drop dead.'

I was stunned. Jane sat panicking. I could tell she was worried.

'All right. I'm ready when you are.'

The doctor told me that most people needed to get this replaced a lot sooner than me. It was a miracle I hadn't collapsed before now. I guess I hadn't had time to fall over. I was too busy trying to kill myself to die of natural causes.

I knew I needed to have the operation immediately. I had to just charge at it. If I thought about it I would want to run away. The date was set. I would be having open heart surgery within a week.

The night before I went into hospital, I sat with my dogs in the lounge room. 'Oh, my little boys. I'm so worried. I need to come back and see you. You guys need me to look after you. Don't worry. I'm coming back.'

The dogs looked at me. It was as if they knew I was scared. They snuggled closer into me. It helped a lot. I walked around the house alone, taking it all in just in case it was for the last time.

EVERYTHING SMELLED OF BLEACH and disinfectant. The walls were white, the nurses' clothes were white and the lights were white. Bright white neon lights. I was being wheeled down a hallway to theatre where my heart would stop beating and then be taken out of my chest and repaired. I might not be coming back. My eyes darted nervously around as if trying to see everything for the last time. The world. My Jane. Jane walked beside me holding my hand. Trying to stay calm so she wouldn't upset me. But I had already been given something by the nurses to calm me down. Maybe they should have given something to Jane too. She looked so beautiful, even with those red eyes. I watched her just in case I never got to see her again. I didn't want to leave. I needed to be with my Jane. The anaesthetist and a few other doctors started milling around.

'Jane, we're sorry, but this is as far as you can go.'

I gripped her hand. 'I'll be all right. I'll be back before you know it. Kiss me, baby.'

I was trying not to cry. I just wanted to be home with my Jane. Safe and sound. The nurse started pushing me away.

'Oh. Wait a minute. Jane, have you got the camera? Take a photo. It might be my last with you.' It was a joke but it wasn't funny. 'Give the camera to them. Can someone take a few snaps in the theatre?'

Jane handed over the camera, squeezed my hand one last time and I was gone. I was taken into another room for some sort of pre-op. I thought about my children, my Jane and my little puppies. I thought about all the things I had done wrong. Everything went black.

I CAME TO IN intensive care. I felt like I had been hit by a freight train. Not the trains that had hit me before. This was not self-inflicted. I knew I needed to be in the ICU because I have never felt so lost or in so much pain in my life. I had made it through.

But I didn't feel like I was going to make it for long. Something had to have gone wrong. I couldn't feel this bad and be on the mend at the same time. I passed out again. I drifted in and out of consciousness for a while, I don't remember how long. Every time I came to, even for a second, there was my Jane. Holding my hand and smiling at me. She looked like an angel.

'How did it go?' My throat was stuck together. I could hardly speak.

'You're going to be all right, baby. Now just sleep.'

Jane touched my face and I slipped away. Eventually they moved me to a ward. Every bump or corner of the trip felt like I was going to die. The pain was excruciating.

'Where's Jane? I need to see her,' I asked.

'Jane has gone home to have a shower but she'll be right back,' the nurse assured me.

When I woke next it was dark outside the window. The room was quiet. I lay on the bed and reflected on the last few days. I had technically died while my heart was being repaired. I didn't see any light. Not even theatre lights, thank God. It was a complete blank. The drugs had worked well. The door opened. I could hardly turn my head. There was Jane dressed in a long overcoat. Our friend Annabelle was with her.

Jane removed her coat to reveal what was underneath. 'I wore this to cheer you up.'

Jane was wearing a rubber nurse's outfit under the coat. Annabelle and Jane thought it was very funny. I couldn't laugh, even though I wanted to. I was in pain just breathing; laughing would have killed me. The girls hugged me and lay next to me taking photos and laughing before they kissed me and headed out into the night. I hoped Jane was going home. The rubber nurse's outfit was for my eyes only. But she didn't go home. Jane was also wearing the nurse's outfit to cheer up a dear friend of ours who was very sick. Richard Bailey had an advanced cancer and was fighting tooth and nail for his life. We loved Richard and his beautiful family, and Jane thought she could bring a smile to his face too. Make me laugh and cheer up Richard at the same time. So that's what she did.

Next day when I saw Jane she told me what had happened. After her bedside visits she had headed home to get an early night. Now I knew this, but Jane obviously didn't. Apparently you need help to take off a rubber dress. They are not to be tackled alone. Jane got home and started pulling the dress off and it got stuck. The more she pulled it up, the tighter it got. She ended up lying on the bed with the rubber dress ungracefully up and over her head, her arms sticking straight up in the air. It wouldn't budge past that point. She lay herself on the bed and pulled the blankets up with her teeth. She tried to get the dogs to help her but they were scared off by the noise and hid in the corner. So there she lay, gasping for air. She was expecting to be found suffocated in the morning. She told me that she could already see the headlines. 'Rock singer's wife found dead in auto-erotic liaison gone wrong. Jimmy Barnes was suffering in hospital while his wife was up to no good.' At least she had the photos to prove that she had worn it to see me in hospital. Eventually she used all her remaining strength to rip the dress up and over her head and off, tearing chunks of hair from her head along the way. She was covered in bruises from where the dress had wrapped too tightly around her. She would never wear that dress again unless I was there to help her get it off.

AFTER ABOUT A WEEK I was ready to go home. I couldn't wait to get out of there and back to my own bed. But it all suddenly went wrong. Instead of celebrating my survival, we got some terrible news. As I was leaving the hospital, a dear friend of mine, a man who was a real hero to me, Billy Thorpe, was being admitted. Since I was a young kid, I had looked up to Billy Thorpe. Billy was the singer I wanted to be like more than anyone else. He was wild and tough and everybody loved him. He made a career doing things his own way. He was flawed and beautiful. Billy had time for young bands and singers like me. I remember when I was starting out back in Adelaide, I ended up at a party in a hotel with Billy and his band. Instead of ignoring me or having me thrown out, Billy took me under his wing and gave me my first lesson on how to survive the music business. From that day on, Billy was like a big brother to me. I really looked up to him.

Just a few months earlier I had sat with Billy, laughing and listening to him tell me how I should write a book. Now here we were. My heart was on the mend, but Billy had had a massive heart attack. He didn't make it. Billy died. I felt like a big part of Australian rock died with him. There was only one Billy Thorpe and I would miss him terribly.

I was told to stay in bed for twelve weeks or at least stay still and calm for that long. But I had to go to Billy's service to say goodbye to my old friend. It hurt to move – but it hurt anyway to sit and think about the loss of Billy. I got out of bed and clutched a pillow to my chest so I could move and went and cried at his funeral.

Meanwhile, my son Jackie was at university in Boston. He was sitting in a class when he spotted something on his computer, saying, 'Australian rock legend dies of heart attack in St Vincent's Hospital'. Jackie knew I was in that hospital and he knew why I was there. He thought it was me. For some unknown reason it took hours for Jackie to get to the bottom of it. He found out I hadn't died, and was of course very happy, but Jackie loved Billy too and so he was sad to hear the news. It was difficult when he was so far from home.

THE DOCTORS TOLD ME I would feel good in about eight or nine weeks, but I should take it easy and not work for at least twelve weeks, just to be sure. I lay in bed and tried to keep still. Jane was my nurse and she would be up and down the stairs all day, checking to see if I needed anything. But I was miserable. I didn't like having so much time to sit and think. As a rule, I would keep myself busy so that I couldn't think about the bad things I had done in my life, but now here I was. I tried to remember anything from the time when my heart was stopped but I couldn't. If there was something to learn from it, it was that your memory isn't much good without your heart. So I slept a lot. My dogs slept on the bed with me, my constant companions. Even Jane, who was happy to look after me, could only stand so much but the dogs never moved.

After about eight weeks I felt like a new man. I had been offered a big show in Malaysia before I was taken in for surgery and I had told my agent, Frank Stivala, not to cancel it, just in case. I rang him and told him it was on.

Frank is my agent and my friend. We have worked together since just after *For the Working Class Man*. But long before that I used to visit his office whenever I was in Melbourne and sit and watch him work. It was fun to see him juggle the books of every big band in the country. 'Fuck them. Cancel that show. We don't like them anymore. This is the fucking band you want. Trust me.'

There is no one in the world like Frank. He is an old school Italian booking agent. He is tough and funny, and if he is on your side, there is a good chance you will be all right. I have seen Frank help out struggling bands and build their careers into something huge. I would trust Frank with my kids' lives. He is like an uncle to them all and they love him as much as Jane and I do.

Frank was wary. 'Have you asked your doctor if you can do it? I can still cancel it if I need to.'

I told him not to cancel. I would be fine. I rang the doctor. 'Hi, Doctor. Listen, I feel terrific and I was wondering if it was all right to do a little show. I'll only sing a little. I'll have my daughter Mahalia and my son David with me.'

The doctor was very hesitant. 'I'm not sure that's a good idea, Jimmy. You should be in bed taking it easy.'

But I had made up my mind. 'Look, Doctor, I'll take it very easy and if I feel tired I'll lay down.' I can be very convincing when I want to be.

'All right then, but just a few songs then back into bed.'

I hung up the phone. It was on. I had neglected to tell the doctor that the show was in Malaysia and that I was booked to play for one and a half hours. I would be fine.

We all travelled to Malaysia. Jane wasn't happy with me. She felt I would be better in bed. But we were going anyway. I got to the show and felt fine. Unfortunately, I was so happy to be singing again that I worked too hard. I screamed and shouted my way through the set. By the time it was over I had bad pains in my chest. I had done too much. The doctor was right and I was wrong. We caught the next plane back to Sydney and I was taken directly to hospital. Fluids had collected in my chest cavity and were pressing on my heart. They would have to open me up and drain the fluids. I was in hospital for four days. The doctor wanted to keep me in but I assured him I would do nothing but rest in my bed. And that's what I intended to do.

After another nine weeks or so I felt brand new again and once again I rang my agent. 'Hey Frank, are there any shows I could do? I'm going fucking crazy sitting in this bed.'

I talked him into it and soon I was breaking the news to Jane and my doctor that I wanted to work again. Both thought I was crazy but I had made up my mind.

Frank gave me two shows in Queensland. I told everyone that it would be like a little holiday in the sun. It would be good for me. So on the Saturday night I played a late show in Brisbane. I was a little sore but I was all right. I didn't tell anyone that

I was in pain. The next day we had a second show. It was a mid-afternoon show in the direct Queensland sun. We played for two hours and then I collapsed. The chest pains were back. We travelled to Sydney and the doctor sent me back to hospital. This time they drained the fluids with long needles they stuck into my chest. At least they didn't have to open me up again.

This time the doctor was adamant. He was keeping me in hospital for twelve weeks.

I begged him to let me go home. 'Please doctor. There'll be no shows, no singing. I promise I'll stay in my bed.'

Jane assured the doctor that she would not let me up again. They sent me home and I was sentenced to twelve weeks in solitary confinement.

What could I do but sit and watch TV? But even I can't watch that much TV and I can watch more than most people. Once again I was going crazy, so I grabbed an acoustic guitar and a tape machine and tried to write some songs. After a couple of weeks, I had written an album. It was a different sort of record. I couldn't scream. I couldn't even sing loud. So all the songs I wrote were soft and a little mournful. I felt sorry for myself lying in that bed and it came out in the songs. *Out in the Blue* was recorded as soon as I could get out of bed. I got some help from Nash Chambers and a few of his mates and I think it was a really good record considering I was dying in bed when I wrote it. The cover shot was taken by my good friend Richard Bailey, the other guy Jane visited in the rubber dress. Richard was a guitar player and a surfer, as well as one of the best fashion photographers in the world. He didn't normally do album covers but for me he made an exception. The cover shows me lying on a marble slab – I had come close to death – with Jane's name tattooed over my heart. It was as if Jane had been there, calling me back from death's door. Now that I think about it, she's been doing that for years. The album, released in November 2007, peaked at number three on the charts, but I didn't expect it to even do that well. I had survived heart surgery and was still kicking.

THAT SAME YEAR MY father, Jim Swan, died. Dad and I had managed to work through a few of our issues before he died. I hope we had worked through enough for him to die in peace. After Dad's visit to John and me at the Largs Pier Hotel – remember I told you about that – things got worse, but they did eventually get better. When he came back into my life, he was drinking way too much. But to his credit, after a few run-ins with Jane and me, he got his life together. My dad died sober. I was proud of him for that. My dad didn't have to do much to make me proud. I *wanted* him to be great. Even at his worst, I could only see the Jim I loved.

He died of emphysema, struggling to get air into his lungs. The Dad I remembered was afraid of no one or nothing, but before he died I could see fear in his eyes. He pretended he wasn't scared but I think that was for us. We pretended we couldn't see that he was scared. He died thinking we thought he was brave. And I did think he was brave. He had been forced to face up to a lot of the shit he had done in his life. And he had had to face it sober.

My brothers and sisters came together for a short time to mourn, but not for long. We couldn't be close anymore. We were shattered like broken glass, scattered every which way, and we could never be put back together. We would get together only when we had to, if someone died or to celebrate one of Mum's birthdays.

CHAPTER FORTY-SEVEN

your dog is always happy to see you

A NOTE ON DOGS

A S A KID, MY dad always had a dog. I think that Dad preferred the company of animals to humans. In fact, even his human friends were like animals when I think about it. Dad would sit out on the back porch after getting home drunk and fighting with Mum, and he would talk to the dog. Maybe the dog was the only one who didn't judge him. The only one who didn't talk back. Anyway, Mum wouldn't let us talk to him when she was fighting with him, so the dog was the only friend he had. My dad was a fighter and never thought twice about hurting another man, but he could never hurt an animal. Dogs were his favourite.

I DON'T THINK THAT a home is complete without a dog around. They remind me of what real love is. Never judging, your dog is always happy to see you, always ready to run to you and accept you as you are. Maybe that's why I love them. Because they have never had to forgive me.

Our first family dog was Theo, a cattle dog-border collie-lab cross. By the time Theo died he was like a coffee table, wide and flat across the back. Theo was gentle and patient with the children. He was never a problem to have around. I even took Theo on tour with me. He would hide in the car until the receptionist wasn't looking, then I would sneak him in and he would stay in the room with me. He used to lay on the bed and watch TV when I was out working. I used to joke that he could watch *Lassie* while I was out. When he died the whole family went into mourning. He was one of us and we still think of him. I get misty when I see his photo.

When the kids were small I got two very big dogs. I thought we needed them for security. But you can't really have a dog for security and have small children around at the same time. We had Rhontu, a huge Rottweiler. He weighed about twelve stone, maybe more. This was a big, fierce-looking dog. Then I got Jessica. She was a bull mastiff and looked like a short-nosed alligator. Either of these dogs could have killed you. But they were docile and child friendly. The kids used to ride on their backs. But I would never leave them alone. Just in case. One bite could have been fatal.

THESE DAYS I HAVE two miniature schnauzers. I always wanted big dogs before these guys. The bigger the better. I felt safer when I had them around. I think that was a leftover from my mum's constant worrying about being attacked. But now I can look after myself. Besides, I have grown out of my fears a little. My boys, Ollie and Snoop, are my best mates. They go everywhere with me. Except on tour. I don't want them to be away from home. They would miss it too much. I think I am projecting onto them a little here. I got these guys after meeting Jep and Mark's dog Rufus. Rufus was their big brother and had to be the coolest dog I had ever met. So I decided I would get one. I asked the breeder for a black puppy and when the day came for delivery, she turned up with a basket full of puppies. I was handed my little black dog, who we had decided would be called Snoop Dog. I asked in passing if the others had homes. She looked at me and said, 'All but this one. No one wants him.'

There was a little fat guy sitting in the corner alone. He was the runt. I loved him immediately. 'I'll take him too. What shall we call him, kids?' They decided on Oliver Twist because he was an orphan.

My dogs have sat with me while I wrestled with my childhood. They guarded over me while I recovered from heart surgery. They have watched me fall apart and then watched as I rebuilt my life. They have shared the good, the bad and the ugly with me. Never once have they judged me. Oliver even bit one of my gay friends when he came into my room while I was sick. I laughed and told my mate he was guarding my honour. My mate now tells the world that my dog is homophobic. But he's not. He just loves me. My dogs have sat and listened as I read my books to them before anyone else. If the dogs liked them, I'd be okay.

I find that I can't be away from home now because I miss them too much. Once we were on holidays in Europe. We were staying at one of the best hotels in the world in Paris when I turned to Jane and said, 'I miss my boys too much. I want to go home.' Jane laughed at me and started packing. We cut our holidays short by two weeks so we could be home with our dogs. It is very hard to even go on tour these days. And just like my dad and his dog, when Jane and I fight, the boys still talk to me. Thank God for that.

CHAPTER FORTY-EIGHT

we'd had a second chance

SYDNEY, 2009–11

COLD CHISEL WAS READY to record again in 2010. It had been a long time between studio albums. *The Last Wave of Summer* seemed to have come and gone a lifetime ago. The *Ringside* live recordings had been and gone. We thought that maybe it was time we got into the studio and put something new down. We started making plans. We had a bunch of songs and we had my studio to try them out in. Kevin Shirley, who worked with us mixing *The Last Wave*, was who we wanted when we really started cutting tracks. But we would start out at my place without him.

As soon as we hit the studio the magic was there. Right where we left it. The minute we picked up our instruments it came pouring out. We were all excited.

A year earlier, we had been asked to get together to play the V8 Supercars at Homebush. This was to be a huge party, celebrating the races coming to Sydney. It was the perfect place for Chisel to do a one-off show to whet the appetites of our audience and get them ready for a new record. Fast cars and fast music had always been a good combination for the band. We started our engines.

But there were a few communication breakdowns at that time, particularly between Rod, our dear friend and long-time manager, and the band. Things were moving fast, too fast for us to take time getting our shit together. We needed to be on, and we needed to be on right now. We made the decision that it was time to change management. This was not an easy decision. Rod had guided us through every step of Chisel's recording career. And he was a close friend to each one of us. We had shared food and families with each other. But we had been together too long. Things needed to be shaken up, and fast. The split was painful but necessary.

Now we needed someone to take the wheel. Someone to take our management and crank it up, ready for the next phase of the band's life. We didn't find one man to do this. We found two. John Watson is a sharp, music-loving guy who has been involved in record companies, management, journalism and even played bass in a band at one time. John O'Donnell is a man of many talents too. He has been a manager, an editor and writer for major rock music magazines, and he has run the record company side of things too. Like John Watson, he lives for music. Either one of these guys could probably have done the job we needed. Together they took the band to a new level. Each brought something unique to our management. They were part of a new wave of music managers. They knew a lot about the power of social media and the ins and outs of digital music and where it was heading. They were exactly what we needed. Besides this, both of these guys loved Cold Chisel and were ready to put their careers on the line to make it work for us.

Everything was going to plan. We sold more than fifty thousand tickets for the Homebush show. The band was charging ahead. We prepared to release our back catalogue into the digital world. Cold Chisel would be available on iTunes for the first time, and on our own terms. We had new music coming from each member of the band and the next record was shaping up to be something special.

The first sessions were great. We had some fantastic recordings that left us excited, ready to get back into the studio and finish them off. I already had an album of my own coming out that year – *Rage & Ruin* – but we all agreed to set aside the whole of 2011 for Cold Chisel recording and touring. To keep the band sharp we played at the 2010 Deni Ute Muster to another massive crowd. We couldn't have been more positive. We had a plan and it was taking us all in the right direction.

IN JANUARY 2011, STEVE was told that he had another brain tumour. He had been complaining of headaches for a while. He tried to shrug them off but we all knew he was worried. I remember him telling me, 'You know, it's weird. I have a feeling this is the same thing I had before. I recognise the feelings. I know it's back.' Then his fears were confirmed.

He didn't make a fuss. He was never fussed about much, unless it was something to do with music. He always knew what he wanted his songs to sound like, what he wanted to play, how he wanted to play it and how he wanted his drums to sound. Steve would fight with producers and anyone else who got in the way of things turning out the way he heard them. But he was quiet about his condition. He had already fought this fight once and the thought of going through it all again must have scared him. It scared me.

'Oh, you know, I don't think it's as bad as last time. Don't worry. I'll be all right,' Steve said. But the headaches were bad.

We all tried to be positive. Steve was tough. He'd be all right. Everything would be okay. The date had been set and he was going in for surgery. Steve didn't want anyone to go to the hospital with him. He didn't want to worry us. He was a very private person and besides, he had his children there.

SUNDAY MORNING, 16 JANUARY 2011, I got the call. My memories of this time are hazy, like a bad dream. It was a typical Sunday morning. A typical any morning actually. Yeah, unfortunately, a typical morning for me meant recovering, because by this time I was off the wagon, so every morning was difficult to greet. I was woken from the haze that was left from the night before when the phone rang.

It was John Watson. 'Listen, I hate to be the one to tell you this but Steve's not going to make it. He's in a coma and he's not going to come out of it.'

I was in shock. I didn't know what to say. 'Has anybody told Rod?'

Rod needed to know before it became public knowledge. I hung up. I sat and tried to process what I'd been told. Steve couldn't die. He wasn't supposed to, not yet. He had his children who needed him. They must have it wrong. I was expecting the phone to ring again. I'd be told it was all a big mistake or a sick joke. 'Steve is going to be fine. He's come out of it and everything's all right.'

But the phone didn't ring. They turned off the life support around 3.30 that afternoon. We had lost our friend. Our brother. I felt a sense of emptiness like never before. From the day we left Adelaide, it was us against everyone. Even when the band broke up, somewhere in the back of my mind I expected us to play together again. Maybe not straightaway, but some day. And we did. *The Last Wave* was a fresh start for Cold Chisel. *Ringside* confirmed that we were back on track. We were lucky. We'd had a second chance to make music. Not every band got this chance. It was an amazing gift to us all. But now that chance was gone.

EACH TIME I LOSE someone close, I can feel a change come over me. There is a sense of grief of course, but there is also a sense of nothing ever getting better. Like the loss has brought about a shift that will ultimately take me down too. And it's not even that it is a bad shift. There is almost a sense of relief about it. 'Right, it will all be over soon.'

I first felt this as a child, when my dog was run over right before my eyes. I wanted to leave too. I was afraid of being left behind alone. I knew that my parents would be angry but they would be all right. They wouldn't want me to feel pain. But it was like a part of me left with the dog and I wanted the rest of me to slip away too.

Later on in life I lost a few friends and remember similar feelings. When Bon died, way back in 1980, I felt it. Bon was a friend, but not like a brother to me. He was a role model. He was kind and funny and I liked him. But the night I found out that he died, it profoundly affected me. And, as I told your earlier, sitting on the edge of the cliffs overlooking the Pacific Ocean, I was almost overcome by the sense of wanting to leave too. I think that maybe, in my mind, death was almost a better option to living with myself, my pain and my guilt. But it wasn't enough to make me want to jump. It was just there, below the surface.

When James Freud died in 2010, I wondered if he was at peace. I hoped he was. I could see the pain and the heartache he'd caused the ones he loved, but he must have weighed that up when he took that final step. And in that moment he thought he made the right choice. Of course I have the benefit of hindsight and can see it should never have been considered. But James was overwhelmed. I had felt like that too.

Like I said earlier, I never realised that I was suicidal though. I thought I was just a bit crazy. But I had felt that way before. It was there when I ran away from home as a child and thought about swimming out to sea. It was there as I sat alone in a hotel room drinking myself into oblivion. And I remember feeling it again when Steve left us. It felt like the fight was over. And I had lost. But these feelings came and went. They never stayed long enough for me to lay down, but that would change.

---

CHAPTER FORTY-NINE

lost at sea

AFTER THE LOSS OF Steve, none of us thought we would ever play together again. It was too much for the band to take. But we still had business to take care of. We would meet and there was an empty seat that seemed like it could never be filled. Steve was gone and we could never replace him. We didn't want to play without him. But after a while the conversation changed.

Steve was the one who always wanted us to get over it and make music together. Sitting at a band meeting without him drove this home. If Steve was there, he would be telling us, 'Come on lads, pick yourselves up and play some music. At least finish the fucking record.'

But it was hard. How do you replace someone like Steve? You can't. We couldn't replace him. So instead of trying to replace him, we thought about who else we could play our music with. No one would be able to fill his shoes, but maybe we could find someone to bring something else, something new, to the band.

That's what Steve would have wanted us to do. There weren't many names tossed around. I'm not sure there were any before Don suggested Charley Drayton. Charley was a musician with incredible feel and depth. He had played on some of the best records I'd heard, with some of the best musicians in the world.

Charley was dealing with his own heartbreak. The love of his life, Chrissy Amphlett, was very sick and he was facing life without her. We couldn't take away the pain Charley was feeling about Chrissy. And Charley couldn't take away the pain we felt at losing Steve, but maybe, just maybe, we could make music together and help each other deal with life. Charley agreed to come down from New York and play with us. He told us, 'You know man, it's weird. Here's the thing. When Chrissy and I heard about Steve passing, just like everybody else we were hurting for you guys. But Chrissy said to me back then that if you guys ever wanted to record again, I should offer to do it. And now here I am.'

Chrissy was close to the band. We loved her and she loved us. We had grown up together. But Chrissy, being Chrissy, felt strongly enough about us to think about sharing Charley at this time, when she needed him most. Maybe she was doing it for Charley as much as for us. He would need something to be part of when she was gone.

We had played without Steve before during the life of the band, but that was through choice or because of a random act of stupidity, like Steve falling over drunk and breaking his wrist. We never wanted to play without him, not really anyway, unless we were fighting. But here we were playing Cold Chisel songs with someone else. Charley didn't play like Steve. He didn't try to. He respected everything that Steve had given to the band and played like himself. Anyone else would have copied Steve, or at least tried to, and that wouldn't have worked. Charley brought new life to the band, and now whenever we play together I can close my eyes and still feel Steve's spirit driving us. But when I open them up I see Charley, proud and soulful. That's one of many things he and Steve have in common. They are both proud and soulful and know how to drive a rock'n'roll band.

BY THIS TIME, I was on a downhill track with no way, that I could see, of turning back. Jane and I had not dealt with all the shit that had come between us during my life of destruction and mayhem. I had somehow got myself straight but I hadn't been able to, or been ready to, deal with the real cause of all my problems. My childhood. My traumas. My life. It was always there, lurking in the shadows, waiting for me to stumble and fall. And it took a little time but I did fall. I couldn't face the pain I had felt as a child, and I couldn't stand the pain I had caused as a man. I started drinking again. Just a little at first. Alone in my hotel room. One drink to help silence the voices in my head. Blur the face that was staring at me from the mirror. Those same feelings of loss, and loss of contact with the world, were back and stronger than they had ever been. I was closer to stepping off than ever. That one drink led to another and then another. And when that didn't work, I needed something harder, something stronger, so I found drugs again. Lots of them. But there weren't enough drugs or booze in the world to block the shame and guilt anymore. No matter what I swallowed, snorted, punched, kissed or ran from. I was back at my darkest place. I felt like I was drowning in a dark pool of pain and someone had pulled the plug and I was spinning down. I could see everything rushing out of control. Nothing could stop it this time. Down into the emptiness I went again. It was over. I couldn't fight it anymore. It was just a matter of time until it took me away for good.

I would stagger into the studio, hardly able to stand up and sing a few takes and then run away and hide in a room where I didn't have to see anybody. The band looked worried whenever I walked in. They had lost Steve and they were expecting to find out they'd lost me too. Jane and I would stay awake for days, trying desperately to work out where it all went wrong again. It wasn't her. She knew that and I certainly knew that. But she loved me and had been trying to save me since we met. She couldn't save me, not this time. No one could but me.

We finished the record that we had started before Steve left us. Kevin Shirley was at the controls, guiding us through the tears and the grief. The result was *No Plans*. The album title said it all. We were all lost at sea. None of us had come to terms with the loss of our brother Steve. We weren't ready to make any long-term plans. We didn't know how it would all work out, or if it would work at all.

MID-2011, I WENT BACK into rehab. This time in Australia. I had to do something or else I would die. The Sanctuary in Byron Bay was a high-end, very expensive way to dry out. But I couldn't do this in the public eye. I had already fallen apart in clear view of everyone in Australia, so I needed privacy if I was to have a chance at getting it together. Four weeks seeing therapists and eating well and taking nothing but supplements gave me enough clarity to make it through the forthcoming Light the Nitro tour. But not long after leaving the place, I started drinking and taking drugs again. It wasn't the fault of the clinic. They would have needed me to stay for a year or two to really help me. Once again, I had scratched the scab off my life and it was weeping. I didn't have time to fix things. Not now anyway. I had work to do.

That reminds me. At my first AA meeting many years earlier, I talked with a well-known actor, who shall remain anonymous – hence the name, Alcoholics Anonymous. After the meeting, he came up to me and said, 'So Jimmy, what's your poison?'

At that time, I wasn't ready to say that I was a drug addict and an alcoholic to just anyone, especially a total stranger, even though it was obvious to everyone who looked at me. So I answered him, 'Look, the only problem I have is when I work. That's when I drink and that's when I take drugs, when I work.'

He looked at me and I had the feeling he understood me. He said, 'Oh, it's so obvious. You're a workaholic.' And laughed and walked away. But he was right. Work had become one of my problems too, but I didn't see it. I was fine as long as I was wrapped in bubble wrap and away from the world.

I left rehab and I went back to work and back to drinking and everything else.

In August 2011, the Light the Nitro tour went on sale and Cold Chisel sold more tickets in a shorter time than any Australian band in history. Thirty-six shows sold out. Three hundred thousand tickets in record time. The public, it seemed, had not had enough of us. Maybe they wanted to share in our grief, help us get through it.

We played much better this time around. Better than the Last Wave tour. And different to Ringside. That had been practically an unplugged tour. This was a rock tour. The band was firing. Charley had breathed new life into us. It was as if he, and the rest of us, tried harder to make it work for Steve, and for ourselves. A certain amount of tension was gone. It was different. Not better than with Steve, but different. I think that losing Steve had made us all grow up. We weren't playing to fight against the world like we had in the past. We were playing to make sense of a world that was spinning faster and faster, as we tried desperately to hold on. Even in my failing state, the shows were still good. Amazingly, I sang much better than I ever had before with Cold Chisel.

Jane and I travelled with the band. Every day we would meet in the lobby of the hotel, eyes covered by the darkest sunglasses we owned. The lack of sleep was beginning to show on my face.

It was even beginning to show on Jane's beautiful face. We would sit next to each other, unable to talk or even look at one another. Every night we would end up consuming everything we could get our hands on and then start going through our life together, looking for clues that would help us mend the wounds that were killing us. We never found any answers, just more wounds. It was a cycle that we repeated every night, for what seemed like years, never getting the answers we wanted.

No one really spoke about me falling back into my old habits, although Eric Robinson, who was again running all our production, didn't pull any punches. 'Good to see you looking so healthy, Jimmy,' he said sarcastically as I fell into the backstage area one day. We both laughed but he was genuinely worried for me. Eric had a tough exterior but we all knew he was a softy inside.

Still, the band was on fire and Light the Nitro was a massive success. The tour was healing some of the loss we felt from the passing of Steve. Then, more bad news. Eric was diagnosed with an aggressive cancer and left the tour to deal with it. We were all worried for our friend.

THE TOUR ROLLED INTO Adelaide. Even the thought of going to Adelaide worried me. I didn't know why. I just knew that it was the key to all the pain I felt. And it was waiting in Adelaide. Every street and building held some sort of memory. I knew that the place where it all started was Elizabeth and I never wanted to go back there, but I was starting to remember things. Things that I had pushed back. Things I didn't want to remember. But they kept coming, scratchy and not really clear enough to get the whole picture, like old super-eight films. I spoke to Jane about my fears. And for the first time I told her I had been abused by a man when I was still very young. I won't go into this anymore now – I spoke about it in the first book. It was so hard to talk to another human being about this time, even Jane, but I knew I had to start talking to someone. I knew then that there was so much more to find out before I could have a chance at healing. The scratchy films were becoming a little clearer every day.

Around the same time, I was up late watching TV in a hotel room. The longer my life went on, the less sleep I was getting. Jane was in bed and I needed to watch something to distract me from myself. The only movie on the TV that I hadn't already seen was set in Adelaide, of all places. It was called *Snowtown*. I knew it was a horrible story but I watched it anyway – it couldn't have been any more horrible than what was already going through my head. It's a movie about serial killers and abuse in Adelaide. The 'bodies in the barrels' case was very famous. I knew the story roughly. But when the movie started I was shocked. The street that this movie was set in looked like the street I lived on in Elizabeth West. Then it moved into the house and the house looked like our house. I became very scared and turned the TV off. But it was too late. The film had unlocked more about my past than I was ready to deal with. I could suddenly smell the way the house used to smell and taste the fear I felt when we lived there. My childhood started flooding back over me.

WITH THE TOUR OUT of the way I got worse. I could only get so bad with Chisel around, but without them there was no end to how low I could go. I fell so far that I thought I would never make it back. The fear kept growing.

I was getting to the point of no return. The shame I felt kept consuming me and the pressure of being in the corner I had painted myself into made me buckle until I didn't know which way was up. In the end that shame and pressure took me to sitting alone in the dark with a cord wrapped around my neck in my hotel suite in New Zealand. Waiting, hoping to die.

CHAPTER FIFTY

we share good times and bad

S OMETHING INSIDE WAS POISONING me and poisoning everything I touched. I tried ignoring it. I tried smothering it. I tried drowning it in booze. I tried chopping it up and snorting it but even the hardest drugs had no effect.

Eventually I started writing. I wrote 100,000 words before I even knew it. It was all finally coming out. At first that made the pain even worse but slowly, page by page, I could feel that thing inside me shrinking until it was almost gone. A bit of it will always remain, of course, but writing turned out to be one of the things that actually helped. It was the missing piece of the puzzle. It allowed me to put some of those demons in their place at last.

I HAD ALSO STARTED seeing a therapist once a week. Sometimes I saw him twice a week. Peter Cox was my therapist and if he could have got me to see him every day of the week he would have. I don't know exactly why but something changed. Peter had connected with me, helped me find a way through the darkness.

One day I woke up and I knew it was over. I had turned a corner. It was up to me to stay on that road. If wanted to stop the car crash from happening, then I had to stop making the same mistakes over and over again. This was not an act of God. It was not a miracle. It was an act of love. I had been supported for years by a loving family and my beautiful wife. They were the ones I wanted to become a better man for. They were the ones who cheered me on. Every little bit of progress I made, they held me and told me how well I was doing. Every year I had more reasons to live. I've been blessed with quite a few grandchildren. Thirteen up to the time of writing this book. As I mentioned, I even have a beautiful great-grandchild. I needed to get over this stuff for all of them. If I didn't, they would have to struggle with demons that I had brought from my childhood into theirs. Jane says the kids are like us with new software. Every time I learn something and update my software, their software gets an automatic update too. They won't have to deal with my baggage.

Over the years that I had been fighting this battle I had worked with, and received information from, a lot of very clever and caring people. I had spent a lot of time listening to Deepak Chopra as he tried to tell me that life was beautiful and worth living. He was such a good friend to me. And I had sat in a cave in Thailand with Buddhist monks, meditating and looking for answers. I'd read nearly all the books written about helping yourself. I had all the information at my fingertips, but never took any of it in. I needed to use it.

I used to get up and do the same thing every day because I couldn't cope. But that would lead to more trouble, more mistakes. If you want to change the way you feel about yourself, especially when you feel as bad as I did about myself, then you have to do things that you are proud of. I was like a rat running on a wheel and getting nowhere but tired. I had to get off the wheel. If I didn't get off now, I would run until I dropped. I tried to stop doing drugs. Well, I stopped doing massive amounts of them. I stopped drinking until I couldn't feel. I had to be alive. I had to feel. I had to fight if I wanted to live. I no longer felt the need to escape. I was ready to try to deal with life. It might not turn out the way I wanted it, but it would be worked out and I could get on with living again. Jane and I slowly got better. I could see how much Jane loved me and, more importantly, I could see how much I loved my Jane. Life was starting to look good. Even the pain wasn't so overwhelming anymore.

It became obvious to me that new life was springing up all around me, and I should stick around.

David had struggled his way through his teens, still reeling from a childhood that was confusing and hard to take. For a short time, like most teenagers, he had seemed a little lost and I had tried to reach out to him. I even had him come on tour and sing a song during the set. But David knew that hard rock was not really for him, and I wonder now if this just confused him even more. Did he have to be like me? He had grown up with a whole different repertoire of songs as the soundtrack to his life, songs that I never heard as a child. Crooners and show tunes, melodic and sweet, not like the music his father was making.

He broke away from us for a while. He stayed in contact but his life was separate to ours. I knew he was making music and involved in musical theatre, but I had no idea what he was singing. When I started to get close to him again it was as if he had gone through a transformation, from a caterpillar to a butterfly. He was no longer an awkward teenager, he was a man.

He had found something he loved. Just like me, he loved to sing, but his style was the complete opposite to mine. He had found his own voice and it was beautiful.

Around 1997, I went to New York to see David sing at a very famous nightclub. The Rainbow Room is sixty-five floors up, overlooking the Big Apple. Some of the greatest cabaret singers in the world have sung on its stage. From what I heard in that room, my son David was the toast of the New York cabaret scene. I sat mesmerised as he sang some songs that I had heard somewhere and others that I had never heard before. Most of the audience was in tears as David took them on an emotional journey. I was so proud of my son.

David went on to find the girl of his dreams, Lisa, and it wasn't long until Leo came along. Leo is a strikingly handsome young man, if I do say so myself. Later they had twins, Betty and Billy. These guys are the most beautiful babies. Funny, cute and smart. David's life is as far away from the northern suburbs of Adelaide as you could get. I know he still has his own stuff to deal with but he is a happy man with a beautiful family. David, like me, has broken the cycle that his family had been trapped in for generations, and life is good for him.

Mahalia married Ben Rodgers, a great guy and a hell of a musician. Ben studied music in Canberra. Bass is his main instrument, but I soon found out that Ben is capable of getting a tune out of anything with strings. I call him Jazz Boy because if anything was challenging to play, I set Jazz Boy onto it and he quickly has it conquered. Ben plays bass with Mahalia and guitar with me. They had a beautiful baby girl, Ruby, and then seven years later, Rosetta came along. She was named after Sister Rosetta Tharpe, an amazing guitar-playing, soul-singing black woman. Ruby and Rosie, as I call her, moved with their parents down to the country recently and live just a short walk from us. This means I get to spend a lot of time spoiling them.

Jackie met and married a beautiful Australian–Malaysian girl, Stephanie. Steph became like a daughter to me from the minute we met. She is loving and warm and has become a fantastic mother. Jackie and Steph have two little girls who look like china dolls. Their names are Isabella and Zoey. I am totally smitten with the pair of them. Jackie studied percussion at Berklee College of Music in Boston and, since graduating, has played drums in my band. He is one of the best drummers I have ever seen but, more importantly, he is a good man and a great father.

Eliza-Jane left home to tour the world with her close friends Liam Finn and Ceci Herbert. They have been friends since they were toddlers. Neil and Sharon Finn have been close to us forever and our children feel as comfortable with them as they do with us. They are a great family. We call them the Finn-laws. EJ has toured and recorded with Liam and also sings with Ceci, her partner in crime for a long time now. She has even been fortunate enough to sing with Neil Finn on and off for a few years. She is very lucky to be performing with one of the world's great singer-songwriters. Working with Liam led her to meet a good friend of the Finn family, Jimmy Metherell. Jimmy is a gentle caring fellow who can cook, and he plays piano and guitar and sings well too. They are not married but I think it's just a matter of time. We think he's a keeper.

Elly-May met Liam Conboy, a tall good-looking Scotsman from Aberdeenshire, when he was on a working holiday in Australia. They had a whirlwind romance and got married and had a beautiful baby they called Dylan. They are both wonderful parents who care for each other and are still in the process of working their lives out. We can't ask for more than that. We just hope that they will all be happy. Elly will hopefully make her first record very soon.

My three girls, Mahalia, EJ and Elly-May, all sing with me. And even Jane has taken to the stage and sings with me every night. I feel truly blessed to be able to make music with my family. Life is good and it's only getting better.

I am a loving grandfather and Jane is the best grandmother I have ever seen. My grandkids just love her and so do I. I can see in their eyes how much they love her, every time they look at her. Just like when my children were small. Her whole life is devoted to them. I'm the same, I can't get enough of them. I am still a rock'n'roll singer and our lives are far from normal but, when it all comes down to it, we are just like any family. We laugh and we cry together. We share good times and bad. But most importantly, we love each other. Now all I need is more time to spend at home with all my children, new and old, and their beautiful families. There are just not enough minutes in the day, and time keeps ticking away.

My grandchildren have sung a few songs and given them to me as Christmas presents. I suspect at some point I will see the new Tin Lids. Just like my children did so many years before, my grandkids think that everybody makes music. Some of them have already let me know that they want to sing and play music too. I wonder if they need a manager.

CHAPTER FIFTY-ONE

I can feel the change

FAREWELLS, 2012–16

THE ROAD HAS TAKEN so many of us. Some die of loneliness. Some die in a crowd. Some die because they just work themselves into the ground. But whatever way they have gone, I have lost a lot of friends.

In March 2012, I got the news that my dear old friend Vince Lovegrove had crashed his Kombi van into a tree. Vince was like me in a lot of ways. He never coped well with pressure either. He had settled into a calmer, peaceful life, living up in the Byron Bay area, but it didn't last. The roads are very bad around there and late one night he died. He had found peace. I sang at his funeral. It was hard. Vince had lived a life full of joy and pain at the same time.

Charley lost his beautiful Chrissy in 2013. It was all too much for her to fight. Multiple sclerosis and breast cancer eventually wore her down. Charley was heartbroken but I thought I could see relief in his eyes. Chrissy wasn't suffering anymore.

The world was sad the day that Chrissy left. She was the toughest girl to take on the music industry, and she did it with a style like no one else. The last time Chrissy sang on stage was with Cold Chisel on Light the Nitro. Chrissy joined us and sang 'Saturday Night'. What a moment it was to share the stage with Chrissy and Charley. We were all meant to be there for each other.

Ian Smith had been part of my life for many years, running tours and managing bands. Everyone in the music business knew him as Smithy. He left us in 2014. Ian battled liver cancer with the same strength and enthusiasm that he'd tackled life. Nothing could beat Smithy. He had fought a raging battle with hard drugs and won. He had been through the wringer a few times. But he still came back smiling. He was a great man and a dear friend. When he thought life couldn't give him any more, he had found the love of his life, Caroline, and was finally happy. That was when the cancer struck.

Smithy used to say to me, 'Look Jim. I've done it all and I'm surprised that something hasn't killed me before. I can face this. I've done all I need to do.'

He was sad to leave his beautiful Caroline behind, but she was like a rock for him. He was never alone. I went to see Smithy when he was in palliative care. He looked calm and at peace. I wanted to feel that at peace too. As I walked in, there were a few old friends of ours waiting to say goodbye. Mark Pope was there along with Richard Clapton. Richard looked like he'd had a big week. As I sat next to Ian's bed holding his hand, I said quietly to him, 'You know what, Ian? You look better than Richard out there. He looks like he should swap places with you.'

I don't know if he heard me but he would have laughed. I did. I laughed for both of us. It was the last time we would have a laugh together.

We all waited to find out about Eric. He was a tough guy. He had worked hard all his life. He was big and afraid of no one but his diagnosis had been too late. The cancer had spread. Eric, as tough as he was, couldn't beat it. He fought for a few years, taking one step forward and two steps back. Eric and Patti, his wife, were never apart over those years. He was lucky to have her with him. She loved him so much.

When Eric died, we were all left with a gaping hole in our hearts. Eric was as much a part of the new touring Cold Chisel as any of us. He had become the big brother of the tour. No matter what camp you were in, the band, the management, the crew, the truck drivers or the merchandising, Eric was a part of your job. He had been the glue that held us all together. We had all laughed, cried, screamed and fought with Eric at some point on the last few tours and now he was gone.

I often sit now and wonder how I made it through and so many didn't.

COLD CHISEL WENT BACK into the recording studio with Kevin Shirley in 2014 and started making *The Perfect Crime*, our first album that Steve didn't play on, though I could feel his spirit on every track that we recorded. By this time Charley was as much a part of the band as I was. We had found our sound again. Making this record was easy. Well, easier than most of the records we'd made. I was no longer smashed for a start. I could sit still and listen to what was going down without wanting to escape from the band or myself. It was funny that the single was called 'Lost', because I wasn't anymore. For the first time in a long time, I knew where I was and where I was going. The song was classic Cold Chisel. Don's chord changes were as tricky to sing over as ever. But once I found the way they moved, the melodies were perfect. In 2015, the song charted. We hadn't been on the singles charts for a long time.

By mid-2015 we were going out on tour and I was ready. I didn't need to dry out or go to rehab. I was focused and fit. I took

Jane and the kids to Thailand for a little break before we started. It had always been a place where we could drop our guard and relax for a while, even in the midst of all the chaos. But this time a bomb went off, right next to where we were staying.

On 17 August, we were walking from our hotel to a restaurant to eat. We had a few of our grandkids with us so it wasn't easy. Bangkok roads are crazy and there were roadworks all around the area. I came up with a plan to get the pram across the main road to the restaurant. It was what my kids call one of my short cuts, which by the way always seem to take much longer to get anywhere. Jane calls it the scenic route. But because of the pram they all agreed to follow my directions. We ended up going a long way around and as we walked between two buildings we heard an almighty bang. No more than fifty yards from us a bomb had exploded, killing at least twenty people and injuring hundreds more. Had we not taken my short cut, we would have walked across the road, exactly where the explosion occurred, and been blown to pieces.

The bomb was hidden in a small shrine where people went to pray and make wishes for their families. When the wish comes true, they go back and give thanks. I had kneeled in that shrine many times asking for peace and help. It seemed like a particularly cruel target.

The reason I'm telling this story is that I can now see that even with all the things that had happened to me as a child and as an adult, I was still a lucky person. Friends and even buildings were falling all around me and I was still standing. When times were at their worst, I found Reg Barnes. When I needed help and a way out, I found Cold Chisel. And on that day in 1979 in Canberra, I found the one person who would give me a reason to go on living. My Jane. I have some sort of inner sense that pulls me from the darkest place at the right time. I missed the 2002 Bali bombing by minutes as well. Someone or something was looking out for me. I know we make our own luck and I know that I am a fighter, but something was helping me.

THE ONE NIGHT STAND tour started with a bang, the sound of pyrotechnics exploding as we played four songs before the NRL Grand Final. The band was set up on the field, within swinging distance of the crowd. I remembered something my father told me, when I played football as a kid. He'd say, 'I don't care if it's leather or human, destroy it.' So we were ready to crash-tackle anybody that moved, and we smashed our way through the set and then headed north, up the coast.

Every night we gave everything. This was what Cold Chisel did. Gave everything. We knew that it could end at any time. We had learned that from the loss of our mates.

The climax was in Sydney in December 2015. We would be the last Australian band to play the Entertainment Centre. Elton John played the very final night, but the place was already crumbling as we played. I could feel the brickwork shaking as the band crashed our way through our final songs. This was where we'd played our final Last Stand so many years before. And we had one last chance to say goodbye to all the memories this building held.

That last night we thought about all our friends who had shared the road with us. Friends who were gone now. Steve, Thorpie, Alan and Billy, Bon, Vince, Hutch, James, Smithy, Chrissy, and of course Eric. So many mates who we wouldn't see again. We had torn this hall apart so many times in the past and now it was the last night. We wanted to tear it down again for everyone who had left us. The encore kept going on and on.

'What about this one?' Don shouted over the roar of the crowd and started another song. We must have played eight songs in the encore that night. I could see Bailey, the production manager, looking at his watch, willing us to stop, but we didn't. We just kept playing. We didn't want to say goodbye. It was too final. We played for ourselves, for the audience and for our old mates who couldn't be there.

Eric had hated it when we finished with 'The Last Wave of Summer'. He thought it was too slow and self-indulgent. 'Leave them with one of your big hits. Oh sorry, you guys never had any,' he'd quip as he got the crew started on packing up the gear. We had all loved him, even when he was tearing strips off us. The last song we would ever play at the Entertainment Centre was especially for our lost mates.

There's a cold winter comin'
I can feel the change
It's the last wave of summer
We'll ever see again
Let's ride

EPILOGUE

I RUSHED TO NEWCASTLE after I received a call from my sister
Lisa. 'You'd better get up here again. I think this is it. The
doctors have given her something to help her pass without pain.
They don't think she will last long.'

I had been up and back a few times that week but I knew that
this time it could be it. She could only fight for so long. Even Mum
wasn't that tough. I arrived and the house was full of family. It
looked like no one had slept. Their eyes were all sunken and ringed
with red. I could taste the tears on their cheeks as I kissed them and
said hello. I walked into Mum's room. The light was low and no
one said a word. We all sat, taking turns to be next to her and hold
her hand. Maybe for the last time. We waited for Mum to die.

'All this silence is killing me. Never mind what it's doing to
Mum,' I joked, but no one laughed. I grabbed my phone to see if
there was something appropriate to play at a time like this. Then
I remembered a playlist I had made the night before. It was as
if I had known I would need it now. I pressed play. The sound of
bagpipes filled the room.

Mum hadn't responded to anything for days but as I held her hand I was sure I could see her eyes flicker. Look, there it was again. It was as if she was trying to fight her way back, away from death's door and back to the light, to her family one last time. She opened her eyes and squeezed my hand.

'She knows you're here, Jim,' my sister Dot whispered.

'Hi Mum. We are all here with you. We love you.'

Dot laughed but her eyes filled with tears at the same time. I couldn't speak. Then Mum closed her eyes again and drifted away. That was the last time my mum was with me.

MUM CHOSE TO BE buried in the ground. Cremation was out of the question. She'd been burned enough by life and didn't need any more in death.

About eight years before she died, Jane and I had given Mum a little schnauzer puppy. She called him Oscar. Oscar would become the only shining light in her life. She adored him and doted over him. Oscar was treated like a prince. He had his own bed next to hers so she could watch over him. It was as if all the love she was too scared to show to another human came pouring out of her and into her 'wee dug'.

Oscar had died suddenly about six months before Mum did, basically of the same types of cancer that she eventually had. If I didn't know better I'd say that he was trying to take her disease and pain away, trying desperately to save her. But he couldn't.

From the moment Oscar died, Mum let go of her life. 'I miss ma wee boy, Jim. I don't want tae be aroon' wi'out him,' she told me. Even her family weren't enough to keep her here. She wanted to go with her wee man, Oscar.

The last time I looked at Mum she was lying in her coffin, clutching Oscar's ashes in a jar tightly to her chest. He was close to her heart. I knew her heart had stopped beating but he had found it when she was alive, when no one else could. I was sure he had found it again. And they were together.

AT THE CEMETERY, THE family waited in silence for Mum to arrive, each of us looking like the old headstones that marked the graves from a hundred years before. Broken and crumbling and falling apart. I stood over the empty grave. I don't know why but I needed to see where she would rest. As I stared down into the cold damp earth, my eyes filled with tears. I swallowed hard and walked back to the car to wait with Jane. I needed to hold her hand and feel the warmth of her touch. Everything seemed to be dying around me. But not Jane.

The hearse pulled into the carpark and we all gathered around the graveside. I couldn't look at my brothers and sisters or anyone else. They were the same. Staring blankly out into space. Lost and alone. We moved to the car and the signal was given to pick up the coffin and walk to the grave. The sound of bagpipes rang out across the cemetery. This was it. It was almost over.

As Mum's coffin was lowered into the ground, a gust of wind swept through the trees. A flock of white cockatoos danced on the breeze, dipping down as if to look on us one last time before disappearing into the distance. Mum was gone.

I expected to feel empty as I left the cemetery, but I didn't. I was left with a strange sense of closure and peace. It was as if the roller coaster I had been riding all my life had slowed down, and in that moment I could breathe.

ACKNOWLEDGMENTS

—————

AND I THOUGHT MY childhood was hard to look at. This was even harder. The mistakes I made and the pain I caused myself and the ones I love have at times been almost too hard to revisit. But that's what I had to do. Just like in my first book, the writing was part of the healing process. In *Working Class Boy*, I learned to let go of a lot of what happened to me as a child. The cover said it was a memoir of running away. As I was editing that book my mother died. I never got to talk to her about all of this. I think it was probably for the best. She saw things through her own eyes, not mine. No one else has seen what I have seen in my life. No one else has been in my shoes.

Writing that book, along with all that I have told you in this one, helped me make sense of my life. I spent almost a year talking about my childhood on my Stories and Songs tour. And I have learned a lot more about myself. I have also learned that some things can't be fixed. But I'm not running away anymore. I'm facing up to everything that life can throw at me and I'm doing all right. You can't run from life or it will run you down.

I used to think I was running out of time. Deepak once said to me, 'You know, Jimmy, people who say they are running out of time, run out of time.'

I've got nothing but time.

IN THIS NEW BOOK, I have had to learn to forgive myself. It hasn't been easy. There is a lot to forgive. And I don't think that the simple act of writing this all down will help me forgive. But it was the key to opening the floodgates this time around. Once it all came out, I had a lot of work to do. I had to start putting my life back on track, facing the hard, sometimes ugly truth and then learning from it. There are some things we do that we can't take back. God knows I've tried. But we can make sure that we never make the same mistakes again. A friend told me once that we never tread in the same river twice. Each time we enter the water it is new and on a new path. That's what I'm doing now. Diving headlong into the river of life and fighting my way up to the surface. If I work hard enough and I can forgive enough then I will be able to breathe. I am determined not to let the things I have done wrong in the past hold me back for a second time. I will break through the dark cold water and find the sunshine once and for all.

As dark as it has been at times, I have been helped through that darkness by my beautiful family. My Jane, my children and my grandchildren have been my light. Whenever things got overwhelming, they knew, and offered their love. I am so blessed. I don't take them for granted. I know how lucky I am to have such a beautiful family. So, thank you all so much. I couldn't have gotten through this without you.

Every day I sat in my study writing. I was left alone to write, but the family were never far away. Jane would walk in and check on me, encouraging me at every step, offering tea and shortbread to give me the strength to keep working. My two little schnauzer brothers, Oliver and Snoop Dog, sat next to my chair. They seemed to know when it was getting too hard and would wag their tails and nudge me with their paws, telling me to take a break and go for a walk. Of course, they might have just needed a walk but I think they were saving me. I couldn't ask for better friends.

Before sending anything to my publisher, I would send it to my dear friend and manager, John Watson, to read first. 'I'm not sure this is any good. I can't tell anymore,' I would say. John would ring and tell me to keep writing. 'It's really good, Jimmy. Can you send more? I feel like I am watching a serial. I need to see how it ends.' But he knew how it ended. He had seen the way it was heading for a long time too, and was willing me to get through it and come out the other side. So, thanks John, for hanging in there when it looked bad and helping me sift through it all.

I would like to thank my publishers. In particular, Helen Littleton for the encouragement. Nicola Robinson my editor. I love working with you, Nicola. You have helped make sense of my ramblings. Karen-Maree Griffiths for keeping me sane on the road. And Rina Ferris for making me work so hard. You are a hard task mistress but we still love you. Scott Forbes, once again, for his Scottish dialect coaching and also for helping Jane sift through all the photos for the book. Jane went through thousands and thousands of photos. If she wasn't sick of my face before she started, there is a good chance she was by the time she finished.

My life has been helped by all of you who love music. The punters out there who go out to watch live bands. The ones who excitedly wait for an album to come out and then rush out and buy it. Not just mine, but all music. You guys give us a reason to sing. I can't thank you enough. I also want to thank everyone who read *Working Class Boy*. I shared that story with a lot of people who had a similar journey to myself. I made it through and so can you.

I would like to say thanks to Michael Lawrence. Your book has been an invaluable fact checker for us all. Robert Hambling deserves a big thank you. He helped search for photos that sometimes didn't exist, and he found most of the ones we needed. Thanks also to Philip Mortlock for his photo work, plus all the other photographers whose work appears here. Thank you to Peter Cox. If ever a therapist worked for his money, it's you, Peter. And thank you to Richard Cobden, my consigliere, for helping bring my family closer together.

I would like to thank my friends who have played in my many bands and have helped me make music over the years. Especially my brothers from Cold Chisel. Don, Ian, Phil and dear Steve. And of course, Charley, who helped put us all back together when we thought we couldn't do it anymore. Also Rod and Gay Willis for their help. And of course, John Watson and John O'Donnell for their continued guidance.

Michael and Sue Gudinski. Frank Stivala. Warren and Leith Costello. You guys have been my Mushroom family. What a trip we've had, eh? Thanks guys.

I want to thank Jane's mum and dad, Kusumphorn and John Mahoney, and their wonderful family for taking me in like a stray cat and putting up with me while I learned how to behave and feel like a normal human being. I love you.

Every single roadie who I worked with. You guys never get enough thanks. Rock'n'roll happens because of you guys. I spent more time travelling and drinking and laughing and crying with you guys than nearly anyone else.

I can't thank everyone that I have worked with personally, and I am sure if I tried I would miss someone and offend them. So I just want to make a broad statement here. I have worked with and for a lot of great people. I have made great friends and I have met a lot of people I wish to never see again. But I genuinely want to thank you all because each of you has helped bring me to where I am today. This book is for all the people that got lost on the road. I was one of them but now I am found.

And I know that I have thanked you earlier, Jane, but from the day I first saw you in the Motel 7 I loved you. I still love you and I will always love you my darling.

Peace and Love
Jimmy

LYRIC CREDITS

'Tutti Frutti' (D.Labostrie/J.Lubin/R.Penniman)
© 1955 Sony/ATV Songs LLC
For Australia and New Zealand: Sony/ATV Music Publishing Australia
Pty Limited.
All rights reserved. Used by Permission.

'Letter to Alan' (D. Walker)
© 1982 Sony/ATV Music Publishing Australia Pty Limited.
All rights reserved. Used by Permission.

'Flame Trees' (D. Walker/S. Prestwich)
© 1984 Sony/ATV Music Publishing Australia Pty Limited/Copyright
Control.
All rights reserved. Used by Permission.

'The Last Wave of Summer' (D. Walker)
© 1998 Sony/ATV Music Publishing Australia Pty Limited.
All rights reserved. Used by Permission.

'On Your Way Down' (A. Toussaint)
© 1972 Screen Gems – EMI Music Inc and Warner-Tamerlane
Publishing Corp.
International copyright secured. All rights reserved. Reproduced by
Permission of EMI Music Publishing Australia Pty Limited and Devirra
Group.